GENDER TYPING
of CHILDREN'S
TOYS

GENDER TYPING of CHILDREN'S TOYS

How Early Play Experiences Impact Development

Edited by Erica S. Weisgram
and Lisa M. Dinella

AMERICAN PSYCHOLOGICAL ASSOCIATION
Washington, DC

Published by
American Psychological Association
750 First Street, NE
Washington, DC 20002
www.apa.org

APA Order Department
P.O. Box 92984
Washington, DC 20090-2984
Phone: (800) 374-2721; Direct: (202) 336-5510
Fax: (202) 336-5502; TDD/TTY: (202) 336-6123
Online: http://www.apa.org/pubs/books
E-mail: order@apa.org

In the U.K., Europe, Africa, and the Middle East, copies may be ordered from
Eurospan Group
c/o Turpin Distribution
Pegasus Drive
Stratton Business Park
Biggleswade Bedfordshire
SG18 8TQ United Kingdom
Phone: +44 (0) 1767 604972
Fax: +44 (0) 1767 601640
Online: https://www.eurospanbookstore.com/apa
E-mail: eurospan@turpin-distribution.com

Typeset in Goudy by Circle Graphics, Inc., Columbia, MD

Printer: Bang Printing, Brainerd, MN
Cover Designer: Nicci Falcone, Gaithersburg, MD

Library of Congress Cataloging-in-Publication Data

Names: Weisgram, Erica S., editor. | Dinella, Lisa M., editor.
Title: Gender typing of children's toys : how early play experiences impact
   development / edited by Erica S. Weisgram and Lisa M. Dinella.
Description: First Edition. | Washington, DC : American Psychological
   Association, [2018] | Includes bibliographical references and index.
Identifiers: LCCN 2017038884| ISBN 9781433828867 | ISBN 1433828863
Subjects: LCSH: Child development. | Child psychology. | Toys—Psychological
   aspects. | Play—Psychological aspects.
Classification: LCC HQ772 .G37 2018 | DDC 155.4—dc23
LC record available at https://lccn.loc.gov/2017038884

British Library Cataloguing-in-Publication Data
A CIP record is available from the British Library.

Printed in the United States of America
First Edition

http://dx.doi.org/10.1037/0000077-000

10 9 8 7 6 5 4 3 2 1

CONTENTS

CONTRIBUTORS

Rebecca S. Bigler, PhD, Professor of Psychology and Women's and Gender Studies, The University of Texas at Austin

Giulia A. Borriello, MS, Doctoral Student, The Pennsylvania State University, University Park

Christia Spears Brown, PhD, Professor of Psychology, University of Kentucky, Lexington, and Director of Social Inequality in Development Research Group

Isabelle D. Cherney, PhD, Dean of the School of Education and Social Policy, Merrimack College, North Andover, MA

Rachel E. Cook, MS, Doctoral Student in Family and Human Development, Arizona State University, Tempe

Emily F. Coyle, PhD, Assistant Professor of Psychology, St. Martin's University, Lacey, WA

Jacqueline Davis, MPhil, Doctoral Student, University of Cambridge, Cambridge, England

Lisa M. Dinella, PhD, Principal Investigator, Gender Development Laboratory; Associate Professor of Psychology; and Affiliated Faculty Member of Gender Studies; Monmouth University, West Long Branch, NJ

Lise Eliot, PhD, Professor of Neuroscience, Chicago Medical School of Rosalind Franklin University of Medicine and Science, Chicago, IL

Megan Fulcher, PhD, Associate Professor of Psychology, Washington and Lee University, and Director, Washington and Lee Gender Psychology Lab, Lexington, VA

Melissa Hines, PhD, Professor of Psychology and Director, Gender Development Research Centre, University of Cambridge, Cambridge, England

Campbell Leaper, PhD, Professor of Psychology, University of California, Santa Cruz

Lynn S. Liben, PhD, McCourtney Professor of Child Studies; Professor of Psychology; Professor of Education; Professor of Human Development & Family Studies; and Director of the Cognitive and Social Development Lab, The Pennsylvania State University, University Park

Carol Lynn Martin, PhD, Cowden Distinguished Professor, T. Denny Sanford School of Social and Family Dynamics; and Executive Director, Link Enterprise: Bringing People Together in a Diverse World, Arizona State University, Tempe

Sarah K. Murnen, PhD, Samuel B. Cummings Professor of Psychology, Kenyon College, Gambier, OH

Diane N. Ruble, PhD, Emeritus Professor of Psychology, New York University, New York

Kingsley M. Schroeder, MS, Doctoral Student, The Pennsylvania State University, University Park

Ellen A. Stone, PhD, Doctoral Student, Department of Psychology, University of Kentucky, Lexington

Erica S. Weisgram, PhD, Professor of Psychology, University of Wisconsin–Stevens Point

Kristina M. Zosuls, PhD, Visiting Faculty/Scholar/Researcher, T. Denny Sanford School of Social and Family Dynamics, Arizona State University, Tempe

GENDER TYPING of CHILDREN'S TOYS

INTRODUCTION

ERICA S. WEISGRAM AND LISA M. DINELLA

Do boys and girls play with different toys? Is there such a thing as a "girl toy" or a "boy toy?" If boys and girls are interested in and play with different toys, why do these differences occur? Are there biological factors that contribute to gender differences in children's toy interests and play? Cognitive factors? Social factors? Is it problematic for boys and girls to play with different toys? What do top scientists say about children's gender-typed toy play? What recommendations do these experts make for parents, educators, and toy developers? As a part of a societal conversation about gender and toys, these questions, among others, have received considerable attention in the last 5 years within the psychological literature, social media, and popular press and have also been considered by parents, scholars, feminist activists, and even the White House. These questions often lead to debate among interested parties and do not have clear-cut answers, as the chapters in this volume illustrate. The scientific literature demonstrates that gender differences in children's toy interests and play are

http://dx.doi.org/10.1037/0000077-001
Gender Typing of Children's Toys: How Early Play Experiences Impact Development, E. S. Weisgram and L. M. Dinella (Editors)

complex in their presence and causes, as well as their consequences for child development.

We do know that gender differences are present in children's toy interests and choices. Numerous studies have shown that boys, on average, are more interested than girls in toys such as vehicles, action figures, and sporting equipment—toys that are often considered by society to be "boys' toys" (or masculine toys, as they will be called throughout this volume). Girls, on average, are more interested than boys in toys such as baby dolls, fashion dolls, and princess dresses and accessories—toys that are often considered by society to be "girls' toys" (i.e., feminine toys). Boys' and girls' toy interests both contribute to and are derived from these classifications, illustrating one of the complex issues within the literature.

What makes a toy a masculine or feminine toy? Imagine a new toy has been developed for an upcoming holiday season. When the new toy is introduced, it is marketed as the "Top New Toy for Girls" and includes a picture of only girls on the pink and purple packaging or marketing materials. The explicit and implicit labels used in the advertising and packaging of the toy may consequently create a greater interest among girls than boys. However, one can imagine an alternative scenario, in which a toy is marketed to both boys and girls by omitting explicit and implicit labels. If girls become more interested in the toy, regardless of the gender-neutral marketing, does the toy become stereotyped by society as a feminine toy? These scenarios illustrate the complexity of gender typing of toys

OUR GOALS

In this volume, we bring together top scholars from the field of developmental psychology to contribute their expertise about gender, toys, and play. These esteemed scholars discuss a constellation of topics about gender and toy play while relying heavily on the scientific literature. The authors in this volume, ourselves included, share the goal of understanding how gender differences in children's interests may emerge, what consequences gender-typed toy play has for children's development, and how we can break down gender stereotypes about toys.

The first part of this volume presents a general introduction to the topic of gender-typed toys and play. Erica S. Weisgram (Chapter 1) begins by discussing the reasons it is important to study gender and children's toy interests, providing a brief history of gender-typed toys, and summarizing the recent conversations in American society about gender typing of children's toys. Lisa M. Dinella (Chapter 2) then presents a review and critique of the methodology that is commonly used to study gender and toys. Kristina M. Zosuls and Diane N. Ruble (Chapter 3) present a thorough discussion of gender differences in infants' toy interests and play patterns, and consider the role of cognitive constructs such as gender identification in these interests and behaviors. Isabelle D. Cherney (Chapter 4) broadly examines gender-typed toys, the implications of gender-typed toys and play, and the features that denote each toy type, such as explicit and implicit gender labels.

In the second part of this volume, the chapter authors illuminate the factors that may contribute to gender differences in children's toy interests and play patterns. Melissa Hines and Jacqueline Davis (Chapter 5) discuss biological factors that may contribute to these differences with an emphasis on the role of prenatal testosterone. Christia Spears Brown and Ellen A. Stone (Chapter 6) discuss the social agents that impact children's interests and behaviors, highlighting the role of parents, peers, and media and advertising. To close Part II, Carol Lynn Martin and Rachel E. Cook (Chapter 7) review prominent theories of gender development, illustrating the importance of gender identity, gender schemas, and stereotype construction and endorsement in the development of children's interests and behaviors.

The final part of this volume reflects on the consequences of gender-typed toy play. In sum, the authors examine how playing predominantly with gender-typed toys may lead to gender differences in development that extend into adulthood. Lise Eliot (Chapter 8) discusses the importance of play from a biological and evolutionary perspective and the potential consequences of gender differentiated play for biological and neural development. Next, Sarah K. Murnen (Chapter 9) highlights the consequences of gender-typed toys and play for social development, including the development of nurturing behaviors, sexualization of girls, and aggressive behaviors. Lynn S. Liben, Kingsley M. Schroeder, Giulia A. Borriello, and Erica S. Weisgram (Chapter 10) discuss the role of toys and play in the development of cognitive skills and how gender differences in toy interests and play patterns may contribute to gender differentiation of these skills. Next, Megan Fulcher and Emily F. Coyle (Chapter 11) discuss the long-term consequences of gender-typed toys and play for individuals' work and family roles as adults. Specifically, they reflect on how play with masculine and feminine toys may differentially prepare men and women for social roles or constrain their visions for their future. Campbell Leaper and Rebecca S. Bigler (Chapter 12) shift the conversation to how society's gender typing of toys can have consequences for the development and maintenance of gender stereotypes. They also highlight evidence-based practices for intervention to encourage diversity in children's toy play and attenuate the negative consequences of gender-typed toy play. In the Conclusion (Chapter 13), the volume editors echo the many authors' calls for additional research on gender, toys, and play. We outline gaps in the scientific literature where further research is needed, and discuss the type of methodology that may best address the issues at hand. We also conclude that evidence supports the need for a reduction of gender stereotypes about toys in our society. Achieving this goal will allow children to follow their own interests without gender limits and help them develop a wide range of skills that will benefit them in the future.

We hope that this volume will inform scholars, parents, educators, feminist activists, policymakers, and executives in the toy industry who seek a deeper understanding of gender and toys. We also hope that these pages will inspire more research into the gendered nature of children's toys and play—research that continuously answers and poses interesting and important questions to advance the psychological literature.

I

TOY PREFERENCES
AND GENDER

1

GENDER TYPING OF TOYS IN HISTORICAL AND CONTEMPORARY CONTEXTS

ERICA S. WEISGRAM

Gender typing of toys has been a focus of recent discussions in the mainstream media and on social media as many parents and feminist activists call for a reduction of gender stereotypes in toys and marketing. Gender typing of toys is the process through which toys become associated with a particular gender within a culture. Many scholars within psychology have considered which factors lead to gender typing of children's toys such as labels, colors, marketing, and other factors (see Chapter 4 for a review). Examining the factors that contribute to gender typing in the current social context is of the utmost importance, especially for designing and advocating for interventions to reduce gender typing and gender stereotypes about toys. Investigating the process of gender typing of toys also has important implications for the broader field of gender development within psychology. In addition, it may be useful to explore the historical context in which gender typing of toys has emerged. Which toys have been gender typed historically? Why were

http://dx.doi.org/10.1037/0000077-002
Gender Typing of Children's Toys: How Early Play Experiences Impact Development, E. S. Weisgram and L. M. Dinella (Editors)

certain toys associated with only one gender in the past? As gender roles have changed over time, particularly in the United States, is this traditional gender typing of toys still relevant?

In this chapter, I first discuss the multiple reasons it is important to study the role of gender in children's toy interests and play from a developmental psychology perspective. Second, I give a brief history of gender-typed toys by describing the toys that were given to and played with by boys and girls at various time points across Western cultures. Last, I summarize the recent conversations in American society about gender typing of children's toys.

WHY STUDY GENDER-TYPED TOYS?

Studying children's gender-typed toys and play may seem like fun and games, but examining children's toys and play continues to be crucial given their importance in children's lives. The toys, activities, and play patterns with which boys and girls engage can differentially impact their development. The study of gender-typed toys and play has implications not only for children but also for numerous stakeholders such as parents and guardians, grandparents and relatives, child care workers and teachers, feminist policymakers and activists, and toy developers and marketing executives. Thus, it is important from a psychological perspective to describe and explain the complex constellation of factors that are both causes and consequences of the gender differentiation in children's toy interests and play.

Toys and Play Are Important Parts of Children's Daily Lives

Most psychologists, educators, and parents and caregivers would agree with Jean Piaget (1962) that play is an important component of children's development. Centuries apart, philosophers Plato and John Locke both emphasized that children's play should be encouraged as part of their education and development (as cited in Cross, 1997), a position reiterated by preeminent psychologists Jean Piaget (1962) and Lev Vygotsky (1967). Children in the United States spend a large portion of their day engaged in play (about 10–15 hours per week according to time diary estimates), an estimate that did not vary significantly across racial/ethnic groups or socioeconomic status (Hofferth, 2009). The amount of time children spend in play at home has decreased since the 1980s, but it still takes up more time than every other activity beyond sleeping and school/day care (these estimates do not account for play in day care or school settings) and is comparable to the amount of time spent watching television (Hofferth, 2009). According to Piaget, children begin engaging in symbolic play in the second and third year of life as their motor and cognitive skills mature and develop. Symbolic play often involves the use of toys, and the toys that children choose may evoke different themes and play patterns. Thus, if boys and girls are engaged in play with different types of toys, the themes and play patterns that make up their symbolic play may also differ.

Gender Differences in Toys Are Large

Gender differences in children's toy interests are among the largest in the psychological literature (Hyde, 2005; see also Chapter 5, this volume). When making between-gender comparisons, boys play with and show more interest in *masculine toys* compared with girls, and girls play with and show more interest in *feminine toys* compared with boys. When making within-gender comparisons, girls show more interest in feminine toys than masculine toys and boys show more interest in masculine toys than feminine toys. In fact, these toys are considered *masculine* and *feminine*, in part, because of gender differences in children's interests, but these categories also encompass groups of toys that are often considered to afford either agentic or communal goals, respectively (Kahlenberg & Hein, 2010). Boys' toy interests are particularly gender typed. In a recent observation of children's free play with toys, Dinella, Weisgram, and Fulcher (2017) found that boys spent over half of their time (52%) playing with masculine toys and girls spent about a third of their time (29%) with feminine toys. Hines and Davis (in Chapter 5, this volume) further discuss the strength and direction of gender differences in children's interest in masculine and feminine toys as they consider the factors that contribute to these differences.

Gender-Typed Toy Play Differentially Impacts Boys' and Girls' Development

Research throughout the fields of philosophy, education, and psychology has investigated the importance of toys and play in children's physical, cognitive, and social development, as well as their emotional and mental health (Singer, Golinkoff, & Hirsh-Pasek, 2009). To the extent that boys and girls are playing with different types of toys, they may be honing and developing different skills contributing to gender differences in adulthood. For example, preschool children who play with puzzles perform better on spatial tasks than their peers (Levine, Ratliff, Huttenlocher, & Cannon, 2012). Play with masculine toys may exercise skills and abilities that feminine toys do not and vice versa. The consequences of gender-typed toy play are discussed in Part III of this volume and are a primary motive for investigating gender differences in children's toys and play.

Toys and Play Are a First Avenue of Gender Role Messages

The relationship between gender roles and gender-typed toys is complex and dynamic. As I discuss below, many toys throughout history have been created to replicate and teach appropriate gender roles to boys and girls (Cross, 1997). For example, toy dolls and swords were common playthings for girls and boys, respectively, in medieval England to prepare them for their future roles as mothers and soldiers. Since the second wave of the feminist movement in the 1970s, gender roles have converged, and there are very few occupational or caregiving roles that are gender specific. Despite the convergence in adult gender roles, many children's toys remain gender stereotyped (Sweet, 2014). The gender typing of children's toys found in today's marketplace may perpetuate the traditional gender roles of the 20th century, rather than promote gender equality. Because toy play is one of the first avenues of experience for children, the explicit and implicit messages that they receive about toys from socializing agents (e.g., parents, peers, media, advertising) may introduce young children to gender roles, lead them to develop stereotypical gender schemas about adult roles, and perpetuate gender roles across generations. Thus, it is possible that toys are gender typed because they reflect the gender roles of society, but it is also simultaneously possible that they create and perpetuate stereotypical gender roles.

Theories of Gender Development Can Be Tested

Numerous theories of gender development have been created to explain gender differences in children's interests and behaviors. Essentialist theories examine biological factors (e.g., evolutionary psychology), environmental theories examine social factors (e.g., social learning theory), and constructivist theories examine cognitive factors (e.g., gender schema theory, social cognitive theory, dual pathways model; Liben & Bigler, 2002). These theories seek to explain gender differences in motivations and behaviors in a wide variety of domains, including occupational choices, achievement-related choices, peer preferences, media consumption, and many others. Toys and play are a developmentally appropriate domain in which researchers can test theories of stereotype construction and utilization, causal influences on interests and behaviors, and the development of gender schemata among very young children who may be unfamiliar with information from other domains (e.g., occupations, academic subjects; Weisgram, 2016).

A BRIEF HISTORY OF GENDER TYPING OF TOYS

The history of children's toys and play can shed light on how historical gender roles have shaped present-day gender typing of children's toys. Archeological evidence of toys has been found since approximately 1000 BCE (Mammas & Spandidos, 2012); throughout history many toys have been created by children and adults, such as rattles, balls, tops, kites, wooden animals, and whistles (Jaffé, 2006). These toys were popular among both boys and girls, and children often played in mixed gender groups. Many toys were not gender differentiated because they were shared with other gender siblings and among children in the neighborhood (Jaffé, 2006; Orme, 2001).

Some toys, however, were more likely to be given to boys or girls because they simulated the roles children would have as adults—roles that were historically very gender differentiated (Cross, 1997; Jaffé, 2006; Orme, 2001). These toys were given to children to allow them to imitate same-gender role models, a behavior that is found in children cross-culturally, and to train children to do the work of adults in a way that was safe and age-appropriate. Girls in ancient Greece, ancient Rome, and medieval England often played with homemade dolls, imitating their mothers as they cared for younger siblings and learning to sew clothing for their dolls—skills that would be needed in adulthood as they took on domestic roles (Cross, 1997). Boys in ancient Rome played with toy soldiers and chariots, and in medieval England played with wooden crossbows, arrows, and swords to emulate the men who were soldiers and the knights who were prominent in their community, and to train them to take on these roles in adulthood (Cross, 1997; Orme, 2001).

With the development of plastics and automated machinery to mass produce toys, and innovations in transportation that increased the trade of items, the toy industry grew rapidly in the 19th and 20th centuries (Cross, 1997; Jaffé, 2006). The automation of many household duties combined with the smaller number of children in each household meant that children had more time to play rather than helping care for younger siblings or doing household chores. As a result, play with toys became more recreational and less about training for future roles, yet still reflected the gender roles of the time (Cross, 1997). In the United States in the 1870s, store catalogs began to include a section with toys that featured tools advertised for boys and dolls and doll accessories advertised for girls (Cross, 1997). With changing technology and automation in the early 1900s, toys associated with boys also changed to emphasize science, industry, and construction, while toys associated with girls continued to emphasize domestic roles (Cross, 1997). Throughout the 20th century, toys marketed toward boys incorporated technology and industry: cars, airplanes, model trains, chemistry sets, toy cameras, construction toys, and toy soldiers and guns. Toys marketed toward girls continued to incorporate domestic roles, though the number of accessories expanded: dolls, dresses, toy washing machines, strollers, doll houses, and play kitchens.

Across the second half of the 20th century, many toys were appealing to both boys and girls, and many new toys were developed for a gender-segregated market. However, the gender roles of women in particular were changing rapidly, which led to the toy industry slightly decreasing its emphasis on domesticity in feminine toys (Orenstein, 2011). As a result of these changing gender roles, fashion dolls were introduced and marketed toward girls, with Barbie quickly becoming the most prominent brand in the United States after her introduction in 1959 (Orenstein, 2011). In the early days of the brand, Barbie countered stereotypes by presenting Barbie as a career woman with masculine and feminine occupations. However, through her appearance, signature pink color, and the fashion styles and accessories, Barbie has emphasized femininity, leading the brand to be one of the foremost gender-typed toys for many years (Orenstein, 2011). In recent years, fashion dolls that emphasize feminine qualities and promote stereotypes and sexualization have continued to be developed (e.g., Bratz, Monster High; Orenstein, 2011), but some fashion dolls that counter stereotypes have very recently been developed as a reaction to the highly sexualized, popular dolls (e.g., Lottie, DC Super Hero Girls, Project MC^2; Martinson, 2012). Soon after the premier of Barbie, G.I. Joe (in 1964) and Action Man (in 1966) were introduced and marketed toward boys as "action figures," a type of toy that continues to be popular, with present-day action figures often representing superheroes and movie characters (Bainbridge, 2010). Action figures have increased in masculinity since their introduction into the toy market as denoted, in part, by the dramatic increase in muscular builds and weapons (Pope, Olivardia, Gruber, & Borowiecki, 1999). These features are also indicators of an increase in masculinity in other toys marketed primarily toward boys (Bartneck, Min Ser, Moltchanova, Smithies, & Harrington, 2016).

A cousin to modern toys, computer and video games are played by many children in the United States (Cherney & London, 2006). On average, boys engage in more video game and computer game play than girls ($d = 1.22$; Cherney & London, 2006) and the top selling video games often have masculine themes and characters (e.g., first person shooter scenarios, simulated sports games; Dill, Gentile, Richter, & Dill, 2005; Morris, 2016) leading to a gender-segregated market. Whether games have masculine themes because boys play video games more than girls or whether more boys play because of the masculine themes has been considered a "chicken and egg problem" by scholars in the field (Gittleson, 2014). The drastic increase of digital content such as mobile applications and social networking games has changed the types of games children play, and thus future research should explore the role of gender in children's engagement with these games.

Gender-targeted marketing of toys has changed over the course of the 20th and 21st centuries. In her work, Elizabeth Sweet (2014) has examined toy advertisements throughout these time periods, noting that in the early 1900s toys marketed toward boys included those that emphasized industry, while toys marketed toward girls emphasized domesticity. Yet, during this same time period, over half of the toys were advertised as appropriate for both boys and girls (Sweet, 2014). Interestingly, some rare advertisements specifically included counterstereotypical messages in the early 1900s. For example, the Sears catalog in 1931 mentioned that "dolls are a tender influence for little boys" (as cited in Cross, 1997). In the 1970s, as the second wave of the feminist movement became prominent and women entered the workforce in larger numbers, gender-targeted marketing of toys decreased dramatically (Sweet, 2014). In her analysis, Sweet found that less than 2% of toys were marketed toward boys or toward girls in the 1975 Sears Catalog and counterstereotypical advertisements were prevalent. In the 1970s, the LEGO corporation specifically noted in a letter to parents that "a lot of boys like dolls houses. They're more human than spaceships. A lot of girls like spaceships. They're more exciting than dolls houses. The most important thing is to put the right material in their hands and let them create whatever appeals to them" (as cited in Bologna, 2014).

Beginning in the 1980s, gender-typed marketing increased once again, a trend that has continued into the 21st century as gender and age differences are exaggerated to create segmented markets and increase sales (Fine & Rush, 2016; Kahlenberg & Hein, 2010; Orenstein, 2011). Products often include explicit gender labels or implicit labels such as gender-typed colors or narratives that are thought to be appealing more to boys or to girls (Auster & Mansbach, 2012; Owen & Pardon, 2015; Sweet, 2014). Even among previously gender-neutral toys, there is a trend toward making two different versions of the same item: one with primary and dark colors aimed at boys and one with pastel and pink-hued colors aimed at girls to increase sales within families that have both boys and girls (Orenstein, 2011). In her thorough analysis of the gender-typed marketing trends, Orenstein (2011) noted, "That pinkification could, I suppose, be read as a good faith attempt at progress . . . [or] it could even remind girls to shun anything that *isn't* pink and pretty as not for them, a mind-set that could eventually prove limiting" (p. 38, italics in original). Indeed, this trend can also prove limiting to boys who may avoid pink toys or toys in pink packaging—toys that may otherwise interest them.

The current toy industry generally considers boys and girls to be different target markets (Jaffé, 2006; Orenstein, 2011), suggesting that gender differences in children's interests create the need for the development of different types of toys and marketing strategies. However, by marketing toys with explicit and implicit gender labels, the toy industry is also simultaneously creating and magnifying gender differences in children's toy interests and, perhaps, marginalizing those children who have counterstereotypical interests (Fine & Rush, 2016; Weisgram, Fulcher, & Dinella, 2014). The intertwined, dynamic factors of gender differences in children's interests, gender-typed marketing strategies, and cultural gender roles and stereotypes all construct the gender typing of children's toys that is present in children's lives.

CONTEMPORARY CONVERSATIONS ABOUT GENDER AND TOYS

In the past several years, conversations about gender and toys have increased in the mainstream media, on social media, and within academic circles. Peggy Orenstein's (2011) book, *Cinderella Ate My Daughter: Dispatches from the Front Lines of the New Girlie-Girl Culture*, discussed the increase of gender-typed marketing of toys, the femininization of toys marketed towards girls, and the messages these toys send to children. In addition, a social media campaign called "Let Toys Be Toys" was launched in 2012 in the United Kingdom encouraging the toy industry to do away with gender-typed marketing and to make suggestions to parents and educators of toys, books, and media that are gender neutral or defy stereotypes ("Let Toys Be Toys," 2017). In part as a result of this campaign, Toys "R" Us (a major toy retailer) eliminated explicit gender labels in its U.K. stores in 2013. Other popular press books were published in 2014 that encouraged reducing gender stereotypes in children's toys and play, such as Melissa Atkins Wardy's (2014) *Redefining Girly: How Parents Can Fight the Stereotyping and Sexualizing of Girlhood, From Birth to Tween* and Christia Spears Brown's (2014) *Parenting Beyond Pink and Blue: How to Raise Your Kids Free of Gender Stereotypes*. The conversation also continued within the popular press and with additional social media campaigns such as "No Gender December," an Australian campaign that aims to "create opportunities for kids to develop a broad range of skills, support them in discovering a whole rainbow of colours, encourage them to learn about themselves and each other, free from the limitations of gender stereotypes" (Play Unlimited, 2017). Scholars within academia have also been discussing these concerns—in fact, there were two panels on gender and toys presented at the 2015 biannual meeting of the Society for Research in Child Development in Philadelphia, Pennsylvania.

In summer 2015, a major U.S. retailer, Target Corporation, announced that they would be removing both explicit and implicit gender labels from the children's toy and bedding sections in its stores. This was in part a response to criticism for having signage reading "Building sets. Girls' building sets" that was noticed and criticized by a mother and posted to social media (Bechtel, 2015). Target's announcement said,

> We never want guests or their families to feel frustrated or limited by the way things are presented. Over the past year, guests have raised important questions about a handful of signs in our stores that offer product suggestions based on gender . . . We heard you, and we agree. Right now, our teams are working across the store to identify areas where we can phase out gender-based signage to help strike a better balance. (Target Corporation, 2015)

Other major retailers quietly followed suit. Following this announcement, major media outlets reached out to scholars and feminist activists, who largely supported the move. Critics of Target's decision, however, claimed that gender differences in children's toy interests were innate and that removing labels would not affect children's interests but would make toys harder to locate (Sieczkowski, 2015). Supporters of Target's decision noted that explicit and implicit gender labels could influence children's decisions and removing the labels may reduce gender stereotypes and increase cross-gender toy interests (Cunha, 2015; Grinberg, 2015; Weisgram, 2015). Thus, this announcement and the popular press "buzz" that followed was a turning point in the societal conversation about gender, toys, and play that continues today.

On April 6, 2016, my coeditor, Lisa Dinella, and I attended a conference at the White House entitled "Helping Our Children Explore, Learn, and Dream Without Limits: Breaking Down Gender Stereotypes in Media and Toys." Officials from the Obama administration gathered together toy industry executives, media executives, academic scholars, and youth-serving and parent organizations to facilitate a conversation between these groups about implications that gender stereotypes about toys and media have for children's development (The White House, Office of the Press Secretary, 2016). The conference included a panel of feminist activists, bloggers, and media experts who advocated for reducing gender stereotypes among different segments of the population and discussed the role of social media in meeting this goal. In addition, scholars from the fields of communications, psychology, and sociology presented research on how boys and girls are often represented in the media and in toy advertisements, and how explicit and implicit messages about gender affect children's interests, self-esteem, and development.

In addition, executives from top toy and media companies (e.g., Mattel, LEGO, Disney Channel, DC Entertainment) discussed the efforts their companies were making to reduce stereotypes and increase diversity within their brands. For example, representatives from Mattel and the Disney Channel discussed increasing within-gender diversity in their female dolls'/characters' body types as well as the occupations, activities, and traits that are afforded by each character (Filippatos, 2016; Pantel, 2016). Representatives from LEGO and DC Entertainment discussed their efforts to increase girls' interest in and participation with toys within their brand with the introduction of the LEGO Friends and LEGO Elves and DC Superhero Girls lines, respectively, and the praise and criticism that have accompanied their "journey" to reduce gender stereotypes in their brands (McNally, 2016; Nelson, 2016). Representatives from DC Entertainment and Disney's Marvel spoke about increasing the representation of girls throughout both superhero lines (Filippatos, 2016; Nelson, 2016). The conference also included up-and-coming toy developers who aim to break down stereotypes, such as Wonder Crew, a company that is developing and marketing dolls to boys, and littleBits, a company that is developing small robotics toys with gender-neutral packaging and marketing them to girls (Bdeir, 2016; Wider, 2016). Throughout the day-long conference, attendees from toy and media companies were able to interact with experts in communications, psychology, and related fields to discuss how the scientific community may inform the decisions that they make in terms of developing and marketing toys. This conference was not only informative and insightful for all involved, but for many corporations and companies, it represented a commitment to consider reducing gender stereotyping of toys that they produce and market and a willingness to continue the conversation about gender typing of toys in the United States.

CONCLUSION

Gender typing of toys is an important and relevant topic for scholars in psychology, individuals and organizations involved in creating and marketing toys to children, parents and relatives who are providing toys to children, and feminist activists who wish to see the reduction of gender stereotypes in children's toys and lives. Although historically, toys were given to allow children to practice the gender-typed roles that dominated their culture and time period, these gender roles have changed dramatically, particularly in the United States. Thus, many questions remain about children's interest in gender-typed toys in the present and how these interests are impacted by changes in the broader culture. The chapters in this volume suggest that the factors that influence children's interest in gender-typed toys are complex and multifaceted. As gender roles continue to evolve, I look forward to seeing the changes that emerge in the toy market, the psychological literature, and in contemporary conversations about the gender typing of toys.

REFERENCES

Auster, C. J., & Mansbach, C. S. (2012). The gender marketing of toys: An analysis of color and type of toy on the Disney store website. *Sex Roles, 67,* 375–388. http://dx.doi.org/10.1007/s11199-012-0177-8

Bainbridge, J. (2010). Fully articulated: The rise of the action figure and the changing face of "children's" entertainment. *Continuum: Journal of Media & Cultural Studies, 24,* 829–842. http://dx.doi.org/10.1080/10304312.2010.510592

Bartneck, C., Min Ser, Q., Moltchanova, E., Smithies, J., & Harrington, E. (2016). Have LEGO products become more violent? *PLoS One, 11,* e0155401. http://dx.doi.org/10.1371/journal.pone.0155401

Bdeir, A. (2016, April). *Case studies: Breaking down gender stereotypes in toys and media* [Panel discussion]. Washington, DC: The White House.

Bechtel, A. (2015, June 1). Don't do this, @Target [Twitter post from @abianne]. Retrieved from http://www.newsweek.com/target-phase-out-gender-based-signs-361353

Bologna, C. (2014, November 24). Letter from LEGO to parents in the '70s makes an important point about gender. *Huffington Post.* Retrieved from http://www.huffingtonpost.com/2014/11/24/lego-letter-from-the-70s_n_6212362.html

Brown, C. S. (2014). *Parenting beyond pink and blue: How to raise your kids free of gender stereotypes.* New York, NY: Ten Speed Press.

Cherney, I. D., & London, K. (2006). Gender-linked differences in the toys, television shows, computer games, and outdoor activities of 5- to 13-year-old children. *Sex Roles, 54,* 717–726. http://dx.doi.org/10.1007/s11199-006-9037-8

Cross, G. (1997). *Kids' stuff: Toys and the changing world of American childhood.* Cambridge, MA: Harvard University Press.

Cunha, D. (2015, August 10). Target's decision to remove gender-based signs is just the start. *Time.* Retrieved from http://time.com/3990442/target-gender-based-signs/

Dill, K. E., Gentile, D. A., Richter, W. A., & Dill, J. C. (2005). Violence, sex, race, and age in popular video games: A content analysis. In E. Cole & J. H. Daniel (Eds.), *Featuring females: Feminist analyses of media* (pp. 115–130). Washington, DC: American Psychological Association. http://dx.doi.org/10.1037/11213-008

Dinella, L. M., Weisgram, E. S., & Fulcher, M. (2017). Children's gender-typed toy interests: Does propulsion matter? *Archives of Sexual Behavior, 46,* 1295–1305. http://dx.doi.org/10.1007/s10508-016-0901-5

Filippatos, T. (2016, April). *Case studies: Breaking down gender stereotypes in toys and media* [Panel discussion]. Washington, DC: The White House.

Fine, C., & Rush, E. (2016). "Why does all the girls have to buy pink stuff?" The ethics and science of the gendered toy marketing debate. *Journal of Business Ethics*. Advance online publication. http://dx.doi.org/10.1007/s10551-016-3080-3

Gittleson, K. (2014, February 18). How did GI Joe become the world's most successful boys' toy? *BBC News*. Retrieved from http://www.bbc.com/news/business-26196760

Grinberg, E. (2015, August 8). Target to move away from gender-based signs. *CNN*. Retrieved from http://www.cnn.com/2015/08/08/living/gender-based-signs-target-feat/index.html

Hofferth, S. L. (2009). Changes in American children's time—1997 to 2003. *Electronic International Journal of Time Use Research, 6*, 26–47. http://dx.doi.org/10.13085/eIJTUR.6.1.26-47

Hyde, J. S. (2005). The gender similarities hypothesis. *American Psychologist, 60*, 581–592. http://dx.doi.org/10.1037/0003-066X.60.6.581

Jaffé, D. (2006). *The history of toys: From spinning tops to robots*. Stroud, England: Sutton Publishing Limited.

Kahlenberg, S. G., & Hein, M. M. (2010). Progression on Nickelodeon? Gender-role stereotypes in toy commercials. *Sex Roles, 62*, 830–847. http://dx.doi.org/10.1007/s11199-009-9653-1

Let Toys Be Toys. (2017). *About the campaign*. Retrieved from http://lettoysbetoys.org.uk/

Levine, S. C., Ratliff, K. R., Huttenlocher, J., & Cannon, J. (2012). Early puzzle play: A predictor of preschoolers' spatial transformation skill. *Developmental Psychology, 48*, 530–542. http://dx.doi.org/10.1037/a0025913

Liben, L. S., & Bigler, R. S. (2002). The developmental course of gender differentiation: Conceptualizing, measuring, and evaluating constructs and pathways. *Monographs of the Society for Research in Child Development, 67*, i–viii. http://dx.doi.org/10.1111/1540-5834.00200

Mammas, I. N., & Spandidos, D. A. (2012). A 3,000-year-old child's toy. *European Journal of Pediatrics, 171*, 1413. http://dx.doi.org/10.1007/s00431-012-1790-9

Martinson, J. (2012, November 27). Make way, Barbie: Let's welcome Lottie, the doll who isn't a little monster. *The Guardian*. Retrieved from https://www.theguardian.com/lifeandstyle/the-womens-blog-with-jane-martinson/2012/nov/27/make-way-barbie-welcome-lottie

McNally, M. (2016, April). *Case studies: Breaking down gender stereotypes in toys and media* [Panel discussion]. Washington, DC: The White House.

Morris, C. (2016, January 14). Here are the top selling video games of 2015: Exactly how strong was The Force for EA? *Fortune*. Retrieved from http://fortune.com/2016/01/14/here-are-the-best-selling-video-games-of-2015/?iid=sr-link1

Nelson, D. (2016, April). *Case studies: Breaking down gender stereotypes in toys and media* [Panel discussion]. Washington, DC: The White House.

Orenstein, P. (2011). *Cinderella ate my daughter: Dispatches from the front lines of the new girlie-girl culture*. New York, NY: Harper Collins.

Orme, N. (2001). *Medieval children*. New Haven, CT: Yale University Press.

Owen, P. R., & Pardon, M. (2015). The language of toys: Gendered language in toy advertisements. *Journal of Research on Women and Gender, 6*, 67–80. Retrieved from https://journals.tdl.org/jrwg/index.php/jrwg/article/view/24

Pantel, L. (2016, April). *Case studies: Breaking down gender stereotypes in toys and media* [Panel discussion]. Washington, DC: The White House.

Piaget, J. (1962). *Play, dreams, and imitation in childhood*. (C. Gattegno & F. M. Hodgson, Trans.). New York, NY: Norton.

Play Unlimited. (2017). *No gender December: Give gifts not stereotypes* [Website]. Retrieved from http://www.nogenderdecember.com/

Pope, H. G., Jr., Olivardia, R., Gruber, A., & Borowiecki, J. (1999). Evolving ideals of male body image as seen through action toys. *International Journal of Eating Disorders, 26*, 65–72. http://dx.doi.org/10.1002/(SICI)1098-108X(199907)26:1<65::AID-EAT8>3.0.CO;2-D

Sieczkowski, C. (2015, August 11). Target angers customers with its stores' new non-gendered policy. *Huffington Post*. Retrieved from http://www.huffingtonpost.com/entry/target-gender-biased-signs_us_55c9ffe6e4b0923c12be0f96

Singer, D. G., Golinkoff, R. M., & Hirsh-Pasek, K. (Eds.). (2009). *Play = learning: How play motivates and enhances children's cognitive and social-emotional growth*. New York, NY: Oxford University Press. http://dx.doi.org/10.1093/acprof:oso/9780195304381.001.0001

Sweet, E. (2014). Toys are more divided by gender now than they were 50 years ago. *The Atlantic*. Retrieved from https://www.theatlantic.com/business/archive/2014/12/toys-are-more-divided-by-gender-now-than-they-were-50-years-ago/383556/

Target Corporation. (2015, August 7). What's in store: Moving away from gender-based signs. *Target: A bullseye view*. Retrieved from https://corporate.target.com/article/2015/08/gender-based-signs-corporate

Vygotsky, L. S. (1967). Play and its role in the mental development of the child. *Soviet Psychology, 5*, 6–18. Retrieved from http://www.tandfonline.com/doi/abs/10.2753/RPO1061-040505036?tab=permissions&scroll=top

Wardy, M. A. (2014). *Redefining girly: How parents can fight stereotyping and sexualizing of girlhood, from birth to tween*. Chicago, IL: Chicago Review Press.

Weisgram, E. S. (2015). Now that Target won't label toys by gender, some alternatives. *The New York Times*. Retrieved from https://parenting.blogs.nytimes.com/2015/08/17/truth-in-signage-in-the-toy-aisle-after-target-removes-gender-labels-whats-next/?_r=0

Weisgram, E. S. (2016). The cognitive construction of gender stereotypes: Evidence for the dual pathways model of gender differentiation. *Sex Roles, 75*, 301–313. http://dx.doi.org/10.1007/s11199-016-0624-z

Weisgram, E. S., Fulcher, M., & Dinella, L. M. (2014). Pink gives girls permission: Exploring the role of explicit gender labels and gender-typed colors on preschool children's toy preferences. *Journal of Applied Developmental Psychology, 35*, 401–409. Retrieved from http://fulcherlab.academic.wlu.edu/files/2015/10/pink-gives-girls-permission-1.pdf

The White House, Office of the Press Secretary. (2016, April 6). *FACT SHEET: Breaking down gender stereotypes in media and toys so that our children can explore, learn, and dream without limits* [Press release]. Retrieved from https://obamawhitehouse.archives.gov/the-press-office/2016/04/06/factsheet-breaking-down-gender-stereotypes-media-and-toys-so-our

Wider, L. (2016, April). *Case studies: Breaking down gender stereotypes in toys and media* [Panel discussion]. Washington, DC: The White House.

2

RESEARCH METHODS IN STUDYING GENDER AND TOY PREFERENCES

LISA M. DINELLA

Toys are prevalent and impactful in children's lives, and we should take a purposeful approach to understand the interplay of gender, toys, and children's development. Three billion toys are sold every year (Toy Industry Association, 2016b), and in 2015 the estimated market size for the United States toy industry was $25 billion (Toy Industry Association, 2016a). In addition to bringing children amusement, toys also serve to teach children academic skills, allow for interpersonal role play, provide career exploration opportunities, and deliver gendered messages about societal expectations. The gender-typed trends in children's interests in toys and the creation and marketing of toys as "for boys" or "for girls" are concerning because the narrowing of children's toy options potentially limits their exposure to toys' benefits.

Lisa M. Dinella thanks the research assistants of the Gender Development Laboratory at Monmouth University for their assistance in manuscript preparation. Maryam A. Srouji made particularly laudable contributions.

http://dx.doi.org/10.1037/0000077-003
Gender Typing of Children's Toys: How Early Play Experiences Impact Development, E. S. Weisgram and L. M. Dinella (Editors)

Given how important toys can be to children's development, the scientific method should be leveraged to inform the creation, marketing, purchasing, and availability of toys.

The goal of the chapter is to explore the scientific methods available to scholars, such as myself, as we investigate all aspects of toys and gender—the causes, correlates, and consequences. This discussion includes information about the advantages and disadvantages of the most common methodologies used in the field. I also identify some of the challenges faced by those scientifically investigating this topic, including the need to attend to and address the role of children's developmental stages and processes, and the difficulties that exist in trying to study gender—a socially constructed variable. Finally, I raise the importance of methodological pluralism in the pursuit to understand the interplay of gender, toys, and children's lives, as well as the role of mixed methodology, replication, and a systematic approach to research investigations. Attention to these aspects of research would allow for more steadfast conclusions to be drawn from the research conducted on gender and toys in childhood and across the lifespan.

TOYS ARE IMPORTANT: SCIENCE SHOULD BE USED TO GUIDE DECISIONS ABOUT THEM

As broadly stated above, toys play an important role in children's development. Throughout this volume, top researchers in the field review the many ways that toys and gender interact and are instrumental in children's lives. It is beyond the scope of this chapter to review this literature here, too. However, it is important to recognize that the psychology field's understanding of all of these associations are derived from scientific investigations using diverse methodologies. Thus, it is imperative to understand the research methods scientists use to gain this knowledge base and the diverse methodologies available to scientists who want to build upon this foundation of information.

The decisions people make about toys are also important. People make decisions about the merit and value of toys all the time. For instance, children make decisions to play with certain toys over others, given the toys provided to them (see Chapter 4, this volume). And adults are the gatekeepers of toys, such that they control the physical availability and purchasing of toys. Without evidence-based answers to questions such as whether girls and boys inherently like different toys, what the impact is of playing with gender-typed toys, and whether marketing gender stereotypes and marketing strategies impact people's beliefs about toys (Blakemore & Centers, 2005; Sweet, 2013; Weisgram, Fulcher, & Dinella, 2014; Wong & Hines, 2015), both children's toy interests and adults' toy choices may be based on gendered assumptions. I argue that toys are too important not to use science as a guide for decision making.

Scientists reading this volume may take the value of scientific investigation for granted as a shared truth. But we should not be cavalier about the role that science can and should play in understanding the connections between gender and toys. Charles S. Peirce (1877), an American philosopher, theorized about the relative virtue of people's strategies for making decisions and constructing belief systems. Peirce proposed four increasingly sophisticated levels of decision making, starting with the method of tenacity at the base, the methods of authority and a priori logic following respectively, and the method of science at the pinnacle. He pointed out the usefulness of each strategic level, but also each level's limitations. I posit that much of the everyday decision making about toys is functioning in the lower three tiers of Peirce's decision-making heuristic. For example, Peirce asserted that at the most basic level of belief setting, tenacity, people hold fast to the beliefs they already have and avoid situations that would induce doubt. Psychological research supports this conjecture, with a body of research existing on confirmation bias (e.g., Wason, 1960) and including more recent fMRI brain scans that illustrate humans' tendencies to make decisions that minimize negative affect and maximize positive affect (Westen, Blagov, Harenski, Kilts, & Hamann, 2006). It is plausible that beliefs about children's toys tenaciously persist regardless of the veracity of these beliefs.

Peirce's (1877) second level, the method of authority, describes how people base their beliefs on those espoused by community institutions and that consequences can follow for those whose beliefs counter this social structure. Peirce's third method, a priori logic, refers to when people choose their beliefs on the basis of which broadly accepted ideas they deem reasonable. It is easy to see how Peirce's second and third methods parallel the role of socialization forces in people's gender-related toy decisions, such as how media and advertising label certain toys to be for girls but others for boys, and that there are social costs associated with children engaging in cross-gender play (see Chapter 6). Importantly, Peirce pointed out that both of these methods of decision making are flawed; they are subject to change with the popular trends of the day, and lack the benefits of the systematic and objective investigation provided by the scientific method.

Purposeful empirical investigation, the fourth and most sophisticated of Peirce's (1877) methods, can help people understand children's decisions about toys, guide adults' decision making, and provide the answers needed to make informed decisions about toys. For example, scientific methods can help identify the characteristics of masculine and feminine (see Chapter 4), what causes the gender differences in children's interests in toys (see Chapters 5–7), and the impact of gender-differentiated toy play (see Chapters 8–12). Thus, the goal of this chapter is to explore the research methodologies used to better understand the causes, correlates, and consequences present in the gender and toy domain.

REVIEW OF RESEARCH METHODS AVAILABLE

A sizeable body of research exists on gender and toys. The methods that are employed are diverse, and each design has its own set of strengths and drawbacks. The following subsections review some common designs and methodologies employed within this research area.

Correlational Designs

Correlational research is a mainstay in the existing body of research on gender and toys. The umbrella category of correlational research refers more to the statistical method used to analyze the data collected than to a particular research design. By definition, the term *correlational design* refers to any study that seeks to understand the association between two variables and, thus, harnesses a correlational statistical analysis to assess the extent to which two variables are linearly related to one another. The English statistician Francis Galton was the first to develop the correlation and the regression line in terms of psychological inquiry (Pearson, 1924), and is credited with developing surveys to better understand psychological constructs. His contribution to today's investigations into gender and toys cannot be understated, given the prevalence of correlation and regression analysis in this area of study.

The advantage of correlational research is the ability to determine both the strength and the direction of the relation between two variables. Multiple types of regression analyses extend these advantages to include the ability to determine the relative predictive power of multiple variables (Martin, Fabes, Hanish, Leonard, & Dinella, 2011), and the ability to identify moderator and mediator effects. A common method in correlational research is for introspective and behavioral data to be gathered via surveys and observations respectively, and then analyzed via correlational methods. These methods are typically not laborious or intrusive, can assess multiple variables at the same time, and allow for aggregate statements to be made about a large number of participants. One correlational study that illustrates the use of these methods is a study designed to explain gender segregation in preschoolers' play (Martin et al., 2011). Observations of children's gender-typed play behaviors (e.g., rough and tumble play) and children's self-reports about how similar to their gender group they felt were used to predict girls' and boys' play with same-gender peers. For both boys and girls, gender cognitions about similarity to their peers was predictive of their actual gender-segregated play; however, only boys' gender-typed play behaviors (not girls' play behaviors) were related to how often they played with same-gender peers. This study and many other studies illustrate how correlational methods can be harnessed to provide a better understanding of gender and children's play.

The advantages of correlational designs are particularly salient when studies involve children. For example, a correlation can provide information about two variables without the need for control and experimental groups or manipulations, design elements that often lead to the need for larger sample sizes that are difficult to obtain with children. Further, there are times when an experimental design requires a manipulation that would be inappropriate for children, who are considered a vulnerable population. For example, a sizable body of research exists laying the foundation that violent video games have negative implications for gamers. Methods used to assert these findings include correlational studies (Fox & Potocki, 2016), content analyses (Dietz, 1998; Dill & Thill, 2007), theoretical investigations (Jansz, 2005), and even experimental studies with young adults (Beck, Boys, Rose, & Beck, 2012; Yao, Mahood, & Linz, 2010). Moreover, meta-analysis confirms the linkages between gender, violence, and video games (Anderson et al., 2010). Given these findings, it is reasonable to question the impact of young children's exposure to violent video games, too. However, experimentally exposing young children to explicitly violent video games could be considered unethical, given that similar linkages have been substantiated in other populations and the vulnerability of the population. Thus, correlational studies of already existing exposure with negative outcomes would be a reasonable approach to answering such a question. The need to understand young children's exposure to video games and violence was recognized in a recent American Psychological Association Task Force on Violent Media (2015) report, and reviews of correlational studies (as well as studies from many other methods) are included. An advantage of correlational designs is that they can be used to fill these types of gaps in the existing literature.

The most prominent disadvantage of correlational studies is the inability to make cause-and-effect conclusions about the variables being studied. Researchers must be careful not to overstate the reach of their correlational studies, and individuals turning to scientific investigations to understand gender, children, and toys should keep the question of whether directional or causal inferences can and should be made at the forefront of their minds. Correlational findings can sometimes indicate the need for additional research into an area to confirm the direction of effects found via a correlational design. In these situations, targeted experimental studies can verify expected causal relations (see the next subsection, Experimental Designs). Further, there are times when smaller scale experimental designs can be followed up with correlational studies to confirm a broader effect. An illustration of the way these studies can work in tandem can be found in Ramani and Siegler's (2008) study on board games and mathematics skills. After a longitudinal, experimental study was conducted showing that the board game *Chutes and Ladders* taught preschool children basic mathematics skills in classroom environments, a follow up correlational study was conducted demonstrating the relation between playing board games at home and increased mathematics skills. The combination of the two designs provides depth of understanding to the question of toys' impact on children's learning.

Experimental Designs

In many disciplines, an experimental design is considered the gold standard of research methodologies. The standards and procedures for designing an experimental study were codified by statistician Ronald Fisher (1935), and although his research was largely agricultural, his work has been far-reaching and influential across scientific disciplines (Stanley, 1966). Within this type of study, true experiments are most highly valued. A true experiment is one that includes a random selection of participants, a control and a treatment group(s) in which only one variable is manipulated, and a random assignment of participants to one of these groups. Strict adherence to these design elements results in high levels of internal validity and, more important, the ability to make causal claims about the relations between independent and dependent variables.

The benefits of experimental designs have been leveraged to better understand many aspects of gender and toys. Research on cognitive influences and skill acquisition illustrates the importance of early play behaviors on learning, and how gendered exposure to these toys can lead to gender differences in academic skills (e.g., Cherney, 2008; Cherney, Bersted, & Smetter, 2014). Experimental studies have also been conducted to investigate the impact of gendered messages embedded in toys, such as whether toys can impact children's career aspirations (e.g., Coyle & Liben, 2016), and the impact of playing with thin dolls on children's own body image (e.g., Anschutz & Engels, 2010). Moreover, experimental studies have also been conducted to better understand the role of toy attributes on gender differences in toy interests (e.g., Dinella, Weisgram, & Fulcher, 2017; Weisgram et al., 2014).

There are common challenges that gender and child development researchers encounter when designing experimental studies on gender and toys. For example, many studies are conducted with child participants who are recruited from school districts or child care centers. Often, this makes the random selection process difficult to complete and results in homogeneity within samples. The existing body of research on gender and toys lacks studies that investigate the intersection of variables such as socioeconomic status, race, and ethnicity, and the difficulty of randomly selecting child participants contributes to this problem. The field needs researchers to proactively design their studies to address this problem.

The process of creating and maintaining control groups is another challenge, especially if the study is being conducted in the field rather than in a laboratory setting. An example of this challenge was discussed in an experimental study designed to test the efficacy of training schoolchildren to combat sexism, such as teaching children retorts like "There's no such thing as a girl [toy]" (Lamb, Bigler, Liben, & Green, 2009). Children in one of the treatment groups were trained to speak out should they encounter remarks designed to limit their behaviors because of their gender. However, it was noted that children in the experimental group taught other children how to respond should they, too, encounter sexist remarks. This spontaneous creation of a "cultural climate" benefited those children who learned how to combat sexism, but this potentially reduced the effect of the control/treatment design.

Scientists using experimental designs to understand gender, toys, and children must be aware of the ethical guidelines of working with a vulnerable population. As mentioned above, ethical considerations must be taken into consideration, especially when designing the study's manipulation and when deciding to incorporate deception. For example, research questions about hormonal influence on children's toy interests, exposure to violent or sexual content via video games or media, and exposure to toys with highly gender-typed messages are all compelling questions that could be answered via experimental studies in theory, but may be deemed inappropriate or unethical to put into practice.

Quasi-Experimental Designs

There are also times when true experiments are not merely impractical, but are impossible. When studying gender and toys, the inability to randomly assign children to a treatment group is a common reason to use a quasi-experimental design, such as when researchers group children by their existing gender because gender cannot be manipulated. Boys and girls may not all experience gender in exactly the same way; however, there is an assumption of commonalities (e.g., gendered messages, experiences, activities) within gender groups. High quality quasi-experimental studies make efforts to control all other aspects other than the grouping variable, such as matching groups on other constructs such as socioeconomic status or academic performance. An example of a study that leveraged a quasi-experimental design was conducted in Canada, and was designed to better understand the impact of commercials on children's toy and product interest and to understand the impact of new regulations that banned commercials during children's programming (Goldberg, 1990). However, children living near the border between Canada and the United States were still receiving American television and, thus, were still being exposed to commercials. In the study, children were grouped by the type of television available to them (rather than being randomly assigned to groups), and differential interest in the toys and products were compared. To address any cultural differences that may have existed between the two groups due to the lack of random assignment, French versus English language was controlled. This study exemplifies how quasi-experimental designs can add to the field's understanding of naturally occurring phenomena, even when a true experimental design is not feasible.

Meta-Analysis

A *meta-analysis* is a study that draws a single conclusion by statistically combining the weighted results of many studies on a given topic. The process of pooling multiple studies' data serves to increase the sample size and diversity of the study, thus increasing power. The pooling of studies also allows for greater generalizability, and downplays any methodological flaws of a particular study (Borenstein, Hedges, Higgins, & Rothstein, 2009). Researchers predetermine the inclusion criteria for studies on the topic, and leverage effect sizes (which take into consideration standard error and sample size) to arrive at a final conclusion. Decisions about which studies to include, and the concern about the phenomenon called *file drawer effect* (i.e., studies not published due to lack of significant findings or results contrary to hypothesized directions) have important implications for this research design.

Meta-analyses have been instrumental in making summative statements to answer research questions and have increased our understanding of gender differences. For instance, a hallmark meta-analysis conducted by Hyde (2005) illustrates the tendency for men and women to be overwhelmingly more similar to one another than different; the study also found many expected gender differences were not statistically evident or were too small to have practical significance when considered across a large number of studies. A wide range of topics have employed meta-analysis, such as the impact of hormones on children's behavior (Constantinescu & Hines, 2012), the role of parent–child similarity and attitudes, differences in activity levels (Eaton & Enns, 1986), and temperament (Else-Quest, Hyde, Goldsmith, & Van Hulle, 2006). More closely related to the topic of gender and toys, researchers have also conducted meta-analyses on the impact of video games on aggression (Anderson et al., 2010) and gender stereotypes in children's television programming (Browne, 1998). Further, Davis and Hines (2017) conducted a meta-analysis on studies from the 1980s until 2014 that found large within-sex preferences for gender-typed toys (see Chapter 5, this volume, for a detailed review). Meta-analyses such as these have the potential to inform our understanding of many aspects of gender and toys; they should be used to help summarize and draw conclusions about what we currently know about the topic.

Content Analysis

Content analysis is a methodology that allows for a systematic description of the content of communication, typically employing a quantitative unit of analysis (Berelson, 1952). Content analysis as a strategy was originally standardized for use in the early 1950s within the social science and communications fields with the goal of being able to draw objective conclusions about the content of a message (Nachmias & Frankfort-Nachmias, 1976). However, a variety of definitions exist for content analysis because the methodology has been adopted for use across various disciplines (Woodrum, 1984), particularly in historical and political research (Holsti, 1968). Content analysis begins with the creation of a coding scheme based on the material intended to be analyzed and determining units of analysis, categorization criteria, and identification of sample parameters (Prasad, 2008). The use of multiple coders and even more sophisticated technological transcription and coding software aids in ensuring the objective nature of the analysis. Inter-rater reliabilities, which are statistics used to determine the level of agreement between raters' codings, are required to be high prior to conclusions being drawn, and statistical analysis of the coded data is then used to synthesize findings. It is not surprising that content analysis has gained popularity across disciplines, given its usefulness in aggregating and synthesizing the information found in large bodies of text, and its applicability to other forms of communication besides written samples.

Researchers have harnessed the advantages of content analysis to aid in the understanding of gender, toys, and children's development. Content analysis in its traditional sense provides information about children's literature, including picture and storybooks (Diekman & Murnen, 2004), magazines (Graff, Murnen, & Krause, 2013; Hatton & Trautner, 2011), and print advertisements (Lynn, Walsdorf, Hardin, & Hardin, 2002; Mager & Helgeson, 2011). However, researchers have been highly creative in using content analysis to glean information from sources not easily collected from traditional sources such as self-report interviews or person-completed surveys. For instance, technological advances have resulted in media potentially impacting children, such as through television shows and their commercials for toys and products (Johnson & Young, 2002; Kahlenberg & Hein, 2010; Kim et al., 2007; Larson, 2001), and more recently, children's access to online content has been investigated through content analysis (Malik & Wojdynski, 2014). Particularly relevant to the investigation of gender, toys, and children are studies conducted on online toy catalogs (Auster & Mansbach, 2012). Gendered trends in video games (Dietz, 1998; Dill & Thill, 2007), which continue to increase in popularity alongside technological advances, have also been studied using this method.

Content analysis affords researchers the opportunity to unlock information from creative and unique sources. For example, one study analyzed the content of children's letters to Santa Claus to evaluate the relation between gender-typed toy choices and social structure (Richardson & Simpson, 1982). This study was replicated a decade later to provide further insights (Marcon & Freeman, 1996). Content analysis of this novel source of data allowed researchers to have access to children's toy preferences, without the concern that children's answers were impacted by social desirability, the way they might have been should the researchers have relied on self-report interview. Another content analysis that was applied to a unique information source was conducted on the toys and possessions found in children's rooms (Rheingold & Cook, 1975). Objective categorization of children's toys and belongings was used as an indicator of parents' gender stereotypical attitudes, reducing self-report and retrospective bias, which is often an advantage of content analysis.

Content analysis may provide unique insights from existing narratives and images in objective and systematic ways, but, like other nonexperimental designs, it does have the limitation of being unable to determine causality or direction of effects (Prasad, 2008). Thus, follow-up studies are often needed to confirm the underlying processes and resulting implications of the studied phenomena. Further, the information provided from a content analysis is largely determined by the quality of the original coding scheme created by the researcher. Therefore, replication of content analyses (much like other methodologies) is necessary.

THE NEED FOR MIXED-METHODOLOGY, METHODOLOGICAL PLURALISM, AND SYSTEMATIC APPROACHES

The majority of the studies reviewed to this point are quantitatively oriented, although content analyses could be viewed as a hybrid of qualitative and quantitative orientations in that many times content analyses apply a quantitative approach to qualitative sources of information. Qualitative methodologies within psychology are not as prevalent as quantitative methods (Alise & Teddlie, 2010), and this is true of the research on gender and toys, too. However, ethnographic and qualitative approaches provide compelling insights, and the methods have been harnessed to provide information on the intersection of socioeconomic status, race, and ethnicity that is often missing from studies conducted using other methodologies. For example,

Niobe Way's (2011) book entitled *Deep Secrets: Boys' Friendships and the Crisis of Connection* collates hundreds of interviews with adolescent African American, Latino, White, and Asian American boys about the way gender stereotypes inaccurately depict the relationships amongst boys and their peers. Similarly, in Barrie Thorne's (1993) book entitled *Gender and Play: Girls and Boys in School*, she describes her experiences observing gender-typed and gender-segregated play amongst children in school settings. Both books provide detailed accounts of trends in children's play and friendships.

The important contributions of such sources support the need for more mixed-methodological studies. A traditional definition of a *mixed-method study* is one that combines qualitative and quantitative approaches within the same investigation (Brewer & Hunt, 1989). The benefit of mixed methods is that the advantage of one design can address the disadvantage of the other. For instance, children being constrained in their responses to categorical, pre-derived answer options about their favorite toy type can be ameliorated by the addition of open-ended focus groups or interviews on the same topic, where they can fully describe their particular toy. Additionally, quantitative assessments can help address the subjectivity inherent in ethnographic methods. Further, convergence of findings from multiple methodologies adds confidence in the findings, whereas divergence can point out areas in need of more investigation (e.g., Torney-Purta, 2009).

Calls for more mixed methods in psychological investigations have been made before (Dattilio, Edwards, & Fishman, 2010; Fine & Elsbach, 2000; Tashakkori, Teddlie, & Sines, 2012; Torney-Purta, 2009; Yoshikawa, Weisner, Kalil, & Way, 2008). Increases in the use of mixed-method designs have been documented (Tashakkori et al., 2012), even within the specific field of developmental psychology (Yoshikawa et al., 2008). However, there are multiple reasons for the slow response to such calls. Potentially the largest barrier to mixed methods is the perception that qualitative and quantitative research are not merely two different methodologies, but rather the methods are representative of orthogonal paradigms (see Greene, 2008, for a review). The tensions between these paradigms have been contentious at times, even characterized as "paradigm wars" (Gage, 1989). Historical analysis of the two perspectives in recent decades shows pendulum swings of support for the two methodologies, dotted with calls from theorists and researchers in various disciplines to recognize the compatibility of the perspectives (e.g., Greene, 2008; Howe, 1988). Notably, in 1977 sociologists Bell and Newby coined the term "methodological pluralism" to refer to the need for scientists to assess the research question at hand, entertain all possible methodologies available, and decide to use the method that best addresses the question. However, debate continues about whether the two perspectives truly represent different paradigms of thought, and if so, whether they are incommensurate and whether qualitative and quantitative methods could or should be separated from these schools of thought (see Table 1 in Greene, 2008, for more information). Researchers such as Niobe Way, who uses quantitative methodologies in addition to her qualitative work to fully explore her research topics (e.g., Way, Stauber, Nakkula, & London, 1994), provide support that the two perspectives can be merged.

Practical barriers to methodological pluralism exist (Greene, 2008; Sandelowski, 2003; Tashakkori et al., 2012). Even researchers who recognize the value of merging quantitative and qualitative research may not have the expertise or training in both research methods. Researchers with the goal of fully understanding the interplay of gender, toys, and children's lives could mitigate many of these concerns by building interdisciplinary partnerships between research programs. Highly trained researchers from diverse philosophical and methodological backgrounds could work together to provide both aggregate and summative information, while also using narrative methods to maintain participants' voices.

THE NEED FOR SYSTEMATIC APPROACHES
TO UNDERSTANDING GENDER AND TOYS

The need for mixed methods in studying gender and toys is not isolated to the use of both qualitative and quantitative methodologies. Rather, integration of diverse research designs within the quantitative tradition is needed, too. The need for replication in psychological research has been a source of discussion and debate, both within the field and in broader outlets (e.g., Marcus, 2013; Open Science Collaboration, 2015). I add that in addition to the need for replication, the pursuit of understanding gender and toys would be aided by approaching one's research question systematically from multiple methodological angles. A recent study I conducted with Erica Weisgram and Megan Fulcher (2017) illustrates the benefits of a diverse-method approach. The goal of the study was to investigate whether boys were interested in toys that had propulsive attributes (i.e., toys that require vigorous forward movement, such as toy vehicles) more than were girls. If boys like toys that they could push or pull more than do girls, it is possible that propulsive attributes could help explain which toys become considered masculine toys and which become thought of as feminine toys. To this end, we designed three different studies to address the same research question. Two were interview-based experimental studies, and the third was an observation-based experiment. First, children were interviewed about their interests in existing toys; we manipulated the gender type of the toy (masculine, feminine, neutral) and whether it required propulsion or not. Children reported their interest on a rating scale. The gender type of the toy was found important to children's interests, but the propulsive properties were not. A second experiment was conducted to address the concern that children's previous experience with the toys could be impacting their interest levels. Thus, novel toys with and without wheels were created (e.g., a wooden elephant), and the children were interviewed again. Propulsive attributes were not found to impact children's interests in this study either. Finally, a third study was designed to address the concern that social desirability in children's responses during direct interviews could impact children's answers. Thus, each child was given the chance to free play with the existing toys and an observation study was conducted. Children actually played with toys based on the toy type, but they were not impacted by whether the toy required propulsion to play with it or not.

Although the findings about propulsive properties were uniform across all three methodologies, children's responses reflected more gender-typed interests when they were being interviewed compared with when their play was unknowingly being observed. This finding illustrates the importance of context in studying children and toys, and studying children in multiple ways. It is possible that studying children's play when they were free playing with their peers would have had different results, and that the gender makeup of the peer group could be influential, too (Fabes, Martin, & Hanish, 2003; see also Chapter 4, this volume). Researchers must consider context when designing studies about gender and children's toy choices. Further, approaching this study from a qualitative perspective could add depth to our understanding of children's interest in propulsive toys, and even give insight into other toy attributes that contribute to gender-differentiated play.

As with most studies in psychology, all three of these studies need to be independently replicated (Open Science Collaboration, 2015). However, the body of research as it stands presently provides a compelling converging pattern of results that would not exist without the systematic use of diverse methods.

THE CHALLENGE OF STUDYING GROWING CHILDREN

Underlying many investigations into gender and toys is the desire to understand how children's toy play changes them and the concern that the gendered nature of play will lead to gender differentiation of children's development and life experiences. Experimental studies illustrate toys' causal influences in learning and gendered behaviors, as noted above. However, longitudinal studies are needed to understand the long-term consequences of playing with toys, such as how they relate to gendered trends in career choices (Dinella, Fulcher, & Weisgram, 2014; Fulcher, Dinella, & Weisgram, 2015; Weisgram, Dinella, & Fulcher, 2011) that subsequently contribute to career segregation in the United States (Blau, Brummund, & Liu, 2013; see also Chapter 11, this volume).

Longitudinal studies on gender-typed toys and children's development illustrate the importance of toys in children's life paths. These studies do not have to follow children throughout their entire lives to be impactful. The developmental stage when a child would play with certain toys and the age at which hypothesized outcomes would best be seen should guide decisions about when to start and end a longitudinal study. For instance, Ramani and Siegler's (2008) short-term longitudinal study on the effects of number-based board games on children's foundational mathematics skill-acquisition began when children were approximately 5 years old, the age when they would both be playing this type of game (e.g., *Chutes and Ladders*) and gaining basic mathematics skills. The 9-week longitudinal aspect of the study confirmed the mastery of the skills being assessed, rather than temporary influence of the game. Similarly, the 1-year longitudinal study on the impact of Disney Princess–oriented play started when children were about 5.5 years old, when many children are interested in the princess genre, and ended prior to an age when kids would have grown out of such play (Coyne, Linder, Rasmussen, Nelson, & Birkbeck, 2016). The benefit of the longitudinal method is that the same children are followed throughout the study, allowing for conclusions to be drawn about changes over time. However, these studies are challenging, in that researchers must wait for results over the course of time and because staying in contact with participants over time can be problematic given that participants will likely change home or e-mail addresses, telephone numbers, or school districts during the study.

One way to avoid the negative impact of attrition (i.e., losing participants over time) is to conduct a cross-sectional study. In cross-sectional studies, groups of participants representing different age groups are all studied at the same time. This allows for results to be readily available without having to follow the participants as they age. For example, an investigation into children's perceptions of princesses, princes, and superheroes interviewed younger children (ages 3–6 years) and older children (ages 7–11 years; Dinella, Claps, & Lewandowski, in press). The two groups of children were chosen to closely resemble one another on all characteristics except age (e.g., socioeconomic status, race/ethnicity, region in which they live, type of school they attend), making it easier to infer that differences in the groups were due to developmental changes. The results indicated that the older children gender-typed princesses as "for girls" more than younger children, and older children considered superheroes to be "for boys and girls" more than younger children did. Although follow-up experimental or longitudinal studies are needed before causal conclusions can be drawn, the findings indicate children's cognitions about these fictional characters may become more gender typed as they age.

However, to confirm the long-term impact of gender-typed play, studies that follow children throughout multiple developmental stages are needed. One of the few studies investigating the lifelong trends of gender-typed play followed children from age 10 years into young adulthood, when children were choosing their first careers (Lee, Lawson, & McHale, 2015). Results indicated that masculine interests in childhood predicted young men entering masculine-typed careers at age 25. For girls, feminine interests predicted their gaining feminine skills, and feminine skills predicted their entry into feminine-typed careers at age 25. This longitudinal study harnesses the benefits of a correlational design and aids understanding of how gendered trends in children's play interests are related to life trajectories, the linkages between toys and long-term outcomes, and the mediators and moderators of these relations.

A methodological challenge raised by longitudinal designs is the need to adapt measures to be age appropriate. It can be difficult to standardize measures, stimuli, and procedures that can be applied throughout the lifespan. Young children's verbal and cognitive abilities change with age, as do the types of play experiences in which they engage. For example, the idea that dolls are a feminine toy has been well-established (Blakemore & Centers, 2005); however, children's interest in baby dolls when they are younger may shift to Barbie dolls (or the more recently popular and highly sexualized Monster High dolls) as they age. Thus, researchers need to attend to the developmental changes occurring within children, but also must consider the ever-changing landscape of children's toys. This includes considering the fluid nature of toy marketing strategies, toy offerings (e.g., whether Monster High dolls are in the same category as baby dolls), and technological advances (i.e., availability of video games, app-based games, and online media). It is clear that, in addition to proactively considering developmental concerns, flexibility and reactivity to sociocultural shifts are necessary, particularly in long-term longitudinal studies.

The prevalence of toys in children's lives also presents a challenge to scientists studying gender and toys. Adults may purchase toys for children's nurseries even before the child is born, and the use of ultrasound technology to identify a baby's sex in utero adds the possibility that the baby could be exposed to gendered toys at birth. The desire to understand the early impact of toys thus requires scientists to design studies that assess children who are preverbal (see Chapter 3 for a review of infant and toddler studies). This often includes measuring babies' and toddlers' looking times (Alexander, Wilcox, & Woods, 2009; Jadva, Hines, & Golombok, 2010; Woods, Wilcox, Armstrong, & Alexander, 2010).

Another developmental concern that impacts many researchers studying gender and toy play is that children's gender development occurs alongside their changing interests in and exposure to toys. Biological, social, and cognitive changes in gender all need to be considered when designing studies, especially those with a longitudinal perspective. Although general statements can be made about children's patterns of gender development, individual variation in these changes exist, and the maturation process is not perfectly linear. For instance, a debate exists on whether gender constancy, a milestone in cognitive gender development, is needed prior to understanding other aspects of gender, such as gender stereotyping and categorization (see Chapter 7). Children reach these cognitive milestones at different ages; thus, assuming a child has achieved a cognitive level of maturity based on age (rather than on assessing each child's cognitive stage) may provide unsatisfactory results. Should a researcher want to make assertions about children based on age, a large enough sample size of similarly aged children is needed to ensure representation of the variability in children's development.

THE CHALLENGE OF GENDER AS A SOCIAL CONSTRUCTION

Gender as a construct changes over time. The distinction between sex and gender separates biological characteristics (e.g., physical sex characteristics, hormonal and genetic characteristics) from socially constructed aspects of being a man or woman, boy or girl. Although these constructs overlap and are sometimes mistakenly used interchangeably, the socially based nature of gender means that as times change so do gender concepts, such as what is deemed to be a masculine trait or a feminine role.

Constructivist theories of gender development are based on the idea that individuals create their own gender schemas based on their personal life experiences and their cognitions about societal messages, and that these schemas act as filters through which life experiences are funneled. Thus, attention, memory, preferences, and behaviors can be guided by these constructed gender schemas (for a review see Dinella, in press; see also Chapter 7, this volume). In addition to the idea that gender is socially constructed, Constantinople (1973) and Bem (1974) revolutionized the conceptualization of masculinity and femininity (previously thought to be the bipolar ends of a single scale), proposing that masculinity and femininity are individual constructs. Thus, all individuals have the capacity to have varying levels of masculinity and femininity, regardless of their self-labeled gender (see Dean & Tate, 2017). Bem (1974) furthered this idea to include that psychological androgyny—or the possession of both masculine and feminine traits—was optimal given the needs of current society. These changes in the way we think about gender illustrate the socially constructed nature of gender and the need for gender researchers to operationalize gender as a construct.

Recently, advances in science and technology have revealed the complex (and nonbinary) nature of the physical characteristics of sex, including a better understanding of the interplay between genes, hormones, brain structures, and physical expression of physical sex characteristics (Fausto-Sterling, Coll, & Lamarre, 2012). Moreover, advocates and popular media have opened the discourse and urged the general public (and science) to better understand gender identity, intersex, and transgender issues. In 2015, *Vanity Fair* released their June magazine with Caitlyn Jenner, Olympic athlete and reality television star, on the cover. The issue included a photo spread and article on Jenner's transition experience as a transgender woman. The public discussion about transgender experiences and rights increased, as did the discussion about how the conceptualization of sex and gender as binary constructs can be limiting and potentially inaccurate. Thus, we are seeing a fresh discussion about sex and gender issues in both the scientific community and society at large.

It is possible that the gender research field is at a crossroads. As scientists, we need to continue to discuss how best to operationalize and conceptualize sex and gender. Two sizable challenges need to be addressed. First, how do you study the concept of sex and gender, given its fluid, dynamic, and socially-constructed nature? Second, how does the field harness statistical and methodological tools to best assess gender and sex? For example, the traditional method of categorizing sex or gender as two-level variables is potentially at odds with the burgeoning perspective of gender as a nonbinary construct. However, researchers trying to describe and understand the world in its current state cannot ignore the categories of male and female, man and woman, boy and girl—they are still prominent in the way our society currently organizes people. Moreover, the scientific and popular developments towards a nonbinary perspective on sex and gender are set against a backdrop of an intensification of gender-typed toys and marketing strategies aimed toward children (Sweet, 2013). Additionally, current gender researchers are building on a foundation of research and methodology based on two categories of gender.

Gender researchers need to grapple with what it means to have multiple and changing perspectives on gender. Dean and Tate (2017) reviewed how Bem's (1974) revolutionary prescription for psychological androgyny (separate from an individual's self-gender label) was a way to free people from gender stereotyped thinking. If the goal was for people to have both masculinity and femininity, the binary gender labels would lose their power to constrain people. They proposed that Bem's ideas should be considered "conceptual advances." Other contributions to the reconceptualization of gender include movements to identify gender identity constructs (e.g., Egan & Perry, 2001) instead of binary gender or sex. Additionally, Tate, Ledbetter, and Youssef

(2013) made recommendations on how to reduce the emphasis on gender categories and stereotypes within the field by revising demographic survey methods. Moreover, Bigler and Leaper (2015) called for the field (and others) to use gender-free pronouns and language to reduce unnecessary emphasis on gender. All of these discussions are pushing the boundaries of how we conceptualize sex and gender as a field. Are small methodological changes enough, or is the field in need of a paradigm shift in the way we envision gender? I assert that the work of gender researchers is to make progress in these discussions.

CONCLUSION

Science can be used to better understand gender, toys, and children's development throughout the lifespan. The prevalence and importance of toys in children's lives should compel scientists to investigate the topic and guide broader decision making about toys. The review of the research methods provided here helps describe the tools available to aid in this pursuit and information that can help match research questions with appropriate methodologies. Further, it poses questions that need to be answered in the future should we desire to fully understand the interplay of gender, toys, and children's development.

REFERENCES

Alexander, G. M., Wilcox, T., & Woods, R. (2009). Sex differences in infants' visual interest in toys. *Archives of Sexual Behavior, 38*, 427–433. http://dx.doi.org/10.1007/s10508-008-9430-1

Alise, M. A., & Teddlie, C. (2010). A continuation of the paradigm wars? Prevalence rates of methodological approaches across the social/behavioral sciences. *Journal of Mixed Methods Research, 4*, 103–126. http://dx.doi.org/10.1177/1558689809360805

American Psychological Association Task Force on Violent Media. (2015). *Technical report on the review of the violent video game literature.* Retrieved from http://www.apa.org/pi/families/violent-media.aspx

Anderson, C. A., Shibuya, A., Ihori, N., Swing, E. L., Bushman, B. J., Sakamoto, A., . . . Saleem, M. (2010). Violent video game effects on aggression, empathy, and prosocial behavior in Eastern and Western countries: A meta-analytic review. *Psychological Bulletin, 136*, 151–173. http://dx.doi.org/10.1037/a0018251

Anschutz, D. J., & Engels, R. C. M. E. (2010). The effects of playing with thin dolls on body image and food intake in young girls. *Sex Roles, 63*, 621–630. http://dx.doi.org/10.1007/s11199-010-9871-6

Auster, C. J., & Mansbach, C. S. (2012). The gender marketing of toys: An analysis of color and type of toy on the Disney store website. *Sex Roles, 67,* 375–388. http://dx.doi.org/10.1007/s11199-012-0177-8

Beck, V. S., Boys, S., Rose, C., & Beck, E. (2012). Violence against women in video games: A prequel or sequel to rape myth acceptance? *Journal of Interpersonal Violence, 27,* 3016–3031. http://dx.doi.org/10.1177/0886260512441078

Bem, S. L. (1974). The measurement of psychological androgyny. *Journal of Consulting and Clinical Psychology, 42,* 155–162. http://dx.doi.org/10.1037/h0036215

Berelson, B. (1952). *Content analysis in communication research.* Glencoe, IL: The Free Press.

Bigler, R. S., & Leaper, C. (2015). Gendered language: Psychological principles, evolving practices, and inclusive policies. *Policy Insights from Behavioral and Brain Sciences, 2,* 187–194. http://dx.doi.org/10.1177/2372732215600452

Blakemore, J. E. O., & Centers, R. E. (2005). Characteristics of boys' and girls' toys. *Sex Roles, 53,* 619–633. http://dx.doi.org/10.1007/s11199-005-7729-0

Blau, F. D., Brummund, P., & Liu, A. Y. (2013). Trends in occupational segregation by gender 1970–2009: Adjusting for the impact of changes in the occupational coding system. *Demography, 50,* 471–492. http://dx.doi.org/10.1007/s13524-012-0151-7

Borenstein, M., Hedges, L. V., Higgins, J. P. T., & Rothstein, H. R. (2009). *Introduction to meta-analysis.* Chichester, England: Wiley. http://dx.doi.org/10.1002/9780470743386

Brewer, J., & Hunt, A. (1989). *Multimethod research: A synthesis of styles.* Newbury Park, CA: Sage.

Browne, B. A. (1998). Gender stereotypes in advertising on children's television in the 1990s: A cross-national analysis. *Journal of Advertising, 27,* 83–96. http://dx.doi.org/10.1080/00913367.1998.10673544

Cherney, I. D. (2008). Mom, let me play more computer games: They improve my mental rotation skills. *Sex Roles, 59,* 776–786. http://dx.doi.org/10.1007/s11199-008-9498-z

Cherney, I. D., Bersted, K., & Smetter, J. (2014). Training spatial skills in men and women. *Perceptual & Motor Skills, 119,* 82–99. http://dx.doi.org/10.2466/23.25.PMS.119c12z0

Constantinescu, M., & Hines, M. (2012). Relating prenatal testosterone exposure to postnatal behavior in typically developing children: Methods and findings. *Child Development Perspectives, 6,* 407–413. http://dx.doi.org/10.1111/j.1750-8606.2012.00257.x

Constantinople, A. (1973). Masculinity–femininity: An exception to a famous dictum? *Psychological Bulletin, 80,* 389–407. http://dx.doi.org/10.1037/h0035334

Coyle, E. F., & Liben, L. S. (2016). Affecting girls' activity and job interests through play: The moderating roles of personal gender salience and game characteristics. *Child Development, 87,* 414–428. http://dx.doi.org/10.1111/cdev.12463

Coyne, S. M., Linder, J. R., Rasmussen, E. E., Nelson, D. A., & Birkbeck, V. (2016). Pretty as a princess: Longitudinal effects of engagement with Disney Princesses on gender stereotypes, body esteem, and prosocial behavior in children. *Child Development, 87*, 1909–1925. http://dx.doi.org/10.1111/cdev.12569

Dattilio, F. M., Edwards, D. J. A., & Fishman, D. B. (2010). Case studies within a mixed methods paradigm: Toward a resolution of the alienation between researcher and practitioner in psychotherapy research. *Psychotherapy: Theory, Research, Practice, Training, 47*, 427–441. http://dx.doi.org/10.1037/a0021181

Davis, J., & Hines, M. (2017). *Gender differences in children's toy preferences: A systematic review and meta-analysis.* Manuscript submitted for publication.

Dean, M. L., & Tate, C. C. (2017). Extending the legacy of Sandra Bem: Psychological androgyny as a touchstone conceptual advance for the study of gender in psychological science. *Sex Roles.* Advance online publication. http://dx.doi.org/10.1007/s11199-016-0713-z

Diekman, A. B., & Murnen, S. K. (2004). Learning to be little women and little men: The inequitable gender equality of nonsexist children's literature. *Sex Roles, 50*, 373–385. http://dx.doi.org/10.1023/B:SERS.0000018892.26527.ea

Dietz, T. L. (1998). An examination of violence and gender role portrayals in video games: Implications for gender socialization and aggressive behavior. *Sex Roles, 38*, 425–442. http://dx.doi.org/10.1023/A:1018709905920

Dill, K. E., & Thill, K. P. (2007). Video game characters and the socialization of gender roles: Young people's perceptions mirror sexist media depictions. *Sex Roles, 57*, 851–864. http://dx.doi.org/10.1007/s11199-007-9278-1

Dinella, L. M. (in press). Cognitive theories of gender development. In K. Nadal (Ed.), *Encyclopedia of psychology and gender.* Thousand Oaks, CA: Sage.

Dinella, L. M., Claps, J., & Lewandowski, G. W. (in press). Princesses, princes, and superheroes: Children's gender cognitions and fictional characters. *The Journal of Genetic Psychology.*

Dinella, L. M., Fulcher, M., & Weisgram, E. S. (2014). Sex-typed personality traits and gender identity as predictors of young adults' career interests. *Archives of Sexual Behavior, 43*, 493–504. http://dx.doi.org/10.1007/s10508-013-0234-6

Dinella, L. M., Weisgram, E. S., & Fulcher, M. (2017). Children's gender-typed toy interests: Does propulsion matter? *Archives of Sexual Behavior, 46*, 1295–1305. http://dx.doi.org/10.1007/s10508-016-0901-5

Eaton, W. O., & Enns, L. R. (1986). Sex differences in human motor activity level. *Psychological Bulletin, 100*, 19–28. http://dx.doi.org/10.1037/0033-2909.100.1.19

Egan, S. K., & Perry, D. G. (2001). Gender identity: A multidimensional analysis with implications for psychosocial adjustment. *Developmental Psychology, 37*, 451–463. http://dx.doi.org/10.1037/0012-1649.37.4.451

Else-Quest, N. M., Hyde, J. S., Goldsmith, H. H., & Van Hulle, C. A. (2006). Gender differences in temperament: A meta-analysis. *Psychological Bulletin, 132*, 33–72. http://dx.doi.org/10.1037/0033-2909.132.1.33

Fabes, R. A., Martin, C. L., & Hanish, L. D. (2003). Young children's play qualities in same-, other-, and mixed-sex peer groups. *Child Development, 74*, 921–932. http://dx.doi.org/10.1111/1467-8624.00576

Fausto-Sterling, A., Coll, C. G., & Lamarre, M. (2012). Sexing the baby: Part 1– What do we really know about sex differentiation in the first three years of life? *Social Science & Medicine, 74*, 1684–1692. http://dx.doi.org/10.1016/j.socscimed.2011.05.051

Fine, G., & Elsbach, K. (2000). Ethnography and experiment in social psychological theory building: Tactics for integrating qualitative field data with quantitative lab data. *Journal of Experimental Social Psychology, 36*, 51–76. http://dx.doi.org/10.1006/jesp.1999.1394

Fisher, R. A. (1935). *The design of experiments*. New York, NY: Hafner.

Fox, J., & Potocki, B. (2016). Lifetime video game consumption, interpersonal aggression, hostile sexism, and rape myth acceptance: A cultivation perspective. *Journal of Interpersonal Violence, 31*, 1912–1931. http://dx.doi.org/10.1177/0886260515570747

Fulcher, M., Dinella, L. M., & Weisgram, E. S. (2015). Constructing a feminist reformation of the heterosexual breadwinner/caregiver family model: College students' plans for their own future families. *Sex Roles, 73*, 174–186. http://dx.doi.org/10.1007/s11199-015-0487-8

Gage, N. L. (1989). The paradigm wars and their aftermath: A "historical" sketch of research and teaching since 1989. *Educational Researcher, 18*, 4–10. http://dx.doi.org/10.3102/0013189X018007004

Goldberg, M. E. (1990). A quasi-experiment assessing the effectiveness of TV advertising directed to children. *Journal of Marketing Research, 27*, 445–454. http://dx.doi.org/10.2307/3172629

Graff, K. A., Murnen, S. K., & Krause, A. K. (2013). Low-cut shirts and high-heeled shoes: Increased sexualization across time in magazine depictions of girls. *Sex Roles, 69*, 571–582. http://dx.doi.org/10.1007/s11199-013-0321-0

Greene, J. C. (2008). Is mixed methods social inquiry a distinctive methodology? *Journal of Mixed Methods Research, 2*, 7–22. http://dx.doi.org/10.1177/1558689807309969

Hatton, E., & Trautner, M. N. (2011). Equal opportunity objectification? The sexualization of men and women on the cover of *Rolling Stone*. *Sexuality & Culture: An Interdisciplinary Quarterly, 15*, 256–278. http://dx.doi.org/10.1007/s12119-011-9093-2

Holsti, O. R. (1968). Content analysis. In G. Lindzey & E. Aronson (Eds.), *The handbook of social psychology* (Vol. II, pp. 596–692). New Delhi, India: Amerind.

Howe, K. R. (1988). Against the quantitative–qualitative incompatibility thesis or dogmas die hard. *Educational Researcher, 17*, 10–16.

Hyde, J. S. (2005). The gender similarities hypothesis. *American Psychologist, 60*, 581–592. http://dx.doi.org/10.1037/0003-066X.60.5.581

Jadva, V., Hines, M., & Golombok, S. (2010). Infants' preferences for toys, colors, and shapes: Sex differences and similarities. *Archives of Sexual Behavior, 39,* 1261–1273. http://dx.doi.org/10.1007/s10508-010-9618-z

Jansz, J. (2005). The emotional appeal of violent video games for adolescent males. *Communication Theory, 15,* 219–241. http://dx.doi.org/10.1111/j.1468-2885.2005.tb00334.x

Johnson, F., & Young, K. (2002). Gendered voices in children's television advertising. *Critical Studies in Media Communication, 19,* 461–480. http://dx.doi.org/10.1080/07393180216572

Kahlenberg, S. G., & Hein, M. M. (2010). Progression on Nickelodeon? Gender-role stereotypes in toy commercials. *Sex Roles, 62,* 830–847. http://dx.doi.org/10.1007/s11199-009-9653-1

Kim, J. L., Sorsoli, C. L., Collins, K., Zylbergold, B. A., Schooler, D., & Tolman, D. L. (2007). From sex to sexuality: Exposing the heterosexual script on prime-time network television. *Journal of Sex Research, 44,* 145–157. http://dx.doi.org/10.1080/00224490701263660

Lamb, L. M., Bigler, R. S., Liben, L. S., & Green, V. A. (2009). Teaching children to confront peers' sexist remarks: Implications for theories of gender development and educational practice. *Sex Roles, 61,* 361–382. http://dx.doi.org/10.1007/s11199-009-9634-4

Larson, M. S. (2001). Interactions, activities, and gender in children's television commercials: A content analysis. *Journal of Broadcasting & Electronic Media, 45,* 41–56. http://dx.doi.org/10.1207/s15506878jobem4501_4

Lee, B., Lawson, K. M., & McHale, S. M. (2015). Longitudinal associations between gender-typed skills and interests and their links to occupational outcomes. *Journal of Vocational Behavior, 88,* 121–130. http://dx.doi.org/10.1016/j.jvb.2015.02.011

Lynn, S., Walsdorf, K., Hardin, M., & Hardin, B. (2002). Selling girls short: Advertising and gender images in *Sports Illustrated for Kids. Women in Sport and Physical Activity Journal, 11,* 77–100. http://dx.doi.org/10.1123/wspaj.11.2.77

Mager, J., & Helgeson, J. G. (2011). Fifty years of advertising images: Some changing perspectives on role portrayals along with enduring consistencies. *Sex Roles, 64,* 238–252. http://dx.doi.org/10.1007/s11199-010-9782-6

Malik, C., & Wojdynski, B. W. (2014). Boys earn, girls buy: Depictions of materialism on US children's branded-entertainment websites. *Journal of Children and Media, 8,* 404–422. http://dx.doi.org/10.1080/17482798.2013.852986

Marcon, R. A., & Freeman, G. (1996). Linking gender-related toy preferences to social structure: Changes in children's letters to Santa since 1978. *Journal of Psychological Practice, 2,* 1–10.

Marcus, G. (2013, May 1). The crisis in social psychology that isn't. *The New Yorker.* Retrieved from http://www.newyorker.com/tech/elements/the-crisis-in-social-psychology-that-isnt

Martin, C. L., Fabes, R. A., Hanish, L., Leonard, S., & Dinella, L. M. (2011). Experienced and expected similarity to same-gender peers: Moving toward a comprehensive model of gender segregation. *Sex Roles, 65*, 421–434. http://dx.doi.org/10.1007/s11199-011-0029-y

Nachmias, D., & Frankfort-Nachmias, C. (1976). *Research methods in the social sciences* (pp. 132–139). London, England: Edward Arnold.

Open Science Collaboration. (2015). Estimating the reproducibility of psychological science. *Science, 349*(6521). http://dx.doi.org/10.1126/science.aac4716

Pearson, K. (1924). *The life, letters, and labours of Francis Galton* (Vols. 2–3). London, England: Cambridge University Press. Retrieved from http://galton.org/galton/pearson/index.html

Peirce, C. S. (1877). The fixation of belief. *Popular Science Monthly*, 1–15. Retrieved from http://www.peirce.org/writings/p107.html

Prasad, B. D. (2008). Content analysis: A method of social science research. In D. K. Lal Das (Ed.), *Research methods for social work* (pp. 174–193). New Delhi, India: Rawat.

Ramani, G. B., & Siegler, R. S. (2008). Promoting broad and stable improvements in low-income children's numerical knowledge through playing number board games. *Child Development, 79*, 375–394. http://dx.doi.org/10.1111/j.1467-8624.2007.01131.x

Rheingold, H. L., & Cook, K. V. (1975). The contents of boys' and girls' rooms as an index of parents' behavior. *Child Development, 46*, 459–463. http://dx.doi.org/10.2307/1128142

Richardson, J. G., & Simpson, C. H. (1982). Children, gender, and social structure: An analysis of the contents of letters to Santa Claus. *Child Development, 53*, 429–436. http://dx.doi.org/10.2307/1128986

Sandelowski, M. (2003). Tables or tableaux? The challenges of writing and reading mixed methods studies. In A. Tashakkori & C. Teddlie (Eds.), *Handbook of mixed methods in social and behavioral research* (pp. 321–350). Thousand Oaks, CA: Sage.

Stanley, J. C. (1966). The influence of Fisher's "The design of experiments" on educational research thirty years later. *American Educational Research Journal, 3*, 223–229. http://dx.doi.org/10.3102/00028312003003223

Sweet, E. V. (2013, August). *Same as it ever was? Gender and children's toys over the 20th century.* Presented at the 108th American Sociological Association meeting, New York, NY.

Tashakkori, A., Teddlie, C., & Sines, M. C. (2012). Utilizing mixed methods in psychological research. In I. B. Weiner, J. A. Schinka, & W. F. Velicer (Eds.), *Handbook of psychology: Vol. II. Research methods in psychology* (pp. 428–451). Hoboken, NJ: John Wiley & Sons.

Tate, C. C., Ledbetter, J. N., & Youssef, C. P. (2013). A two-question method for assessing gender categories in the social and medical sciences. *Journal of Sex Research, 50*, 767–776. http://dx.doi.org/10.1080/00224499.2012.690110

Thorne, B. (1993). *Gender and play: Girls and boys in school.* New Brunswick, NJ: Rutgers University Press.

Torney-Purta, J. V. (2009). International psychological research that matters for policy and practice. *American Psychologist, 64,* 825–837. http://dx.doi.org/10.1037/0003-066X.64.8.825

Toy Industry Association, Inc. (2016a). *Annual U.S. sales data* [Data file]. Retrieved from http://www.toyassociation.org/ta/research/data/annual/toys/research-and-data/data/annual-us-sales-data.aspx

Toy Industry Association, Inc. (2016b). *Economic impact of the toy industry* [Data file]. Retrieved from http://www.toyassociation.org/app_themes/tia/pdfs/economicimpact/unitedstates.pdf

Wason, P. (1960). On the failure to eliminate hypotheses in a conceptual task. *The Quarterly Journal of Experimental Psychology, 12,* 129–140. http://dx.doi.org/10.1080/17470216008416717

Way, N. (2011). *Deep secrets: Boys' friendships and the crisis of connection.* Cambridge, MA: Harvard University Press. Retrieved from http://dx.doi.org/10.4159/harvard.9780674061361

Way, N., Stauber, H., Nakkula, M., & London, P. (1994). Depression and substance use in two diverse populations: A quantitative and qualitative analysis. *Journal of Youth and Adolescence, 23,* 331–357. http://dx.doi.org/10.1007/BF01536723

Weisgram, E. S., Dinella, L. M., & Fulcher, M. (2011). The role of masculinity/femininity, values, and occupational value affordances in shaping young men's and women's occupational choices. *Sex Roles, 65,* 243–258. http://dx.doi.org/10.1007/s11199-011-9998-0

Weisgram, E. S., Fulcher, M., & Dinella, L. M. (2014). Pink gives girls permission: Exploring the roles of explicit gender labels and gender-typed colors on preschool children's toy preferences. *Journal of Applied Developmental Psychology, 35,* 401–409. http://dx.doi.org/10.1016/j.appdev.2014.06.004

Westen, D., Blagov, P. S., Harenski, K., Kilts, C., & Hamann, S. (2006). Neural bases of motivated reasoning: An fMRI study of emotional constraints on partisan political judgment in the 2004 U.S. Presidential election. *Journal of Cognitive Neuroscience, 18,* 1947–1958. http://dx.doi.org/10.1162/jocn.2006.18.11.1947

Wong, W. I., & Hines, M. (2015). Effects of gender color-coding on toddlers' gender-typical toy play. *Archives of Sexual Behavior, 44,* 1233–1242. http://dx.doi.org/10.1007/s10508-014-0400-5

Woodrum, E. (1984). "Mainstreaming" content analysis in social science: Methodological advantage, obstacles, and solutions. *Social Science Research, 13,* 1–9. Retrieved from http://www.sciencedirect.com/science/article/pii/0049089X84900012

Woods, R. J., Wilcox, T., Armstrong, J., & Alexander, G. (2010). Infants' representations of three-dimensional occluded objects. *Infant Behavior and Development,* *33,* 663–671. Retrieved from http://www.sciencedirect.com/science/article/pii/S0163638310001001

Yao, M. Z., Mahood, C., & Linz, D. (2010). Sexual priming, gender stereotyping, and likelihood to sexually harass: Examining the cognitive effects of playing a sexually-explicit video game. *Sex Roles,* *62,* 77–88. http://dx.doi.org/10.1007/s11199-009-9695-4

Yoshikawa, H., Weisner, T. S., Kalil, A., & Way, N. (2008). Mixing qualitative and quantitative research in developmental science: Uses and methodological choices. *Developmental Psychology,* *44,* 344–354. http://dx.doi.org/10.1037/0012-1649.44.2.344

3

GENDER-TYPED TOY PREFERENCES AMONG INFANTS AND TODDLERS

KRISTINA M. ZOSULS AND DIANE N. RUBLE

More than just objects, children's toys are infused with cultural beliefs and expectations. When they play with toys, young children practice and enact social roles and scripts, and toy objects themselves can become highly prized possessions and even symbols of identity. Gender is a primary dimension along which toys are characterized and marketed, and this leads them to be important cultural tools for teaching and reinforcing gender stereotypes and gender identity (e.g., Kahlenberg & Hein, 2010; Li & Wong, 2016). In fact, it is difficult to identify another behavioral characteristic, other than clothing choices (Halim, Ruble, Lurye, Greulich, & Zosuls, 2014), that more clearly differentiates boys and girls than do toy preferences (Blakemore, Berenbaum, & Liben, 2009).

It is widely taken for granted that gender differences in behavior emerge early in life, and even gender researchers confidently state that gender differences in toy preferences are clearly present in the toddler years, if not earlier.

http://dx.doi.org/10.1037/0000077-004
Gender Typing of Children's Toys: How Early Play Experiences Impact Development, E. S. Weisgram and
L. M. Dinella (Editors)

Yet, until recently, research exploring the question of when and how the earliest gender differences in children's play appear and develop has been surprisingly sparse. Our own research has brought some clarity to this issue while highlighting the need to attend to reasons for variability in the timing of these processes, rather than relying on an "ages and stages" framework, and attending to what types of toys and toy play are gender differentiated at different phases of development (Zosuls, Ruble, & Tamis-LeMonda, 2014; Zosuls et al., 2009).

Various theoretical orientations make predictions about when and why gender differences might develop; however, current empirical evidence is limited in its ability to fully integrate and weigh these perspectives. There are relatively few studies, with limitations that are discussed throughout this chapter, including substantial variation in the methods used, toys examined, and ages that are separated or grouped together in analyses. This chapter aims to bring clarity to the issues of what is and is not known about when in the course of development gender differences appear in children's toy preferences, the nature of such differences, and to provide guidance for future research.

THEORIES OF GENDER DIFFERENCES IN TOY PREFERENCES

Cognitive or self-socialization perspectives (e.g., Bem, 1981; Kohlberg, 1966; Maccoby & Jacklin, 1974; Martin & Halverson, 1981; Ruble, 1994; Tobin et al., 2010) posit that gender development involves an active construction of gender identity, and this sense of belonging to a gender group motivates children to align their behaviors and preferences, including toy play, with their own gender (see Chapter 7, this volume, for a review). Increasing evidence shows that children begin to acquire gender category concepts and establish their gender identities before the age of 2, and that this knowledge is linked to the development of gender-stereotyped preferences (Zosuls et al., 2009). Social–cognitive learning perspectives (Bussey & Bandura, 1999; Mischel, 1966) place relatively more weight on the role of social agents who model and reinforce gender-stereotyped behaviors (see Chapter 6). According to this view in its simplest form, children acquire gender-stereotyped behaviors by observing models that exemplify activities that are considered appropriate for their gender. Social–cognitive learning theorists have asserted that gender differences in play behavior appear prior to the development of gender identity, and have pointed to this developmental sequencing as evidence in support of their ideas and against self-socialization theories (Bussey & Bandura, 1999). However, more recent research has called this developmental sequence into question (Zosuls et al., 2009). From a theoretical standpoint, self-socialization researchers have also questioned why children would differentially attend to and acquire behaviors of same-gender models without having an understanding of gender as a social category linked to their own identities (Martin, Ruble, & Szkrybalo, 2004).

There is also clear support for the role of biological processes in gender development (Alexander & Hines, 2002; Berenbaum & Beltz, 2016; Wallen, 2005; see also Chapter 5, this volume, for a review). Cross-species comparisons and studies using human populations with atypical hormone levels, especially girls with congenital adrenal hyperplasia (CAH), have been particularly relevant to the literature on gender differences in play. In classical CAH, girls have been exposed to abnormally high concentrations of androgens during fetal development, which typically causes genetic females to be born with some degree of genital virilization (Merke & Bornstein, 2005; see also Chapter 5, this volume). The question for our purposes is whether or not these hormone differences relate to behavioral differences, such as toy play. Investigations of gender-stereotyped play in girls with CAH have observed children who are 3 years and older and have found that girls with CAH are more interested in male-typical toys than are female controls (Cohen-Bendahan, van de Beek, & Berenbaum, 2005). Studies examining typical variations of hormones have also found evidence for a relation between prenatal hormone exposure and postnatal behaviors (Hines et al., 2002). In addition, research on nonhuman primates suggests that biological factors play an important role in the development of gender-stereotyped toy preferences (Alexander & Hines, 2002; Hassett, Siebert, & Wallen, 2008). For instance, a study of rhesus monkeys found that males (but not females) showed a significant preference for wheeled toys over plush toys (Hassett et al., 2008). In sum, research using a number of different approaches has found evidence for the role of biological processes, especially the role of hormones, in the development of early gender differences in toy preferences.

THE CHANGING DEVELOPMENTAL CONTEXT

Taken together, this body of literature raises the possibility that gender differences in toy play that occur prior to an understanding of gender categories could be due to a complex interplay of social experiences and biological factors, as has been found in research on nonhuman primates (Wallen, 1996; Wallen & Hassett, 2009). As such, it is important to consider how the influence of different processes might vary with development.

Gender differences in toy preferences that are apparent in infancy suggest that biological processes are in effect. In addition, certain rudimentary socialization processes might be important in the first year of life. For example, starting at approximately 9 months, when infants begin to show an appreciation for the way in which objects are intended to be played with (e.g., rolling a toy car across the floor; Lamb, Bornstein, & Teti, 2002) and have greatly increased motor abilities (Adolph & Joh, 2007), children's experiences with objects might shape their interest based on mere familiarity (Zajonc, 2001) and enjoyment derived from those interactions. Furthermore, because children are now able to manipulate toys in ways that better approximate how they might see older children and adults play with such objects, they might receive greater reinforcement for playing with own-gender-stereotyped objects.

The strengthening and evolution of interests when children become toddlers opens the possibility that self-socialization processes can play a formative role in the second year of life. As mentioned earlier, at 18 to 24 months, toddlers begin to develop an understanding of gender categories and form a gender identity (Zosuls et al., 2009). Their play also increases in complexity and incorporates symbolic play (e.g., Fenson & Ramsay, 1980; Tamis-LeMonda & Bornstein, 1996), through which they can now enact gender-stereotyped scripts, such as pretending to calm a crying baby (using a doll) that they learn from same-gender models (Bussey & Bandura, 1999). Such behaviors might be reinforced or discouraged by others in ways that may or may not be similar to what children experience earlier in infancy. For example, a parent who did not pay much mind to his son picking up dolls at a young age might object to doll play that evolves into nurturing activities, such as dressing a baby doll. As children enter preschool and develop more advanced social skills, peers might become particularly influential in shaping preferences, leading to a further evolution in toy play.

A more thorough descriptive understanding of the phenomenon that theories of gender development try to explain—gender-stereotyped toy preferences—is a critical starting point for the advancement of research to tease apart these theoretical issues. Studies that explore toy play with a nuanced consideration of the cognitive, social, and physical context of children's early development are vital, and as we describe in this review, still lacking.

APPROACH TO THE STUDIES REVIEWED IN THIS CHAPTER

This chapter focuses on a relatively small but critical period of time when foundational processes of gender development are thought to take place: infancy through the age of 2 years. At the age of 3, studies show consistent gender-stereotyped toy preferences among both boys and girls (e.g., Bussey & Bandura, 1992; Perry, White, & Perry, 1984; Schau, Kahn, Diepold, & Cherry, 1980; Servin, Bohlin, & Berlin, 1999; Smetana & Letourneau, 1984; Weinraub et al., 1984), as well as the establishment of other gender-related behavioral preferences, such as the preference for same-gender peers (i.e., gender segregation; LaFreniere, Strayer, & Gauthier, 1984; Maccoby & Jacklin, 1974; Powlishta, Serbin, & Moller, 1993).

Infants and toddlers cannot state their interests and preferences; thus, the bulk of our review focuses on observational studies of children's toy play. We place emphasis on studies in which children played alone and made independent choices using experimenter-provided toys, as these represent the highest level of control in terms of ruling out the influence of others (parents, peers, teachers) and toy availability.

OBSERVATIONAL STUDIES

Observational studies of young children's toy play encompass a broad range of methodological differences that make them challenging to synthesize. Studies have employed a variety of toys that differ in the degree to which they are gender-stereotyped, and in many cases, scant details are provided about important features (e.g., color). Methods for measuring toy play have also varied (e.g., time sampling methods, total time in contact with toys), as have operationalizations of behavioral preferences (e.g., touching toys, looking at toys). Some studies also have serious limitations to their statistical power and reliability due to very small sample sizes. Age-related conclusions can also be difficult to draw because studies often collapse across broad age ranges, and few use cross-sectional or longitudinal designs. We were careful to consider all of these factors when weighing the evidence of gender differences in toy play.

Our outcome of interest, gender differences in toy play, was also approached differently in different studies. Some studies either reported within-gender toy preferences or between-gender differences (but not both), and thus used *gender-stereotyped play* to mean somewhat different things. This is an important, yet often overlooked, distinction in the literature. We suggest that although between-gender differences surely reflect meaningful group-level differences in preferences, the within-gender analysis is the more precise measurement of difference for testing and understanding the individual-level gender development processes outlined in the previous section. For example, a primate study emphasized gender differences in how much time primates spend playing with a doll (Alexander & Hines, 2002). However, within-gender differences showed that males had a similar level of play with masculine and feminine toys, indicating that between-gender differences were largely driven by the preferences of one, but not the other gender. By focusing on between-gender differences, important information, such as asymmetries in gender development, is lost that could be of theoretical importance. In this chapter, we refer to within-gender analyses of children's preferences for gender-stereotyped toys (e.g., differences in girls' play with dolls vs. trucks) as *gender-stereotyped preferences/play*, and we use *between-gender differences* to refer to differences between girls and boys in their play with the same toys (e.g., girls' vs. boys' play with dolls). The term *gender differences* is used more broadly to discuss findings in aggregate, but we have taken care to specify which type of difference was reported in each individual study that was reviewed.

Gender Differences in Observed Play Before Age 2

As described earlier, children undergo remarkable developmental changes in their motor and cognitive abilities in the first 2 years of life, and different mechanisms likely affect their gender-related play at different ages. Thus, in this section we separately consider research of children younger and older than 18 months.

Studies Examining Play Before 18 Months

Despite its theoretical importance, conducting observational studies of play preferences in children younger than 12 months has clear challenges (e.g., fussiness, reaching toys). Thus, it is not surprising that studies of this age group mostly involve substantial parental involvement or use experimental approaches. Studies meeting our criteria for little parent involvement all observed children who were slightly older than 12 months.

One early study using a very small sample size found no gender differences in play with male and female plastic cowboy figurines in this age group (Corter & Jamieson, 1977). Several other older studies reported rather idiosyncratic gender differences (stuffed dog in Goldberg & Lewis, 1969; robot in Jacklin, Maccoby, & Dick, 1973), and some found counterstereotypic findings (blocks in Goldberg & Lewis, 1969, and X-men in Servin et al., 1999). However, if more weight is given to the three most recent and arguably rigorous studies (Servin et al., 1999; Todd, Barry, & Thommessen, 2016; van de Beek, van Goozen, Buitelaar, & Cohen-Kettenis, 2009), there is evidence for at least modest gender differences in toy preferences at around 1 year of age.

One of the more recent studies (Todd et al., 2016) found both between-gender differences and gender-stereotyped preferences in expected directions with a car, digger (truck), doll, and cooking pot among a small sample (18 boys, 11 girls) of British children who averaged 13 months old, but ranged from 9 to 17 months. Analyses were conducted on gender-stereotyped groupings of toys; thus, it is unclear whether differences in this age group were driven by particular toys (e.g., doll vs. cooking pot). Gender-neutral toys were not provided, thus potentially magnifying differences. Further data were not provided on play with a ball (despite modest, but significant, gender differences across children in three age groups ranging from 9 to 32 months) and pink and blue teddy bears for this age group.

Another study found that boys played longer than girls with several male-stereotyped toys (vehicles, Lincoln Logs), and that girls played more with a tea set than boys, but gender differences were not found with the most stereotypically female toys (Barbie and Ken dolls, soft female doll with accessories, beauty set; Servin et al., 1999). Within-gender stereotyped preferences were not reported in this study. The other study that reported the clearest gender differences was a Dutch study that found that 13-month-old boys spent a significantly greater proportion of time playing with male-stereotyped toys (transportation toys) than did girls, and that girls played significantly more with the female-stereotyped toys (doll-related, tea set) than did the boys (van de Beek et al., 2009). As with the Todd et al. (2016) study, analyses were not conducted on play times with individual toys, leaving unknown whether play with particular toys drove the effects. Nonetheless, it does appear across a few studies that when vehicles and kitchen items were available (Servin et al., 1999; Todd et al., 2016; van de Beek et al., 2009), gender differences were observed among children who are slightly over 12 months.

We found two observational studies with limited statistical evidence that examined children younger than 12 months in contexts that made parental involvement likely (Katz & Kofkin, 1997; Roopnarine, 1986). One study using very small sample sizes found that at 10 and 14 months, girls were more likely to play with dolls than were boys, but the study found no significant gender differences in play with other female- (domestic) and male- (vehicles, blocks) stereotyped toys (Roopnarine, 1986). It is important to note that parents were instructed to interact with their children and the results indicated differences in parents' interactions with girls versus boys. For example, parents attended more to the block play of boys, and fathers engaged more in the doll play of girls. The other study, in which children were observed in their own homes, did not find any gender differences at 6, 9, and 12 months (Katz & Kofkin, 1997). The results of this study are difficult to evaluate because they were not published in a peer-reviewed journal, and are missing some critical details. The authors did not provide statistics other than a few percentages and did not supply detailed information on the methodology, including information on the involvement of family members and descriptions of all of the toys. Thus, none of these studies in which parental involvement was likely provide particularly compelling evidence for gender differences in play before 12 months.

We also identified two studies that included parent involvement in the toy play of children at around 12 months. A study using a small sample of 12- to 15-month-old children observed playing at home with their own toys found between-gender differences in play with transportation toys and dolls in the expected direction (Smith & Daglish, 1977). Also, girls in this age group played more with soft toys than did boys. No gender differences were found in play with blocks. The other study, in which fathers had to reach on a shelf to provide children with desired toys, found that 12-month-old girls played more than boys with dolls and boys played more than girls with a toy vacuum cleaner, but reported no gender differences in play with vehicles (Snow, Jacklin, & Maccoby, 1983). Given that fathers served as gatekeepers to toys in this study, it is possible that they might have directly (e.g., initiating play, prohibiting play) or indirectly (e.g., body position relative to given toys) influenced play. In sum, both studies found stereotype-consistent toy preferences at around 12 months, but it is unclear how much those differences were driven by parental behaviors.

Taken together, the studies that did and did not entail likely parent involvement suggest that by about 12 to 15 months, boys often, but not always, show greater interest in vehicles (Servin et al., 1999; Smith & Daglish, 1977; van de Beek et al., 2009), and that girls possibly show greater interest in dolls (though this might be more dependent on parental influence) (Roopnarine, 1986; Smith & Daglish, 1977; Todd et al., 2016; van de Beek et al., 2009) and tea sets/kitchen items (Servin et al., 1999; Todd et al., 2016; van de Beek et al., 2009). Other findings appeared to be more isolated and peculiar (perhaps artefactual). Some of the studies suggested that aside from vehicles, boys might have a broader preference for mechanical and hard toys (vacuum cleaner, robot; Jacklin et al., 1973; Snow et al., 1983), whereas girls are more interested in soft toys such as stuffed animals (Smith & Daglish, 1977). However, consistent support was not found for these ideas in a follow-up investigation (Jacklin et al., 1973). Blocks and similar construction toys were not included as often as vehicles and dolls, and one study found that boys played more with Lincoln Logs than girls (Servin et al., 1999), another found that girls played more with blocks than did boys (Goldberg & Lewis, 1969), and a third reported no significant gender difference in block play (Smith & Daglish, 1977).

Conclusions about children under 12 months do not seem possible because of the serious limitation of the two existing studies we identified (Katz & Kofkin, 1997; Roopnarine, 1986) and the grouping of children in this age range with children over 12 months (e.g., Todd et al., 2016). Nonetheless, the existence of studies that did find gender differences by the time children are a year old suggests the possibility of early biological and social influences (based on exposure and reinforcement) on infants' toy preferences. Given that self-socialization and arguably, social-cognitive learning processes have not yet been set in motion at this age, it is not surprising that even though gender differences might exist, they are subtle and difficult to detect.

More research is clearly needed during this early developmental period, including research that examines play both before and after 12 months with a comprehensive range of gender-stereotyped and gender-neutral toys. It is also worth noting that most of the studies of children's toy play under 18 months were conducted before the end of the 20th century and many are decades older than 2000. While it is not clear how historical timing might have affected results, toy marketing has become more gender-stereotyped during the past few decades despite growing awareness of the effects of gender stereotyping and discrimination (Sweet, 2014). Comparing toy play of children being raised in households that discourage and (actively or passively) encourage gender-stereotyped toys would provide important information to understand developmental processes during these early years of development.

Studies Examining Play From 18 Through 24 Months

The 18- through 24-month span is of particular interest to researchers because of the conceptual gains made by children during this period, and it has been a specific focus in our own research. Conclusions are more easily drawn from these studies compared with those examining younger children.

We identified five papers that observed children without any clear parental involvement. Gender differences were apparent in doll play as children approach 24 months (Alexander & Saenz, 2012; Fein, Johnson, Kosson, Stork, & Wasserman, 1975; Zosuls et al., 2009, 2014) and differences in play with trucks were found in four out of the five studies (Alexander & Saenz, 2012; Todd et al., 2016; Zosuls et al., 2009, 2014). Interestingly, significant (within-gender) stereotyped preferences among boys were only found in the studies with the oldest age groups (21 months, Todd et al., 2016; 24 months, Zosuls et al., 2014), while within-gender preferences were found among girls (preference for dolls vs. trucks) at ages younger than 24 months.

Conclusions are more difficult to draw about gender differences in play with toys other than dolls and trucks (e.g., hammer, bracelet used in Fein et al., 1975). Those objects have not been not used across studies, although phone play was observed in two of the studies (Zosuls et al., 2009, 2014) and showed between-gender gender differences in only one of them (Zosuls et al., 2009).

In our own research (Zosuls et al., 2009), we classified toys as strongly and moderately male- and female-stereotyped and neutral (according to studies investigating adults' stereotyped toy ratings) to gain a more nuanced understanding of early gender differences. As indicated above, gender differences only emerged in play with the two most highly gender-stereotyped toys: a doll and a truck. Specifically, boys played significantly more than girls with the truck at both 17 and 21 months, and girls played more with the doll than boys at 21 months. Furthermore, while the proportion of truck play remained at the essentially same high (boys) and low (girls) levels from 17 to 21 months, doll play decreased among boys and increased among girls from 17 to 21 months. This pattern of results is particularly interesting in light of theories of gender development; it suggests that self-socialization processes that emerge as children approach the age of 2 may spur the development of more apparent gender-stereotyped preferences.

A handful of studies with parent involvement showed at least one stereotype-consistent gender difference, and those involving children closer to 24 months typically showed multiple differences. Most of the studies looked at gender differences with dolls and vehicles, and a few found gender differences in play with both of these toys (Alexander & Saenz, 2012; Fagot, 1978; Smith & Daglish, 1977). Two studies found gender differences in play with blocks (favoring boys; Fagot, 1974, 1978). As in the previous studies, a few found asymmetries related to girls and female-stereotyped toys. The studies by Roopnarine (1986) and Katz and Kofkin (1997) discussed earlier both found that at 18 months, gender differences in play were only apparent with female-stereotyped toys. However, another study only found stereotyped play preferences among 19- to 27-month-old boys (analyses were not conducted at the individual toy level; Eisenberg, Wolchik, Hernandez, & Pasternack, 1985). Two studies (Fagot, 1974, 1978) also found differences with soft toys, although another study did not (Smith & Daglish, 1977).

Our study reviewed above (Zosuls et al., 2009) also separately observed children playing with their mothers with the same set of toys, thus enabling a direct comparison of children's play alone with and without parental involvement. When playing with their mothers, gender stereotyped preferences were found in play with a truck and doll among girls at 18 and 21 months, but counterstereotypic preferences were found among boys at 18 months, suggesting that mothers in this (white middle- to upper-middle class urban) sample might have been actively countering gender-stereotyped play. Our results stand in contrast with Alexander and Saenz (2012), who found children's play did not differ depending on parent involvement.

Taken together, between 18 and 24 months, gender differences in toy play emerge more consistently, with girls spending more time playing with female-stereotyped toys (especially dolls) than boys, and boys spending more time playing with male-stereotyped toys (especially trucks) than girls. These differences also appeared to be more apparent among children who were closer to 24 months. Studies that investigated within-gender differences also found stereotyped preferences among both girls and boys, although they were more dependably found among girls, especially at younger ages and when children were playing alone.

Only two studies in this review were longitudinal investigations with at least two time points of children 24 months and younger (Katz & Kofkin,

1997; Zosuls et al., 2009). These studies indicate an emergence of gender differences across time, with differences appearing and increasing from 18 to 21 months. Thus, across studies, although gender differences are apparent even before children reach 2 years, differences become more clear and stable as children approach 24 months.

Gender Differences in Observed Play of 2-Year-Olds

Most studies observing children's play in the 24- to 36-month-old age range have been conducted in preschool or day care settings, making them difficult to compare with studies of younger children. However, these studies reflect the dramatic change in the play context children often experience by this age. Therefore, in this section we also include a brief discussion of research on children's toy play in preschool or day care settings (restricted to children with an average age under 36 months) to provide a more rounded perspective on toy play during this period.

We identified three studies that observed children without the likely influence of parents or peers. One study found stable between-gender differences at 26 and 31 months in play with a subset of male-stereotyped toys (vehicles) and all of the included female-stereotyped toys (all doll related; Weinraub et al., 1984) and another study found that girls played significantly more than boys with a doll (Campbell, Shirley, & Caygill, 2002). The most recent study—a cross-sectional study mentioned in previous sections—found both between-gender differences and gender-stereotyped preferences with a car, digger (truck), doll, and cooking pot among a small sample (16 boys and 16 girls) of children who range from 24 to 32 months (Todd et al., 2016).

Two studies that were conducted in home contexts with parent involvement likely or encouraged reported conflicting findings and are difficult to evaluate due to a lack of detail in their reports. Eisenberg et al. (1985) found gender-stereotyped play preferences among 26- to 33-month-old boys, but not girls, while Katz and Kofkin (1997) found the reverse.

Overall, these studies, especially the ones involving alone play, suggest relatively similar findings to those involving children approaching the age of 2. In fact, our own research shows that gender differences do not necessarily become more pronounced from 24 to 36 months, and that considerable variations remain in children's knowledge of gender categories during this age range (Zosuls et al., 2014). Thus, the 18- to 36-month age range might be thought of as a period when gender differences solidify as children settle into a sense of belonging to a gender group. Then, as children progress toward higher levels of gender understanding (i.e., gender constancy) over the next 2 to 4 years, their gender-stereotyped toy preferences may continue to strengthen (Szkrybalo & Ruble, 1999).

The six studies we identified in which peer influence was likely all showed gender differences. These studies also included toys that were rarely, if ever, examined in the studies reviewed to this point. For example, all of the studies except for one (Campbell et al., 2002) showed gender differences in play with tools (Etaugh, Collins, & Gerson, 1975; Fagot, Leinbach, & Hagan, 1986; Moller & Serbin, 1996; O'Brien & Huston, 1985; O'Brien, Huston, & Risley, 1983). In addition, a few of these studies found that, compared with boys, girls showed a preference for art-related items (Etaugh et al., 1975; Moller & Serbin, 1996). Clearly, in addition to the influence of peers as models and reinforcers of behavior, the diversity of items available to children in preschool settings is likely to influence children's gender-related play. The preschool setting could also affect asymmetries that are observed in children's gender-stereotyped preferences. For example, given that boys are likely to face greater sanctions for engaging in cross-gender activities and that activity preferences (vs. appearance and social behaviors) are more central to the definition of masculinity than femininity (e.g., Smetana, 1986), they might be more likely to restrict their behaviors to own-gender stereotyped activities. In fact, research has found girls' preferences for gender-stereotyped toys decrease across elementary school more so than do such preferences among boys (e.g., Cherney & London, 2006; Etaugh & Liss, 1992).

STUDIES USING EXPERIMENTAL METHODS TO ASSESS TOY PREFERENCES

Behavioral preferences are challenging to study in infants and toddlers because of limitations in their verbal skills and mobility. As a result, researchers interested in the earliest stages of development have increasingly turned to experimental laboratory techniques, especially visual preference tasks to assess preferences for gender-stereotyped stimuli. Some studies have also used tasks that involve pointing to or otherwise choosing between two or more toys and conducted systematic touching analyses.

Studies employing these methods have suggested that infant boys and girls differ in what toys, typically dolls versus vehicles, attract their visual interest. Gender differences were more consistently present at ages 18 months and older in these studies (Jadva, Hines, & Golombok, 2010; Serbin, Poulin-Dubois, Colburne, Sen, & Eichstedt, 2001), although they were also present at earlier ages in a few cases. One looking time study using photos found stereotyped preferences among boys at 9 and 18 months (Campbell, Shirley, Heywood, & Crook, 2000), and another found stereotyped preferences for line drawings of dolls relative to trucks among girls at 12 months (Jadva et al., 2010). In addition, a study using eye tracking technology to measure

3- to 8-month-old infants' visual attention to a three-dimensional doll and a three-dimensional toy truck showed some indications of gender differences in visual fixations, with significant gender-stereotyped preferences only among girls and nonsignificant between-gender differences for the doll and toy truck (Alexander, Wilcox, & Woods, 2009). Two older studies that involved asking 2-year-old children to indicate their preferences only found stereotyped preferences among boys (Blakemore, LaRue, & Olejnik, 1979, Study 1; Perry et al., 1984), and the other study using a choice paradigm did not find any stereotyped preferences in 1-year-olds (Servin et al., 1999).

In sum, although one study found some indication of preferences among infants under 9 months (Alexander et al., 2009), as a whole, gender differences were more apparent at older ages. As in the observational studies of the youngest children, findings were mixed, and more consistent patterns of gender differences were observed with vehicles and dolls at 18 months and older. Of course, caution is warranted when drawing summary conclusions across observational and experimental paradigms, as these methods have qualities that might affect children's behaviors in different ways. For example, the experimental methods overwhelmingly pitted dolls and trucks, without the use of other gender-stereotyped and neutral toys, and this forced-choice method in a strange setting might affect behavior in a way that might not reflect preferences in more naturalistic contexts. Importantly, crucial questions surround the meaning of differences in response to two-dimensional representations of toys. For instance, infants have difficulty understanding how two-dimensional representations correspond to three-dimensional objects, and thus children under the age of 3 have trouble transferring learning from two-dimensional representations, even when they are animated (Barr, 2010). Thus, while infants can see and even respond in gender-differentiated ways to these experimental scenarios, it is unclear what their responses actually mean if they are not able to understand those representations' link to actual toys. This question is also pertinent to the research discussed in the following section.

OTHER GENDER DIFFERENCES IN PREFERENCES

Given that some of the most clearly gender-stereotyped toys differ on the dimensions of social versus nonsocial stimuli and mechanical motion (i.e., dolls and vehicles), research demonstrating gender differences in interest in human or social stimuli and mechanical motion is particularly germane to research on children's toy preferences. This research has primarily focused on neonates with the goal of understanding the biological basis of gender-related preferences (i.e., before socialization processes have been able to exert their influence). Prominent (and controversial) research by Baron-Cohen and his colleagues has found gender differences on these dimensions using looking-time paradigms. In a study in which neonates were presented with a human female face or a mobile that matched the face in color, size, and shape, male babies tended to have a preference for the mobile whereas girls had either a preference for the face or no preference (Connellan, Baron-Cohen, Wheelwright, Batki, & Ahluwalia, 2000). Analyses were based on preferences that were calculated by subtracting the percentage of time spent looking at the mobile from the percentage of time spent looking at the face and using a cutoff to classify infants as having a face preference, mobile preference, or no preference. The authors attributed the findings to strong innate differences in interest in social versus nonsocial stimuli, with males showing a preference for mechanical motion. Although this is an interesting possibility, the weak results among female infants, coupled with methodological limitations, including the use of the experimenter's face as a stimulus, has led to considerable criticism. The findings of a study involving better controls (i.e., video clips; Lutchmaya & Baron-Cohen, 2002) were consistent with the results of the previous study, but represented a significant departure from that study because it used 12-month-olds rather than neonates. More recent research by a different research group has investigated gender differences among 4- to 5-month-olds using eye tracking and multiple stimuli for each category tested (Escudero, Robbins, & Johnson, 2013). This assessed infants' preferences for stimuli from four categories (photographs of real/toy cars, real female/doll faces in Study 1a, and real/toy stoves, real male/doll faces in Study 1b), thereby addressing previous findings involving social versus nonsocial stimuli as well as dolls and vehicles more specifically. This study failed to confirm gender differences among young infants and, instead, found that both genders preferred real and doll faces over real and toy cars. In sum, assertions about the existence of clear gender differences among young infants are not warranted from this small body of research. Nonetheless, the possibility that young boys and girls respond differentially to social and nonsocial stimuli is an interesting way to characterize the essence of gender differences in play and is relevant to a broad range of research on this topic.

Taken together, research investigating infants' and young children's interest in social stimuli does perhaps provide some tentative, preliminary evidence that girls' greater interest in dolls might stem from a more general and early emerging interest in social stimuli. Results among neonates are not sufficiently consistent, however, to indicate that such differences have a clear biological antecedent, present from birth. Instead, it appears from at least one study that both female and male infants have a preference for social stimuli (Escudero et al., 2013).

DISCUSSION

Despite evidence of gender differences as early as 8 months (Alexander et al., 2009), numerous studies we reviewed did not show clear evidence of gender differences before 12 months and consistent support did not emerge until the 18- to 24-month age range. Across studies, gender differences were most apparent with vehicles and dolls (and to some extent tea sets), and studies with 2-year-old children indicated that gender differences expand to other toys during the 24- to 36-month age range, especially in the context of peer groups. Because vehicles and dolls, and to some extent tea sets, were used across many studies, we can more confidently draw conclusions about these toys. Conclusions are more difficult to make about construction toys (e.g., Lincoln Logs, blocks), tools (e.g., hammers), and domestic toys (e.g., toy vacuum cleaners), which showed gender differences in only a few studies. Findings from studies using experimental methodologies also indicated gender differences in interest in dolls and trucks, especially among children 18 months and older. Thus, across both types of studies, answers about gender differences in children under 18 months are elusive, both because of inconsistent findings and because relatively few studies have investigated children this young.

A more definitive conclusion that can be drawn is that early gender differences are typically subtle, and overall, infants and toddlers are more similar than different in their play, with girls and boys often spending the most time playing with the same toys (e.g., O'Brien et al., 1983; Zosuls et al., 2009). Studies that do not include neutral stimuli (as most of the experimental studies we reviewed) also tend to obscure this point, as children in such studies must choose between stereotype-consistent and counterstereotypic toys, thereby potentially exaggerating gender differences. In other words, in the absence of gender-neutral options, children might default to gender-stereotyped toys due to greater familiarity with these toys or slight preferences that might not reflect how much they would prefer such toys given a wider array of options.

Although we might conclude (though without a substantial degree of confidence) from this review that there is evidence for some very early gender differences in children's toy preferences (especially with vehicles), the subtlety of these gender differences and their strengthening over time indicates that it is possible and likely that multiple processes are at work, and that researchers and theorists need to use caution when making arguments based on developmental sequencing. Overall, this review indicates more strongly what is not known, rather than what is known, about the development of early gender differences in toy preferences.

Limitations of the Approaches to Research

Aside from a relative lack of well-controlled studies of children playing alone, the observational studies reviewed often lacked attention to toy classifications and features and to the ways in which such factors might relate to gender differences in preferences (or a lack thereof).

For one, a critical consideration in the design of studies assessing gender-stereotyped play is the degree to which toys designated as male- and female-stereotyped are in fact stereotyped. Two classes of toys, building toys or blocks and domestic toys such as kitchen or tea sets, are common in studies of gender-stereotyped play, yet it is unclear how strongly such toys are stereotyped. For example, although some studies placed blocks clearly in the male-stereotyped category (Campbell, Shirley, & Candy, 2004; Fagot et al., 1986), others considered them as only moderately male-stereotyped (Bussey & Bandura, 1992). Similarly, some studies designated toy kitchen sets and other toy domestic items (e.g., appliances, cookware) as definitively feminine (e.g., Todd et al., 2016; van de Beek et al., 2009) and others as only moderately feminine (e.g., Bussey & Bandura, 1992). Research examining the issue has found that classifications vary depending on the qualities of the exact item considered (e.g., tea set vs. kitchen set; Blakemore & Centers, 2005).

The superficial qualities (e.g., colors, themes) and functions (e.g., plates and spoons vs. blender) of toys are also likely to vary in their appeal to boys versus girls (Weisgram, Fulcher, & Dinella, 2014). Interestingly, a study examining sex differences in vervet monkeys' preferences for human toys found differences in expected directions with a set of female-stereotyped toys that included a cooking pot (the other female-stereotyped toy was a doll), which is surprising given that this object does not have features that are presumably relevant to monkeys' gender roles (in contrast, it might be argued that a soft doll might also appear baby monkeylike to a monkey; Alexander & Hines, 2002). However, this study also did not report separate analyses for individual toys; therefore, it is also unclear whether effects were driven by one of the two toys (Alexander & Hines, 2002).

Increasingly, researchers have turned their attention to basic features of toys that might be plausibly linked to biological- versus socialization-based reasons for differentially appealing to girls and boys. For example, mechanical features of toys might largely explain very early gender differences in vehicles, whereas the toy labels *car* or *truck* might exert relatively more influence on maintaining and increasing gender differences at later ages, once boys link these objects with males through stereotyped associations (Zosuls et al., 2014). Toy color is another important attribute that can affect children's toy preferences, and the color pink is a particularly salient marker of female-stereotyped objects. Although some have proposed evolutionary hypotheses about girls' preferences for reddish colors (Alexander, 2003), one of the studies reviewed here did not find these expected gender differences in color preferences among young children (Jadva et al., 2010). Other research has found that human children do not develop gender-stereotyped color preferences until about age 2, with girls showing a preference for pink and boys showing an avoidance of pink (LoBue & DeLoache, 2011). As electronic toys become increasingly prevalent for children at younger and younger ages, it will also be important to understand how the characteristics of these toys might differentially appeal to girls and boys.

A related question concerns the ways in which children play with toys. Given the same toy, will boys and girls play with it the same way? Exploring the types of play children engage in could be helpful to understanding how biological, social, and cognitive factors influence play. Wallen and his colleagues took an innovative step in their research to better explore the features of objects that might be differentially appealing to males versus females (Hassett et al., 2008). To do this, they observed juvenile rhesus monkeys and 3- and 4-year-old children play with wheeled and plush objects that differed in their feel (i.e., plush vs. hard) and movable parts (i.e., wheels that spin vs. wheel-shaped feature that does not spin) but had the same overall shape. Children, but not younger monkeys, showed the expected gender-stereotyped preferences (boys interacted more with the wheeled hard object than girls; within gender preferences were also noted; Hassett et al., 2008).

In our own research, we have also found subtle but significant gender differences in types of play. In an unpublished analysis, we were intrigued to find that when playing with a doll, boys engaged in more play that involved the mechanical features of this toy—opening and closing its "sleeping" eyes—whereas girls engaged in more nurturing and role-playing activities, such as cuddling and feeding the doll. We followed up on this observation in a subsequent study using a different sample and found that girls engaged in more nurturing activities (e.g., cuddling a doll) and boys engaged in more motion-related activities (e.g., spinning wheels of a vehicle) with a standardized set of toys, and that motion-related activities were greater at 36 months compared with 24 months (Zosuls et al., 2014). However, we hasten to add that these forms of play, especially nurturing activities, only made up a small portion of the time children spent playing with the toys, and that these behaviors (especially nurturing) might take longer to appear as they involve more complex gendered scripts. Additionally, we did not find differences in rough handling of toys, despite stereotypic predictions we heard from both colleagues and friends convinced that we would see boys throwing and hitting other objects with the doll, and research on boys' rough and tumble play (e.g., DiPietro, 1981). These findings underscored for us the ongoing need for rigorous studies of children's play behaviors.

CONCLUSION

The surprising lack of clarity on the developmental course of early gender differences in children's toy play, and the processes underlying them, especially before 18 months, is not a trivial concern, as toy preferences are a window into fundamental processes of gender development. Although biological, social, and self-socialization mechanisms have been linked to gender-stereotyped toy preferences, researchers still have much to learn about how and whether these processes influence children's behaviors at different phases of development. Infancy is an especially challenging period to study, but it is also vital to elucidating the role of biological relative to socialization processes. Experimental methodologies have become a popular and ingenious solution to understanding infant cognition; however, it is difficult to know how behaviors such as preferentially looking at an image of a doll over a truck translate into actual gender-linked preferences. High-quality observational studies are also still needed, especially for gaining a more nuanced understanding of how children interact with toys across development.

REFERENCES

Adolph, K. E., & Joh, A. S. (2007). Motor development: How infants get into the act. In A. Slater & M. Lewis (Eds.), *Introduction to infant development* (2nd ed., pp. 63–80). New York, NY: Oxford University Press. Retrieved from http://psych.nyu.edu/adolph/publications/2007AdolphJoh%20LearningDevelopmentInInfantLocomotion.pdf

Alexander, G. M. (2003). An evolutionary perspective of sex-typed toy preferences: Pink, blue, and the brain. *Archives of Sexual Behavior, 32,* 7–14. http://dx.doi.org/10.1023/A:1021833110722

Alexander, G. M., & Hines, M. (2002). Sex differences in response to children's toys in nonhuman primates (*Cercopithecus aethiops sabaeus*). *Evolution and Human Behavior, 23,* 467–479. http://dx.doi.org/10.1016/S1090-5138(02)00107-1

Alexander, G. M., & Saenz, J. (2012). Early androgens, activity levels and toy choices of children in the second year of life. *Hormones and Behavior, 62,* 500–504. Retrieved from https://www.ncbi.nlm.nih.gov/pubmed/22955184

Alexander, G. M., Wilcox, T., & Woods, R. (2009). Sex differences in infants' visual interest in toys. *Archives of Sexual Behavior, 38,* 427–433. http://dx.doi.org/10.1007/s10508-008-9430-1

Barr, R. (2010). Transfer of learning between 2D and 3D sources during infancy: Informing theory and practice. *Developmental Review, 30,* 128–154. Retrieved from https://www.ncbi.nlm.nih.gov/pmc/articles/PMC2885850/

Bem, S. L. (1981). Gender schema theory: A cognitive account of sex typing. *Psychological Review, 88*, 354–364. http://dx.doi.org/10.1037/0033-295X.88.4.354

Berenbaum, S. A., & Beltz, A. M. (2016). How early hormones shape gender development. *Current Opinion in Behavioral Sciences, 7*, 53–60. Retrieved from http://www.sciencedirect.com/science/article/pii/S2352154615001515

Blakemore, J. E. O., Berenbaum, S. A., & Liben, L. S. (2009). *Gender development.* New York, NY: Taylor & Francis.

Blakemore, J. E. O., & Centers, R. E. (2005). Characteristics of boys' and girls' toys. *Sex Roles, 53*, 619–633. http://dx.doi.org/10.1007/s11199-005-7729-0

Blakemore, J. E. O., LaRue, A. A., & Olejnik, A. B. (1979). Sex-appropriate toy preference and the ability to conceptualize toys as sex-role related. *Developmental Psychology, 15*, 339–340. http://dx.doi.org/10.1037/0012-1649.15.3.339

Bussey, K., & Bandura, A. (1992). Self-regulatory mechanisms governing gender development. *Child Development, 63*, 1236–1250. http://dx.doi.org/10.2307/1131530

Bussey, K., & Bandura, A. (1999). Social cognitive theory of gender development and differentiation. *Psychological Review, 106*, 676–713. http://dx.doi.org/10.1037/0033-295X.106.4.676

Campbell, A., Shirley, L., & Candy, J. (2004). A longitudinal study of gender-related cognition and behaviour. *Developmental Science, 7*, 1–9. http://dx.doi.org/10.1111/j.1467-7687.2004.00316.x

Campbell, A., Shirley, L., & Caygill, L. (2002). Sex-typed preferences in three domains: Do two-year-olds need cognitive variables? *British Journal of Psychology, 93*, 203–217. http://dx.doi.org/10.1348/000712602162544

Campbell, A., Shirley, L., Heywood, C., & Crook, C. (2000). Infants' visual preference for sex-congruent babies, children, toys and activities: A longitudinal study. *British Journal of Developmental Psychology, 18*, 479–498. http://dx.doi.org/10.1348/026151000165814

Cherney, I. D., & London, K. (2006). Gender-linked differences in the toys, television shows, computer games, and outdoor activities of 5- to 13-year-old children. *Sex Roles, 54*, 717–726. http://dx.doi.org/10.1007/s11199-006-9037-8

Cohen-Bendahan, C. C., van de Beek, C., & Berenbaum, S. A. (2005). Prenatal sex hormone effects on child and adult sex-typed behavior: Methods and findings. *Neuroscience and Biobehavioral Reviews, 29*, 353–384. http://dx.doi.org/10.1016/j.neubiorev.2004.11.004

Connellan, J., Baron-Cohen, S., Wheelwright, S., Batki, A., & Ahluwalia, J. (2000). Sex differences in human neonatal social perception. *Infant Behavior and Development, 23*, 113–118. http://dx.doi.org/10.1016/S0163-6383(00)00032-1

Corter, C., & Jamieson, N. (1977). Infants' toy preferences and mothers' predictions. *Developmental Psychology, 13*, 413–414. http://dx.doi.org/10.1037/0012-1649.13.4.413

DiPietro, J. A. (1981). Rough and tumble play: A function of gender. *Developmental Psychology, 17*, 50–58. http://dx.doi.org/10.1037/0012-1649.17.1.50

Eisenberg, N., Wolchik, S. A., Hernandez, R., & Pasternack, J. F. (1985). Parental socialization of young children's play: A short-term longitudinal study. *Child Development, 56*, 1506–1513. http://dx.doi.org/10.2307/1130469

Escudero, P., Robbins, R. A., & Johnson, S. P. (2013). Sex-related preferences for real and doll faces versus real and toy objects in young infants and adults. *Journal of Experimental Child Psychology, 116*, 367–379. http://dx.doi.org/10.1016/j.jecp.2013.07.001

Etaugh, C., Collins, G., & Gerson, A. (1975). Reinforcement of sex-typed behaviors of two-year-old children in a nursery school setting. *Developmental Psychology, 11*, 255. http://dx.doi.org/10.1037/h0076461

Etaugh, C., & Liss, M. B. (1992). Home, school, and playroom: Training grounds for adult gender roles. *Sex Roles, 26*, 129–147. http://dx.doi.org/10.1007/BF00289754

Fagot, B. I. (1974). Sex differences in toddlers' behavior and parental reaction. *Developmental Psychology, 10*, 554–558. http://dx.doi.org/10.1037/h0036600

Fagot, B. I. (1978). The influence of sex of child on parental reactions to toddler children. *Child Development, 49*, 459–465. http://dx.doi.org/10.2307/1128711

Fagot, B. I., Leinbach, M. D., & Hagan, R. (1986). Gender labeling and the adoption of sex-typed behaviors. *Developmental Psychology, 22*, 440–443. http://dx.doi.org/10.1037/0012-1649.22.4.440

Fein, G., Johnson, D., Kosson, N., Stork, J., & Wasserman, L. (1975). Sex stereotypes and preferences in the toy choices of 20-month-old boys and girls. *Developmental Psychology, 11*, 527–528. http://dx.doi.org/10.1037/h0076675

Fenson, L., & Ramsay, D. S. (1980). Decentration and integration of the child's play in the second year. *Child Development, 51*, 171–178. http://dx.doi.org/10.2307/1129604

Goldberg, S., & Lewis, M. (1969). Play behavior in the year-old infant: Early sex differences. *Child Development, 40*, 21–31. http://dx.doi.org/10.2307/1127152

Halim, M. L., Ruble, D. N., Lurye, L. E., Greulich, F. K., & Zosuls, K. M. (2014). Pink frilly dresses and the avoidance of all things "girly": Children's appearance rigidity and cognitive theories of gender development. *Developmental Psychology, 50*, 1091–1101. http://dx.doi.org/10.1037/a0034906

Hassett, J. M., Siebert, E. R., & Wallen, K. (2008). Sex differences in rhesus monkey toy preferences parallel those of children. *Hormones and Behavior, 54*, 359–364. Retrieved from https://www.ncbi.nlm.nih.gov/pmc/articles/PMC2583786/

Hines, M., Golombok, S., Rust, J., Johnston, K. J., Golding, J., & the Avon Longitudinal Study of Parents and Children Study Team. (2002). Testosterone during pregnancy and gender role behavior of preschool children: A longitudinal, population study. *Child Development, 73*, 1678–1687. http://dx.doi.org/10.1111/1467-8624.00498

Jacklin, C. N., Maccoby, E. E., & Dick, A. E. (1973). Barrier behavior and toy preference: Sex differences (and their absence) in the year-old child. *Child Development, 44*, 196–200. http://dx.doi.org/10.2307/1127703

Jadva, V., Hines, M., & Golombok, S. (2010). Infants' preferences for toys, colors, and shapes: Sex differences and similarities. *Archives of Sexual Behavior, 39,* 1261–1273. http://dx.doi.org/10.1007/s10508-010-9618-z

Kahlenberg, S. G., & Hein, M. M. (2010). Progression on Nickelodeon? Gender role stereotypes in toy commercials. *Sex Roles, 62,* 830–847. http://dx.doi.org/10.1007/s11199-009-9653-1

Katz, P. A., & Kofkin, J. A. (1997). Race, gender, and young children. In S. S. Luthar, J. A. Burack, D. Cicchetti, & J. Weisz (Eds.), *Developmental psychopathology: Perspectives on adjustment, risk, and disorder* (pp. 51–74). New York, NY: Cambridge University Press.

Kohlberg, L. A. (1966). A cognitive-developmental analysis of children's sex role concepts and attitudes. In E. E. Maccoby (Ed.), *The development of sex differences* (pp. 82–173). Stanford, CA: Stanford University Press.

LaFreniere, P., Strayer, F. F., & Gauthier, R. (1984). The emergence of same-sex affiliative preferences among preschool peers: A developmental/ecological perspective. *Child Development, 55,* 1958–1965. http://dx.doi.org/10.2307/1129942

Lamb, M. E., Bornstein, M. H., & Teti, D. M. (2002). *Development in infancy: An introduction* (4th ed.). Mahwah, NJ: Lawrence Erlbaum.

Li, R. Y. H., & Wong, W. I. (2016). Gender-typed play and social abilities in boys and girls: Are they related? *Sex Roles, 74,* 399–410. http://dx.doi.org/10.1007/s11199-016-0580-7

LoBue, V., & DeLoache, J. S. (2011). Pretty in pink: The early development of gender-stereotyped colour preferences. *British Journal of Developmental Psychology, 29,* 656–667. http://dx.doi.org/10.1111/j.2044-835X.2011.02027.x

Lutchmaya, S., & Baron-Cohen, S. (2002). Human sex differences in social and non-social looking preferences, at 12 months of age. *Infant Behavior and Development, 25,* 319–325. Retrieved from https://pdfs.semanticscholar.org/1b50/e90a417960eaf3e57b4092f619411d9e60e3.pdf

Maccoby, E. E., & Jacklin, C. N. (1974). *The psychology of sex differences* (Vol. 1). Stanford, CA: Stanford University Press.

Martin, C. L., & Halverson, C. F. (1981). A schematic processing model of sex typing and stereotyping in children. *Child Development, 52,* 1119–1134. http://dx.doi.org/10.2307/1129498

Martin, C. L., Ruble, D. N., & Szkrybalo, J. (2004). Recognizing the centrality of gender identity and stereotype knowledge in gender development and moving toward theoretical integration: Reply to Bandura and Bussey (2004). *Psychological Bulletin, 130,* 702–710. http://dx.doi.org/10.1037/0033-2909.130.5.702

Merke, D. P., & Bornstein, S. R. (2005). Congenital adrenal hyperplasia. *The Lancet, 365,* 2125–2136. http://dx.doi.org/10.1016/S0140-6736(05)66736-0

Mischel, W. (1966). A social-learning view of sex differences in behavior. In E. E. Maccoby (Ed.), *The development of sex differences* (pp. 57–81). Stanford, CA: Stanford University Press.

Moller, L. C., & Serbin, L. A. (1996). Antecedents of toddler gender segregation: Cognitive consonance, gender-typed toy preferences and behavioral compatibility. *Sex Roles, 35,* 445–460. http://dx.doi.org/10.1007/BF01544131

O'Brien, M., & Huston, A. C. (1985). Development of sex-typed play behavior in toddlers. *Developmental Psychology, 21,* 866–871. http://dx.doi.org/10.1037/0012-1649.21.5.866

O'Brien, M., Huston, A. C., & Risley, T. R. (1983). Sex-typed play of toddlers in a day care center. *Journal of Applied Developmental Psychology, 4,* 1–9. Retrieved from http://www.sciencedirect.com/science/article/pii/0193397383900540

Perry, D. G., White, A., & Perry, L. C. (1984). Does early sex typing result from children's attempts to match their behavior to sex role stereotypes? *Child Development, 55,* 2114–2121. http://dx.doi.org/10.2307/1129784

Powlishta, K. K., Serbin, L. A., & Moller, L. C. (1993). The stability of individual differences in gender typing: Implications for understanding gender segregation. *Sex Roles, 29,* 723–737. http://dx.doi.org/10.1007/BF00289214

Roopnarine, J. L. (1986). Mothers' and fathers' behaviors toward the toy play of their infant sons and daughters. *Sex Roles, 14,* 59–68. http://dx.doi.org/10.1007/BF00287848

Ruble, D. N. (1994). A phase model of transitions: Cognitive and motivational consequences. *Advances in Experimental Social Psychology, 26,* 163–214. http://dx.doi.org/10.1016/S0065-2601(08)60154-9

Schau, C. G., Kahn, L., Diepold, J. H., & Cherry, F. (1980). The relationship of parental expectations and preschool children's verbal sex typing to their sex-typed toy play behavior. *Child Development, 51,* 266–270. http://dx.doi.org/10.2307/1129620

Serbin, L. A., Poulin-Dubois, D., Colburne, K. A., Sen, M. G., & Eichstedt, J. A. (2001). Gender stereotyping in infancy: Visual preferences for and knowledge of gender-stereotyped toys in the second year. *International Journal of Behavioral Development, 25,* 7–15. http://dx.doi.org/10.1080/01650250042000078

Servin, A., Bohlin, G., & Berlin, L. (1999). Sex differences in 1-, 3-, and 5-year-olds' toy-choice in a structured play-session. *Scandinavian Journal of Psychology, 40,* 43–48. http://dx.doi.org/10.1111/1467-9450.00096

Smetana, J. G. (1986). Preschool children's conceptions of sex-role transgressions. *Child Development, 57,* 862–871. http://dx.doi.org/10.2307/1130363

Smetana, J. G., & Letourneau, K. J. (1984). Development of gender constancy and children's sex-typed free play behavior. *Developmental Psychology, 20,* 691–696. http://dx.doi.org/10.1037/0012-1649.20.4.691

Smith, P. K., & Daglish, L. (1977). Sex differences in parent and infant behavior in the home. *Child Development, 48,* 1250–1254. http://dx.doi.org/10.2307/1128482

Snow, M. E., Jacklin, C. N., & Maccoby, E. E. (1983). Sex-of-child differences in father–child interaction at one year of age. *Child Development, 54,* 227–232. http://dx.doi.org/10.2307/1129880

Sweet, E. (2014). Toys are more divided by gender now than they were 50 years ago. *The Atlantic.* Retrieved from https://www.theatlantic.com/business/archive/2014/12/toys-are-more-divided-by-gender-now-than-they-were-50-years-ago/383556/

Szkrybalo, J., & Ruble, D. N. (1999). "God made me a girl": Sex-category constancy judgments and explanations revisited. *Developmental Psychology, 35,* 392–402. http://dx.doi.org/10.1037/0012-1649.35.2.392

Tamis-LeMonda, C. S., & Bornstein, M. H. (1996). Variations in children's exploratory, nonsymbolic, and symbolic play: An explanatory multidimensional framework. In C. Rovee-Collier, L. P. Lipsitt, & H. Hayne (Eds.), *Advances in infancy research* (Vol. 10, pp. 37–78). Santa Barbara, CA: Praeger.

Tobin, D. D., Menon, M., Menon, M., Spatta, B. C., Hodges, E. V., & Perry, D. G. (2010). The intrapsychics of gender: A model of self-socialization. *Psychological Review, 117,* 601–622. http://dx.doi.org/10.1037/a0018936

Todd, B. K., Barry, J. A., & Thommessen, S. A. (2016). Preferences for "gender-typed" toys in boys and girls aged 9 to 32 Months. *Infant and Child Development.* Advance online publication. Retrieved from http://www.pitt.edu/~bertsch/Todd_et_al-2016-Infant_and_Child_Development.pdf

van de Beek, C., van Goozen, S. H. M., Buitelaar, J. K., & Cohen-Kettenis, P. T. (2009). Prenatal sex hormones (maternal and amniotic fluid) and gender-related play behavior in 13-month-old infants. *Archives of Sexual Behavior, 38,* 6–15. http://dx.doi.org/10.1007/s10508-007-9291-z

Wallen, K. (1996). Nature needs nurture: The interaction of hormonal and social influences on the development of behavioral sex differences in rhesus monkeys. *Hormones and Behavior, 30,* 364–378. http://dx.doi.org/10.1006/hbeh.1996.0042

Wallen, K. (2005). Hormonal influences on sexually differentiated behavior in nonhuman primates. *Frontiers in Neuroendocrinology, 26,* 7–26. http://dx.doi.org/10.1016/j.yfrne.2005.02.001

Wallen, K., & Hassett, J. M. (2009). Sexual differentiation of behaviour in monkeys: Role of prenatal hormones. *Journal of Neuroendocrinology, 21,* 421–426. http://dx.doi.org/10.1111/j.1365-2826.2009.01832.x

Weinraub, M., Clemens, L. P., Sockloff, A., Ethridge, T., Gracely, E., & Myers, B. (1984). The development of sex role stereotypes in the third year: Relationships to gender labeling, gender identity, sex-typed toy preference, and family characteristics. *Child Development, 55,* 1493–1503. http://dx.doi.org/10.2307/1130019

Weisgram, E. S., Fulcher, M., & Dinella, L. M. (2014). Pink gives girls permission: Exploring the roles of explicit gender labels and gender-typed colors on preschool children's toy preferences. *Journal of Applied Developmental Psychology, 35,* 401–409. http://dx.doi.org/10.1016/j.appdev.2014.06.004

Zajonc, R. B. (2001). Mere exposure: A gateway to the subliminal. *Current Directions in Psychological Science, 10,* 224–228. http://dx.doi.org/10.1111/1467-8721.00154

Zosuls, K. M., Ruble, D. N., & Tamis-LeMonda, C. S. (2014). Self-socialization of gender in African American, Dominican immigrant, and Mexican immigrant toddlers. *Child Development, 85,* 2202–2217. Retrieved from https://www.ncbi.nlm.nih.gov/pubmed/24977945

Zosuls, K. M., Ruble, D. N., Tamis-Lemonda, C. S., Shrout, P. E., Bornstein, M. H., & Greulich, F. K. (2009). The acquisition of gender labels in infancy: Implications for gender-typed play. *Developmental Psychology, 45,* 688–701. http://dx.doi.org/10.1037/a0014053

4

CHARACTERISTICS OF MASCULINE AND FEMININE TOYS AND GENDER-DIFFERENTIATED PLAY

ISABELLE D. CHERNEY

Toys play a very important role in young children's development (e.g., Leaper, 2015). They stimulate pretend play, and in many ways, interaction with toys is an important gateway to many aspects of children's social and cognitive development in early childhood (e.g., Hirsh-Pasek, Golinkoff, Berk, & Singer, 2008; see also Chapters 9 and 10, this volume). Toys, however, are highly gendered, particularly in the United States. It is thus important to understand how these toys are gendered, and how they influence children's development. In addition, toy manufacturers use different strategies to market toys to boys and to girls. Strolling down the toy aisles, children and parents can typically choose a toy among a "sea of blue and pink." Frequently, the same toy is available in "boy colors" or "girl colors." This chapter explores the research on the development of children's play, differentiated play patterns that emerge from playing with gendered toys, characteristics of gendered and neutral toys, and the skills children may develop from playing with certain

http://dx.doi.org/10.1037/0000077-005
Gender Typing of Children's Toys: How Early Play Experiences Impact Development, E. S. Weisgram and L. M. Dinella (Editors)

toys. This chapter also investigates effect sizes of gender differences in toy preferences and play styles and factors that influence those under varying conditions.

THE DEVELOPMENT OF CHILDREN'S PLAY

Play is a crucial aspect of healthy development (e.g., Hirsh-Pasek et al., 2008). Children are active learners who acquire new knowledge by exploring their environment through play. Although young children spend about 90% of their time playing with toys, there is little empirical evidence on how the (gendered) toys influence children's development (Trawick-Smith, Wolff, Koschel, & Vallarelli, 2015). Research in many parts of the world has shown robust gender differences in children's play and toy preferences (e.g., Martin, Eisenbud, & Rose, 1995; Nelson, 2005; Serbin, Poulin-Dubois, Colburne, Sen, & Eichstedt, 2001). On average, girls prefer and play more than boys with dolls, kitchens or other domestic toys, fashion accessories, and stuffed animals, whereas boys prefer and play more than girls with transportation and construction toys, military toys and toy guns, sports-related toys, and building sets (e.g., Cherney & London, 2006). The correlations between gender and type of toy are very reliable as measured across different methodologies (see Chapter 2), and are consequently often called "boys' toys" (masculine toys) or "girls' toys" (feminine toys; Blakemore & Centers, 2005).

Gender differences in children's toy preferences reliably emerge around the age of 2 (e.g., Caldera, Huston, & O'Brien, 1989; Campbell, Shirley, & Caygill, 2002; see also Chapter 3, this volume, for a review), although evidence using eye-tracking technology indicates that 3- to 8-month-old girls look longer at a doll than a toy truck ($d > 1.0$; Alexander, Wilcox, & Woods, 2009) and infant boys compared with girls look longer at a toy truck than a doll ($d = .78$). These looking preferences may be experience-dependent, as parents often provide own-gender-stereotyped toys to young infants. On the other hand, these preferences may also be experience-independent, as other research has shown that shortly after birth, girls prefer to look at a human face and boys prefer to look a mechanical motion of a mobile (Connellan, Baron-Cohen, Wheelwright, Batki, & Ahluwalia, 2000).

Around the age of 2, gender roles and basic knowledge about gender norms develop (Martin, Wood, & Little, 1990; Ruble & Martin, 1998; Thompson, 1975). The magnitude and extent of gender differences in toys, play activities, and interests increase during the preschool years (Cherney & Dempsey, 2010; Cherney, Harper, & Winter, 2006; Leaper, 2015; Ruble, Martin, & Berenbaum, 2006). Toy preferences among children are one of the largest gender differences ($d = 2.7$, Cherney & London, 2006; Servin,

Bohlin, & Berlin, 1999). Five-year-olds, especially boys, have very clear preferences for gender-typed toys (Bussey & Bandura, 1992; Cherney & London, 2006).

Gendered toy preferences show different patterns after the preschool years. Boys' preferences for gender-stereotyped toys remain consistent, as they grow older, whereas girls' preferences for gender-stereotyped toys decreases (Cherney & London, 2006). Cherney and London (2006) investigated gender differences in leisure activity preferences in 5- to 13-year-olds. They established a gender index for each activity to identify developmental trends across four leisure activities (toys, television, sports, and video/computer games) and three age groups (5- to 7-year-olds, 8- to 10-year-olds, 11- to 13-year-olds). As far as toys were concerned, boys and girls had a greater preference for toys stereotyped as own-gender than for cross-gender-stereotyped or gender-neutral toys (e.g., Carter & Levy, 1988; Cherney, Kelly-Vance, Glover, Ruane, & Ryalls, 2003; Martin et al., 1995). Furthermore, on average, boys preferred manipulative toys, vehicles, and action figures, whereas girls preferred dolls, stuffed animals, and educational toys.

GENDER-DIFFERENTIATED PLAY STYLES

Gender differences in play styles are well documented. Children around the world interact in similar ways with same-gender peers (e.g., Pellegrini & Smith, 1998). Young children in the United States spend about half of their social interactions in same-gender interactions (Martin, Fabes, Hanish, Leonard, & Dinella, 2011). Girls tend to prefer to play in dyads (two people) or at most triads (three people), whereas boys prefer larger groups (Benenson, 1993; Markovits, Benenson, & Dolenszky, 2001).

Boys and girls play different kinds of games and activities and also have characteristic play styles. Preschool boys in groups are likely to engage in rough-and-tumble play, a boisterous, high-energy type of play that may involve yelling and play fights (Pellegrini & Smith, 1998). Girls, on the other hand, are more likely to take turns and cooperate with each other (Maccoby, 1998). Lindsey and Colwell (2013) analyzed the play of preschool children's pretend and physical play with same-gender, other-gender, and mixed-gender peers. Girls' same-gender peer play emphasized fantasy and sociodramatic play, whereas boys' same-gender peer play was made up of exercise play, fantasy play, and rough-and-tumble play. Similarly, other researchers found that girls' fantasy play tends to revolve around make-believe play reflecting parenting and other reciprocal social relationships, whereas boys' fantasy play is more likely to emphasize power, dominance, and aggression (Gredlein & Bjorklund, 2005), often incorporated in rough-and-tumble play. These play styles could easily be related to the type of activities (e.g., dress-up vs. football) and the type of toys with which girls and boys play.

Girls and boys may also use the same toys in different ways. For example, Pitcher and Schultz (1983) reported that girls cuddled, fed, and diapered dolls, whereas boys probed the dolls' hair, manipulated the dolls' legs, and removed the dolls' clothing. These styles continue into elementary school years with boys emphasizing dominance and girls focusing more on social relationships (Blakemore, Berenbaum, & Liben, 2008).

Another type of gender-differentiated play can be found during solitary as opposed to social play. Boys are more likely than girls to engage in object-oriented play (e.g., Caldera et al., 1999). In an observational study involving same-gender dyads of children, boys immediately started playing with blocks and used more complex building strategies than girls. In contrast, girls spent more time engaged in conversation before playing with the blocks, and they showed less complex techniques (Sluss, 2002).

These differentiated play styles may be related to cognitive and social development (e.g., Pellegrini & Bjorklund, 2004). For instance, because boys engage in more rough-and-tumble play than girls, Pellegrini and Smith (1998) suggested that this prepares them for adult male-on-male competition. Similarly, boys tend to have more experience in outdoor play with props and tasks requiring eye–hand coordination. Several researchers (e.g., Bjorklund & Brown, 1998; Cherney, 2008; Doyle, Voyer, & Cherney, 2012) have suggested that this type of play and ensuing experiences may prepare them for spatial cognition. Spatial skills are important for success in science and mathematics (e.g., Ceci, Williams, & Barnett, 2009; Cherney & Campbell, 2011; Halpern et al., 2007). Because male-dominated jobs are associated with mathematical, mechanical or scientific skills, aggressiveness, and risk taking (Blakemore et al., 2008), early play with masculine toys may inspire boys to pursue these careers. For girls, the differentiated play style may prepare them well for careers that emphasize language-related domains and nurturing skills (see Chapter 11).

Thus, boys' and girls' play groups differ in size, themes in pretend or fantasy play, play styles, activities, competition, aggression and conflict, dominance, and use of language (Maccoby, 1998). These differentiated experiences may be related to gender roles and social, emotional, and cognitive development, and may also develop different career aspirations.

WHAT MAKES A TOY "MASCULINE" OR "FEMININE"?

Play provides opportunities for practicing particular behaviors. This repeated practice develops expertise. Thus, recurring gendered play activities may shape children's expectations and preferences (Leaper, 2000b). On average, masculine- and feminine-stereotyped play activities tend to differentially focus on self-assertive (masculine toys) and affiliative (feminine toys) behavior (Leaper, 2000a).

Early studies have shown that children often own different types of toys. Rheingold and Cook (1975) examined boys' and girls' bedrooms and found that they contained different types of toys. Another way to measure what toys boys and girls have is to identify the toys parents purchase for their children or those that children request for Christmas (Bradbard, 1985; Richardson & Simpson, 1982). Parents' choices are frequently less gender stereotyped because they often choose educational or artistic materials suitable to all genders (Robinson & Morris, 1986). Salespersons, however, tend to steer customers in the direction of gender-appropriate toys (Reynolds, 1994; Ungar, 1982). In addition, toy distributors and online vendors frequently steer consumers to gendered toys (Auster & Mansbach, 2012). Online purchasers will typically find that toys are classified by age and gender. However, this trend may lessen over time. For example, recently, Target, a major U.S. retailer, decided to eliminate gendered toy aisles in their stores (Target Corporation, 2015). Although there have been some slight changes over the years in children's toy requests (Marcon & Freeman, 1996), girls continue to be more likely to ask for dolls and domestic toys, and boys continue to be more likely to ask for toy vehicles, military toys, action figures, and spatial toys. Although both genders play with figurines, it is interesting to note that when comparing how Barbie dolls and G. I. Joe and other action figures are marketed, accessories for Barbie are usually used to act on the doll rather than for the doll to use. In contrast, weapons are often part of the action figure's own body and involve "bad guys fighting good guys" (Klugman, 1999).

Color

Color is an important way that marketing companies signify that their products are intended for boys or girls (Auster & Mansbach, 2012; Orenstein, 2011). Gender schema theory (Martin & Halverson, 1981; see also Chapter 7, this volume) and developmental intergroup theory (Bigler & Liben, 2006) predict that color can signify whether a toy is "for girls" or "for boys." There seems to be less empirical information on gender-stereotyped color preferences than on other gender-stereotyped childhood behaviors (Wong & Hines, 2015), such as toy and activity preferences, but there is some evidence that the development of gender-stereotyped color preferences differs from that of gender-stereotyped toy and activity preferences. For instance, boys and girls show gender-stereotyped toy preferences prior to the emergence of gender-stereotyped color preferences (Jadva, Hines, & Golombok, 2010). In contrast, Alexander's (2003) evolutionary perspective might suggest that very young children evolved specialized visual biases that optimize the development of sex-dimorphic behaviors, which develop even earlier than anticipated. According to such a hypothesis, ancestral hunting for males would suggest that the male visual system (M-cell pathway) may have evolved to be more sensitive to tracking spatial movement of objects, whereas females' ancestral foraging for food may have prepared them to be more sensitive to object features—in particular, color (P-cell pathway; Alexander, 2003). In other words, girls might be more perceptually cued into color, whereas boys might be more attracted to movement.

Gender-related cognitive processes have been implicated in the acquisition of gender-stereotyped color preferences. Specifically, gender-stereotyped behaviors may be acquired through self-socialization after children have developed gender identity (Marcus & Overton, 1978; Ruble et al., 2007), and become self-motivated to adopt gender norms (Kohlberg, 1966; Martin & Halverson, 1981; Martin, Ruble, & Szkrybalo, 2002). Chiu et al. (2006) showed that in line with cognitive developmental and gender schema theories (Martin & Halverson, 1981), the gender difference in preferences for pink/purple and blue in 3- to 12-year-old boys and girls with gender dysphoria were similar to preferences in their cisgender (i.e., nontransgender) boys and girls, respectively. Given that infants and toddlers are often dressed in a gendered color-coded way, and are also exposed to other aspects of their environment that are color-coded, it is possible that this has an influence on color preference for the familiar prior to the emergence of gender identity self-labeling (Chiu et al., 2006).

One of the multiple ways children classify toys to gender is through color. In a study of children 7 months to 5 years, LoBue and DeLoache (2011) showed that by 2 years, girls tend to show a preference for pink over other colors. This preference to the detriment of other colors is even more pronounced by 2.5 years. Boys, in contrast, show a clear avoidance of pink by that age. In a series of studies, Cherney and her colleagues (e.g., Cherney et al., 2006; Cherney & Herr, 2016) examined children's reasoning for classifying toys into "girl toy" and "boy toy" categories. They were interested in preschoolers' understanding and framework of gendered toys, and their features including color. In one of her earlier studies, Cherney and her colleagues (2006) studied 49 preschoolers who classified 28 pictures of masculine, feminine, neutral, and ambiguous toys (toys that may have a masculine function and feminine color such as a pink airplane) and reasoned why the toys were gendered. Gender associations, egocentric thinking, and specific characteristics of toys were the preschoolers' dominant responses. Color was mentioned 11% of the time as a reason for why a toy was gendered. In a subsequent study, 64 preschoolers were asked to classify the toys into "boy toys" and "girl toys" by having children sort pictures of toys into piles. They were asked the reasons for their choices before and after they played with the toys alone in a play laboratory that contained 40 carefully chosen gender-stereotyped, neutral, and ambiguous toys. Overall, children's reasoning fell into the following categories: (a) toy characteristics or schema (32.39%; e.g., the child mentioned a particular aspect of a toy that falls into a gender schema); (b) egocentric thinking (24.04%; e.g., children assigned the gender of the toy because it was a toy they liked—thus, "I'm a girl/boy and I like it, so all girls/boys will like it"); (c) other, or don't know, or just is, or because (22.21%; children often just do not know or cannot verbalize why they assigned a toy to a particular gender); (d), gender role or gender association (17.82%; e.g., a gender participates in an associated job or task); (e) and color (3.54%).

To further analyze the influence of color on preschoolers' toy categorizations, Cherney and Herr (2016) showed 42 preschoolers gendered toy pictures. Half of the toy pictures were shown in their original color (typically blue or pink), and half of the toy pictures were shown in the counterstereotypical color. Thus, each child saw a blue car and the same car in pink. On average, preschoolers in the picture sorting study were more likely to use color (15.18%) as a reason for categorization than in the play lab study described above (3.45%). Manipulating the color was particularly salient for girls, and color was used as a reason for categorization significantly more for masculine toys that looked like feminine toys than the reverse (Cherney & Herr, 2016). Anecdotally, this is what toy manufacturers are exploiting: they are more likely adding a pink version of a masculine toy than a blue version of a feminine toy in order to increase sales (Orenstein, 2011).

The gender color-coding of toys has been thought to magnify gender differences in cognitive and social developmental outcomes (e.g., Orenstein, 2011). As yet, however, there is little empirical evidence that gender color-coding of gender-stereotyped toys alters boys' or girls' interest in them or enlarges the differences between boys' and girls' toy interests. Weisgram, Fulcher, and Dinella (2014) examined children's interest in and judgments of toys by toy type and toy color. Preschoolers were shown eight toys: two masculine toys with masculine colors, two masculine toys with feminine colors, two feminine toys with feminine colors, and two feminine toys with masculine colors. After playing with each toy for 30 seconds, children rated their interest in the toy, their stereotype endorsement, and judgments of the toy. Their findings showed that "pink gave girls permission to interact with a masculine toy" (Weisgram et al., 2014, p. 404), however, boys' choices were not significantly influenced by color. Feminine colors also tended to elicit more stereotypes than masculine colors. Even masculine toys presented in feminine colors were categorized as "only for girls" and for "both boys and girls."

Overall, these studies suggest that color plays a relatively small role in children's classifications of toys, especially when other characteristics or toy attributes are present. The findings also suggest that the pink color changes the way that children think about a toy, with boys avoiding the toy even if it would be considered a masculine toy (e.g., pink block, pink car).

Explicit and Implicit Labels

Besides visual cues, such as physical appearance and color, verbal labels are other important cues for learning social categories at a young age (Bigler & Liben, 2006). As articulated in developmental intergroup theory (Bigler & Liben, 2006), environmental gender cues such as perceptual discriminability, and labeling, for example, may increase the psychological salience of gender and make it more likely that children use gender to categorize and stereotype others. One way children acquire the knowledge about the gender stereotyping of toys is through explicit gendered labels used by children's parents, peers, teachers, and media. Toys that are labeled "appropriate" for one's gender will be incorporated into one's gender schema (Martin & Halverson, 1981), which increases one's interest in those toys (Martin et al., 2002) but leads to avoidance of toys labeled as "appropriate" for the other gender (e.g., Martin et al., 1995). For example, studies have demonstrated that preschool children are more interested in novel items that are labeled as for their own gender than those that are labeled as for the other gender (Bradbard, Martin, Endsley, & Halverson, 1986). Martin and her colleagues (1995) termed that phenomenon the "hot potato effect." In their study, preschool children avoided even attractive toys when they were considered appropriate for the other gender.

A growing body of research in developmental and social psychology has shown that salience of social categories (e.g., verbal labeling) affects perceptions of differences among social categories (Zosuls et al., 2009). Gender is typically one of children's first social categories with which they identify, and they learn the stereotypes that are associated with it (Ruble et al., 2006). A gender label initiates a process of social learning that includes modeling and reinforcement of gender-stereotyped (toy) preferences (Bussey & Bandura, 1999), and gender-appropriate (play) behaviors (Maccoby, 1988; Martin & Halverson, 1981). The developmental pattern for early learning of gender categories and associated attributes (stereotypes) can be characterized by three sequenced phases of (a) learning about gender-related characteristics during toddler and preschool years, (b) consolidating the newly acquired gender knowledge in a rigid dichotomous world until 5 to 7 years, and (c) moving away from the rigidity into a more flexible paradigm (Trautner et al., 2005).

Zosuls and her colleagues (2009) wanted to know at what age children acquire gender category labels and how this knowledge related to their toy preferences and play behaviors. Their longitudinal study showed that infants used gender labels by 18 to 21 months, and by 21 months, most used multiple labels; infants also exhibited some gender-stereotyped play behaviors. Interestingly, gender category knowledge acquired during the second year was related to raises in gender-stereotyped play from 17 to 21 months (Zosuls et al., 2009; see also Chapter 3, this volume).

In two recent studies, Weisgram and her colleagues (2014) examined 3- to 5-year-old children's interest in and judgments of toys that varied in color labels and type. Specifically, in Study 2, the role of explicit gender labels and toy color on children's interest in and judgments of novel toys were examined. Novel toys were labeled as "for boys" or "for girls." Their results showed that the verbal label given to a novel item and its color influenced girls' interests in that item significantly. Explicit labels also influenced children's stereotypes. On average, children categorizing an item labeled as "only for girls" or "only for boys" reflected the experimenter's verbal label of the item (see also Weisgram, 2016). Clearly, verbal labels prime and influence young children's thinking and behaviors about gendered toys.

Feminine Toys and Play

Although there are differences in what toys boys and girls own, only a few studies have specifically examined the general characteristics of gendered toys (Blakemore & Centers, 2005; Cherney & Dempsey, 2010; Cherney & London, 2006; Miller, 1987). In these studies, characteristics of girls' toys were most associated with appearance and attractiveness. For example, accessories such as frilly clothes, perfume, and shoes make dolls "look more attractive." Feminine toys were also generally rated as nurturing and encouraging domestic and household skills (e.g., Blakemore & Centers, 2005), although strongly feminine toys were rated as less likely to encourage cooperation than any other type of toy.

In a recent study, Li and Wong (2016) examined whether first-grade children's play with feminine toys was related to social abilities such as empathy and comforting skills. They observed Chinese boys' and girls' play with gender-stereotyped toys and measured empathy and comforting skills with existing paradigms. Regression analyses showed that feminine toy play predicted comforting skills more strongly than comforting skills predicted feminine toy play. According to the authors, playing with feminine toys (e.g., baby dolls) and generating comforting strategies such as nurturing and "playing nice" with others (Maccoby, 1998) are about generating ideas for prosocial interaction (Li & Wong, 2016). However, it is important to note that the relationship between gender-stereotyped play and social skills was gender specific in the sample of Chinese first-graders. None of the correlations with feminine toy play were significant for boys, probably in part because they played less frequently with feminine toys. Alternatively, perhaps when boys play with feminine toys, they play with a weaker element of nurturance than girls (Li & Wong, 2016). There were no gender differences in empathy.

An important characteristic of any toy is also what type of play it may elicit. Cherney et al. (2003) examined preschoolers' interaction with gendered toys and measured play complexity (the number of multischeme combinations of short play sequences/behaviors combined in a logical order: for example, a child may cook food on the oven, get a fork, feed the baby doll, and lay her to bed). Their results showed that only feminine toys reached the two highest complexity play rankings. In other words, children (boys and girls) who played with feminine toys (e.g., kitchen set, doll, nesting cups, phone) displayed the most complex play behaviors. One implication of this finding was that stereotyped feminine toys should be provided to boys because they bring forth more complex play behaviors when compared with stereotyped masculine or neutral toys. This is important because boys tend to display stronger own-gender-stereotyped preferences (e.g., Carter & Levy, 1988; Cherney & London, 2006) and may avoid playing with feminine toys, thus not manifesting high complex play behavior (Cherney et al., 2003), even though they are just as capable of complex play as girls (e.g., Cherney & Dempsey, 2010). Cherney and Dempsey (2010) observed preschoolers' play with neutral and ambiguous (an ambiguous toy has aspects of both genders—e.g., pink airplane) toys to determine play complexity and play substitution (i.e., play creativity). Their findings showed that girls displayed significantly higher levels of play sequencing than did boys. This was probably due to the observation that girls used the toys in a more scripted way than did boys. In other words, girls used the toys in the ways the toy manufacturers intended the toy to be used. However, when play behavior was measured for play substitutions (i.e., when a toy gets used in unscripted or multiple ways), there were no gender differences. The authors noted that play substitution may present an alternative to measuring gendered play. Thus, on average, feminine toys tend to promote domestic fantasy play, verbal skills, affiliative and nurturing behaviors, comforting skills (Li & Wong, 2016), and play complexity (Cherney et al., 2003).

Masculine Toys and Play

In contrast, characteristics of boys' toys were most associated with aggression, violence (Hellendoorn & Harinck, 1997; Watson & Peng, 1992), competition, dangerousness, manipulation, construction, assertiveness, and active exploration (Bradbard & Parkman, 1984; Cherney & London, 2006; Leaper, 2015; Miller, 1987). For example, boys' toys generally include guns, bombs, swords, and military equipment that could all be used to "kill others." Interestingly, a recent study by Bartneck, Min Ser, Moltchanova, Smithies and Harrington (2016) showed that LEGO products have become more violent over time, supporting the claim that masculine toys may be more associated with aggression.

Additional attributes associated more with masculine than feminine toys are movement (e.g., balls and vehicles; Alexander & Hines, 2002), spatial skill, construction, transportation, and science (e.g., Blakemore, Berenbaum, & Liben, 2008). Masculine toys tend to encourage symbolic fantasy play that is removed from daily life, as well as building and creating something new. Another attribute that has been associated with mostly moderately masculine toys is "feedback." According to Block (1983) and Blakemore and Centers (2005), some masculine and neutral toys provide feedback to the child, that is, the toy responds to a child's manipulation. For example, radio-controlled cars, robots, electric trains, and computer games provide feedback based on the child's input and controls. These types of toys tend to be associated more with boys than girls. Interestingly, Blakemore and Centers found that masculine toys were more likely than feminine toys to be seen as more fun and exciting, more sustaining of attention, riskier, and requiring more adult supervision.

Boys, on average, also spend a lot more time playing with video and computer games than girls. Cherney and London's (2006) study showed that boys played significantly longer than girls across all age groups (5–13 years), and their video games were perceived as becoming more masculine as they grew older. Girls' video game content was perceived as changing from neutral to more masculine. In other words, adults rated the content of the video and computer games more masculine than feminine or neutral. These findings were consistent with those of other studies, which found that video games were, on average, considered masculine, and that boys spent more time engaged with computer and video games (e.g., Cherney, Bersted, & Smetter, 2014; Terlecki & Newcombe, 2005).

As previously mentioned, masculine toys tend to encourage and elicit spatial skills. Several studies suggest that play with masculine toys enhances spatial abilities (e.g., Blakemore & Centers, 2005; Doyle et al., 2012) and may contribute to gender differences in later spatial cognitive and social development outcomes (Block, 1983; Caldera et al., 1989; Sprafkin, Serbin, Denier, & Connor, 1983; see also Chapters 9 and 10, this volume). Spatially oriented video games are generally regarded as masculine in quality (Terlecki & Newcombe, 2005), most video games are targeted at a male audience, and girls find the content unappealing rather than the activity itself (Jansz, 2005). Research has shown that training with video games for even a short duration (1–4 hours) decreases a robust gender difference in mental rotation (e.g., Cherney, 2008; Cherney et al., 2014). Because playing with masculine-stereotyped toys is thought to enhance spatial skills important for success in science and mathematics (e.g., Ceci et al., 2009; Cherney & Campbell, 2011; Halpern et al., 2007), some researchers and parents advocate encouraging girls to play more often with masculine toys in attempts to narrow gender gaps (e.g., Eliot, 2009; Fine, 2010). Although not discussed as extensively, encouraging boys to play with feminine toys could enhance their social and verbal skills, and as seen previously, play complexity (Cherney et al., 2003).

IMPLICATIONS

Research suggests that strongly stereotyped toys may have some undesirable attributes for boys and girls. For example, in a recent study, Coyne, Linder, Rasmussen, Nelson, and Birkbeck (2016) showed that children who engaged more frequently with Disney Princesses were more likely to display female-gender-stereotypical behavior 1 year later, even after controlling for initial levels of gender-stereotypical behavior (Coyne, Linder, Rasmussen, Nelson, & Birkbeck, 2016). This finding was true for both boys and girls. Although female-gender-stereotypical behavior is not undesirable in itself, Coyne et al. noted that strong adherence to female stereotypical behavior may limit children's exploration of various activities or even occupations and can also increase focus on one's appearance. Even when parents discussed media content (active mediation) with their children, the results were the same, showing that princess engagement predicted higher female stereotypical behaviors in boys and girls. However, princess engagement was not associated with body esteem for either boys or girls. Finally, the study also showed that Disney Princess engagement was not associated with higher levels of prosocial behavior for girls, but it was for boys when there was active parental mediation.

Conversely, strongly masculine toys can lead boys to more violence and aggression (Hellendoorn & Harinck, 1997; Watson & Peng, 1992). At the same time, many educational and enriching toys seem to be moderately masculine (e.g., science, construction, spatial toys) and neutral (music, art) and help to develop important cognitive skills, whereas moderately feminine toys are associated with learning other useful skills such as nurturance and domestic skills (Blakemore et al., 2008).

Overall, these studies provide some support for the socialization perspective that feminine toys as well as masculine toys contribute to gendered developmental outcomes (Block, 1983; Caldera et al., 1989; Cherney & London, 2006, Li & Wong, 2016).

METHODOLOGICAL ISSUES

It is difficult to draw conclusions from the studies presented, in part because of different operationalization of gender-typical play, differences in context (e.g., adult present or not, coding of behaviors, assessments used), sample sizes within age groups, age differences, culture, preexisting experiences, types of toys used, methodology and procedures, identification by adults or children of feminine and masculine toys, and types of questions asked to name a few (see Chapter 2). As previously mentioned, depending on the methodology, there are gender differences in the emergence of gender-typed preferences. Some studies have found early gender-typed preferences among girls but not boys (e.g., Katz & Kofkin, 1997), whereas others have found early gender-typed preferences mostly among boys (e.g., Servin et al., 1999). As previously seen, children may categorize by color when the task involves sorting pictures of toys, rather than when the children play with a toy in a naturalistic environment.

Meta-analyses or longitudinal analyses of developmental changes across development from infancy to adulthood of gender differences in play, toy or career interests, or time use are needed in the literature to illustrate patterns of development (Blakemore et al., 2008). It may be that some of these gender differences increase or decrease over time or fluctuate at certain ages. Overall, the absence of meta-analyses might be indicative of the lack of controversy about whether the gender and age differences exist. Researchers disagree about what causes them and how they develop, but the lack of analysis of developmental change may reflect the inherent difficulties involved in comparing gender differences in activities across age (Blakemore et al., 2008). The types of toys and activities children prefer change with age. For example, adolescent girls are not likely playing with dolls any longer, and young girls are not likely going to use makeup. Similarly, adolescent boys are not likely playing with trucks any longer. Developmental change is difficult to measure, especially when the activities of younger and older children differ so drastically.

Not surprisingly, research methodologies also affect the research outcomes significantly (see Chapter 2). As seen previously, whether children are observed in a naturalistic or laboratory environment matters. The types of toys utilized and whether children are familiar with those toys or not alters research findings. The presence or absence of same-gender or opposite-gender peers also changes the results. Research has shown that both boys and girls were less likely to play with gender-stereotyped toys or engage in less stereotyped activities when playing in mixed-gender groups than when playing exclusively with children of their own gender (Fabes, Martin, & Hanish, 2003).

CONCLUSION

During their childhood years, children spend thousands of hours playing with toys, watching television and playing video games, and engaging in play with peers. These gendered activities are important in the development of children's socialization, cognitive skills, and self-concept. They are also important in shaping children's gender stereotypes and possible careers. Research shows that children's toys are gender stereotyped. Girls are more likely to own and play with dolls, domestic items, and toys that focus on nurturance and appearance. Boys are more likely to own and play with vehicles and sports equipment, spatial and temporal toys, building sets, video games, and toys that are violent. These differences are seen no matter how they are measured: in observations of children's play in laboratories, at home, in (pre)schools, in reports by parents and teachers, in the children's preferences when viewing pictures of toys, or in the toys children own. Because these gender differences are consistent, the terms "boy toys" and "girl toys" have entered the vocabulary (Blakemore & Centers, 2005; Cherney et al., 2006). These gendered experiences shape how children think, act, and feel. It behooves researchers, parents, teachers, and others who work with children to further examine how these experiences contribute to long-term gender stereotypes, and how those can be mitigated by encouraging boys to play more frequently with feminine toys and girls to play more frequently with masculine toys. At the same time, it is important to minimize gendered labeling and associating certain colors with either gender.

REFERENCES

Alexander, G. M. (2003). An evolutionary perspective of sex-typed toy preferences: Pink, blue, and the brain. *Archives of Sexual Behavior, 32,* 7–14. http://dx.doi.org/10.1023/A:1021833110722

Alexander, G. M., & Hines, M. (2002). Sex differences in response to children's toys in nonhuman primates (Cercopithecus aethiops sabaeus). *Evolution and Human Behavior, 23,* 467–479. Retrieved from http://biososial.org/wp-content/uploads/2010/03/Alexander-Hines-2002.pdf

Alexander, G. M., Wilcox, T., & Woods, R. (2009). Sex differences in infants' visual interest in toys. *Archives of Sexual Behavior, 38,* 427–433. http://dx.doi.org/10.1007/s10508-008-9430-1

Auster, C. J., & Mansbach, C. S. (2012). The gender marketing of toys: An analysis of color and type of toy on the Disney store website. *Sex Roles, 67,* 375–388. http://dx.doi.org/10.1007/s11199-012-0177-8

Bartneck, C., Min Ser, Q., Moltchanova, E., Smithies, J., & Harrington, E. (2016). Have LEGO products become more violent? *PLoS One, 11*(5), e0155401. http://dx.doi.org/10.1371/journal.pone.0155401

Benenson, J. F. (1993). Greater preference among females than males for dyadic interaction in early childhood. *Child Development, 64*, 544–555. http://dx.doi.org/10.2307/1131268

Bigler, R. S., & Liben, L. S. (2006). A developmental intergroup theory of social stereotypes and prejudice. In R. V. Kail (Ed.), *Advances in child development and behavior* (Vol. 34, pp. 39–89). London, England: Elsevier.

Bjorklund, D. F., & Brown, R. D. (1998). Physical play and cognitive development: Integrating activity, cognition, and education. *Child Development, 69*, 604–606. http://dx.doi.org/10.1111/j.1467-8624.1998.tb06229.x

Blakemore, J. E. O., Berenbaum, S. A., & Liben, L. S. (2008). *Gender development.* New York, NY: Psychology Press.

Blakemore, J. E. O., & Centers, R. E. (2005). Characteristics of boys' and girls' toys. *Sex Roles, 53*, 619–633. http://dx.doi.org/10.1007/s11199-005-7729-0

Block, J. H. (1983). Differential premises arising from differential socialization of the sexes: Some conjectures. *Child Development, 54*, 1335–1354. http://dx.doi.org/10.2307/1129799

Bradbard, M. R. (1985). Sex differences in adults' gifts and children's toy requests at Christmas. *Psychological Reports, 56*, 969–970. http://dx.doi.org/10.2466/pr0.1985.56.3.969

Bradbard, M. R., Martin, C. L., Endsley, R. C., & Halverson, C. F. (1986). Influence of sex stereotypes on children's exploration and memory: A competence versus performance distinction. *Developmental Psychology, 22*, 481–486. http://dx.doi.org/10.1037/0012-1649.22.4.481

Bradbard, M. R., & Parkman, S. A. (1984). Gender differences in preschool children's toys requests. *The Journal of Genetic Psychology, 145*, 283–284. http://dx.doi.org/10.1080/00221325.1984.10532277

Bussey, K., & Bandura, A. (1992). Self-regulatory mechanisms governing gender development. *Child Development, 63*, 1236–1250. http://dx.doi.org/10.2307/1131530

Bussey, K., & Bandura, A. (1999). Social cognitive theory of gender development and differentiation. *Psychological Review, 106*, 676–713. http://dx.doi.org/10.1037/0033-295X.106.4.676

Caldera, Y. M., Culp, A. M., O'Brien, M., Truglio, R., Alvarez, M., & Huston, A. C. (1999). Children's play preferences, construction play with blocks, and visual–spatial skills: Are they related? *International Journal of Behavioral Development, 23*, 855–872. http://dx.doi.org/10.1080/016502599383577

Caldera, Y. M., Huston, A. C., & O'Brien, M. (1989). Social interactions and play patterns of parents and toddlers with feminine, masculine, and neutral toys. *Child Development, 60*, 70–76. http://dx.doi.org/10.2307/1131072

Campbell, A., Shirley, L., & Caygill, L. (2002). Sex-typed preferences in three domains: Do two-year-olds need cognitive variables? *British Journal of Psychology*, *93*, 203–217. http://dx.doi.org/10.1348/000712602162544

Carter, D. B., & Levy, G. D. (1988). Cognitive aspects of early sex-role development: The influence of gender schemas on preschoolers' memories and preferences for sex-typed toys and activities. *Child Development*, *59*, 782–792. http://dx.doi.org/10.2307/1130576

Ceci, S. J., Williams, W. M., & Barnett, S. M. (2009). Women's underrepresentation in science: Sociocultural and biological considerations. *Psychological Bulletin*, *135*, 218–261. http://dx.doi.org/10.1037/a0014412

Cherney, I. D. (2008). Mom, let me play more computer games: They improve my mental rotation skills. *Sex Roles*, *59*, 776–786. http://dx.doi.org/10.1007/s11199-008-9498-z

Cherney, I. D., Bersted, K., & Smetter, J. (2014). Training spatial skills in men and women. *Perceptual and Motor Skills*, *119*, 82–99. http://dx.doi.org/10.2466/23.25.PMS.119c12z0

Cherney, I. D., & Campbell, K. (2011). A league of their own: Do single-sex schools increase girls' participation in the physical sciences? *Sex Roles*, *65*, 712–724. http://dx.doi.org/10.1007/s11199-011-0013-6

Cherney, I. D., & Dempsey, J. (2010). Young children's classification, stereotyping and play behavior for gender neutral and ambiguous toys. *Educational Psychology*, *30*, 651–669. http://dx.doi.org/10.1080/01443410.2010.498416

Cherney, I. D., Harper, H. J., & Winter, J. A. (2006). *Nouveaux jouets: Ce que les enfants identifient comme "jouets de garçons" et "jouets de filles"* [New toys for tots: What preschoolers identify as "boy toys" and "girl toys"]. *Enfance*, *3*, 266–282. http://dx.doi.org/10.3917/enf.583.0266

Cherney, I. D., & Herr, D. (2016, May). *Boys don't play with pink: How gender stereotyping affects preschoolers' reasoning and play*. Poster presented at the 28th Annual Association of Psychological Science conference in Chicago, IL.

Cherney, I. D., Kelly-Vance, L., Glover, K. G., Ruane, A., & Ryalls, B. O. (2003). The effects of stereotyped toys and gender on play assessment in children aged 18–47 months. *Educational Psychology*, *23*, 95–106. http://dx.doi.org/10.1080/01443410303222

Cherney, I. D., & London, K. (2006). Gender-linked differences in the toys, television shows, computer games, and outdoor activities of 5- to 13-year-old children. *Sex Roles*, *54*, 717–726. http://dx.doi.org/10.1007/s11199-006-9037-8

Chiu, S. W., Gervan, S., Fairbrother, C., Johnson, L. J., Owen-Anderson, A. F. H., Bradley, S. J., & Zucker, K. J. (2006). Sex-dimorphic color preference in children with gender identity disorder: A comparison to clinical and community controls. *Sex Roles*, *55*, 385–395. http://dx.doi.org/10.1007/s11199-006-9089-9

Connellan, J., Baron-Cohen, S., Wheelwright, S., Batki, A., & Ahluwalia, J. (2000). Sex differences in human neonatal social perception. *Infant Behavior and Devel-*

opment, 23, 113–118. Retrieved from http://www.sciencedirect.com/science/article/pii/S0163638300000321

Coyne, S. M., Linder, J. R., Rasmussen, E. E., Nelson, D. A., & Birkbeck, V. (2016). Pretty as a princess: Longitudinal effects of engagement with Disney Princesses on gender stereotypes, body esteem, and prosocial behavior in children. *Child Development, 87*, 1909–1925. http://dx.doi.org/10.1111/cdev.12569

Doyle, R., Voyer, D., & Cherney, I. D. (2012). The relation between childhood spatial activities and spatial abilities in adulthood. *Journal of Applied Developmental Psychology, 33*, 112–120. http://dx.doi.org/10.1016/j.appdev.2012.01.002

Eliot, L. (2009). *Pink brain, blue brain: How small differences grow into troublesome gaps—and what we can do about it.* Oxford, England: Oneworld.

Fabes, R. A., Martin, C. L., & Hanish, L. D. (2003). Young children's play qualities in same-, other-, and mixed-sex peer groups. *Child Development, 74*, 921–932. http://dx.doi.org/10.1111/1467-8624.00576

Fine, C. (2010). *Delusions of gender.* New York, NY: W. W. Norton.

Gredlein, J. M., & Bjorklund, D. F. (2005). Sex differences in young children's use of tools in a problem-solving task: The role of object-oriented play. *Human Nature, 16*, 211–232. http://dx.doi.org/10.1007/s12110-005-1004-5

Halpern, D. F., Benbow, C. P., Geary, D. C., Gur, R. C., Hyde, J. S., & Gernsbacher, M. A. (2007). The science of sex differences in science and mathematics. *Psychological Science in the Public Interest, 8*, 1–51. http://dx.doi.org/10.1111/j.1529-1006.2007.00032.x

Hellendoorn, J., & Harinck, F. J. H. (1997). War toy play and aggression in Dutch kindergarten children. *Social Development, 6*, 340–354. http://dx.doi.org/10.1111/j.1467-9507.1997.tb00110.x

Hirsh-Pasek, K., Golinkoff, R. M., Berk, L. E., & Singer, D. G. (2008). *A mandate for playful learning in preschool: Presenting the evidence.* New York, NY: Oxford University Press.

Jadva, V., Hines, M., & Golombok, S. (2010). Infants' preferences for toys, colors, and shapes: Sex differences and similarities. *Archives of Sexual Behavior, 39*, 1261–1273. http://dx.doi.org/10.1007/s10508-010-9618-z

Jansz, J. (2005). The emotional appeal of violent video games for adolescent males. *Communication Theory, 15*, 219–241. http://dx.doi.org/10.1111/j.1468-2885.2005.tb00334.x

Katz, P. A., & Kofkin, J. A. (1997). Race, gender, and young children. In S. S. Luthar, J. A. Burack, D. Cicchetti, & J. R. Weisz (Eds.), *Developmental psychopathology: Perspectives on adjustment, risk, and disorder* (pp. 51–74). Cambridge, England: Cambridge University Press.

Klugman, K. (1999). A bad hair day for G. I. Joe. In B. L. Clark & M. R. Higonnet (Eds.), *Girls, boys, books, toys* (pp. 169–182). Baltimore, MD: The Johns Hopkins University Press.

Kohlberg, L. A. (1966). A cognitive–developmental analysis of children's sex role concepts and attitudes. In E. E. Maccoby (Ed.), *The development of sex differences* (pp. 82–173). Stanford, CA: Stanford University Press.

Leaper, C. (2000a). Gender, affiliation, assertion, and the interactive context of parent–child play. *Developmental Psychology, 36,* 381–393. http://dx.doi.org/10.1037/0012-1649.36.3.381

Leaper, C. (2000b). The social construction and socialization of gender. In P. H. Miller & E. K. Scholnick (Eds.), *Toward a feminist developmental psychology* (pp. 127–152). New York, NY: Routledge.

Leaper, C. (2015). Gender and social-cognitive development. In L. S. Liben & U. Muller (Eds.), *Handbook of child psychology and developmental science: Vol. 2. Cognitive processes* (7th ed., pp. 806–853). New York, NY: Wiley. http://dx.doi.org/10.1002/9781118963418.childpsy219

Li, R. Y. H., & Wong, W. I. (2016). Gender-typed play and social abilities in boys and girls: Are they related? *Sex Roles, 74,* 399–410. http://dx.doi.org/10.1007/s11199-016-0580-7

Lindsey, E. W., & Colwell, M. J. (2013). Pretend and physical play: Links to preschoolers' affective social competence. *Merrill–Palmer Quarterly, 59,* 330–360. http://dx.doi.org/10.1353/mpq.2013.0015

LoBue, V., & DeLoache, J. S. (2011). Pretty in pink: The early development of gender-stereotyped colour preferences. *British Journal of Developmental Psychology, 29,* 656–667. http://dx.doi.org/10.1111/j.2044-835X.2011.02027.x

Maccoby, E. E. (1988). Gender as a social category. *Developmental Psychology, 24,* 755–765. http://dx.doi.org/10.1037/0012-1649.24.6.755

Maccoby, E. E. (1998). *The two sexes: Growing up apart, coming together.* Cambridge, MA: Harvard University Press.

Marcon, R. A., & Freeman, G. (1996). Linking gender-related toy preferences to social structure: Changes in children's letters to Santa since 1978. *Journal of Psychological Practice, 2,* 1–10.

Marcus, D. E., & Overton, W. F. (1978). The development of cognitive gender constancy and sex role preferences. *Child Development, 49,* 434–444. http://dx.doi.org/10.2307/1128708

Markovits, H., Benenson, J., & Dolenszky, E. (2001). Evidence that children and adolescents have internal models of peer interactions that are gender differentiated. *Child Development, 72,* 879–886. http://dx.doi.org/10.1111/1467-8624.00321

Martin, C. L., Eisenbud, L., & Rose, H. (1995). Children's gender-based reasoning about toys. *Child Development, 66,* 1453–1471. http://dx.doi.org/10.2307/1131657

Martin, C. L., Fabes, R. A., Hanish, L., Leonard, S., & Dinella, L. M. (2011). Experienced and expected similarity to same-gender peers: Moving toward a comprehensive model of gender segregation. *Sex Roles, 65,* 421–434. http://dx.doi.org/10.1007/s11199-011-0029-y

Martin, C. L., & Halverson, C. F. (1981). A schematic processing model of sex typing and stereotyping in children. *Child Development, 52*, 1119–1134. http://dx.doi.org/10.2307/1129498

Martin, C. L., Ruble, D. N., & Szkrybalo, J. (2002). Cognitive theories of early gender development. *Psychological Bulletin, 128*, 903–933. http://dx.doi.org/10.1037/0033-2909.128.6.903

Martin, C. L., Wood, C. H., & Little, J. K. (1990). The development of gender stereotype components. *Child Development, 61*, 1891–1904. http://dx.doi.org/10.2307/1130845

Miller, C. L. (1987). Qualitative differences among gender-stereotyped toys: Implications for cognitive and social development in girls and boys. *Sex Roles, 16*, 473–487. http://dx.doi.org/10.1007/BF00292482

Nelson, A. (2005). Children's toy collections in Sweden—A less gender-typed country? *Sex Roles, 52*, 93–102. http://dx.doi.org/10.1007/s11199-005-1196-5

Orenstein, P. (2011). *Cinderella ate my daughter: Dispatches from the front lines of the new girlie-girl culture.* New York, NY: HarperCollins.

Pellegrini, A. D., & Bjorklund, D. F. (2004). The ontogeny and phylogeny of children's object and fantasy play. *Human Nature, 15*, 23–43. http://dx.doi.org/10.1007/s12110-004-1002-z

Pellegrini, A. D., & Smith, P. K. (1998). Physical activity play: The nature and function of a neglected aspect of playing. *Child Development, 69*, 577–598. http://dx.doi.org/10.1111/j.1467-8624.1998.tb06226.x

Pitcher, E. G., & Schultz, L. H. (1983). *Boys and girls at play: The development of sex roles.* New York, NY: Praeger [Harvester Press].

Reynolds, K. (1994). Toys for boys and girls. *Science Scope, 17*, 64. Retrieved from http://www.jstor.org/stable/43176921

Rheingold, H. L., & Cook, K. V. (1975). The contents of boys' and girls' rooms as an index of parents' behavior. *Child Development, 46*, 459–463. http://dx.doi.org/10.2307/1128142

Richardson, J. G., & Simpson, C. H. (1982). Children, gender, and social structure: An analysis of the contents of letters to Santa Claus. *Child Development, 53*, 429–436. http://dx.doi.org/10.2307/1128986

Robinson, C. C., & Morris, J. T. (1986). The gender-stereotyped nature of Christmas toys received by 36-, 48-, and 60-month-old children: A comparison between nonrequested vs. requested toys. *Sex Roles, 15*, 21–32. http://dx.doi.org/10.1007/BF00287529

Ruble, D. N., & Martin, C. L. (1998). Gender development. In N. Eisenberg (Ed.), *Handbook of child psychology: Vol. 3. Social, emotional, and personality development* (5th ed., pp. 933–1016). New York, NY: John Wiley & Sons.

Ruble, D. N., Martin, C. L., & Berenbaum, S. A. (2006). Gender development. In N. Eisenberg (Ed.), *Handbook of child psychology: Vol. 3. Social, emotional, and personality development* (6th ed., pp. 858–932). Hoboken, NJ: John Wiley & Sons.

Ruble, D. N., Taylor, L. J., Cyphers, L., Greulich, F. K., Lurye, L. E., & Shrout, P. E. (2007). The role of gender constancy in early gender development. *Child Development, 78,* 1121–1136. http://dx.doi.org/10.1111/j.1467-8624.2007.01056.x

Serbin, L. A., Poulin-Dubois, D., Colburne, K. A., Sen, M. G., & Eichstedt, J. A. (2001). Gender stereotyping in infancy: Visual preferences for and knowledge of gender-stereotyped toys in the second year. *International Journal of Behavioral Development, 25,* 7–15. http://dx.doi.org/10.1080/01650250042000078

Servin, A., Bohlin, G., & Berlin, L. (1999). Sex differences in 1-, 3-, and 5-year-olds' toy-choice in a structured play-session. *Scandinavian Journal of Psychology, 40,* 43–48. http://dx.doi.org/10.1111/1467-9450.00096

Sluss, D. J. (2002). Block play complexity in same-sex dyads of preschool children. In J. L. Roopnarine (Ed.), *Conceptual, social-cognitive, and contextual issues in the fields of play* (pp. 77–91). Westport, CT: Ablex Publishing.

Sprafkin, C., Serbin, L. A., Denier, C., & Connor, J. M. (1983). Sex-differentiated play: Cognitive consequences and early interventions. In M. B. Liss (Ed.), *Social and cognitive skills: Sex roles and child's play* (pp. 167–192). New York, NY: Academic Press.

Target Corporation. (2015, August 7). What's in store: Moving away from gender-based signs. *Target: A bullseye view.* Retrieved from https://corporate.target.com/article/2015/08/gender-based-signs-corporate

Terlecki, M. S., & Newcombe, N. S. (2005). How important is the digital divide? The relation of computer and videogame usage to gender differences in mental rotation ability. *Sex Roles, 53,* 433–441. http://dx.doi.org/10.1007/s11199-005-6765-0

Thompson, S. K. (1975). Gender labels and early sex role development. *Child Development, 46,* 339–347. http://dx.doi.org/10.2307/1128126

Trautner, H. M., Ruble, D. N., Cyphers, L., Kirsten, B., Behrendt, R., & Hartmann, P. (2005). Rigidity and flexibility of gender stereotypes in childhood: Developmental or differential? *Infant and Child Development, 14,* 365–381. http://dx.doi.org/10.1002/icd.399

Trawick-Smith, J., Wolff, J., Koschel, M., & Vallarelli, J. (2015). Effects of toys on the play quality of preschool children: Influence of gender, ethnicity, and socioeconomic status. *Early Childhood Education Journal, 43,* 249–256. http://dx.doi.org/10.1007/s10643-014-0644-7

Ungar, S. B. (1982). The sex-typing of adult and child behavior in toy sales. *Sex Roles, 8,* 251–260. http://dx.doi.org/10.1007/BF00287309

Watson, M. W., & Peng, Y. (1992). The relation between toy gun play and children's aggressive behavior. *Early Education and Development, 3,* 370–389. http://dx.doi.org/10.1207/s15566935eed0304_7

Weisgram, E. S. (2016). The cognitive construction of gender stereotypes: Evidence for the dual pathways model of gender differentiation. *Sex Roles, 75*, 301–313. http://dx.doi.org/10.1007/s11199-016-0624-z

Weisgram, E. S., Fulcher, M., & Dinella, L. M. (2014). Pink gives girls permission: Exploring the roles of explicit gender labels and gender-typed colors on preschool children's toy preferences. *Journal of Applied Developmental Psychology, 35*, 401–409. http://dx.doi.org/10.1016/j.appdev.2014.06.004

Wong, W. I., & Hines, M. (2015). Effects of gender color-coding on toddlers' gender-typical toy play. *Archives of Sexual Behavior, 44*, 1233–1242. http://dx.doi.org/10.1007/s10508-014-0400-5

Zosuls, K. M., Ruble, D. N., Tamis-Lemonda, C. S., Shrout, P. E., Bornstein, M. H., & Greulich, F. K. (2009). The acquisition of gender labels in infancy: Implications for gender-typed play. *Developmental Psychology, 45*, 688–701. http://dx.doi.org/10.1037/a0014053

II

CAUSES OF CHILDREN'S GENDER-TYPED TOY PLAY

5

SEX HORMONES AND CHILDREN'S GENDER-TYPED TOY PLAY

MELISSA HINES AND JACQUELINE DAVIS

Boys and girls tend to play with different toys, and the evidence that social factors influence children's gender-typed toy choices is abundant. For example, children are rewarded for engagement with gender-typed toys (Etaugh & Liss, 1992; Idle, Wood, & Desmarais, 1993; Jacklin, DiPietro, & Maccoby, 1984; Lytton & Romney, 1991), and children's gender-typed toy preferences are influenced by the preferences and behavior of parents and peers (Goble, Martin, Hanish, & Fabes, 2012; Peretti & Sydney, 1986; Schau, Kahn, Diepold, & Cherry, 1980; Serbin, Connor, Burchardt, & Citron, 1979). It might seem surprising, therefore, that factors that come into play before birth influence these toy choices, too. This chapter provides a critical review of the research attempting to evaluate the hypothesis that hormonal factors present before and shortly after birth influence children's subsequent gender-typed toy preferences. First, we provide an overview of general principles of sex determination and sexual differentiation in nonhuman mammals, with

http://dx.doi.org/10.1037/0000077-006
Gender Typing of Children's Toys: How Early Play Experiences Impact Development, E. S. Weisgram and L. M. Dinella (Editors)

particular attention to the role of sex chromosomes and sex hormones. We further explore how these general principles lead to specific hypotheses linking the sex hormone testosterone with the development of gender-typed toy preferences in humans. Second, we describe the nature and magnitude of gender-typed differences in children's toy preferences. Third, we provide a critical review of studies that have investigated the hypothesis that early testosterone exposure contributes to children's gender-typed toy preferences. In the fourth and final section, we discuss possible directions for future research.

PRINCIPLES OF MAMMALIAN SEX DETERMINATION AND SEXUAL DIFFERENTIATION

The processes involved in sex determination and sexual differentiation of the body, of the brain, and of behavior have been studied extensively in nonhuman mammals. Results of the thousands of experiments that have been conducted suggest some general principles. The first is that genetic information on the sex chromosomes plays a crucial role in sex determination, determining whether the gonads, which are originally identical in males and females, develop as testes or ovaries (Johnson, 2013). If the sex-determining region Y gene, *SrY*, is present, as it normally is on the Y chromosome, the gonads develop as testes. In the presence of two X chromosomes and no *SrY*, the gonads develop as ovaries. The chromosomes are thus responsible for the development of the gonads in a way that differs for male and female animals. As will be explained below, these early processes related to sex determination may contribute to children's later gender-typed toy preferences.

Apart from directing gonadal development, genetic information on the sex chromosomes might also have direct influences on the mammalian brain and on behavior, as suggested by research in rodents (Arnold, 2009). In humans, no such direct influences have been described for behavior, but there is evidence supporting indirect influences on behavior through sex hormones. Genetic information on the sex chromosomes determines the direction of gonadal development, which in turn influences the sex hormone environment in which the individual develops (Hines, 2015). The testes begin to produce testosterone and other androgens at about week 8 of gestation, whereas the ovaries do not (Wilson, George, & Griffin, 1981). In adulthood, the ovaries produce estrogens, but before birth the ovaries do not appear to produce substantial amounts of any sex hormone. As a consequence of this difference in sex hormone production, testosterone concentrations are higher in male than in female fetuses, and this sex difference in testosterone may influence later gender-typed toy preferences.

The difference in testosterone between male and female fetuses appears to be most marked from about week 8 to week 16 or 24 of gestation (Smail, Reyes, Winter, & Faiman, 1981). However, testosterone is also somewhat higher in males than in females later in gestation, and a small sex difference in testosterone remains present at the time of birth. There is also a period shortly after birth, from about the first month to about the third to sixth month postnatal, when testosterone is again higher in boys than in girls (Forest, Cathiard, & Bertrand, 1973; Kuiri-Hänninen et al., 2011). Both of these periods of testosterone elevation, prenatal and shortly after birth, are times when testosterone influences human development.

During prenatal development, testosterone and other androgens cause the external genitalia, which, like the gonads, are initially identical in males and females, to develop in the male pattern (e.g., scrotum and testes). If concentrations of testosterone and other androgens are low, these tissues develop in the female pattern (e.g., clitoris and labia; Wilson et al., 1981). These outcomes occur because testosterone and other androgens interact with androgen receptors in the genital tissues to promote male-typical development. Androgen receptors are not present in every cell of the human body, but they are present in cells in some regions of the mammalian, including the human, brain. The hypothesis that testosterone acts through neural receptors to promote male-typical development of the human brain and human behavior has been suggested based on evidence that this is what occurs in other mammals.

The brain regions and behaviors that are influenced by early testosterone exposure in nonhuman mammals are those that show average differences between the sexes (Hines, 2004). In humans, there is evidence that some subcortical brain regions differ on average in volume for males and females, and these sex differences resemble differences seen in the rodent brain (Hines, 2004). In addition, meta-analytic findings suggest that there may be sex differences in volume and tissue density in some cortical regions that include the amygdala, hippocampus, and insula, although this study did not report on specific cortical regions within these larger areas (Ruigrok et al., 2014). Cortical complexity also has been reported to differ in men and women (Luders et al., 2004). However, there is almost no evidence regarding possible influences of early testosterone exposure on these sex differences in the human brain, and the few existing studies are underpowered and/or do not fit with hypotheses based on findings in other species. They also have not yet been replicated.

Behaviors affected by early testosterone exposure in nonhuman mammals include reproductive behaviors (e.g., male animals mounting female animals), as well as other behaviors that differ on average for the sexes (e.g., physical aggression toward unfamiliar animals, which is more typical of male animals than female animals; parenting behaviors, which are more typical of female animals than male animals; and juvenile rough-and-tumble play behavior, which is more typical of male animals than of female animals). These findings raise the possibility that human behaviors that show sex differences would be influenced by early testosterone exposure, and there is a substantial body of evidence investigating this hypothesis. Here, we review the evidence for influences of early testosterone exposure on children's toy preferences, and other aspects of children's play.

SEX DIFFERENCES IN CHILDREN'S PLAY

Boys and girls differ on average in their frequency of play with certain toys. For example, boys tend to play with toy vehicles more than girls do, and girls tend to play with dolls more than boys do (see Chapter 4 for a review). In addition to these differences between the sexes, there are gender-related differences in toy preferences within each sex; for example, boys prefer toy vehicles to dolls, and girls prefer dolls to toy vehicles. Results of a meta-analysis of studies from the middle of the 1980s to 2014 suggest that these differences are large ($d = 1.21$ to $d = 3.48$; Davis & Hines, 2017). Height provides a familiar sex difference to which these behavioral differences can be compared. The size of the sex difference in height in the United States and in the United Kingdom is $d = 2.0$ (International Committee on Radiological Protection, 1975; Tanner, Whitehouse, & Takaishi, 1966).

The sex differences in children's toy preferences are larger than sex differences in other areas of child behavior that have been subjected to meta-analysis, such as physical aggression ($d = 0.50$, higher in boys than in girls; Hyde, 1984), temperament, in particular, effortful control ($d = 1.01$, higher in girls than in boys; Else-Quest, Hyde, Goldsmith, & Van Hulle, 2006), and verbal abilities ($d \leq 0.33$, higher in girls than in boys; Hyde & Linn, 1988). Sex differences in children's toy preferences also are larger than sex differences in areas of adult behavior that have been subjected to meta-analyses, such as mental rotation ability ($d = .66$; Voyer, Voyer, & Bryden, 1995) with males scoring higher than females, and personality characteristics, where the largest sex difference is seen on some measures of empathy ($d = .95$; Costa & McCrae, 1992; Feingold, 1994) with females scoring higher than males. Although the sex difference in erotic interest in males (androphilia) and the sex difference in identification with the male gender have been reported to be larger

($d > -6.0$ and $d > 11.0$, respectively; Hines, 2015) than the gender-related differences in children's toy preferences, no meta-analyses of sex differences in sexual orientation or gender identity are available, to our knowledge.

The magnitude of gender-related differences in children's toy preferences can be investigated by conducting (a) between-sex comparisons and (b) within-sex comparisons (Davis & Hines, 2017). Between-sex comparisons suggest effect sizes of $d = 1.83$ for boys' greater preference than girls for boy-typed toys (masculine toys), and $d = 1.60$ for girls' greater preference than boys for girl-typed toys (feminine toys; Davis & Hines, 2017). Within sex comparisons suggest effect sizes of $d = 3.48$ for boys' preference for masculine toys over feminine toys and $d = 1.21$ for girls' preference for feminine toys over masculine toys. Meta-analytic results for dolls and vehicles only, rather than broader groups of masculine and feminine toys, produce even larger effect sizes ($d = 2.14$ to $d = 4.12$; Davis & Hines, 2017). The comparisons that have been used most frequently in studies of hormonal influences on toy preferences are those comparing girls to boys in regard to preferences for dolls and vehicles, or, more commonly, to larger groups of masculine toys and feminine toys. The effect sizes that most researchers have been studying, therefore, are large, in the range of about $d = 1.60$ to 1.83.

In addition to differing in their toy preferences, girls and boys differ in some other aspects of their play behavior, including interest in rough-and-tumble play, a style of play that involves body contact and playful aggression, active play, and playmate preferences. On average, boys engage in more rough-and-tumble play, are more active, and tend to play with boys more than do girls, although these aspects of play appear to show smaller effect sizes for sex differences than do toy preferences (DiPietro, 1981; Eaton & Enns, 1986; Hines, 2004; Maccoby & Jacklin, 1987). However, composite measures that assess gender-typed toy, activity, and playmate preferences together can show sex differences that are as large or larger than those in toy preferences. One such measure that has been used in many studies of children's gender-related behavior is the Pre-School Activities Inventory (PSAI; Golombok & Rust, 1993). This measure has been standardized for use in children ages 2 to 7 years. Parents or caretakers are asked to estimate how often the child participates in masculine activities (e.g., play with a tool set or rough-and-tumble play), and feminine activities (e.g., play with jewelry or play with girls; Golombok & Rust, 1993). The scoring procedure is such that higher scores represent more masculine and less feminine behavior. In a study of a population sample of children, the PSAI was found to show a large sex difference ($d \geq 2.4$; Golombok et al., 2008). The PSAI is of particular relevance to this chapter because it has been used in many studies of early testosterone exposure and children's gender-typed behavior.

STUDIES OF GENETIC OR EARLY HORMONAL INFLUENCES ON CHILDREN'S PLAY BEHAVIOR

The effects of testosterone exposure on sexual differentiation of behavior have been documented in a wide range of mammals, including numerous species of rodents, as well as nonhuman primates (Arnold, 2009; Hines, 2004; McCarthy, De Vries, & Forger, 2009). For instance, researchers have administered testosterone or placebo to pregnant rhesus monkeys, and have found that the female offspring of the testosterone-treated pregnancies show more masculine sexual behavior and more juvenile rough-and-tumble play behavior than do the female offspring of the placebo-treated pregnancies. The general principles that have emerged from this large body of research are that administering testosterone to female animals during early development promotes masculine behavioral outcomes and reduces feminine behavioral outcomes, whereas removing testosterone from developing male animals has the opposite effects, reducing masculine outcomes and increasing feminine outcomes. Studies using different doses of hormone indicate that the effects are graded in a linear fashion. For example, administering large doses of hormones to developing female animals produces larger effects than administering small doses, and administering medium-sized doses produces effects in between those of the large and small doses.

The studies showing the effects of early testosterone exposure on later behavior in nonhuman mammals used rigorous experimental procedures. For instance, animals were assigned at random to receive testosterone or placebo treatments. Similar rigorous procedures would not be ethical in humans. Instead, researchers have looked at individuals who developed in atypical hormone environments, for example, because of genetic conditions or because their mothers were prescribed hormones during pregnancy. Researchers also have attempted to measure testosterone exposure in typically developing children during early life and have related these measures to later behavior. We critically evaluate this research in the following sections.

Genetic Conditions Causing Atypical Hormone Exposure Prenatally

The genetic condition that has been studied most extensively in regard to possible influences of testosterone on human development is classical congenital adrenal hyperplasia (CAH). Classical CAH is an autosomal, recessive condition that occurs in about one in 10,000 to one in 15,000 births in Western Europe and North America (Merke & Bornstein, 2005). The condition involves deficiency in an enzyme, usually 21-OH, and results in impaired ability to produce cortisol. As a consequence, hormones that normally would be used to produce cortisol are shunted into a pathway that leads to the production of androgens, including testosterone. Female fetuses with classical CAH are exposed to markedly elevated concentrations of testosterone and other androgens, with androgen concentrations at midgestation similar to those of male fetuses. Boys with classical CAH appear to have androgen concentrations during gestation that are similar to those of typically developing boys (Pang et al., 1980; Wudy, Dörr, Solleder, Djalali, & Homoki, 1999). Research in this area has tended to focus on girls because, unlike boys, their prenatal androgen exposure is dramatically altered by CAH.

Girls with classical CAH are born with ambiguous, partially masculinized, external genitalia (e.g., fused labia, enlarged clitoris). Typically, this genital ambiguity leads to rapid diagnosis and subsequent treatment with glucocorticoid hormones to reduce the hormone irregularity. Girls with classical CAH are typically assigned and reared as girls, and may have surgery to feminize their external genitalia. However, their exposure to high levels of testosterone and other androgens before birth might be hypothesized to masculinize their behavior (Hines, 2015).

Initial studies of girls with CAH used interviews, primarily with the girls' mothers, to assess gender-typed behavior. These studies reported that girls with CAH liked masculine toys, and other boy-typical play activities, more than did other girls (Ehrhardt & Baker, 1974; Money & Ehrhardt, 1973). Other researchers suggested, however, that mothers of girls with CAH might perceive their daughters as more behaviorally masculine, because the mothers knew that the girls had been born with partially masculinized genitalia, and that they were exposed to high concentrations of testosterone and other androgens (male hormones) prenatally (Fausto-Sterling, 1992; Quadagno, Briscoe, & Quadagno, 1977). Similarly, it was suggested that the girls themselves might misperceive their own behavior as masculine. It was, therefore, important to observe the behavior of girls with CAH directly, instead of relying only on data from interviews.

An initial study observed girls and boys with and without CAH in a playroom with a range of masculine toys, feminine toys, and gender-neutral toys (Berenbaum & Hines, 1992). Controls in this study, as in many studies of children with CAH, were unaffected relatives (sisters or first cousins) of children with CAH. Relatives are used as controls, because they provide some control for family background and genetic factors other than those causing CAH. Results showed the expected gender-related differences in children's toy preferences. Unaffected boys played with the masculine toys more than did unaffected girls, and they played with the feminine toys less than did unaffected girls. In addition, girls with CAH played more with the masculine toys and less with the feminine toys than did the unaffected girls. Also as expected, there were no group differences in play with the neutral toys, and boys with and without CAH did not differ from one another in time spent playing with masculine toys, feminine toys, or neutral toys. Similar findings were reported for a subgroup of this sample at an older age by one of the authors of the original study (Berenbaum & Snyder, 1995). The results for girls with and without CAH also have been replicated by an independent research team (Servin, Nordenström, Larsson, & Bohlin, 2003), although this replication did not include boys. Finally, the results have been replicated in a new sample of children with and without CAH by one of the authors of the original study (Pasterski et al., 2005).

Other studies of gender-typed play behavior in children with and without CAH have used questionnaires and interviews to assess toy interests, as well as other aspects of gender-typed play. These studies have come from researchers in New York, Baltimore, Los Angeles, and Chicago in the United States, from researchers in London and Manchester in the United Kingdom, and from researchers in Canada, Sweden, the Netherlands, Germany, and Japan (Berenbaum & Hines, 1992; Dittmann et al., 1990; Ehrhardt & Baker, 1974; Frisén et al., 2009; Hall et al., 2004; Hines, Brook, & Conway, 2004; Hines & Kaufman, 1994; Iijima, Arisaka, Minamoto, & Arai, 2001; Meyer-Bahlburg, 1999; Meyer-Bahlburg, Dolezal, Baker, Ehrhardt, & New, 2006; Meyer-Bahlburg et al., 2004; Nordenström, Servin, Bohlin, Larsson, & Wedell, 2002; Pasterski et al., 2005, 2011, 2015; Slijper, 1984; Zucker et al., 1996). The studies from all of these different countries have produced results that are similar to those of the studies that observed toy choices in a playroom. Girls with CAH consistently show increased masculine play and decreased feminine play compared with unaffected female relative controls or with controls matched for background factors, such as age, sex, and socioeconomic background. Boys with CAH have not always been included in these studies, but when they have been, their play behavior has been found to be similar to that of other boys.

The magnitude of the difference in gender-typed play behavior between girls with and without CAH also appears to relate to the severity of the CAH condition. Girls with the most severe forms of CAH, as indicated by genotype, by symptom severity, or by degree of genital masculinization at birth, show the most dramatic masculinization of behavior (Dittmann et al., 1990; Frisén et al., 2009; Hall et al., 2004).

Other disorders that cause atypical hormone environments early in life are rarer than classical CAH and have not been studied as extensively. However, there is some relevant information about the behavior of XY individuals with complete androgen insensitivity syndrome (CAIS). CAIS is an X-linked, recessive condition characterized by an impairment in the functioning of androgen receptors (Grumbach, Hughes, & Conte, 2003). It is rare, with its exact incidence unknown. Because XY individuals with CAIS lack functional androgen receptors, they are born with feminine-appearing external genitalia. They have functioning testes, but these are undescended at birth, and the cells of their body cannot respond to the androgenic hormones, including testosterone, produced by the testes. Individuals with CAIS are often not diagnosed until adolescence, because they appear to be female but do not menstruate. They also are sometimes diagnosed in childhood because of presentation with inguinal hernia. The lack of functional androgen exposure before birth in XY individuals with CAIS might be expected to reduce their masculine behavior and increase their feminine behavior.

Indeed, XY females who do not have functional androgen receptors because of CAIS have been found to show female-typical childhood play behavior, at least as assessed retrospectively using a questionnaire focusing on toy interests (Hines, Ahmed, & Hughes, 2003). Similarly, a study grouped girls with CAIS and another XY girl, who resembled the XY girls with CAIS in having been born with feminine-appearing external genitalia but who had a different disorder (an androgen biosynthesis defect), and found that both types of XY girls showed increased feminine and decreased masculine toy and activity preferences, measured using a questionnaire completed by a parent, compared with a group of typically developing boys (Jürgensen, Hiort, Holterhus, & Thyen, 2007). Like the findings from girls with CAH, these results suggest that androgenic hormones contribute to male-typical childhood toy and play interests. All of these XY girls were assigned and reared as girls, however, so their lack of effective exposure during early development to testosterone and other androgens cannot be separated from their socialization as female in understanding the causes of their female-typical childhood play behavior. The results do demonstrate, however, that female-typical childhood play behavior can develop despite the presence of a Y chromosome.

Offspring of Pregnancies During Which Hormones Were Prescribed

This section reviews development of gender-typed play in children whose mothers were prescribed hormones during pregnancy for clinical reasons. Some pregnant women were prescribed hormones that stimulated androgen receptors (androgenic hormones, typically androgenic progestins), and some were prescribed hormones that blocked these receptors (antiandrogenic hormones, typically antiandrogenic progestins). The children of women who were prescribed androgenic progestins might be expected to show increased masculine behavior and reduced feminine behavior, and the children of those who were prescribed antiandrogenic progestins might be expected to show decreased masculine behavior and increased feminine behavior.

The pattern of results in studies so far appears to provide some support for these hypotheses. Girls born with virilized external genitalia, following maternal treatment with androgenic progestins, have been reported to show high levels of masculine play behavior (Ehrhardt & Money, 1967), although this study did not include a control group for comparison. A subsequent study found that girls whose mothers had taken antiandrogenic progestins during pregnancy showed reduced masculine play and increased feminine play (Ehrhardt, Grisanti, & Meyer-Bahlburg, 1977). Unlike girls with CAH, these girls did not have a disorder, and they were born with feminine external genitalia. These studies, therefore, provide some convergent evidence of androgenic influences on play behavior, augmenting the findings from girls with CAH and XY females with CAIS, although the findings for children whose mothers were prescribed hormones during pregnancy have not yet been replicated.

Variability in Hormones in Typically Developing Children

Another approach to studying the possible influences of the early hormone environment on children's gender-related play behavior has been to measure testosterone in typically developing children. These studies have measured testosterone in maternal blood during pregnancy, in amniotic fluid during gestation, in umbilical cord blood at the time of birth, or in blood, urine, or saliva during the early postnatal period. These last approaches, which involve measuring testosterone during early infancy, are based on the evidence that there is a surge of testosterone in boys not only prenatally but also shortly after birth. This postnatal surge appears to peak at about 1 month postnatal, with testosterone declining to baseline by about 3 to 6 months postnatal (Forest, 1990; Forest et al., 1973; Winter, Hughes, Reyes, & Faiman, 1976).

One study found that testosterone in amniotic fluid significantly and positively predicts masculine play behavior in boys and in girls as assessed using a parent report questionnaire, the PSAI (Auyeung et al., 2009). However, a similar result was not seen when play was measured using a different parent report measure (Knickmeyer et al., 2005), or observation in a free play paradigm (van de Beek, van Goozen, Buitelaar, & Cohen-Kettenis, 2009). It is not yet known if the one positive finding is unreliable or if smaller samples or less sensitive measures account for the negative results in the two studies that did not see a relationship. A review of the available research using amniotic fluid to measure testosterone and relate it to subsequent behavior suggested that the amniotic fluid approach may not be sensitive or reliable enough to detect hormone behavior relationships, except perhaps in very large samples (Constantinescu & Hines, 2012).

Studies relating maternal testosterone during pregnancy to later gender-typed play have produced similarly mixed findings. An initial study, involving a general population sample of thousands of pregnant women and their offspring, found that maternal testosterone at midpregnancy positively and significantly predicted later masculine behavior as assessed using the PSAI in female, but not in male, offspring (Hines et al., 2002). The relationship in girls, but not boys, was thought to have occurred because of genetic related-ness. Testosterone is not thought to transfer during pregnancy from mothers to fetuses, and mothers pregnant with girls have similar testosterone concentra-tions to mothers pregnant with boys, suggesting that testosterone also does not transfer from fetuses to mothers. Testosterone production is highly heritable in mothers and daughters, but not mothers and sons, perhaps because girls and their mothers share the same sources of testosterone, the adrenal glands and the ovaries, whereas boys produce most of their testosterone in their tes-tes. Thus, mothers producing relatively high concentrations of testosterone may also have female fetuses producing relatively high concentrations of testosterone, explaining the relationship of maternal testosterone to off-spring behavior that was seen in girls. A second study did not see a similar relationship between maternal testosterone and daughters' toy preferences, however (van de Beek et al., 2009). This study used a different measure of behavior, and a far smaller sample, than the initial study. As with the findings relating testosterone in amniotic fluid samples to later behavior, additional research is needed to determine if the initial report was unreliable, or if small sample size and weak measurement explain the failures to replicate.

Research that measured testosterone in urine samples during early infancy and related testosterone concentrations at this time to later gender-typed behavior found results for testosterone concentrations that resembled those seen in prior studies using blood samples (Kuiri-Hänninen et al., 2011; Lamminmäki et al., 2012). Testosterone peaked at about age 1 month postna-tal and declined to baseline by about age 3 to 6 months postnatal. Testosterone during the first 6 months postnatal also positively predicted masculine play at age 14 months in boys, as assessed using a parent report questionnaire, the PSAI (Lamminmäki et al., 2012). The correlation between testosterone and masculine play was also positive in girls, but it was not statistically significant. Also, when observed with toys in a playroom, boys played more with a train than girls did, and girls played more with a doll than boys did. In addition, testosterone positively predicted play with the train in girls, but not in boys, and negatively predicted play with the doll in boys, but not in girls. However, these significant relationships involved relatively small groups of children (15 boys for the parent report questionnaire [PSAI], 22 girls for play with the train, and 20 boys for play with the doll). In addition, there have not yet been any attempts to replicate these findings to our knowledge.

Variability in Physical Characteristics in Typically Developing Children

A final set of approaches to assessing influences of early exposure to tes-tosterone or other androgens on children's play has involved relating physical characteristics that are influenced by androgens, or thought to be influenced by androgens, to behavior. The most popular approach has been to use the ratio of the second digit to the fourth digit of the hand (2D:4D). The rationale behind this approach is that this ratio shows a sex difference, being larger (i.e., closer to 1.0) in females than in males. Because this sex difference in the finger ratio is thought to be determined prenatally, it has been assumed to reflect prenatal androgen exposure (Manning, 2002).

Three studies have related gender-typed play to the 2D:4D finger ratio. The first study (Hönekopp & Thierfelder, 2009) found that left hand 2D:4D correlated significantly and negatively with scores on the PSAI in boys, but right hand 2D:4D did not, nor did either left or right hand 2D:4D correlate with PSAI scores in girls. Interpretation of these results is difficult because the standardized scoring system for the PSAI was not used. The second study (Mitsui et al., 2016) reported somewhat similar results in that 2D:4D correlated significantly and negatively with PSAI scores in boys but not in girls. The third study (Wong & Hines, 2016) studied children on two occasions, separated by several months, and looked at play with gender-typed toys, as well as at PSAI scores. Of 24 gender-related variables assessed in the study, one correlated significantly with 2D:4D, but results for relationships between finger ratios and behavior were inconsistent across the two occasions when children were assessed. Because of this inconsistency, and for other reasons, the authors concluded that finger ratios do not provide a reliable approach to assessing prenatal androgen exposure. Other researchers have also argued against the use of finger ratios to measure early androgen exposure (Berenbaum, Bryk, Nowak, Quigley, & Moffat, 2009; Constantinescu & Hines, 2012) based on evidence that finger ratios do not consistently show predicted relations to early androgen exposure, that they show far smaller sex differences than the sex difference in androgen concentrations prenatally, and that the method is not sufficiently sensitive to individual variability.

Another approach has been to measure characteristics of the external genitalia that are known to be influenced by testosterone and other androgens, and relate these characteristics to later behavior. Anogenital distance (AGD) is the distance from the anus to the genitalia. It is larger in females than in males, and its magnitude relates negatively to prenatal androgen exposure (Dean & Sharpe, 2013; Thankamony, Pasterski, Ong, Acerini, & Hughes, 2016). Researchers have also measured penile growth during the first 3 months postnatal, as a biomarker of early postnatal androgen exposure. The early postnatal testosterone surge influences penile growth, and testosterone concentrations in male infants at age 3 months have been found to correlate with penile growth during this period (Boas et al., 2006; van den Driesche et al., 2011), supporting the use of this measure as an indicator of early postnatal androgen exposure.

Pasterski and colleagues (2015) used penile growth during the first 3 months postnatal to provide an estimate of early postnatal androgen exposure, and used AGD at birth to provide an estimate of prenatal androgen exposure. Results suggested that androgen exposure both prenatally and during the first 3 months postnatal made significant and separate contributions to later gender-typed behavior, assessed at age 3 to 4 years using the PSAI. There have not yet been any attempts to replicate these findings, but the use of AGD at birth, and penile growth during the early postnatal period, could provide a useful, relatively noninvasive, methodology for assessing androgen exposure during each of these two potentially important periods for gender-related development.

RESEARCH DIRECTIONS

Interactions of Early Hormones With the Social Environment and Cognitive Developmental Processes

The social environment also contributes to children's gender-typed play (see Chapter 6). In addition, children's developing cognitive understanding of gender plays a role in children's gender-typed play (see Chapter 7). These social and cognitive processes are described in detail in other chapters of this volume, and will not be treated in detail here. However, we are interested in understanding how hormones, socialization, and cognitive developmental processes might interact to influence the development of children's gender-related play behavior. Girls with CAH might provide some insight into these interactive processes because these girls have unusual androgen exposure prenatally but look like girls. They might, therefore, have increased male-typical prenatal androgen exposure but largely female-typical postnatal socialization by parents, siblings, peers, and society at large. In addition, however, they might differ from other girls to some degree in postnatal socialization of gender or in the cognitive processes involved in gender-related development.

Two studies have observed the toy preferences of girls with CAH not only on their own, but also with their parents, in attempts to look at the impact of parental socialization on toy preferences in these girls. The first study found that the presence of a parent in the playroom did not prevent the reduced preference for feminine toys and the increased preference for masculine toys that is typically seen in girls with CAH (Servin et al., 2003). The study also found that comparison of parents' desired behavior in their daughters and their perceived behavior in their daughters did not support an effect of parental expectations on behavior. The second study looked at parental encouragement of play with feminine toys and masculine toys in girls and boys with and without CAH (Pasterski et al.,

2005). This study found that parents encouraged their daughters with CAH to play with feminine toys more than they encouraged their daughters without CAH to play with feminine toys, at least when they were observed in a playroom with masculine toys, neutral toys, and feminine toys all available. A third study used questionnaires to assess parental encouragement of male-typical and female-typical activities in childhood in girls and boys with and without CAH (Wong, Pasterski, Hindmarsh, Geffner, & Hines, 2013). The researchers found that parents recalled having encouraged their daughters with CAH to engage in male-typical play more so than their daughters without CAH. Taken together, these findings suggest that parents of girls with CAH, like most parents, generally encourage their children to engage in activities that the children enjoy, but, when they are in a setting with access to feminine toys, toys that the girls with CAH might not normally seek out, they encourage their daughters with CAH to play with these conventionally feminine toys.

In addition to showing altered toy preferences, girls with CAH have been found to show reduced female gender identity (Hines, 2015). This suggests the possibility that girls with CAH might be less responsive to some types of influences on gender-related play. One study investigated this possibility by examining how girls with CAH responded to gender labels identifying neutral toys as "for girls" or "for boys," and to male and female models choosing neutral items (Hines et al., 2016). Specifically, balloons and xylophones in different colors were labeled as for one sex or the other (e.g., green balloons are for girls and silver balloons are for boys), and male or female models were seen consistently choosing different neutral items, such as pencils versus pens, or plush squirrels versus plush hedgehogs. Results suggested that girls without CAH and boys with and without CAH responded to these social cues as expected, showing verbal and behavioral preferences for items that they had been taught were for their own sex, or that they had seen chosen by other people of their own sex, whereas girls with CAH did not. These results suggest that the prenatal androgen exposure caused by CAH may not only influence girls' later behavior by altering brain development prenatally, but may also have cascading influences caused by the initial neural changes resulting in altered social environments and altered responses of the girls themselves to the social environment.

Another question is whether animals, which are not subject to the same social and cognitive influences on gender-related behavior as are seen in our society, have sex-typed play or toy preferences. One approach to this question has been to examine the play behavior of nonhuman primates. As mentioned above, juvenile male rhesus monkeys show more rough-and-tumble play behavior than do female rhesus monkeys, and prenatal androgen exposure increases rough-and-tumble play in female rhesus monkeys (Goy, 1978, 1981). In regard to toys, male and female vervet monkeys have been found to differ in their toy preferences, with female animals spending more time than male animals do with toys like dolls, and male animals spending more time than female animals do with toys like vehicles, whereas the male and female animals did not differ in regard to time spent with neutral toys (Alexander & Hines, 2002). A second study of nonhuman primates, in this case rhesus monkeys, replicated the finding of greater male than female preference for wheeled toys, and also found no sex difference in preference for gender neutral (plush) toys (Hassett, Siebert, & Wallen, 2008). These findings all suggest that sex-related toy preferences can develop in the absence of many of the social and cognitive processes that have been found to be influential in children; the nonhuman primates had no prior experience with the toys, and assumedly had no cognitive understanding of gender, particularly in relation to the toys.

These studies raise new questions. For instance, what are the characteristics of children's toys that make them more or less appealing to male and female animals, who have never seen the toys before? Could it be color, or shape, or the affordance of movement? These are among the questions that are currently being investigated.

Testosterone in Typically Developing Children During Infancy and Later Gender-Related Behavior

Another area of active investigation is the influence of testosterone during the early neonatal period when androgens are elevated in boys. Although there is convergent evidence from children who developed in atypical hormone environments that androgens contribute to children's gender-related toy choices and other aspects of gender-typed play, it is important to know if androgen exposure within the typical range has similar influences. Answering this question has been challenging. Several approaches to studying the impact of typical variability in prenatal androgen exposure, including measuring testosterone in amniotic fluid and in maternal blood, and using finger ratios (2D:4D) as proxies for prenatal androgen exposure, have produced inconsistent results. All of these measures may be too unreliable to detect relationships between androgen exposure and later behavior, other than, perhaps, in very large samples of participants.

Unlike amniotic fluid, which is almost always available only in a single sample, taken at an uncontrolled time of day, testosterone can be measured repeatedly in samples taken from infants during the early postnatal testosterone surge and can be obtained under controlled conditions, using not only blood sampling but also noninvasive techniques such as urine or saliva sampling (Constantinescu & Hines, 2012). Thus, sampling during this early postnatal period could provide more definitive information on the effects early androgen exposure has on children's gender-typical toy preferences in the general population. In addition, because this approach is noninvasive, it could allow studies of large samples of children, and thus enable research investigating interactions between early androgen exposure and social and cognitive influences on children's gender-related play behavior.

CONCLUSION

In summary, the sex hormone testosterone is higher during early development in males than in females, and testosterone exposure appears to contribute to children's gender-related play behavior, including children's preferences for masculine and feminine toys. Socialization also contributes to the development of children's gender-related toy preferences, and recent evidence suggests that in addition to influencing early occurring processes of brain development, prenatal testosterone exposure may alter socialization processes related to gender-typed play. Research suggesting that early testosterone exposure influences later gender-typed toy preferences, as well as research showing gender-typed toy preferences in nonhuman primates, raises questions about the characteristics and affordances of toys, such as dolls and vehicles, that make them more appealing to one sex or the other.

However, research to date has not examined some potentially important questions. For instance, relatively little research in this area has focused on video games. Video games could not be included in studies that were conducted before these games were available. Future studies, however, might usefully investigate hormonal and other possible influences on children's interest in these games. In addition, there has been little research on intersectionalities between gender and other types of factors, such as ethnicity, race, culture, or socioeconomic status. Investigation of these intersectionalities, and their particular relation to sex hormones and gender-typed toy play, might also be an interesting focus for future research on children's gender-related toy preferences.

Finally, although much research has focused on the prenatal sex difference in testosterone and its relationship to later play behavior, recent findings suggest that a postnatal surge in testosterone may also relate to later gender-typed play. This early postnatal surge may provide an opportunity for additional studies examining interactions between early testosterone exposure and social and cognitive influences on gender-related toy preferences and other aspects of children's behavior.

REFERENCES

Alexander, G. M., & Hines, M. (2002). Sex differences in response to children's toys in nonhuman primates (*Cercopithecus aethiops sabaeus*). *Evolution and Human Behavior, 23,* 467–479. Retrieved from http://www.ehbonline.org/article/S1090-5138%2802%2900107-1/fulltext

Arnold, A. P. (2009). The organizational–activational hypothesis as the foundation for a unified theory of sexual differentiation of all mammalian tissues. *Hormones and Behavior, 55,* 570–578. Retrieved from http://www.sciencedirect.com/science/article/pii/S0018506X09000646

Auyeung, B., Baron-Cohen, S., Ashwin, E., Knickmeyer, R., Taylor, K., Hackett, G., & Hines, M. (2009). Fetal testosterone predicts sexually differentiated childhood behavior in girls and in boys. *Psychological Science, 20,* 144–148. http://dx.doi.org/10.1111/j.1467-9280.2009.02279.x

Berenbaum, S. A., Bryk, K. K., Nowak, N., Quigley, C. A., & Moffat, S. (2009). Fingers as a marker of prenatal androgen exposure. *Endocrinology, 150,* 5119–5124. http://dx.doi.org/10.1210/en.2009-0774

Berenbaum, S. A., & Hines, M. (1992). Early androgens are related to childhood sex-typed toy preferences. *Psychological Science, 3,* 203–206. http://dx.doi.org/10.1111/j.1467-9280.1992.tb00028.x

Berenbaum, S. A., & Snyder, E. (1995). Early hormonal influences on childhood sex-typed activity and playmate preferences: Implications for the development of sexual orientation. *Developmental Psychology, 31,* 31–42. http://dx.doi.org/10.1037/0012-1649.31.1.31

Boas, M., Boisen, K. A., Virtanen, H. E., Kaleva, M., Suomi, A. M., Schmidt, I. M., . . . Main, K. M. (2006). Postnatal penile length and growth rate correlate to serum testosterone levels: A longitudinal study of 1962 normal boys. *European Journal of Endocrinology, 154,* 125–129. http://dx.doi.org/10.1530/eje.1.02066

Constantinescu, M., & Hines, M. (2012). Relating prenatal testosterone exposure to postnatal behavior in typically developing children: Methods and findings. *Child Development Perspectives, 6,* 407–413. http://dx.doi.org/10.1111/j.1750-8606.2012.00257.x

Costa, P. T., & McCrae, R. R. (1992). Normal personality assessment in clinical practice: The NEO Personality Inventory. *Psychological Assessment, 4,* 5–13. http://dx.doi.org/10.1037/1040-3590.4.1.5

Davis, J., & Hines, M. (2017). *Gender differences in children's toy preferences: A systematic review and meta-analysis.* Manuscript submitted for publication.

Dean, A., & Sharpe, R. M. (2013). Clinical review: Anogenital distance or digit length ratio as measures of fetal androgen exposure: relationship to male reproductive development and its disorders. *The Journal of Clinical Endocrinology and Metabolism, 98,* 2230–2238. http://dx.doi.org/10.1210/jc.2012-4057

DiPietro, J. A. (1981). Rough and tumble play: A function of gender. *Developmental Psychology, 17,* 50–58. http://dx.doi.org/10.1037/0012-1649.17.1.50

Dittmann, R. W., Kappes, M. H., Kappes, M. E., Börger, D., Meyer-Bahlburg, H. F. L., Stegner, H., . . . Wallis, H. (1990). Congenital adrenal hyperplasia. II: Gender-related behavior and attitudes in female salt-wasting and simple-virilizing patients. *Psychoneuroendocrinology, 15,* 421–434. Retrieved from http://www.psyneuen-journal.com/article/0306-4530(90)90066-I/fulltext

Eaton, W. O., & Enns, L. R. (1986). Sex differences in human motor activity level. *Psychological Bulletin, 100,* 19–28. http://dx.doi.org/10.1037/0033-2909.100.1.19

Ehrhardt, A. A., & Baker, S. W. (1974). Fetal androgens, human central nervous system differentiation, and behavior sex differences. In R. C. Friedman, R. M. Richart, & R. L. van de Wiele (Eds.), *Sex differences in behavior* (pp. 33–52). New York, NY: John Wiley & Sons.

Ehrhardt, A. A., Grisanti, G. C., & Meyer-Bahlburg, H. F. L. (1977). Prenatal exposure to medroxyprogesterone acetate (MPA) in girls. *Psychoneuroendocrinology, 2,* 391–398. http://dx.doi.org/10.1016/0306-4530(77)90010-5

Ehrhardt, A. A., & Money, J. (1967). Progestin-induced hermaphroditism: IQ and psychosexual identity in a study of ten girls. *Journal of Sex Research, 3,* 83–100. http://dx.doi.org/10.1080/00224496709550517

Else-Quest, N. M., Hyde, J. S., Goldsmith, H. H., & Van Hulle, C. A. (2006). Gender differences in temperament: A meta-analysis. *Psychological Bulletin, 132,* 33–72. http://dx.doi.org/10.1037/0033-2909.132.1.33

Etaugh, C., & Liss, M. B. (1992). Home, school, and playroom: Training grounds for adult gender roles. *Sex Roles, 26,* 129–147. http://dx.doi.org/10.1007/BF00289754

Fausto-Sterling, A. (1992). *Myths of gender.* New York, NY: Basic Books.

Feingold, A. (1994). Gender differences in personality: A meta-analysis. *Psychological Bulletin, 116,* 429–456. http://dx.doi.org/10.1037/0033-2909.116.3.429

Forest, M. G. (1990). Pituitary gonadotropin and sex steroid secretion during the first two years of life. In M. M. Grumbach, P. C. Sizonenko, & M. L. Aubert (Eds.), *Control of the onset of puberty* (pp. 451–477). Baltimore, MD: Williams & Wilkins.

Forest, M. G., Cathiard, A. M., & Bertrand, J. A. (1973). Evidence of testicular activity in early infancy. *The Journal of Clinical Endocrinology and Metabolism, 37,* 148–151. http://dx.doi.org/10.1210/jcem-37-1-148

Frisén, L., Nordenström, A., Falhammar, H., Filipsson, H., Holmdahl, G., Janson, P. O., . . . Nordenskjöld, A. (2009). Gender role behavior, sexuality, and psychosocial adaptation in women with congenital adrenal hyperplasia due to CYP21A2 deficiency. *The Journal of Clinical Endocrinology and Metabolism, 94,* 3432–3439. http://dx.doi.org/10.1210/jc.2009-0636

Goble, P., Martin, C. L., Hanish, L. D., & Fabes, R. A. (2012). Children's gender-typed activity choices across preschool social contexts. *Sex Roles, 67,* 435–451. http://dx.doi.org/10.1007/s11199-012-0176-9

Golombok, S., & Rust, J. (1993). The Pre-School Activities Inventory: A standardized assessment of gender role in children. *Psychological Assessment, 5,* 131–136. http://dx.doi.org/10.1037/1040-3590.5.2.131

Golombok, S., Rust, J., Zervoulis, K., Croudace, T., Golding, J., & Hines, M. (2008). Developmental trajectories of sex-typed behavior in boys and girls: A longitudinal general population study of children aged 2.5–8 years. *Child Development, 79,* 1583–1593. http://dx.doi.org/10.1111/j.1467-8624.2008.01207.x

Goy, R. W. (1978). Development of play and mounting behaviour in female rhesus virilized prenatally with esters of testosterone or dihydrotestosterone. In D. J. Chivers & J. Herbert (Eds.), *Recent advances in primatology* (pp. 449–462). New York, NY: Academic Press.

Goy, R. W. (1981). Differentiation of male social traits in female rhesus macaques by prenatal treatment with androgens: Variation in type of androgen, duration and timing of treatment. In M. J. Novy & J. A. Resko (Eds.), *Fetal endocrinology* (pp. 319–339). New York, NY: Academic Press.

Grumbach, M. M., Hughes, I. A., & Conte, F. A. (2003). Disorders of sex differentiation. In P. R. Larsen, H. M. Kronenberg, S. Melmed, & K. S. Polonsky (Eds.), *Williams textbook of endocrinology* (Vol. 10, pp. 842–1002). Philadelphia, PA: W. B. Saunders.

Hall, C. M., Jones, J. A., Meyer-Bahlburg, H. F. L., Dolezal, C., Coleman, M., Foster, P., . . . Clayton, P. E. (2004). Behavioral and physical masculinization are related to genotype in girls with congenital adrenal hyperplasia. *The Journal of Clinical Endocrinology and Metabolism, 89*, 419–424. http://dx.doi.org/10.1210/jc.2003-030696

Hassett, J. M., Siebert, E. R., & Wallen, K. (2008). Sex differences in rhesus monkey toy preferences parallel those of children. *Hormones and Behavior, 54*, 359–364. Retrieved from https://www.ncbi.nlm.nih.gov/pmc/articles/PMC2583786/

Hines, M. (2004). *Brain gender.* New York, NY: Oxford University Press.

Hines, M. (2015). Gendered development. In R. M. Lerner & M. E. Lamb (Eds.), *Handbook of child development and developmental science: Vol. 3. Socioemotional processes* (7th ed., pp. 842–887). Hoboken, NJ: John Wiley & Sons.

Hines, M., Ahmed, S. F., & Hughes, I. A. (2003). Psychological outcomes and gender-related development in complete androgen insensitivity syndrome. *Archives of Sexual Behavior, 32*(2), 93–101. http://dx.doi.org/10.1023/A:1022492106974

Hines, M., Brook, C., & Conway, G. S. (2004). Androgen and psychosexual development: Core gender identity, sexual orientation and recalled childhood gender role behavior in women and men with congenital adrenal hyperplasia (CAH). *Journal of Sex Research, 41*, 75–81. http://dx.doi.org/10.1080/00224490409552215

Hines, M., Golombok, S., Rust, J., Johnston, K., Golding, J., & Avon Longitudinal Study of Parents and Children Study Team. (2002). Testosterone during pregnancy and gender role behavior of preschool children: A longitudinal, population study. *Child Development, 73*, 1678–1687. http://dx.doi.org/10.1111/1467-8624.00498

Hines, M., & Kaufman, F. R. (1994). Androgen and the development of human sex-typical behavior: Rough-and-tumble play and sex of preferred playmates in children with congenital adrenal hyperplasia (CAH). *Child Development, 65*, 1042–1053. http://dx.doi.org/10.2307/1131303

Hines, M., Pasterski, V., Spencer, D., Neufeld, S., Patalay, P., Hindmarsh, P. C., . . . Acerini, C. L. (2016). Prenatal androgen exposure alters girls' responses to information indicating gender-appropriate behaviour. *Philosophical Transactions of the Royal Society B: Biological Sciences, 371*, 20150125. http://dx.doi.org/10.1098/rstb.2015.0125

Hönekopp, J., & Thierfelder, C. (2009). Relationships between digit ratio (2D:4D) and sex-typed play behavior in pre-school children. *Personality and Individual Differences, 47*, 706–710. http://dx.doi.org/10.1016/j.paid.2009.06.007

Hyde, J. S. (1984). How large are gender differences in aggression? A developmental meta-analysis. *Developmental Psychology, 20*, 722–736. http://dx.doi.org/10.1037/0012-1649.20.4.722

Hyde, J. S., & Linn, M. C. (1988). Gender differences in verbal ability: A meta-analysis. *Psychological Bulletin, 104*, 53–69. http://dx.doi.org/10.1037/0033-2909.104.1.53

Idle, T., Wood, E., & Desmarais, S. (1993). Gender role socialization in toy play situations: Mothers and fathers with their sons and daughters. *Sex Roles, 28*, 679–691. http://dx.doi.org/10.1007/BF00289987

Iijima, M., Arisaka, O., Minamoto, F., & Arai, Y. (2001). Sex differences in children's free drawings: A study on girls with congenital adrenal hyperplasia. *Hormones and Behavior, 40*, 99–104. http://dx.doi.org/10.1006/hbeh.2001.1670

International Committee on Radiological Protection. (1975). *Report of the task group on reference man.* New York, NY: Pergamon Press.

Jacklin, C. N., DiPietro, J. A., & Maccoby, E. E. (1984). Sex-typing behavior and sex-typing pressure in child/parent interaction. *Archives of Sexual Behavior, 13*, 413–425. http://dx.doi.org/10.1007/BF01541427

Johnson, M. H. (2013). *Essential reproduction* (7th ed.) West Sussex, England: Wiley-Blackwell.

Jürgensen, M., Hiort, O., Holterhus, P. M., & Thyen, U. (2007). Gender role behavior in children with XY karyotype and disorders of sex development. *Hormones and Behavior, 51*, 443–453. http://dx.doi.org/10.1016/j.yhbeh.2007.01.001

Knickmeyer, R. C., Wheelwright, S., Taylor, K., Raggatt, P., Hackett, G., & Baron-Cohen, S. (2005). Gender-typed play and amniotic testosterone. *Developmental Psychology, 41*, 517–528. http://dx.doi.org/10.1037/0012-1649.41.3.517

Kuiri-Hänninen, T., Seuri, R., Tyrväinen, E., Turpeinen, U., Hämäläinen, E., Stenman, U. H., . . . Sankilampi, U. (2011). Increased activity of the hypothalamic–pituitary–testicular axis in infancy results in increased androgen action in premature boys. *The Journal of Clinical Endocrinology and Metabolism, 96*, 98–105. http://dx.doi.org/10.1210/jc.2010-1359

Lamminmäki, A., Hines, M., Kuiri-Hänninen, T., Kilpeläinen, L., Dunkel, L., & Sankilampi, U. (2012). Testosterone measured in infancy predicts subsequent sex-typed behavior in boys and in girls. *Hormones and Behavior, 61*, 611–616. http://dx.doi.org/10.1016/j.yhbeh.2012.02.013

Luders, E., Narr, K. L., Thompson, P. M., Rex, D. E., Jancke, L., Steinmetz, H., & Toga, A. W. (2004). Gender differences in cortical complexity. *Nature Neuroscience, 7,* 799–800. http://dx.doi.org/10.1038/nn1277

Lytton, H., & Romney, D. M. (1991). Parents' differential socialization of boys and girls: A meta-analysis. *Psychological Bulletin, 109,* 267–296. http://dx.doi.org/10.1037/0033-2909.109.2.267

Maccoby, E. E., & Jacklin, C. N. (1987). Gender segregation in children. In H. W. Reece (Ed.), *Advances in child development and behavior* (Vol. 20, pp. 239–287). New York, NY: Academic Press.

Manning, J. T. (2002). *Digit ratio: A pointer to fertility, behavior, and health.* New Brunswick, NJ: Rutgers University Press.

McCarthy, M. M., De Vries, G. J., & Forger, N. G. (2009). Sexual differentiation of the brain: mode, mechanisms, and meaning. In D. W. Pfaff, A. P. Arnold, A. M. Etgen, S. E. Fahrbach, & R. T. Rubin (Eds.), *Hormones, brain, and behavior* (Vol. 2, pp. 1707–1746). San Diego, CA: Academic Press.

Merke, D. P., & Bornstein, S. R. (2005). Congenital adrenal hyperplasia. *The Lancet, 365,* 2125–2136. Retrieved from http://www.thelancet.com/journals/lancet/article/PIIS0140673605667360/abstract

Meyer-Bahlburg, H. F. L. (1999). Variants of gender differentiation. In H. C. Steinhausen & F. C. Verhulst (Eds.), *Risks and outcomes in developmental psychopathology* (pp. 298–313). New York, NY: Oxford University Press.

Meyer-Bahlburg, H. F. L., Dolezal, C., Baker, S. W., Ehrhardt, A. A., & New, M. I. (2006). Gender development in women with congenital adrenal hyperplasia as a function of disorder severity. *Archives of Sexual Behavior, 35,* 667–684. http://dx.doi.org/10.1007/s10508-006-9068-9

Meyer-Bahlburg, H. F. L., Dolezal, C., Baker, S. W., Carlson, A. D., Obeid, J. S., & New, M. I. (2004). Prenatal androgenization affects gender-related behavior but not gender identity in 5–12-year-old girls with congenital adrenal hyperplasia. *Archives of Sexual Behavior, 33,* 97–104. http://dx.doi.org/10.1023/B:ASEB.0000014324.25718.51

Mitsui, T., Araki, A., Goudarzi, H., Miyashita, C., Ito, S., Sasaki, S., . . . Nonomura, K. (2016). Effects of adrenal androgens during the prenatal period on the second to fourth digit ratio in school-aged children. *Steroids, 113,* 46–51. Retrieved from https://www.ncbi.nlm.nih.gov/pubmed/27343975

Money, J., & Ehrhardt, A. (1973). *Man and woman, boy and girl: Differentiation and dimorphism of gender identity from conception to maturity.* Baltimore, MD: Johns Hopkins University Press.

Nordenström, A., Servin, A., Bohlin, G., Larsson, A., & Wedell, A. (2002). Sex-typed toy play behavior correlates with the degree of prenatal androgen exposure assessed by CYP21 genotype in girls with congenital adrenal hyperplasia. *The Journal of Clinical Endocrinology and Metabolism, 87,* 5119–5124. http://dx.doi.org/10.1210/jc.2001-011531

Pang, S., Levine, L. S., Cederqvist, L. L., Fuentes, M., Riccardi, V. M., Holcombe, J. H., ... New, M. I. (1980). Amniotic fluid concentrations of delta 5 and delta 4 steroids in fetuses with congenital adrenal hyperplasia due to 21 hydroxylase deficiency and in anencephalic fetuses. *The Journal of Clinical Endocrinology and Metabolism, 51,* 223–229. http://dx.doi.org/10.1210/jcem-51-2-223

Pasterski, V., Geffner, M. E., Brain, C., Hindmarsh, P., Brook, C., & Hines, M. (2011). Prenatal hormones and childhood sex segregation: Playmate and play style preferences in girls with congenital adrenal hyperplasia. *Hormones and Behavior, 59,* 549–555. Retrieved from https://www.ncbi.nlm.nih.gov/pubmed/21338606

Pasterski, V., Zucker, K. J., Hindmarsh, P. C., Hughes, I. A., Acerini, C., Spencer, D., ... Hines, M. (2015). Increased cross-gender identification independent of gender role behavior in girls with congenital adrenal hyperplasia: Results from a standardized assessment of 4–11-year-old children. *Archives of Sexual Behavior, 44,* 1363–1375. http://dx.doi.org/10.1007/s10508-014-0385-0

Pasterski, V. L., Geffner, M. E., Brain, C., Hindmarsh, P., Brook, C., & Hines, M. (2005). Prenatal hormones and postnatal socialization by parents as determinants of male-typical toy play in girls with congenital adrenal hyperplasia. *Child Development, 76,* 264–278. http://dx.doi.org/10.1111/j.1467-8624.2005.00843.x

Peretti, P. O., & Sydney, T. M. (1986). The influence of parental toy choice on child toy preference and sex-role typing. *Pediatrics International, 28,* 55–58. http://dx.doi.org/10.1111/j.1442-200X.1986.tb00697.x

Quadagno, D. M., Briscoe, R., & Quadagno, J. S. (1977). Effect of perinatal gonadal hormones on selected nonsexual behavior patterns: A critical assessment of the nonhuman and human literature. *Psychological Bulletin, 84,* 62–80. http://dx.doi.org/10.1037/0033-2909.84.1.62

Ruigrok, A. N. V., Salimi-Khorshidi, G., Lai, M. C., Baron-Cohen, S., Lombardo, M. V., Tait, R. J., & Suckling, J. (2014). A meta-analysis of sex differences in human brain structure. *Neuroscience and Biobehavioral Reviews, 39,* 34–50. Retrieved from http://www.sciencedirect.com/science/article/pii/S0149763413003011

Schau, C. G., Kahn, L., Diepold, J. H., & Cherry, F. (1980). The relationships of parental expectations and preschool children's verbal sex typing to their sex-typed toy play behavior. *Child Development, 51,* 266–270. http://dx.doi.org/10.2307/1129620

Serbin, L. A., Connor, J. M., Burchardt, C. J., & Citron, C. C. (1979). Effects of peer presence on sex-typing of children's play behavior. *Journal of Experimental Child Psychology, 27,* 303–309. http://dx.doi.org/10.1016/0022-0965(79)90050-X

Servin, A., Nordenström, A., Larsson, A., & Bohlin, G. (2003). Prenatal androgens and gender-typed behavior: A study of girls with mild and severe forms of congenital adrenal hyperplasia. *Developmental Psychology, 39,* 440–450. http://dx.doi.org/10.1037/0012-1649.39.3.440

Slijper, F. M. E. (1984). Androgens and gender role behaviour in girls with congenital adrenal hyperplasia (CAH). In G. J. De Vries, J. P. C. De Bruin, H. B. M. Uylings, & M. A. Corner (Eds.), *Progress in brain research* (Vol. 61, pp. 417–422). Amsterdam, The Netherlands: Elsevier.

Smail, P. J., Reyes, F. I., Winter, J. S. D., & Faiman, C. (1981). The fetal hormonal environment and its effect on the morphogenesis of the genital system. In S. J. Kogan & E. S. E. Hafez (Eds.), *Pediatric andrology* (Vol. 7, pp. 9–19). Boston, MA: Martinus Nijhoff. http://dx.doi.org/10.1007/978-94-010-3719-8_2

Tanner, J. M., Whitehouse, R. H., & Takaishi, M. (1966). Standards from birth to maturity for height, weight, height velocity, and weight velocity: British children, 1965. Part I. *Archives of Disease in Childhood, 41,* 454–471. http://dx.doi.org/10.1136/adc.41.219.454

Thankamony, A., Pasterski, V., Ong, K. K., Acerini, C. L., & Hughes, I. A. (2016). Anogenital distance as a marker of androgen exposure in humans. *Andrology, 4,* 616–625. http://dx.doi.org/10.1111/andr.12156

van de Beek, C., van Goozen, S. H. M., Buitelaar, J. K., & Cohen-Kettenis, P. T. (2009). Prenatal sex hormones (maternal and amniotic fluid) and gender-related play behavior in 13-month-old infants. *Archives of Sexual Behavior, 38,* 6–15. http://dx.doi.org/10.1007/s10508-007-9291-z

van den Driesche, S., Scott, H. M., MacLeod, D. J., Fisken, M., Walker, M., & Sharpe, R. M. (2011). Relative importance of prenatal and postnatal androgen action in determining growth of the penis and anogenital distance in the rat before, during and after puberty. *International Journal of Andrology, 34,* e578–e586. http://dx.doi.org/10.1111/j.1365-2605.2011.01175.x

Voyer, D., Voyer, S., & Bryden, M. P. (1995). Magnitude of sex differences in spatial abilities: A meta-analysis and consideration of critical variables. *Psychological Bulletin, 117,* 250–270. http://dx.doi.org/10.1037/0033-2909.117.2.250

Wilson, J. D., George, F. W., & Griffin, J. E. (1981). The hormonal control of sexual development. *Science, 211,* 1278–1284. http://dx.doi.org/10.1126/science.7010602

Winter, J. S. D., Hughes, I. A., Reyes, F. I., & Faiman, C. (1976). Pituitary–gonadal relations in infancy: 2. Patterns of serum gonadal steroid concentrations in man from birth to two years of age. *The Journal of Clinical Endocrinology and Metabolism, 42,* 679–686. http://dx.doi.org/10.1210/jcem-42-4-679

Wong, W. I., Pasterski, V. L., Hindmarsh, P. C., Geffner, M. E., & Hines, M. (2013). Are there parental socialization effects on the sex-typed behavior of individuals with congenital adrenal hyperplasia? *Archives of Sexual Behavior, 42,* 381–391. http://dx.doi.org/10.1007/s10508-012-9997-4

Wong, W. I., & Hines, M. (2016). Interpreting digit ratio (2D:4D)–behavior correlations: 2D:4D sex difference, stability, and behavioral correlates and their replicability in young children. *Hormones and Behavior, 78*, 86–94. http://dx.doi.org/10.1016/j.yhbeh.2015.10.022

Wudy, S. A., Dörr, H. G., Solleder, C., Djalali, M., & Homoki, J. (1999). Profiling steroid hormones in amniotic fluid of midpregnancy by routine stable isotope dilution/gas chromatography–mass spectrometry: Reference values and concentrations in fetuses at risk for 21-hydroxylase deficiency. *The Journal of Clinical Endocrinology and Metabolism, 84*, 2724–2728. https://doi.org/10.1210/jcem.84.8.5870

Zucker, K. J., Bradley, S. J., Oliver, G., Blake, J., Fleming, S., & Hood, J. (1996). Psychosexual development of women with congenital adrenal hyperplasia. *Hormones and Behavior, 30*, 300–318. http://dx.doi.org/10.1006/hbeh.1996.0038

6

ENVIRONMENTAL AND SOCIAL CONTRIBUTIONS TO CHILDREN'S GENDER-TYPED TOY PLAY: THE ROLE OF FAMILY, PEERS, AND MEDIA

CHRISTIA SPEARS BROWN AND ELLEN A. STONE

Children are repeatedly bombarded by social and environmental messages about toys that are appropriate for boys and toys that are appropriate for girls. Indeed, children are encouraged to play with gender-typed toys by their parents and siblings, their peers, and the media. At times, these messages are explicit, such as when children are told, "Only girls play with dolls!" Other times, these messages are more implicit, and children infer what toys they should play with based on the examples within their environment.

These explicit and implicit social messages are important because encouraging children to play with gender-specific toys is an important mechanism for socializing boys and girls to develop gender stereotypical behaviors, traits, and skills (Caldera, Huston, & O'Brien, 1989). Playing with toys is critical in how children develop enduring skills and abilities (Trawick-Smith, Russell, & Swaminathan, 2011; Vygotsky, 1967; see also Chapters 8–11, this volume). Typically, toys that are deemed appropriate for girls promote nurturance and

http://dx.doi.org/10.1037/0000077-007
Gender Typing of Children's Toys: How Early Play Experiences Impact Development, E. S. Weisgram and L. M. Dinella (Editors)

role-play, whereas toys that are deemed typical for boys promote spatial skills, independence, and aggression (e.g., Caldera et al., 1989; Serbin & Connor, 1979). Thus, although promoting and encouraging play with specific toys may seem trivial, it is a key element in the promotion and perpetuation of gender stereotypes that starts in infancy and continues through the lifespan. Fostering different skills based on gender in childhood exacerbates and solidifies lasting gender differences in adulthood—limiting an individual's potential (Eliot, 2010).

In this chapter, we review past and current research on how children are socialized to engage in gender-typed toy play. Specifically, we examine the role of (a) the family, including parents and siblings; (b) peers in school; and (c) media and advertising. In each section, we review the existing research and discuss the mechanisms through which each socializing agent contributes to the differentiation of children's toy choices. Finally, we point to gaps in the extant literature and offer suggestions for future research.

THE ROLE OF THE FAMILY

Families, including parents and siblings, play an important role in children's gender role stereotypes, including their engagement in gender-typed toy play. Research on children's gender-typed toy choices has focused heavily on the role of parents, as they are the primary socializers during children's first few years of life (i.e., Caldera et al., 1989; Campenni, 1999; Freeman, 2007). Indeed, a meta-analysis assessing parents' differential socialization of boys and girls found that the primary way that parents differ in how they treat their sons and daughters is through the encouragement of gender-typed play and activities (Lytton & Romney, 1991). Specifically, parents seem to promote children's gender-typed toy play by providing greater access to gender-typed toys than cross-typed toys, and by positively reinforcing play with gender-typed toys and punishing play with cross-typed toys.

Research has been clear in showing that parents indeed endorse gender stereotypes about the appropriateness of gender-specific toys for boys and girls. For instance, parents believe that toys such as dolls, makeup, and tea sets are feminine toys and thus are more appropriate for girls than boys, and toys such as trucks and tools are masculine and thus more appropriate for boys than girls (Campenni, 1999; Fisher-Thompson, 1990; Wood, Desmarais, & Gugula, 2002). Furthermore, even before the child is born, parents believe that their child will like gender-specific toys, suggesting that parents hold stereotypical beliefs about toy play before their children actually express any gender-typed interests (Peretti & Sydney, 1984). How exactly parents developed gender stereotypes about toy play is complex in its own right, and likely based on

(a) their own parents and culture, (b) their observations of other children's toy interests, and (c) their own culturally influenced interests in toys as a child. For example, research has shown that children's interests in toys can lead them to construct gender stereotypes about toy play (Weisgram, 2016). Thus, it is possible that parents' own toy interests as a child may have affected their construction of gender stereotypes regarding their children's interests. Most important, children are aware of their parents' gender stereotypes about the appropriateness of gender-specific toys for boys and girls, reporting that gender-typed play would be seen as "good" or "doesn't matter" by both their parents, but that cross-typed play would be seen as "bad" by their fathers (Raag & Rackliff, 1998).

Because parents hold stereotypical beliefs about gender-specific toys, and parents control children's early environments and access to toys, it is not surprising that children have greater access to gender-specific toys. For example, children's rooms are predominantly furnished with gender-typed toys and objects (O'Brien & Huston, 1985; Pomerleau, Bolduc, Malcuit, & Cossette, 1990; Rheingold & Cook, 1975). Even when a range of toys is available, parents direct children, starting in infancy, to gender-specific toys. In one of the first studies to examine the influence of parents on gender-typed toy play, parents were asked to play with an unknown 3-month-old infant and were told that the baby was either a girl or a boy, or they were given no gender information (Seavey, Katz, & Zalk, 1975). Parents who thought the baby was a specific gender offered more gender-typed toys than neutral or cross-typed toys for the baby to play with (Seavey et al., 1975). Even outside of lab settings, children are more likely to receive gender-typed toys as gifts from their parents than cross-typed toys, regardless of what types of toys they requested (Etaugh & Liss, 1992). This research suggests that parents, because they control access to toys, can socialize children to prefer gender-typed toys by simply granting greater access to those types of toys than more cross-typed toys.

There is asymmetry, however, in parents' stereotypic beliefs about toy play and their providing their children greater access to gender-typed toys. Specifically, parents typically believe that it is appropriate for boys *and* girls to play with masculine toys, but only girls can play with feminine toys (Campenni, 1999; Wood et al., 2002). In other words, it is more acceptable for parents when their daughter plays with a truck than when their son plays with a doll. In addition, when buying toys for children, adults are more likely to buy a gender-typed toy than a cross-typed toy, and they are even more likely to do so for a boy than for a girl (Fisher-Thompson, 1993). Relatedly, boys are less likely than girls to receive cross-typed toys as gifts, even when boys request them (Robinson & Morris, 1986). This asymmetry parallels the belief that masculine traits are desirable for both boys and girls, but feminine traits are only desirable for girls. Thus, while both boys and girls have limited access to cross-typed toys, boys are especially unlikely to have access to these toys.

Not only are boys more restricted in their access to gender-typed toys than girls, but fathers are more likely than mothers to be the primary enforcer of gender-typed play. In general, fathers hold more rigid gender role beliefs and enforce more gender-typed behaviors than mothers (Bradley & Gobbart, 1989; Langlois & Downs, 1980; Leaper & Friedman, 2007). Further, although both mothers and fathers encourage gender-typed play among their children, meta-analyses indicate that the effects are strongest for fathers (Leaper & Friedman, 2007; Lytton & Romney, 1991). For example, research has shown that fathers were more likely than mothers to present their children with gender-typed toys than neutral or cross-typed toys during an observed play session (Bradley & Gobbart, 1989). Fathers are especially important in socializing their children's gendered play behaviors because the time they spend with their children is predominately spent in play, compared with mothers' primary focus on caregiving activities (e.g., Cabrera, Tamis-LeMonda, Bradley, Hofferth, & Lamb, 2000). Interestingly, and perhaps not surprisingly given this previous research, children from households without a father present are less gender typed in their toy choices than children from households with both a father and mother (Brenes, Eisenberg, & Helmstadter, 1985; Hupp, Smith, Coleman, & Brunell, 2010).

Additionally, while fathers spend more time playing with their children than do mothers, they also spend more time in physical play than do mothers (Crawley & Sherrod, 1984). Specifically, fathers, more so than mothers, frequently engage in rough-and-tumble play with their children (Crawley & Sherrod, 1984). Furthermore, while both boys and girls enjoy rough-and-tumble play, fathers are more likely to engage in rough-and-tumble play with their sons than with their daughters (Jacklin, DiPietro, & Maccoby, 1984). Boys are then more likely to engage in rough-and-tumble play with their peers (DiPietro, 1981). Thus, fathers play an important role in the socialization of children's play.

In addition to providing differential access to gender-typed toys, parents also positively reinforce children when they play with gender-typed toys and punish children when they play with cross-typed toys. In one of the most frequently cited studies regarding parents' socialization of gender-typed toys, Langlois and Downs (1980) found that mothers and fathers rewarded children for playing with gender-typed toys and punished children for playing with cross-typed toys. For example, mothers were more likely to offer praise and affection when their daughters played with a dollhouse or cooking set than with cars or an army set of soldiers; in contrast, fathers were more likely to verbally ridicule their sons when they played with the dolls or cooking set. This suggests that children are quite accurate when they predicted that their parents would be approving of gender-typed toy play but disapproving of cross-typed toy play (Freeman, 2007; Raag & Rackliff, 1998). Consistent with traditional learning theories, research for the past 50 years has consistently shown that children shape their behavior based on the reinforcements and punishments they receive (Bandura, 1986; Lamb, Easterbrooks, & Holden, 1980). Thus, parents can shape children's play preferences by the differential reinforcement and punishment of gender-specific play.

Research has also shown that the reinforcement of gender-typed toy play may, at times, be more subtle than overt. Yvonne Caldera and her colleagues (1989) at the University of Kansas brought parent–toddler pairs into the lab. There were mothers with daughters, mothers with sons, fathers with daughters, and fathers with sons. They asked the parents to open a series of boxes and play with whatever toys were in them. Some boxes contained masculine toys, such as trucks and wooden blocks, and some boxes contained feminine toys, such as dolls and a kitchen set. Caldera et al. noted that parents, especially fathers, were noticeably more excited when they opened a box containing a toy that was consistent with their child's gender than when it was cross gendered. One dad of a daughter, upon opening a box with a truck in it, said, "Oh, they must have boys in this study." He promptly closed the truck box and went back to playing with the dolls from the previous box. He never gave his daughter a chance to play with the truck. Eight parents actually had to be excluded from the analyses because they did not even play with the cross-typed toys long enough to be analyzed. Again, fathers seem to encourage gender-typed toy play more than mothers (Langlois & Downs, 1980; Leaper, 2000).

Parents are not the only family members to socialize gender-typed toy play; siblings play a role as well (McHale, Crouter, & Whiteman, 2003). Older siblings are salient models of behavior for younger siblings, and they model gender-typed behavior that is then imitated by the younger sibling (McHale et al., 2003). In addition to modeling gender-typed play, the older siblings, because of their greater power in the relationship, may also control the types of play in which the siblings engage. For example, children with older same-gender siblings are more likely to be gender stereotypical in their play than children with older other-gender siblings and children with no siblings (Rust et al., 2000). Specifically, sibling pairs in which the oldest sibling is a brother are more likely to play with vehicles, balls, and weapons, whereas sibling pairs in which the older sibling is a sister are more likely to engage in doll play (Stoneman, Brody, & MacKinnon, 1986).

Taken together, research has shown that families socialize children to play with gender-typed toys by providing greater access to those toys, by reinforcing gender-typed toy choices and play (and punishing cross-typed play), and by modeling gender-typed play behaviors. Although prior research has primarily focused on heterosexual, White parents, more recent research has begun to examine how more diverse families socialize children's gender-typed toy play. For example, research with children from different ethnic groups (e.g., Mexican, African American, and Dominican) has shown that ethnically diverse children and parents show more similarities than differences in their levels of gender-typed play (Halim, Ruble, Tamis-LeMonda, & Shrout, 2013; Leavell, Tamis-LeMonda, Ruble, Zosuls, & Cabrera, 2012). There do appear to be differences, however, among families of differing sexual orientation. Specifically, Goldberg, Kashy, and Smith (2012) found that children of gay or lesbian parents were less likely to engage in gender-typed toy play than children of heterosexual parents. Future research is needed to examine whether this lower level of gender-typed toy play is due to differences in the gender stereotypes of parents, differences in the degree to which parents differentially reinforce gender-typed play, or differences in the available models of gender-stereotypical behavior. Furthermore, it is likely that other family members (e.g., grandparents, aunts, uncles) also affect children's access to toys. Because they know the child less well than parents, they may be particularly inclined to rely on gender stereotypes when buying toys for the child. Future research should examine how the broader family system contributes to children's toy play.

THE ROLE OF PEERS IN SCHOOL

Once children enter school, parents and siblings are no longer the only available socializers in their lives. Peers become an important source of information about gender-appropriate information. Beginning in preschool, children segregate themselves into same-gender peer groups (Maccoby, 1988; Powlishta, Serbin, & Moller, 1993). More than 50% of all children's play involves *only* same-gender children (Martin & Fabes, 2001). Boys typically play in large groups of other boys, away from teachers, with an emphasis on rough-and-tumble styles of play; in contrast, girls are more likely to play in small groups and dyads, closer to teachers, in play that emphasizes cooperation. Children play in these gender-segregated play groups, regardless of their individual activity level or temperament (Maccoby, 1990; Martin et al., 2013). Importantly, children self-segregate by gender and, over time, socialize each other to become more gender-typed by reinforcing gender-typed behavior and punishing cross-typed behavior (Langlois & Downs, 1980; Martin & Fabes, 2001; Martin et al., 2013). In other words, beginning in preschool, girls are more likely to play with other girls, and boys to play with other boys, regardless of their individual differences in personality.

Because of this strict gender segregation, children are heavily socialized by same-gender playmates (Martin et al., 2013). This segregation increases children's preferences for gender-typed toys in several ways. First, like older siblings, peers model gender-typed play. Children are more likely to model a same-gender peer than an other-gender peer (Rubinstein, 1978), and children prefer objects they have seen being used by a same-gender model compared with an other-gender model (Bussey & Perry, 1982). Second, children's play preferences become increasingly gender-typed over time, as they become more experienced and adept at gender-specific types of play, and less experienced and comfortable with cross-typed play. Martin and Fabes (2001) found that the more children played in same-gender peer groups, the more they preferred gender-typed play, over and above their earlier play preferences. Indeed, observational research has shown that, compared with children playing in mixed-gender play groups, children playing in same-gender play groups engaged in more gender-typed toy play (Fabes, Martin, & Hanish, 2003; Martin et al., 2013). Conversely, children playing in mixed-gender peer groups increased their gender-neutral play (Goble, Martin, Hanish, & Fabes, 2012). In addition, because their play is gender segregated and gender specific, children are restricted to only play with the toys with which their same-gender peers are also playing. In other words, similarly to how parents limit children's access to only gender-typed toys, peers limit children's access to only gender-typed toys because that is what is available and what is being used within their heavily gender-segregated play group.

Peers also enforce gender-typed toy play by rewarding gender-typed behaviors and punishing cross-typed behaviors. For instance, Langlois and Downs (1980) found that peers were even more likely than parents to punish cross-typed toy choices, often ignoring or avoiding the child who played with a cross-typed toy. In contrast, children who played with gender-typed toys were more likely to be praised by their peers and more likely to be rated as "popular" than less gender-typed children (Lamb & Roopnarine, 1979; Moller, Hymel, & Rubin, 1992). Furthermore, peers' reinforcement impacted children's subsequent behavior, such that children were more likely to play with the gender-typed toy than a cross-typed toy for a longer period of time after reinforcement (Lamb & Roopnarine, 1979).

Peers also play an indirect role in promoting gender-typed toy play because of children's own self-presentation goals. Perhaps because of the rewarding of gender-typed play and punishing of cross-typed play, children are motivated to appear gender typical to their peers, and thus present themselves to others in ways that are consistent with gender stereotype norms. For example, some research has shown that children are more likely to play with gender-typed toys, and less likely to play with a cross-typed toy, when in the presence of an opposite-gender peer than when alone (Serbin, Connor,

Burchardt, & Citron, 1979; Trautner, 1995). Other work has found that preschool-aged boys (who also endorsed the most rigid gender stereotypes) actually engaged in more gender-typed toy play when in front of a same-gender peer audience than when alone (Banerjee & Lintern, 2000). Thus, although research is not completely clear about which type of peer audience is the most influential in shaping children's behavior, it is clear that children, particularly boys who endorse rigid gender stereotypes, exhibit gender-conforming self-presentation goals in front of peers (Banerjee & Lintern, 2000). Because preschool age children are frequently in the presence of peers, this motivation to appear gender typical to others exacerbates and reinforces children's gender-typed toy play.

It is also important to recognize that schools, because they establish the context in which children are most heavily exposed to their peers, are also complicit in socializing children's gender-typed play. For example, preschool classrooms provide gender-typed toys and offer opportunities for play with peers. Thus, the preschool classroom is a prime location for children to be rewarded for gender-typed behaviors and punished for cross-typed behaviors. Furthermore, teachers allow children to segregate themselves by gender. Indeed, research has shown that children are more heavily gender segregated at school than at home (Maccoby, 1988). At home, children play with who is available, regardless of gender; at school, playgroups are heavily divided by gender. Although this division is not mandated by teachers, it is not discouraged either (Leaper, 1994). When teachers encourage playing with other-gender peers, segregation decreases. In one experimental study, when teachers positively reinforced preschool children who were seen playing with other-gender peers, the amount of cross-gender play increased, at least while the reinforcement was in effect (Serbin, Tonick, & Sternglanz, 1977). When the reinforcement stopped, the children returned to their gender-segregated play. This suggests that teachers who are highly motivated to encourage boys and girls to play together can achieve that goal in their classroom.

Taken together, it appears that the role of peers—and schools—in the socializing of gender-typed toy play is both direct and indirect. Because peer groups at schools tend to be largely gender segregated, children's toy preferences also tend to be segregated by gender. Additionally, peers at school reinforce gender-typed behaviors and punish cross-typed behaviors, which shapes both what toys children choose to play with and how long they will play with them. Furthermore, peers serve as a potent model for gender-typed behaviors and individuals are motivated to be perceived as gender typical in front of their peers. Thus, peers create a "gender-segregation cycle," wherein individuals choose peers based on similar gender-typed interests and their own beliefs about how boys and girls should act, which over time leads to increased gender-typed interests and play (Martin, Fabes, Hanish, Leonard, & Dinella, 2011).

THE ROLE OF MEDIA AND ADVERTISING

Finally, in addition to family and peers, media and advertising can influence children's gender-typed toy choices. As Bandura outlined in his social cognitive theory, media is a salient cultural symbol that transmits information about values and appropriate behaviors (Bandura, 1986, 2002). Children learn about the world and model their own thoughts and behaviors after the images they see in media (Bandura, 2002).

The media, particularly television, is a particularly powerful socializer of behavior because children spend so much time watching it, with children aged 2 to 5 years watching as much as 32 hours of television per week (McDonough, 2009). More specifically, there is evidence that television viewing about toys affects children's behavior. Children have been found to request the specific toys that they view on television and are more likely to request brand name toys than generic toys, suggesting that children are paying attention to and want to play with toys that are portrayed in media (Pine & Nash, 2003; Robinson, Saphir, Kraemer, Varady, & Haydel, 2001). Thus, media and advertising can play an important role in shaping children's gender-typed toy choices, largely by modeling behaviors that children then emulate and by showing specific toys that children then request.

As media is a powerful socializer for children's behavior, it is important to examine the exact content of children's media. Numerous studies have robustly documented that most media are gender stereotypical in content. Content analyses reveal that characters in children's cartoon shows, books, video games, websites, and advertisements reflect gender-stereotyped roles (Auster & Mansbach, 2012; Browne, 1998; Diekman & Murnen, 2004; Dietz, 1998; Leaper, Breed, Hoffman, & Perlman, 2002; Lynn, Walsdorf, Hardin, & Hardin, 2002; Thompson & Zerbinos, 1995). Advertisements, in particular, attend to children's gender by using male voiceovers for ads targeting boys and female voiceovers for ads targeting girls (Johnson & Young, 2002; Smith, 1994). Furthermore, children who appear on television are often portrayed as gender stereotypical. For example, girls are more likely to be shown inside, playing cooperatively, or shopping, whereas boys are more likely to be shown engaging in antisocial behaviors, such as stealing and fighting (Larson, 2001; Macklin & Kolbe, 1984; Smith, 1994).

Among all media, toy commercials are especially likely to be gender typed. In the late 1970s, research found that commercials featuring boys were more likely to contain highly active toys than commercials featuring girls (Welch, Huston-Stein, Wright, & Plehal, 1979). Thirty years later, research finds remarkably similar trends, and in some cases suggests that toy marketing has become even more gender stereotypical (Sweet, 2013; see also Chapter 1, this volume). For example, Kahlenberg and Hein (2010) examined the gender composition of children playing with specific toys in commercials on Nickelodeon, a children's television channel. They found that, overall, most commercials featured only boys or only girls, with fewer than one fifth of all analyzed commercials featuring boys and girls playing together (Kahlenberg & Hein, 2010). They also found that dolls were never shown in commercials that included a group of boys, and *no* commercials for action figures and transportation/construction toys featured *any* girls (and commercials featuring sports toys very rarely included girls).

Thus, it appears that media and advertisements are crafted in ways that promote gender-typed toy play among children. Similar to what happens with siblings and peers, gender-typed media portrayals provide models of which toys are appropriate for each gender. Children are then motivated to obtain and play with toys perceived as meant for their gender group. For instance, after viewing gender-typed toy commercials, boys rated female-typed toys as more appropriate for girls than for boys (Klinger, Hamilton, & Cantrell, 2001). Paralleling the research on the influence of family and peers, boys are less flexible in their perceptions of toy appropriateness, rating female-typed toys as more appropriate for girls than did girls (Klinger et al., 2001). This suggests that media, such as commercials, introduce young children to same-gender role models for gender-typed behaviors. In one of the few experimental tests of the influence of media on children's preference for gender-typed toys, Pike and Jennings (2005) found that when children were presented with cross-typed toy commercials (i.e., a boy playing with a feminine toy or a girl playing with a masculine toy), they were more likely to report that the toy was appropriate for *both* boys and girls instead of gender typed. Importantly, children who viewed gender-typed toy commercials reported the toy as being appropriate only for the observed gender (Pike & Jennings, 2005). This is important considering the content analysis showing most toy commercials are heavily gender segregated and gender typed (Kahlenberg & Hein, 2010).

One of the most prevalent ways in which children's media and merchandising is gender typed is in the near-ubiquitous "princess culture" targeting girls (England, Descartes, & Collier-Meek, 2011). Longitudinal research has shown that girls who engage with princess culture (e.g., by watching Disney Princess movies and playing with Disney Princess toys) are more likely to show gender stereotypical behavior and toy play 1 year later than girls who do not engage with princess culture, even controlling for earlier levels of gender stereotypical behavior (Coyne, Linder, Rasmussen, Nelson, & Birkbeck, 2016).

Media can also increase gender-typed toy play indirectly by increasing children's overall gender stereotypes. Children who watch more television have been shown to endorse stronger gender stereotypes (Morgan, 1987; Morgan & Rothschild, 1983). In experimental studies, children who viewed counterstereotypical commercials (e.g., involving a woman as an engineer) endorsed fewer gender stereotypes than children who saw more stereotypical commercials (Pingree, 1978). Thus, children who watch more gender stereotypical media may be engaging in more gender-typed toy play *because* they are becoming more gender stereotypical in general.

CONCLUSION AND FUTURE DIRECTIONS

It is clear that there are multiple environmental and social contributors to the gender differentiation of toy choices. In particular, in the first few years of life, parents play an important role in controlling access to toys, reinforcing gender-typed behavior, and punishing cross-typed behaviors. The composition of the family is also important, as older siblings can both model gender-typed behavior and direct gender-typed play. Peers, particularly in the school context, become an important socializer as children enter preschool and throughout elementary school. Peers shape children's play behaviors because of their high levels of gender segregation, which inherently restricts access to cross-typed toys and fosters gender-specific play styles. Peers also reinforce gender-typed behavior and punish cross-typed behaviors, and children present themselves to their peers in ways that exacerbate gendered norms. While parents, siblings, and peers are socializing children to engage in gender-typed toy play, children are simultaneously affected by media messages. Because media is so gender stereotypical, some toys are portrayed as only for girls and some as only for boys. Children's own gender stereotypes are strengthened, and they are motivated to obtain and play with only the toys depicted as specific to their gender. Although research has clearly shown that environmental and social messages can shape children's toy choices, there are still specific gaps in the field that should be addressed by future research.

Prior research has been limited by focusing primarily on the toy and play choices of preschool-aged children (under the age of 5). This leads to two specific gaps. First, many of the toys aimed at this age group are clearly gender typed, such as dolls and kitchen sets versus trucks and army soldiers. It is unclear how families and peers socialize older children's toy play, when the play is more complex and the toy choices are less clearly gender typed. Although this has yet to be studied, families may also socialize how and when boys and girls play video games, science-based toys, specific types of board games or technological devices such as iPads and smartphones. This is especially important as technological toys are viewed as more appropriate for boys than for girls, and boys engage with technology more so than do girls (Cherney & London, 2006; Francis, 2010). Parents may be more inclined to buy science-based toys for boys than girls, in the same way they are more inclined to buy construction toys for boys. This can in turn reduce girls' preferences for technological toys, and eventually their interest in technology-related career paths (Francis, 2010).

Relatedly, research should specifically examine the influence of gender-typed video games on children's gender stereotypes. For example, video games, especially popular among older children and adolescents, are viewed as more masculine than feminine (Cherney & London, 2006); boys are represented more often than girls as video game characters (Dill & Thill, 2007; Miller & Summers, 2007); and by adolescence, boys spend twice as long playing video games than do girls (Cherney & London, 2006; Greenberg, Sherry, Lachlan, Lucas, & Holmstrom, 2010; Kovess-Masfety et al., 2016). Future research should explore how the content of video games influences children's development.

Second, and related to the call for more research with older children, future research should examine the increasingly important role of peers in shaping older children's and adolescents' behavior. For example, peers continually become more important to children as they move into middle childhood, and may become more influential than parents in impacting gender-typed choices. As children get older, much of their play focuses on video games, often games that are socially connected to their peers via the Internet (i.e., online multiplayer games; Granic, Lobel, & Engels, 2014). In this context, peers have the potential to continue to shape gendered choices, albeit not face-to-face. For example, on many online multiplayer games, players can give virtual rewards to other players whom they like. Adolescents who are engaging in more gender-typical behavior may be rewarded more often than adolescents engaging in less typical behavior. In this way, the same mechanisms that shaped preschool children's choices may also be shaping adolescents' choices (Granic et al., 2014).

Third, there is a need for more cross-cultural research and research with non-White children, as gender-typed toy play reflects culturally held stereotyped beliefs about the abilities and interests of boys and girls. Currently, most research has focused on children in the United States, Australia, or Canada (e.g., Browne, 1998; Goldberg, 1990). Because media can influence children's gender-typed toy preferences by both modeling gender-typed play and impacting children's gender stereotype endorsement, cross-cultural differences in media content may affect children's preference for gender-typed toys. Furthermore, there are cross-cultural differences in parenting practices that may affect children's gender-typed toy preferences. For example, research has shown that Latino families are typically more traditional in socializing gender roles than European American families (Azmitia & Brown, 2000; Baca Zinn & Wells, 2000; Valenzuela, 1999). Thus, future research should examine how children's gender-typed play choices are socialized in cultures that vary in their gender role socialization norms.

Although research has clearly shown that children are impacted by media, and media is heavily gender stereotypical, more experimental research is needed on the role of media. Thus far, researchers have focused nearly exclusively on content analyses of various types of media, finding that nearly all media portrays gender-stereotyped roles. Furthermore, toy advertisements, in particular, portray gender-typed behaviors, which is related to children's preference for gender-typed toys. However, experimental research has mostly focused on children's perception of gender-appropriate play after viewing gender-typed media and not on children's actual toy choices and play. Thus, future research needs to address experimentally whether media affects children's actual toy choices. Furthermore, research needs to address the influence of different types of media such as websites, social media platforms, and various gaming platforms on children's choices.

Gender-typed play in childhood is both the result of and a contributor to the continuation of gender stereotypes. For children, toys are important and valuable assets in their cognitive, social, and intellectual development. However, both environmental and social factors can direct children's toy selections in ways that exacerbate gender stereotypes, thereby limiting children's potential to learn a range of traits and skills. Because skills such as empathy, perspective taking, spatial relations, and gross and fine motor skills should be fostered in all children, toys that foster positive qualities should be available to and encouraged for both boys and girls, regardless of gender.

REFERENCES

Auster, C. J., & Mansbach, C. S. (2012). The gender marketing of toys: An analysis of color and type of toy on the Disney store website. *Sex Roles, 67,* 375–388. http://dx.doi.org/10.1007/s11199-012-0177-8

Azmitia, A., & Brown, J. R. (2000). Latino immigrant parents' beliefs about the "path of life" of their adolescent children. In J. M. Contreras, K. A. Kerns, & A. M. Neal-Barnett (Eds.), *Latino children and families in the United States* (pp. 77–106). Westport, CT: Praeger Press.

Baca Zinn, M., & Wells, B. (2000). Diversity within Latino families: New lessons for family social science. In D. H. Demo, K. R. Allen, & M. A. Fine (Eds.), *Handbook of family diversity* (pp. 252–273). New York, NY: Oxford University Press.

Bandura, A. (1986). *Social foundations of thought and action: A social cognitive theory.* Englewood Cliffs, NJ: Prentice-Hall.

Bandura, A. (2002). Social cognitive theory of mass communication. In J. Bryant & D. Zillmann (Eds.), *Media effects: Advances in theory and research* (2nd ed., pp. 121–153). Mahwah, NJ: Lawrence Erlbaum.

Banerjee, R., & Lintern, V. (2000). Boys will be boys: The effect of social evaluation concerns on gender-typing. *Social Development, 9*, 397–408. http://dx.doi.org/10.1111/1467-9507.00133

Bradley, B. S., & Gobbart, S. K. (1989). Determinants of gender-typed play in toddlers. *The Journal of Genetic Psychology, 150*, 453–455. http://dx.doi.org/10.1080/00221325.1989.9914612

Brenes, M. E., Eisenberg, N., & Helmstadter, G. C. (1985). Sex role development of preschoolers from two-parent and one-parent families. *Merrill–Palmer Quarterly, 31*, 33–46. Retrieved from https://www.jstor.org/stable/23086133

Browne, B. A. (1998). Gender stereotypes in advertising on children's television in the 1990s: A cross-national analysis. *Journal of Advertising, 27*, 83–96. http://dx.doi.org/10.1080/00913367.1998.10673544

Bussey, K., & Perry, D. G. (1982). Same-sex imitation: The avoidance of cross-sex models or the acceptance of same-sex models? *Sex Roles, 8*, 773–784. http://dx.doi.org/10.1007/BF00287572

Cabrera, N., Tamis-LeMonda, C. S., Bradley, R. H., Hofferth, S., & Lamb, M. E. (2000). Fatherhood in the twenty-first century. *Child Development, 71*, 127–136. http://dx.doi.org/10.1111/1467-8624.00126

Caldera, Y. M., Huston, A. C., & O'Brien, M. (1989). Social interactions and play patterns of parents and toddlers with feminine, masculine, and neutral toys. *Child Development, 60*, 70–76. http://dx.doi.org/10.2307/1131072

Campenni, E. C. (1999). Gender stereotyping of children's toys: A comparison of parents and nonparents. *Sex Roles, 40*, 121–138. http://dx.doi.org/10.1023/A:1018886518834

Cherney, I. D., & London, K. (2006). Gender-linked differences in the toys, television shows, computer games, and outdoor activities of 5- to 13-year-old children. *Sex Roles, 54*, 717. http://dx.doi.org/10.1007/s11199-006-9037-8

Coyne, S. M., Linder, J. R., Rasmussen, E. E., Nelson, D. A., & Birkbeck, V. (2016). Pretty as a princess: Longitudinal effects of engagement with Disney princesses on gender stereotypes, body esteem, and prosocial behavior in children. *Child Development, 87*, 1909–1925. http://dx.doi.org/10.1111/cdev.12569

Crawley, S. B., & Sherrod, K. B. (1984). Parent–infant play during the first year of life. *Infant Behavior and Development, 7*, 65–75. http://dx.doi.org/10.1016/S0163-6383(84)80023-5

Diekman, A. B., & Murnen, S. K. (2004). Learning to be little women and little men: The inequitable gender equality of nonsexist children's literature. *Sex Roles, 50*, 373–385. http://dx.doi.org/10.1023/B:SERS.0000018892.26527.ea

Dietz, T. L. (1998). An examination of violence and gender role portrayals in video games: Implications for gender socialization and aggressive behavior. *Sex Roles, 38*, 425–442. http://dx.doi.org/10.1023/A:1018709905920

Dill, K. E., & Thill, K. P. (2007). Video game characters and the socialization of gender roles: Young people's perceptions mirror sexist media depictions. *Sex Roles, 57*, 851–864. http://dx.doi.org/10.1007/s11199-007-9278-1

DiPietro, J. A. (1981). Rough and tumble play: A function of gender. *Developmental Psychology, 17*, 50–58. http://dx.doi.org/10.1037/0012-1649.17.1.50

Eliot, L. (2010). *Pink brain, blue brain: How small differences grow into troublesome gaps—and what we can do about it.* London, England: Oneworld.

England, D. E., Descartes, L., & Collier-Meek, M. A. (2011). Gender role portrayal and the Disney princesses. *Sex Roles, 64*, 555–567. http://dx.doi.org/10.1007/s11199-011-9930-7

Etaugh, C., & Liss, M. B. (1992). Home, school, and playroom: Training grounds for adult gender roles. *Sex Roles, 26*, 129–147. http://dx.doi.org/10.1007/BF00289754

Fabes, R. A., Martin, C. L., & Hanish, L. D. (2003). Young children's play qualities in same-, other-, and mixed-sex peer groups. *Child Development, 74*, 921–932. http://dx.doi.org/10.1111/1467-8624.00576

Fisher-Thompson, D. (1990). Adult sex typing of children's toys. *Sex Roles, 23*, 291–303. http://dx.doi.org/10.1007/BF00290050

Fisher-Thompson, D. (1993). Adult toy purchases for children: Factors affecting sex-typed toy selection. *Journal of Applied Developmental Psychology, 14*, 385–406. http://dx.doi.org/10.1016/0193-3973(93)90016-O

Francis, B. (2010). Gender, toys and learning. *Oxford Review of Education, 36*, 325–344. http://dx.doi.org/10.1080/03054981003732278

Freeman, N. K. (2007). Preschoolers' perceptions of gender appropriate toys and their parents' beliefs about genderized behaviors: Miscommunication, mixed messages, or hidden truths? *Early Childhood Education Journal, 34*, 357–366. http://dx.doi.org/10.1007/s10643-006-0123-x

Goble, P., Martin, C. L., Hanish, L. D., & Fabes, R. A. (2012). Children's gender-typed activity choices across preschool social contexts. *Sex Roles, 67*, 435–451. http://dx.doi.org/10.1007/s11199-012-0176-9

Goldberg, A. E., Kashy, D. A., & Smith, J. Z. (2012). Gender-typed play behavior in early childhood: Adopted children with lesbian, gay, and heterosexual parents. *Sex Roles, 67*, 503–515. http://dx.doi.org/10.1007/s11199-012-0198-3

Goldberg, M. E. (1990). A quasi-experiment assessing the effectiveness of TV advertising directed to children. *Journal of Marketing Research, 27*, 445–454. http://dx.doi.org/10.2307/3172629

Granic, I., Lobel, A., & Engels, R. C. (2014). The benefits of playing video games. *American Psychologist, 69*, 66–78. http://dx.doi.org/10.1037/a0034857

Greenberg, B. S., Sherry, J., Lachlan, K., Lucas, K., & Holmstrom, A. (2010). Orientations to video games among gender and age groups. *Simulation & Gaming, 41*, 238–259. http://dx.doi.org/10.1177/1046878108319930

Halim, M. L., Ruble, D., Tamis-LeMonda, C., & Shrout, P. E. (2013). Rigidity in gender-typed behaviors in early childhood: A longitudinal study of ethnic minority children. *Child Development, 84*, 1269–1284. http://dx.doi.org/10.1111/cdev.12057

Hupp, J. M., Smith, J. L., Coleman, J. M., & Brunell, A. B. (2010). That's a boy's toy: Gender-typed knowledge in toddlers as a function of mother's marital status. *The Journal of Genetic Psychology, 171*, 389–401. http://dx.doi.org/10.1080/00221325.2010.500637

Jacklin, C. N., DiPietro, J. A., & Maccoby, E. E. (1984). Sex-typing behavior and sex-typing pressure in child/parent interaction. *Archives of Sexual Behavior, 13*, 413–425. http://dx.doi.org/10.1007/BF01541427

Johnson, F., & Young, K. (2002). Gendered voices in children's television advertising. *Critical Studies in Media Communication, 19*, 461–480. http://dx.doi.org/10.1080/07393180216572

Kahlenberg, S. G., & Hein, M. M. (2010). Progression on Nickelodeon? Gender-role stereotypes in toy commercials. *Sex Roles, 62*, 830–847. http://dx.doi.org/10.1007/s11199-009-9653-1

Klinger, L. J., Hamilton, J. A., & Cantrell, P. J. (2001). Children's perceptions of aggressive and gender-specific content in toy commercials. *Social Behavior and Personality: An International Journal, 29*, 11–20. http://dx.doi.org/10.2224/sbp.2001.29.1.11

Kovess-Masfety, V., Keyes, K., Hamilton, A., Hanson, G., Bitfoi, A., Golitz, D., . . . Pez, O. (2016). Is time spent playing video games associated with mental health, cognitive and social skills in young children? *Social Psychiatry and Psychiatric Epidemiology, 51*, 349–357. http://dx.doi.org/10.1007/s00127-016-1179-6

Lamb, M. E., Easterbrooks, M. A., & Holden, G. W. (1980). Reinforcement and punishment among preschoolers: Characteristics, effects, and correlates. *Child Development, 51*, 1230–1236. http://dx.doi.org/10.2307/1129565

Lamb, M. E., & Roopnarine, J. L. (1979). Peer influences on sex-role development in preschoolers. *Child Development, 50*, 1219–1222. http://dx.doi.org/10.2307/1129353

Langlois, J. H., & Downs, C. A. (1980). Mothers, fathers, and peers as socialization agents of sex-typed play behavior in young children. *Child Development, 51*, 1237–1247. http://dx.doi.org/10.2307/1129566

Larson, M. S. (2001). Interactions, activities, and gender in children's television commercials: A content analysis. *Journal of Broadcasting & Electronic Media, 45*, 41–56. http://dx.doi.org/10.1207/s15506878jobem4501_4

Leaper, C. (Ed.). (1994). *Childhood gender segregation: Causes and consequences.* (New directions for child development, No. 65). San Francisco, CA: Jossey-Bass.

Leaper, C. (2000). Gender, affiliation, assertion, and the interactive context of parent–child play. *Developmental Psychology, 36*, 381–393. http://dx.doi.org/10.1037/0012-1649.36.3.381

Leaper, C., Breed, L., Hoffman, L., & Perlman, C. A. (2002). Variations in the gender-stereotyped content of children's television cartoons across genre. *Journal of Applied Social Psychology, 32*, 1653–1662. http://dx.doi.org/10.1111/j.1559-1816.2002.tb02767.x

Leaper, C., & Friedman, C. K. (2007). The socialization of gender. In J. E. Grusec & P. D. Hastings (Eds.), *Handbook of socialization: Theory and research* (pp. 561–587). New York, NY: Guilford Press.

Leavell, A. S., Tamis-LeMonda, C. S., Ruble, D. N., Zosuls, K. M., & Cabrera, N. J. (2012). African American, White, and Latino fathers' activities with their sons and daughters in early childhood. *Sex Roles, 66*, 53–65. http://dx.doi.org/10.1007/s11199-011-0080-8

Lynn, S., Walsdorf, K., Hardin, M., & Hardin, B. (2002). Selling girls short: Advertising and gender images in *Sports Illustrated for Kids*. *Women in Sport and Physical Activity Journal, 11*, 77–100. http://dx.doi.org/10.1123/wspaj.11.2.77

Lytton, H., & Romney, D. M. (1991). Parents' differential socialization of boys and girls: A meta-analysis. *Psychological Bulletin, 109*, 267–296. http://dx.doi.org/10.1037/0033-2909.109.2.267

Maccoby, E. E. (1988). Gender as a social category. *Developmental Psychology, 24*, 755–765. http://dx.doi.org/10.1037/0012-1649.24.6.755

Maccoby, E. E. (1990). Gender and relationships. A developmental account. *American Psychologist, 45*, 513–520. http://dx.doi.org/10.1037/0003-066X.45.4.513

Macklin, M. C., & Kolbe, R. H. (1984). Sex role stereotyping in children's advertising: Current and past trends. *Journal of Advertising, 13*, 34–42. http://dx.doi.org/10.1080/00913367.1984.10672885

Martin, C. L., & Fabes, R. A. (2001). The stability and consequences of young children's same-sex peer interactions. *Developmental Psychology, 37*, 431–446. http://dx.doi.org/10.1037/0012-1649.37.3.431

Martin, C. L., Fabes, R. A., Hanish, L., Leonard, S., & Dinella, L. M. (2011). Experienced and expected similarity to same-gender peers: Moving toward a comprehensive model of gender segregation. *Sex Roles, 65*, 421–434. http://dx.doi.org/10.1007/s11199-011-0029-y

Martin, C. L., Kornienko, O., Schaefer, D. R., Hanish, L. D., Fabes, R. A., & Goble, P. (2013). The role of sex of peers and gender-typed activities in young children's peer affiliative networks: A longitudinal analysis of selection and influence. *Child Development, 84*, 921–937. http://dx.doi.org/10.1111/cdev.12032

McDonough, P. (2009, October 26). *TV viewing among kids at an eight-year high*. Retrieved from http://www.nielsen.com/us/en/insights/news/2009/tv-viewing-among-kids-at-an-eight-year-high.html

McHale, S. M., Crouter, A. C., & Whiteman, S. D. (2003). The family contexts of gender development in childhood and adolescence. *Social Development, 12*, 125–148. http://dx.doi.org/10.1111/1467-9507.00225

Miller, M. K., & Summers, A. (2007). Gender differences in video game characters' roles, appearances, and attire as portrayed in video game magazines. *Sex Roles, 57*, 733–742. http://dx.doi.org/10.1007/s11199-007-9307-0

Moller, L. C., Hymel, S., & Rubin, K. H. (1992). Sex typing in play and popularity in middle childhood. *Sex Roles, 26*, 331–353. http://dx.doi.org/10.1007/BF00289916

Morgan, M. (1987). Television, sex-role attitudes, and sex-role behavior. *The Journal of Early Adolescence, 7,* 269–282. http://dx.doi.org/10.1177/0272431687073004

Morgan, M., & Rothschild, N. (1983). Impact of the new television technology: Cable TV, peers, and sex-role cultivation in the electronic environment. *Youth & Society, 15,* 33–50. http://dx.doi.org/10.1177/0044118X83015001003

O'Brien, M., & Huston, A. C. (1985). Development of sex-typed play behavior in toddlers. *Developmental Psychology, 21,* 866–871. http://dx.doi.org/10.1037/0012-1649.21.5.866

Peretti, P. O., & Sydney, T. M. (1984). Parental toy choice stereotyping and its effects on child toy preference and sex-role typing. *Social Behavior and Personality: An International Journal, 12,* 213–216. http://dx.doi.org/10.2224/sbp.1984.12.2.213

Pike, J. J., & Jennings, N. A. (2005). The effects of commercials on children's perceptions of gender appropriate toy use. *Sex Roles, 52,* 83–91. http://dx.doi.org/10.1007/s11199-005-1195-6

Pine, K. J., & Nash, A. (2003). Barbie or Betty? Preschool children's preference for branded products and evidence for gender-linked differences [Abstract]. *Journal of Developmental and Behavioral Pediatrics, 24,* 219–224. http://dx.doi.org/10.1097/00004703-200308000-00001

Pingree, S. (1978). The effects of nonsexist television commercials and perceptions of reality on children's attitudes about women. *Psychology of Women Quarterly, 2,* 262–277. http://dx.doi.org/10.1111/j.1471-6402.1978.tb00507.x

Pomerleau, A., Bolduc, D., Malcuit, G., & Cossette, L. (1990). Pink or blue: Environmental gender stereotypes in the first two years of life. *Sex Roles, 22,* 359–367. http://dx.doi.org/10.1007/BF00288339

Powlishta, K. K., Serbin, L. A., & Moller, L. C. (1993). The stability of individual differences in gender typing: Implications for understanding gender segregation. *Sex Roles, 29,* 723–737. http://dx.doi.org/10.1007/BF00289214

Raag, T., & Rackliff, C. L. (1998). Preschoolers' awareness of social expectation of gender: Relationships to toy choices. *Sex Roles, 38,* 685–700. http://dx.doi.org/10.1023/A:1018890728636

Rheingold, H. L., & Cook, K. V. (1975). The content of boys' and girls' rooms as an index of parents' behavior. *Child Development, 46,* 459–463. http://dx.doi.org/10.2307/1128142

Robinson, C. C., & Morris, J. T. (1986). The gender-stereotyped nature of Christmas toys received by 36-, 48-, and 60-month-old children: A comparison between nonrequested vs requested toys. *Sex Roles, 15,* 21–32. http://dx.doi.org/10.1007/BF00287529

Robinson, T. N., Saphir, M. N., Kraemer, H. C., Varady, A., & Haydel, K. F. (2001). Effects of reducing television viewing on children's requests for toys: A randomized controlled trial. *Journal of Developmental and Behavioral Pediatrics, 22,* 179–184. Retrieved from http://journals.lww.com/jrnldbp/Abstract/2001/06000/Effects_of_Reducing_Television_Viewing_on.5.aspx

Rubinstein, E. (1978). Television and the young viewer. *American Scientist, 66*, 685–693. Retrieved from http://www.jstor.org/stable/27848957?seq=1#page_scan_tab_contents

Rust, J., Golombok, S., Hines, M., Johnston, K., Golding, J., & the ALSPAC Study Team. (2000). The role of brothers and sisters in the gender development of preschool children. *Journal of Experimental Child Psychology, 77*, 292–303. http://dx.doi.org/10.1006/jecp.2000.2596

Seavey, C. A., Katz, P. A., & Zalk, S. R. (1975). Baby X: The effect of gender labels on adult responses to infants. *Sex Roles, 1*, 103–109. http://dx.doi.org/10.1007/BF00288004

Serbin, L. A., & Connor, J. M. (1979). Sex-typing of children's play preferences and patterns of cognitive performance. *The Journal of Genetic Psychology, 134*, 315–316. http://dx.doi.org/10.1080/00221325.1979.10534065

Serbin, L. A., Connor, J. M., Burchardt, C. J., & Citron, C. C. (1979). Effects of peer presence on sex-typing of children's play behavior. *Journal of Experimental Child Psychology, 27*, 303–309. http://dx.doi.org/10.1016/0022-0965(79)90050-X

Serbin, L. A., Tonick, I. J., & Sternglanz, S. H. (1977). Shaping cooperative cross-sex play. *Child Development, 48*, 924–929. http://dx.doi.org/10.2307/1128342

Smith, L. J. (1994). A content analysis of gender differences in children's advertising. *Journal of Broadcasting & Electronic Media, 38*, 323–337. http://dx.doi.org/10.1080/08838159409364268

Stoneman, Z., Brody, G. H., & MacKinnon, C. E. (1986). Same-sex and cross-sex siblings: Activity choices, roles, behavior, and gender stereotypes. *Sex Roles, 15*, 495–511. http://dx.doi.org/10.1007/BF00288227

Sweet, E. V. (2013). *Boy builders and pink princesses: Gender, toys, and inequality over the twentieth century* (Doctoral dissertation). Retrieved from ProQuest Dissertations and Theses. (Accession No. 3614279)

Thompson, T. L., & Zerbinos, E. (1995). Gender roles in animated cartoons: Has the picture changed in 20 years? *Sex Roles, 32*, 651–673. http://dx.doi.org/10.1007/BF01544217

Trautner, H. M. (1995). Boys' and girls' play behavior in same-sex and opposite-sex pairs. *The Journal of Genetic Psychology, 156*, 5–15. http://dx.doi.org/10.1080/00221325.1995.9914801

Trawick-Smith, J., Russell, H., & Swaminathan, S. (2011). Measuring the effects of toys on the problem-solving, creative, and social behaviors of preschool children. *Early Child Development and Care, 181*, 909–927. http://dx.doi.org/10.1080/03004430.2010.503892

Valenzuela, A., Jr. (1999). Gender roles and settlement activities among children and their immigrant families. *American Behavioral Scientist, 42*, 720–742. http://dx.doi.org/10.1177/0002764299042004009

Vygotsky, L. S. (1967). Play and its role in the mental development of the child. *Soviet Psychology, 5*, 6–18. http://dx.doi.org/10.2753/RPO1061-040505036

Weisgram, E. S. (2016). The cognitive construction of gender stereotypes: Evidence for the dual pathways model of gender differentiation. *Sex Roles, 75,* 301–313. http://dx.doi.org/10.1007/s11199-016-0624-z

Welch, R. L., Huston-Stein, A., Wright, J. C., & Plehal, R. (1979). Subtle sex-role cues in children's commercials. *Journal of Communication, 29,* 202–209. http://dx.doi.org/10.1111/j.1460-2466.1979.tb01733.x

Wood, E., Desmarais, S., & Gugula, S. (2002). The impact of parenting experience on gender stereotyped toy play of children. *Sex Roles, 47,* 39–49. http://dx.doi.org/10.1023/A:1020679619728

7

COGNITIVE PERSPECTIVES ON CHILDREN'S TOY CHOICES

CAROL LYNN MARTIN AND RACHEL E. COOK

For Christmas several years ago, the presents one author (Carol Lynn Martin) of this chapter gave to her 3-year-old friend Rachel represented a range of gendered options—a dashboard of a car, complete with a key that turned, windshield wipers, horn, and steering wheel; and a flying "fairy" doll. Rachel burst into tears when she opened the box holding the car dashboard. Her strong reaction was surprising. She did not want to play with the car, and she did not like it. When asked, Rachel did not believe that this car dashboard could be considered a "girl toy" even though she was told that it was a favorite toy of Carol's when she was a child. Gendered associations such as these are made salient through explicit verbal labels and the colors associated with toys, and these gendered associations can influence children's play preferences. Questions remain, however, about why some children rely so strongly on these associations and why they influence their interactions

http://dx.doi.org/10.1037/0000077-008
Gender Typing of Children's Toys: How Early Play Experiences Impact Development, E. S. Weisgram and L. M. Dinella (Editors)

with toys and activities. The questions we address in this chapter concern the cognitive processes that influence the development of these gendered links and how these cognitive processes motivate children's engagement with certain toys and activities while reducing motivation and contact with toys or activities believed to be for the other gender (e.g., the car dashboard). Although short-term consequences may not seem important, children's motivation to avoid activities such as science projects, building blocks, or math, for instance, may have far-reaching and negative impacts on their skill development, as well as their educational and occupational trajectories and success (see Chapters 9, 10, and 11, this volume).

In this chapter, we focus on a set of theories that describe children as actively constructing and making sense of their worlds—theories we label as *cognitive approaches to gender development*. Most theories of gender development now include consideration of cognitive factors; however, we concentrate on those that have historically emphasized the active role of the child and those that have sparked most of the research on toys and activities. We begin with a review of the common features of these theories, including a brief historical review, and discuss why these theories have been heuristic in formulating research on toys and activities. Next, we review the relevant features of each theory and discuss the evidence concerning toys and activities that derived from research conducted to test each of these theories. For each theory, we review what is known and what questions require more research attention. Finally, we discuss more general issues and future directions for researchers interested in cognitive perspectives on gender development.

FEATURES OF COGNITIVE PERSPECTIVES ON GENDER DEVELOPMENT

Cognitive perspectives initially emerged within a research environment largely dominated by learning theories. In the field of gender development, the learning perspective focused attention on parents and the social environment, with the assumption that information was passively absorbed by children (Mischel, 1966). The learning perspective assumes that gendered associations with toys are due only to the observed pairings of gender with each toy. The cognitive perspective laid out initially by Kohlberg (1966) assumed that children actively process information rather than passively absorbing it; however, it specifies that children do not take an active role in learning gender associations until they have a firm understanding of the stability and constancy of gender over time and situation (i.e., "I'm a girl now and will stay that way even when I grow up," "I'm a girl even if I play with boys' toys"; e.g., Slaby & Frey, 1975). This means that once children have developed this firm understanding of gender being stable and unchanging, they become active in exploring the gendered associations between people and toys and activities rather than merely observing these associations.

This perspective was given new direction by gender schema theories (GSTs; Bem, 1981; Martin & Halverson, 1981) and was supported by early research on gender schemas (Liben & Signorella, 1980). In GST, contrary to Kohlberg's (1966) view, even very young children with only the most basic understanding of gender (i.e., "I'm a girl") attend to gender associations as they try to make sense of their own identity as a girl or boy. These early perspectives were successful and contributed to the cognitive revolution within psychology. Although Kohlberg's cognitive–developmental theory (CDT) and Martin and Halverson's (1981) GST had somewhat differing views on how gender understanding plays a role in gender development, they shared the view that children were self-socializers of gender; that is, they are actively involved in learning and processing gender-related information from their social worlds. In essence, children act as gender detectives whose goal is to search out information and learn about gender, especially their own gender (Martin & Ruble, 2004). Given the preponderance of gendered cues in the social environment, they have a vast array of "data" to which they can attend. However, not all schemas conform to the social environment. Children will also construct illusory associations where they generalize too broadly (e.g., mom likes tea, so all girls like tea) or they may distort information to better fit their schemas (Martin & Halverson, 1983).

By acting as detectives, over time, children form stereotypic associations between gender and toys. These gendered associations are essential features of cognitive perspectives. Each perspective shares the idea that these gender cognitions provide guidance to children about toys, activities, roles, occupations, and behaviors that they might like. How and why these cognitions mediate behavior varies across theories. For instance, one motivating force may be an assumption of shared interests within gender—that is, children may believe that same-gender peers liked those toys because of an underlying common essence. These abstract "gender theories" held by children (Gelman, Collman, & Maccoby, 1986; Martin, Eisenbud, & Rose, 1995; Taylor & Gelman, 1993) provide a way to make assumptions and best guesses when confronted with unfamiliar situations or activities as well as providing guidance in more familiar situations.

Of course, not all children are highly motivated detectives, and not all children share the same degree of gendered associations with toys and activities. Although Kohlberg (1966) did not focus attention on these individual differences, each of the other cognitive perspectives acknowledges that children differ in the salience and strength of gender cognitions. For instance, Martin and Halverson (1981) discussed that gender may be more salient for certain individuals, which would then influence the likelihood that gender-related processing would be used. Bem (1981) proposed that some individuals are gender *aschematic*, meaning that they do not see the world through a gendered lens (Bem, 1993). Also, later research (in particular, the dual pathways model; Liben & Bigler, 2002; Martin & Dinella, 2012; Martin et al., 1995) focused on individual differences in schematicity and provided explanations of when children's own preferences may disrupt gendered associations and increase recognition of exceptions to stereotypes. Later research provided additional elaboration about how social categories become salient thereby leading to stereotyping. For example, developmental intergroup theory (DIT) focuses on the factors that lead to category salience, such as explicit labeling of gender and perceptual discriminability of a category (Bigler & Liben, 2006, 2007).

COGNITIVE PERSPECTIVES ON HOW GENDER COGNITIONS INFLUENCE BEHAVIOR

Cognitive–Developmental Theory

One of the earliest cognitive perspectives on gender was proposed by Kohlberg (1966). In contrast to the strong social learning views of the times (Mischel, 1966), Kohlberg proposed a CDT of gender in which children were seen to take an active role in becoming gendered through what was described as a self-socialization process. Upon mastering an understanding of gender—the stability of gender over time and its consistency across situations—children use gender categories to motivate learning of behaviors related to their gender. Kohlberg outlined three stages of gender development through which children progress to achieve a sophisticated understanding of gender identity. First, children learn about gender identity, or about the existence of gender categories. Here they begin to label themselves according to the gender they believe or feel they are ("I'm a girl"). Around ages 3 to 4, they learn about gender stability—that these gender categories remain stable over time, and apply this to themselves ("I was a girl baby and will stay a girl"). Around the ages of 4 to 6, guided by Piaget's principle of conservation, children learn about gender consistency: An individual's gender remains the same regardless of clothing or situation ("I am a girl even when I play with trucks"; although these ages are controversial and depend on measurement strategy; see Slaby & Frey, 1975).

Kohlberg (1966) proposed that children's gender cognitions guide their attitudes and behaviors regarding gender roles, interests, and preferences. However, he made no specific predictions about children's differential gender-typed preferences after attaining gender identity, stability, and consistency. Regardless, many empirical studies that have used this theoretical framework have been based on the assumption that, as children's understanding of gender becomes more sophisticated, they correspondingly become more focused on gaining additional gender knowledge (e.g., learning more stereotypes). That is, studies have focused on assessing how roles of stability and consistency of understanding of gender influence development and how increasing levels of understanding of gender relate to changes in behavior (e.g., Ruble, Balaban, & Cooper, 1981). Newer formulations of the theory suggest that increased understanding gender is associated with increases in responsiveness to gender cues within the environment (Stangor & Ruble, 1987; 1989; Warin, 2000) and that the influence of understanding gender is particularly evident when toy attractiveness and gender typing are in conflict (Frey & Ruble, 1992). For instance, children with more sophisticated gender understanding should be more likely to select unattractive but gender-typed toys over highly attractive countertypical toys, and evidence is suggestive of this pattern (Frey & Ruble, 1992).

Cognitive Developmental Theory and Toy Choices

Researchers who have tested CDT in relation to children's toy choices have found mixed results regarding its utility. The most consistent finding is that gender category knowledge, or basic knowledge of gender identity, is related to gender-typed preferences in activities and peers (Fagot, 1985; Fagot & Leinbach, 1989; see also evidence presented in the section on GST). However, the relation of gender stability and consistency to preferences is less clear and may depend on methods used to test preferences (e.g., is there a conflict situation?; for reviews, see Martin, Ruble, & Szkrybalo, 2002; Ruble & Martin, 1998; Szkrybalo, 1998). Some studies show that gender-typed preferences increase with levels of gender constancy (Ruble et al., 1981; Slaby & Frey, 1975), and some show correlations between stability and toy preferences (Martin & Little, 1990; Ruble et al., 2007), whereas others show no relation (Emmerich & Shepard, 1984; Fagot, 1985; Marcus & Overton, 1978) or that gender constancy is associated with a decrease in gender typing (Smetana & Letourneau, 1984; Urberg, 1982; Yee & Brown, 1994). Thus, CDT may not provide the clearest framework for predicting differential toy preferences.

Issues and Future Directions

Kohlberg's (1966) CDT had the honor of being the first theory of gender development to emphasize cognitions; as such, it was the first to highlight children's active role in developing gender-typed preferences—that is, self-socialization of gender roles. Thus, a central contribution of this theory was the notion that children's cognitive structures are gendered and that this directs their interests and behaviors.

Despite the groundbreaking novel view of children as self-socializers of gender, the conceptualization that Kohlberg (1966) described needs revisiting. Given the increasing visibility of transgender and gender-fluid individuals, additional research on how people conceptualize gender would be interesting to conduct. Issues that continue to be unsettled in CDT include the motivational process by which progression through the three stages of gender development would influence children's gender-related attitudes and behavior (Szkrybalo, 1998). Kohlberg mentioned a few potential possibilities. He emphasized children's need to develop competence in their gender role; by adopting the appropriate behaviors for their gender, children might attain this competence. Kohlberg also highlighted the need to conform to one's gender role to maintain a positive self-image. Thus, children might select gender-appropriate toys to improve their self-evaluations. Furthermore, the research findings also seemed to suggest that not all stages of gender understanding were motivational. Specifically, identity and stability related to gender-typed preferences more often and more clearly than did gender consistency. This gender pattern suggested that perhaps a sophisticated understanding of gender is not necessary for it to affect children's toy choices; instead, children need only basic categorical cognitive structures to organize gender-related knowledge and motivate behavior. This is the principle on which GST was based.

Gender Schema Theories

In the early 1980s, several GSTs (Bem, 1981; Liben & Signorella, 1980; Martin & Halverson, 1981) emerged on the scene at about the same time. Because the Martin and Halverson (1981) version of GST focused on developmental issues and specifically on toy preferences, we use that theory as a basis for reviewing the literature on how GST relates to toy preferences. The Martin and Halverson GST approach has been tested by many researchers (see below) and has been elaborated upon in more recent versions of the theory (e.g., Martin, 1991, 1994, 2000). Here, we focus attention on the essential features of the theory as they relate to children's toy choices.

GST is based on the idea that children develop gender schemas and that these schemas guide and motivate attention, behavior, and memory once children identify with a gender group (Martin & Halverson, 1981). That is, only basic information about gender identity is needed for schemas to serve a motivational function, such as increasing attention to, and interest in, some toys and decreasing attention to and interest in other toys. Gender schemas motivate behavior because children want to learn about themselves and others like themselves; thus, children are motivated to learn about toys appropriate for their gender.

In addition, gendered toy choice is motivated by an assumption of shared similarities within each gender group. Just as cognitive scientists have proposed that children develop theories about naive psychology that provides them with testable but imperfect ideas about the nature of humans in social situations (Keil, 1989, 2010), children appear to develop "gender theories" that provide testable ideas about the nature of males and females. Martin and colleagues (Martin, 2000; Martin et al., 1995) proposed these gender theories as very general, abstract theories about the genders that promote the use of gender schemas. The conceptual coherence to each category is presumed based on the idea that category members (e.g., females) share deeper properties or essences because they share a category label (e.g., Gelman, 1989; Gelman et al., 1986). At their simplest, children may form a "within-group similarity" theory and a "between-groups differences" theory, and these theories provide additional information about gender categories, which in turn influences their behavior (see the section on gender theories). For instance, a girl on a playground may reason, "There's a girl playing hopscotch. We probably would like the same activities so I should try hopscotch." Thus, GST proposes that a child's basic gender identity, combined with gender theories of shared similarities within gender categories, motivates behaviors such as toy choices.

In the next section, we discuss two types of schemas and how they influence exploration of toys. Next, we consider how schemas influence memory for toy names, gender typing of toys (e.g., their labels), and in-depth information about toys. Then, we address the role of gender similarity and gender theories in children's preferences. Next, we consider how personal preferences and individual differences relate to toy choices. Finally, the issues and future directions for GST research are considered.

Types of Schemas and Motivation to Explore Toys

Martin and Halverson (1981) described two types of schemas: a *superordinate* schema and an *own-sex* schema. The superordinate schema consists of associations between gender and activities, toys, behaviors, traits, and roles (e.g., boys like trucks, girls like dolls). The own-sex schema contains plans of action to help individuals know how to engage with the toys or activities associated with their own sex (e.g., for girls, the own-sex schema may contain a script for the roles that various characters like mom, dad, children might take in "playing house"; Martin & Halverson, 1981). The superordinate schema provides gender-typed labels about what is considered "for me" versus "not for me," which can act as a standard for behavior ("I'm a girl, so I will probably like playing with dolls"). As a result, both types of schemas direct and motivate children's engagement with toys. The superordinate schema provides information about whether a toy is worth approaching ("toys for me") or avoiding ("toys not for me"), and the own-sex schema provides information about how to engage with the toy or activity. In both cases, the assumption is that children are acting to conform to the schemas they hold (also called "schematic consistency").

Even if children like a particular toy or activity, if it becomes associated with the other gender, children may lose interest in it, something Martin et al. (1995) called the "hot potato" effect. They found that 3- to 6-year-old children (Study 3) actively avoided a very attractive toy they previously found interesting when it was given a gender-typed label that it was a toy that other gender children really like. This effect was apparent only for children who remembered the gender-typed labels, which provides support for the idea that children's behavior is guided by toys' labels. The implications of the hot potato effect are that once children or adolescents come to believe that a toy or even an academic subject is "for the other gender," their interest in it likely will drop.

Schemas Direct Memory

Using GST, one can hypothesize that children show strong memory for gender-typed labels associated with toys and increased interest in toys presumed to be own-gender relevant (i.e., "for me"). A few early studies provided provocative evidence in support of these ideas using familiar objects and games (Montemayor, 1974; Stein, Pohly, & Mueller, 1971). However, using familiar toys was a problem because of potential reinforcement histories with these toys. To avoid issues with familiar toys, many studies have been conducted with novel objects/toys (i.e., that children have no prior knowledge of or exposure to) in which gender-typed labels have been given to the toys (e.g., "this is a toy that boys like"). In these experimental studies, the toys given each type of label are counterbalanced so that the particular features of the toys are not used by children to make decisions about whether they would like them (e.g., toy X is labeled as a toy that girls like for some participants and labeled as a toy that boys like for other participants). By doing so, exploration of objects, memory for labels, and recall of these gender-labeled toys have been assessed in children without biases of prior exposure or of toy features (e.g., Bradbard & Endsley, 1983; Bradbard, Martin, Endsley, & Halverson, 1986).

Studies that use the novel object/toy procedures provide evidence consistent with GST predictions. Children showed differential memory for toy names, illustrating the use of the own-sex schema; they preferred and remembered more names for same-gender-labeled toys than other-gender-labeled toys, and toys labeled for both genders tended to fall between the two. In addition, recall of the gender label (who the toy is "for") for all the toys provides support for the use of the superordinate schema in processing information. Specifically, in Bradbard and Endsley (1983), children were 80% accurate in remembering toys' gender labels. These labels were powerful: Some children expressed negative responses about getting near the table holding the other-gender toys (e.g., said "yuck"). In another study (Bradbard et al., 1986), differential memory favoring recall of names of own-gender-typed toys was somewhat stronger for younger children (4–5 years old) than for older (6–7 years old) children, and this was especially the case for girls. And similar to the previous study, children showed excellent memory for gender-typed labels, suggesting that they are interested in and attentive to which gender is described as liking the toys more.

Gender-typed labels direct exploration of toys and memory for the names of toys, and the gender typing of toys also directs how much children learn about how to use toys. On the basis of the children's knowledge of the own-sex schema and their accompanying motivation to learn about own-sex information, GST would predict that children would pay more attention when told about how to use own-gender toys than other-gender toys, and that attention would help them to encode and better remember the in-depth information for own-gender toys than for other-gender toys. GST also posits that the lack of in-depth knowledge about how to use other-gender toys might lead to avoidance of playing with those toys.

Results of the Bradbard et al. (1986) study supported GST predictions. Children were given detailed information about how to use novel toys labeled as either for their own gender or the other gender. For instance, to use one of the toys, children had to push a button on it and then pull a string. Children remembered more of this in-depth information about the own-gender toys than the other-gender toys, even when incentivized (by offers of special gifts) if they tried really hard to fully describe all that they remember, including information about the other-gender toys. These findings suggest that children may fail to encode information (i.e., they may not have paid attention to them well enough to learn and remember) about other-gender toys, which can lead to a lack of competence in their use and the avoidance of other-gender toys. That is, as soon as a toy is labeled as being liked by the other gender, children appear to stop paying attention to any further information about the toy. They do not fail to remember or withhold information—they never even learned the information about other-gender toys. This lack of attention to, and failure to, encode other-gender information has implications: If children fail to pay attention when confronted with topics, activities, or academic subjects that they believe to be relevant only to the other gender (e.g., girls not being interested in math), they are limiting their range of knowledge and interests to only those things believed to be own-gender related.

All Girls Are Alike: Assumptions of Gender Similarity

In addition to shaping children's attention and memory, gender schemas can influence children's beliefs about other boys' and girls' interests in toys. Specifically, children appear to develop gender-related beliefs based on the assumption that all girls share some similar essence and all boys share a different essence. These "essentialist" gender theories about similarity within a gender and differences between the genders contribute to the formation of gender schemas. Martin et al. (1995, Studies 1 and 2) tested the use of gender similarity–difference theories by giving children novel toys and asking them how much they liked them. Then they were asked to judge how much other boys and girls might like the toys. If children use an own-gender-similarity theory, then one would expect them to believe that their own gender would share their liking and disliking of toys; if they used an other-gender-dissimilarity theory, then children should expect that the other gender would disagree with their evaluation of the toy. Children showed strong evidence of the own-gender-similarity theory. They thought their own gender would like the toys they liked. Less evidence was found for the other-gender-dissimilarity theory.

Children also use gender theories when making decisions about whether they might be interested in unfamiliar toys and activities based on what they learn when these toys are described as being liked by other girls or boys (Shutts, Banaji, & Spelke, 2010). After viewing a video of Mary who loves playing with "spoodle" versus Kevin who loves playing with "blicket," children were asked which toy girls or boys might select. Based on assumptions of gender similarity, even very young children tend to select objects liked by same-gender peers more than those liked by other-gender peers, suggesting that gender theories play a role in influencing children's preferences.

Personal Preferences and Individual Differences

In most of the studies described above, the focus was on uncovering normative patterns rather than illustrating or defining individual differences in tendencies to use gender schemas. Nonetheless, GST includes consideration of how and why some children and adults may be unlikely to use gender schemas as they process information. For instance, Bem (1974, 1975) described and conducted research on gender aschematic individuals—also called androgynous individuals—who are able to use either masculine or feminine characteristics or behaviors as needed by the situation. Although a few studies tested these ideas in adults (Bem, 1975), measurement of androgyny was controversial and its measurement did not match the proposed construct (see Martin, Cook, & Andrews, 2016). Furthermore, few studies were conducted to explore androgyny in children and its relation to stereotypic toy play. Instead, the focus was on the roles of masculine and feminine personality characteristics as predictors of sex-typed play, and results were mixed (Boldizar, 1991; Silvern & Katz, 1986).

Another approach to understanding individual variation in children has been to conduct research on a subset of girls who are gender nonnormative in their behavior—tomboys. Because GST proposed that cognitions and behavior should be related, if a girl believes that boys play football, cognitive approaches suggest she is unlikely to like football. But tomboys engage in cross-gender activities. Why might tomboys like activities or toys that do not fit their schemas? Do they modify their schemas to make their interests congruent with them, or do they eventually change their behavior to match their schemas? Research described above about how children may use theories of within-gender similarity to contribute information to their gender schemas (see Martin et al., 1995, Studies 1 and 2) suggests that children's own interests influence schemas. However, those studies used novel objects that were not stereotyped by the broader society, whereas tomboys often have interests that are widely believed to be cross-gendered. Does the cultural pressure offset a child's own interest in this case?

To study this question, Martin and Dinella (2012) compared self-identified tomboys' and nontomboys' activity preferences with their stereotypes about activities. Overall, girls exhibited congruence with stereotypes (i.e., they preferred activities stereotyped for their own gender versus for other gender). This activity-preference congruence was much higher for nontomboys (14 times more likely to show congruence with own-gender stereotypes vs. other-gender stereotypes) than for tomboys (4 times more likely). The meaning of this pattern is unclear, but it may suggest that being a tomboy weakens gender schemas; even so, there is some degree of consistency between tomboys' beliefs and their behaviors. The idea that tomboys might hold different gender schemas was also supported by a trend showing that tomboys tend to have more inclusive stereotypes about girls as compared with nontomboys (they thought more activities would be liked by both boys and girls), suggesting some modification of their stereotypes by their interests (see also the section on the dual pathways model; Liben & Bigler, 2002). Thus, it appears that children's interests have potential to modify their schemas.

Issues and Controversies

Several studies have critiqued GST using an argument that the timing of gender-typed interests in children precedes their development of stereotypes or schemas (e.g., Bussey & Bandura, 1999; Campbell, Shirley, & Caygill, 2002). As has been explained elsewhere (Martin et al., 2002), GST allowed for early gender-typed behavior, even before the onset of gender schemas.

These early interests may result from biological influences, such as hormones, or socialization forces, such as parental or peer influences (Martin et al., 2002). The focus of GST is whether gender schemas provide additional motivation for the development of gendered behaviors. Some of the evidence for this is Zosuls et al.'s (2009) findings that gender-typed play increased with the onset of gender labeling in young infants ages 17 to 21 months. Other studies with young preschool-age children show that with increasing understanding of gender, gender-typed interests increase, consistent with GST (e.g., Martin & Little, 1990).

The novel object studies provide evidence that children use gender-typed labels to guide their behavior, to give them insights into which toys they are likely to engage with, play with, and remember information about. But these studies do not identify the cues children use to determine toy preferences when toys are familiar to them. Do children focus on toy-label associations (e.g., trucks are for boys), function-label associations (e.g., things that move are for boys), features of toys such as color or softness (e.g., pink things are for girls), or all of the above?

Weisgram, Fulcher, and Dinella (2014) set out to answer this question. In Study 1, they assessed the roles of multiple cues (toy gender-type and colors) on interest and judgments about toys with preschool-age children. They bought two sets of toys (e.g., jet, tea set) and modified one set of toys by painting them gender-typed or countertyped colors (e.g., pink jet, black-and-blue tea set). Children were presented with all types of toys in both color combinations and were asked to rate interest in the toy, stereotype endorsement, and judgments of others' liking of the toy. Overall, both gender typing of the toy and colors were influential on children's interests. Some gender differences were also found: Pink toys gave girls more permission to play with countergender-typed toys than did black-and-blue–colored feminine toys for boys. Thus, gender typing of toys played a stronger role than did color. In Study 2, the roles of explicit gender labels and color were examined in young children using novel toys. Gender labels influenced both boys' and girls' toy interest, but girls' interest was also influenced by toy color. Once again, pink seemed to give girls permission to play with cross-gender toys. Overall, the results of the study were consistent with expectations from GST and from prior studies showing the power of labels to influence children's toy choices, although this study extends prior work by also demonstrating the effectiveness of colors, especially pink, in influencing interests of girls.

Future Directions

Research on GST could be expanded in several interesting ways. One way is to give more attention to developmental changes in schemas' influence on behavior. More research is needed to explore whether schemas hold stronger power as a motivator at some developmental periods than at others. Another direction is to explore individual differences more fully, including the salience of gender in children's lives. This might require consideration of more nuanced types of gender cognitions as contributors to gender-typed play. For example, most research has considered how own-sex schemas influence behavior, but what if the own-sex schema includes behaviors, activities, or toys that might be typically considered for the other gender?

Researchers might consider asking children more about their "for me" category to discover whether they have this broader own-sex schema. It is also important to discover how counterstereotypic toys can be incorporated into an own-sex schema, so that children attend to, learn about, and remember how to engage with these activities and toys and thus, gain a wider range of cognitive and social benefits from their toy play.

Another interesting expansion of GST would be to consider a wider array of functions of schemas. An important contribution of GST was to outline ways in which gender schemas lead to faulty conclusions and memory distortions. For instance, children tend to distort inconsistent information into information that is consistent with their schemas—they do not remember being shown a picture of a man holding a purse; instead, they remember and are confident that they saw a woman holding the purse (e.g., Martin & Halverson, 1983). Research has not yet addressed how these distortions influence children's toy choices. To the extent that children show this type of bias, one might predict that they would be less interested in cross-gender activities and toys. Furthermore, schemas lead to illusory correlations in which individuals falsely associate two events that happen to co-occur. If children engage in more illusory correlations about who plays with particular toys (i.e., exaggerate the gender-typed correlations), we might expect they would show more gender-typed interests.

In addition, little research has been conducted on the cognitive motivations behind gendered choices in video games, but GST provides a helpful framework for doing so. Because of the gendered content in games and the differential gender representation in game characters, there exist clear cues as to which gender group corresponds to each game (Dietz, 1998; Funk & Buchman, 1996; Greenberg, Sherry, Lachlan, Lucas, & Holmstrom, 2010; Homer, Hayward, Frye, & Plass, 2012; Lucas & Sherry, 2004; Miller & Summers, 2007). Thus, children likely include video games in their own-sex or other-sex schema, instructing them that a particular game is "for" them or "not for" them. Future research should explicitly address whether this pattern generalizes from other toys to video games and the particular aspects of games that contribute to their gender categorization.

Future research should also address the GST proposition that, given children's failure to encode information about other-gender-typed objects, a lack of competence with other-gender toys contributes to their avoidance of other-gender toys. From a social learning perspective, children learn many things, including cross-gender activities, but they withhold performing them because of social sanctions. The GST perspective proposes that increasing cross-gender play requires that children become competent in cross-gender play. This would require children to have exposure to, focus attention on, and be motivated to learn about cross-gender toys and activities. We must discover how to overcome these barriers to broaden children's interests.

Dual Pathways Model

An extension of ideas from GST, the dual pathways model (Liben & Bigler, 2002) provides a description of the ways in which children's understanding of gender norms and stereotypes relate to their own interests and preferences. Via the attitudinal pathway, stereotypes and norms about others' interest in a particular toy affect a child's likelihood to engage with that toy. Conversely, through the personal pathway, a child's preference for a toy influences the stereotypes they form about others' interest. Outcomes of both pathways vary based on the gender schematicity of the child, or the degree to which gender schemas play a role in information processing or decision making. For example, if a child is gender schematic, their knowledge of a toy's stereotypical appropriateness for their gender is likely to affect their interest and engagement with that toy; however, if a child is aschematic, their own interest is likely to drive their engagement with a toy rather than general stereotypes regarding it. In addition, both of these pathways play a role in determining children's gendered toy preferences; each likely influences attitudes and preferences in different situations and at different times.

Dual Pathways to Toy Choice

Empirical evidence supports both of these hypothesized theoretical pathways. For the attitudinal pathway, the studies that support GST provide support for this pathway because both are based on the idea that children's schemas and attitudes influence behavior (see GST for supporting studies and see Liben & Bigler, 2002; Weisgram, 2016). For the personal pathway, if children are interested in a toy, they report that others of the same gender would like that toy and children of the other gender would not (Lam & Leman, 2003; Liben & Bigler, 2002; Martin & Dinella, 2012; Martin et al., 1995; Weisgram, 2016). If toys are labeled for the other gender, children are less likely to engage with them, particularly if the children are gender schematic (attitudinal pathway; Liben & Bigler, 2002; Martin et al., 1995; Weisgram, 2016).

Recent empirical work testing both pathways established the utility of the dual pathways model in influencing children's gendered toy choices (Weisgram, 2016). After being presented with novel toys, children formed stereotypes about the toys that were congruent with their interest in them (illustrating the personal pathway); if children were more interested in a toy, they were more likely to rate it as being appropriate for their own gender (or both boys and girls). The attitudinal pathway was illustrated by children being more interested in novel toys that had been labeled as appropriate for their gender than other-gender-labeled novel toys; this pattern, however, was only present for gender schematic children. Thus, evidence indicates effects from both pathways, with support for the proposed differences based on children's gender schematicity.

Additional work has highlighted the importance of gender schematicity in a dual pathways model for predicting children's toy preferences. In a test of the attitudinal pathway, Coyle and Liben (2016) tested whether high- and low-gender schematic girls' activity interests were differentially affected by attending to feminized (Barbie) and nonfeminized (Jane) video game models. If girls were highly gender schematic, their interests were expected to become more feminine if they observed Barbie because Barbie's feminization would be more salient to highly gender schematic girls. Indeed, after viewing videos of Barbie, gender-schematic girls reported greater overall interest in feminine activities and a greater increase in feminine interests than gender-aschematic girls. In fact, low-gender-schematic girls' feminine activity interest decreased after viewing the Barbie video, indicating an interesting avoidance of own-gender-typed activities for these girls. Thus, the dual pathways model's emphasis on individual differences, especially in gender schematicity, is empirically useful for predicting gendered toy preferences.

Understanding how gender schematicity, interests, and identity relate to behavior is an issue explored in a recent study. Endendijk, Beltz, McHale, Bryk, and Berenbaum (2016) compared interests, identity, and attitudes in girls with more and less severe cases of congenital adrenal hyperplasia (CAH), which results from increased exposure to androgens during prenatal development (see Chapter 5, this volume, for an in-depth description). Girls with the more serious conditions expressed female gender identities but had more interest in masculine activities than did girls with less serious conditions. It is interesting to note that in these naturally occurring cases of androgen exposure that led to increased masculine interests, the girls did not show more egalitarian or flexible attitudes, contrary to what might be expected from the dual pathways personal pathway. Some evidence was found, however, that suggests that gender identity mediated both attitudes and interests and led to some congruence between stereotypes and interests.

The other cognitive theories described in this chapter share similarity with this model's attitudinal pathway in that they highlight the effects of children's understanding of gender on their motivation and behavior. The dual pathways model extends earlier ideas by clearly emphasizing the importance of children's own interests in the development of stereotypes. In addition, this model includes a description of possible variation in the processes based on differences in schematicity and interests. As such, the dual pathways model provides a framework that most explicitly allows for incorporating individual differences into predicting toy choices.

Future directions for the dual pathways model include additional testing of the ways in which each pathway relates to behavior and to stereotype development, which then may either constrain or provide flexibility for an individual's later behavior. Because so much more attention has been given to the attitudinal/GST pathway, researchers interested in promoting flexibility in behavior should continue exploring the personal pathway and how individual differences in toys and activities relate to and can promote changes in children's stereotypes and increases in behavioral flexibility. Questions of how individual differences in schematicity relate to pathways also require further exploration.

Developmental Intergroup Theory

Another cognitive theory that contributes to understanding gendered toy choices is DIT (Bigler & Liben, 2006, 2007). This theory emphasizes that children actively seek and use cues from socializing agents, such as parents, peers, teachers, and the media, to infer the importance of social categories, form cognitive representations of members of important social groups, and associate attributes with these groups. This theory can be broken into three component parts. First, children determine which characteristics of individuals are relevant and should be used to create meaningful cognitive representations of social categories. This is influenced not only by the perceptual discriminability of the characteristic but also by its implicit and explicit use in social interactions. Once meaningful social categories have been identified, children sort individuals into these groups by the dimensions made salient. Then, children develop stereotypes and prejudices regarding the social groups, both by implicit and explicit associations made between group membership and attributes and by tendencies for ingroup bias and essentialism.

Developmental Intergroup Theory and Toy Choices

Because DIT was initially conceptualized to understand the development of children's stereotypes and prejudices about social groups, it is somewhat unclear how its tenets would support specific predictions about children's gendered toy choices. It can be inferred that once stereotypes are developed about social groups and the activities, interests, and objects associated with them, these stereotypes then guide children's behavior. Perhaps the portions of this theory most relevant to gender-typed preferences involve the salience of the category of gender and the perceptual discriminability of the characteristics indicating gender's importance. For example, if children are aware that gender is an important organizing category, cues indicating the appropriateness of toys for one gender (either explicitly by labeling, or implicitly by showing children of one gender playing with the toy or with toys being gender-stereotypical colors) should become influential on children's toy choices. In this way, DIT explains how gender can become an important and salient category by which children's toy and activity choices might be guided.

Indeed, empirical studies that have used this theoretical framework have focused on the fact that some toys are stereotypically associated with one gender and that this motivates children to choose toys that match these associations. For example, Arthur (2008) posited that children develop preferences for toys appropriate for their ingroup, based on characteristics of categories made salient (in this case, gender). However, although gender salience (established by parents' frequent explicit labeling of the category) was related to children's category knowledge and labeling, it did not increase their gender-typed play. Cherney and Dempsey (2010) used DIT to suggest that perhaps characteristics of the toys indicated gender's perceptual salience, which would lead to a clearer distinction of gender-typed toy categories, which would then lead to greater interest in gender-typed toys. Children tended to play with toys they labeled as own-gender typed more than with other-gender toys. When children were asked to explain why they labeled a toy appropriate for one gender, they often mentioned the toy's color, which is a characteristic that has strong associations with gender categories, illustrating its use as a cue for a salient social group. A key component of DIT is that social categories that are made salient are used for categorizing information, to the exclusion of unimportant categories. Toys have multiple characteristics that children could use to determine gender-typed categories for toys, so the fact that children often provide color as an explanation provides support for the DIT idea that perceptual salience enhances gender salience for children.

Issues and Future Directions

Unique contributions of DIT include its focus on contextual influences, including the degree to which gender is salient in the environment and the cues for the salience of gender. In addition, it complements GST by explaining how gender becomes an important dimension along which information is organized. This theory does not focus on toy or activity preferences but gives a broader account of how stereotypes about social groups develop and consequently affect behavior. For that reason, it may not be surprising that the motivational mechanisms connecting the cognitive associations between gender and toys with the preferences or behavioral toy choice remains unclear. However, the theory and related research provide strong evidence for how social information becomes internalized into gender-related cognitions (Bigler & Liben, 2006, 2007).

COGNITIVE PERSPECTIVES: CONCLUSIONS, QUALIFICATIONS, AND CONSIDERATIONS

The major cognitive perspectives reviewed here share similar views about children's roles as active participants in the gender socialization process, as they attend to, interpret, and explore the social world to learn more about their gender. These theories presume that individuals make meaning of the many gendered cues in their social environment, search for covariations or co-occurrences of gender with other cues to add to their lists of gendered associations, and refine and develop gender theories about how girls share similarities to one another and boys to one another. This strong cognitive and interpretive focus does not deny, replace, or preclude the roles of social agents or biological factors (e.g., hormonal, genetic) as contributors to gender development, nor does it deny individual variation in gender salience. Theories must recognize all these sources of influence on gender development (Berenbaum, Blakemore, & Beltz, 2011).

The cognitive processes outlined in this chapter vary across children: Not all show the same strong motivation to adhere to their beliefs about what they consider "appropriate" and what might be fun for them to play with. Having a deeper understanding of how information about gender is processed and how individual variations in gender salience is essential for the development of interventions to promote in children a wider range of interests and activities.

Recent research suggests that understanding where gender identification comes from and how it contributes to these processes is less straightforward than has been imagined (see also the section on CDT and gender constancy). Many socially transitioning transgender children have strong and clear gender identities that do not match their assigned gender, yet these children have toy preferences and show patterns of gendered behavior that differ little from other children of their asserted gender. These findings suggest that asserted identity matters more than assigned identity for these children (Olson, Key, & Eaton, 2015), and in terms of cognitive perspectives, these children appear to hold strong "own-gender" schemas that fit their asserted identities rather than that of their assigned gender. Such findings suggest that what the social world ascribes to a person as their gender identity is not necessarily the identity that motivates their behavior.

Ultimately, cognitive perspectives initially filled a gap by describing what occurred within children's minds as they process information about the social world. Rather than presuming that natal gender is the identity that children will strive to understand, these theories should move toward increasing recognition of the complexities of identity and work to better understand how identity motivates behavior.

REFERENCES

Arthur, A. E. (2008). *Does social categorization affect toddlers' play preferences? An experimental test* (Unpublished doctoral dissertation). The University of Texas at Austin.

Bem, S. L. (1974). The measurement of psychological androgyny. *Journal of Consulting and Clinical Psychology, 42*, 155–162. http://dx.doi.org/10.1037/h0036215

Bem, S. L. (1975). Sex role adaptability: One consequence of psychology androgyny. *Journal of Personality and Social Psychology, 31*, 634–643. http://dx.doi.org/10.1037/h0077098

Bem, S. L. (1981). Gender schema theory: A cognitive account of sex typing. *Psychological Review, 88*, 354–364. http://dx.doi.org/10.1037/0033-295X.88.4.354

Bem, S. L. (1993). *The lenses of gender: Transforming the debate on sexual inequality.* New Haven, CT: Yale University Press.

Berenbaum, S. A., Blakemore, J. E. O., & Beltz, A. M. (2011). A role for biology in gender-related behavior. *Sex Roles, 64*, 804–825. http://dx.doi.org/10.1007/s11199-011-9990-8

Bigler, R. S., & Liben, L. S. (2006). A developmental intergroup theory of social stereotypes and prejudice. In R. V. Kail (Ed.), *Advances in child development and behavior* (Vol. 34, pp. 39–89). San Diego, CA: Elsevier. http://dx.doi.org/10.1016/S0065-2407(06)80004-2

Bigler, R. S., & Liben, L. S. (2007). Developmental intergroup theory: Explaining and reducing children's social stereotyping and prejudice. *Current Directions in Psychological Science, 16*, 162–166. http://dx.doi.org/10.1111/j.1467-8721.2007.00496.x

Boldizar, J. P. (1991). Assessing sex typing and androgyny in children: The Children's Sex Role Inventory. *Developmental Psychology, 27*, 505–515. http://dx.doi.org/10.1037/0012-1649.27.3.505

Bradbard, M. R., & Endsley, R. C. (1983). The effects of sex-typed labeling on preschool children's information-seeking and retention. *Sex Roles, 9*, 247–260. http://dx.doi.org/10.1007/BF00289627

Bradbard, M. R., Martin, C. L., Endsley, R. C., & Halverson, C. F. (1986). Influence of sex stereotypes on children's exploration and memory: A competence versus performance distinction. *Developmental Psychology, 22*, 481–486. http://dx.doi.org/10.1037/0012-1649.22.4.481

Bussey, K., & Bandura, A. (1999). Social cognitive theory of gender development and differentiation. *Psychological Review, 106*, 676–713. http://dx.doi.org/10.1037/0033-295X.106.4.676

Campbell, A., Shirley, L., & Caygill, L. (2002). Sex-typed preferences in three domains: Do two-year-olds need cognitive variables? *British Journal of Psychology, 93*, 203–217. http://dx.doi.org/10.1348/000712602162544

Cherney, I. D., & Dempsey, J. (2010). Young children's classification, stereotyping, and play behavior for gender neutral and ambiguous toys. *Educational Psychology, 30*, 651–669. http://dx.doi.org/10.1080/01443410.2010.498416

Coyle, E. F., & Liben, L. S. (2016). Affecting girls' activity and job interests through play: The moderating roles of personal gender salience and game characteristics. *Child Development, 87*, 414–428. http://dx.doi.org/10.1111/cdev.12463

Dietz, T. L. (1998). An examination of violence and gender role portrayals in video games: Implications for gender socialization and aggressive behavior. *Sex Roles, 38*, 425–442. http://dx.doi.org/10.1023/A:1018709905920

Emmerich, W., & Shepard, K. (1984). Cognitive factors in the development of sex-typed preferences. *Sex Roles, 11*, 997–1007. http://dx.doi.org/10.1007/BF00288129

Endendijk, J. J., Beltz, A. M., McHale, S. M., Bryk, K., & Berenbaum, S. A. (2016). Linking prenatal androgens to gender-related attitudes, identity, and activities: Evidence from girls with congenital adrenal hyperplasia. *Archives of Sexual Behavior, 45*, 1807–1815. http://dx.doi.org/10.1007/s10508-016-0693-7

Fagot, B. I. (1985). Changes in thinking about early sex role development. *Developmental Review, 5*, 83–98. http://dx.doi.org/10.1016/0273-2297(85)90031-0

Fagot, B. I., & Leinbach, M. D. (1989). The young child's gender schema: Environmental input, internal organization. *Child Development, 60*, 663–672. http://dx.doi.org/10.2307/1130731

Frey, K. S., & Ruble, D. N. (1992). Gender constancy and the "cost" of sex-typed behavior: A test of the conflict hypothesis. *Developmental Psychology, 28*, 714–721. http://dx.doi.org/10.1037/0012-1649.28.4.714

Funk, J. B., & Buchman, D. D. (1996). Children's perceptions of gender differences in social approval for playing electronic games. *Sex Roles, 35*, 219–231. http://dx.doi.org/10.1007/BF01433108

Gelman, S. A. (1989). Children's use of categories to guide biological inferences. *Human Development, 32*, 65–71. http://dx.doi.org/10.1159/000276364

Gelman, S. A., Collman, P., & Maccoby, E. E. (1986). Inferring properties from categories versus inferring categories from properties: The case of gender. *Child Development, 57*, 396–404. http://dx.doi.org/10.2307/1130595

Greenberg, B. S., Sherry, J., Lachlan, K., Lucas, K., & Holmstrom, A. (2010). Orientations to video games among gender and age groups. *Simulation & Gaming, 41*, 238–259. http://dx.doi.org/10.1177/1046878108319930

Homer, B. D., Hayward, E. O., Frye, J., & Plass, J. L. (2012). Gender and player characteristics in video game play of preadolescents. *Computers in Human Behavior, 28*, 1782–1789. http://dx.doi.org/10.1016/j.chb.2012.04.018

Keil, F. C. (1989). *Concepts, kinds, and cognitive development*. Cambridge, MA: MIT Press.

Keil, F. C. (2010). The feasibility of folk science. *Cognitive Science, 34*, 826–862. http://dx.doi.org/10.1111/j.1551-6709.2010.01108.x

Kohlberg, L. (1966). A cognitive-developmental analysis. In E. Maccoby (Ed.), *The development of sex differences* (pp. 82–173). Stanford, CA: Stanford University Press.

Lam, V. L., & Leman, P. J. (2003). The influence of gender and ethnicity on children's inferences about toy choice. *Social Development, 12*, 269–287. http://dx.doi.org/10.1111/1467-9507.00233

Liben, L. S., & Bigler, R. S. (2002). The developmental course of gender differentiation. In W. Overton (Ed.), *Monographs of the society for research in child development* (Vol. 67). Boston, MA: Blackwell.

Liben, L. S., & Signorella, M. L. (1980). Gender-related schemata and constructive memory in children. *Child Development, 51*, 11–18. http://dx.doi.org/10.2307/1129584

Lucas, K., & Sherry, J. L. (2004). Sex differences in video game play: A communication-based explanation. *Communication Research, 31*, 499–523. http://dx.doi.org/10.1177/0093650204267930

Marcus, D. E., & Overton, W. F. (1978). The development of cognitive gender constancy and sex role preferences. *Child Development, 49*, 434–444. http://dx.doi.org/10.2307/1128708

Martin, C. L. (1991). The role of cognition in understanding gender effects. In W. R. Hayne (Ed.), *Advances in child development and behavior* (Vol. 23, pp. 113–149). San Diego, CA: Academic Press. http://dx.doi.org/10.1016/S0065-2407(08)60024-5

Martin, C. L. (1994). Cognitive influences on the development and maintenance of gender segregation. In C. Leaper (Ed.), *Childhood gender segregation: Causes and consequences* (New directions for child development, No. 65, pp. 35–51). San Francisco, CA: Jossey-Bass. http://dx.doi.org/10.1002/cd.23219946505

Martin, C. L. (2000). Cognitive theories of gender development. In T. Eckes & H. M. Trautner (Eds.), *The developmental social psychology of gender* (pp. 91–121). Mahwah, NJ: Erlbaum.

Martin, C. L., Cook, R. E., & Andrews, N. C. Z. (2016). Reviving androgyny: A modern day perspective on flexibility of gender identity and behavior. *Sex Roles, 76*, 592–603. http://dx.doi.org/10.1007/s11199-016-0602-5

Martin, C. L., & Dinella, L. M. (2012). Congruence between gender stereotypes and activity preference in self-identified tomboys and non-tomboys. *Archives of Sexual Behavior, 41,* 599–610. http://dx.doi.org/10.1007/s10508-011-9786-5

Martin, C. L., Eisenbud, L., & Rose, H. (1995). Children's gender-based reasoning about toys. *Child Development, 66,* 1453–1471. http://dx.doi.org/10.2307/1131657

Martin, C. L., & Halverson, C. F. (1981). A schematic processing model of sex typing and stereotyping in children. *Child Development, 52,* 1119–1134. http://dx.doi.org/10.2307/1129498

Martin, C. L., & Halverson, C. F. (1983). The effects of sex-typing schemas on young children's memory. *Child Development, 54,* 563–574. http://dx.doi.org/10.2307/1130043

Martin, C. L., & Little, J. K. (1990). The relation of gender understanding to children's sex-typed preferences and gender stereotypes. *Child Development, 61,* 1427–1439. http://dx.doi.org/10.2307/1130753

Martin, C. L., & Ruble, D. N. (2004). Children's search for gender cues: Cognitive perspectives on gender development. *Current Directions in Psychological Science, 13,* 67–70. http://dx.doi.org/10.1111/j.0963-7214.2004.00276.x

Martin, C. L., Ruble, D. N., & Szkrybalo, J. (2002). Cognitive theories of early gender development. *Psychological Bulletin, 128,* 903–933. http://dx.doi.org/10.1037/0033-2909.128.6.903

Miller, M. K., & Summers, A. (2007). Gender differences in video game characters' roles, appearances, and attire as portrayed in video game magazines. *Sex Roles, 57,* 733–742. http://dx.doi.org/10.1007/s11199-007-9307-0

Mischel, W. (1966). A social learning view of sex differences in behavior. In E. Maccoby (Ed.), *The development of sex differences* (pp. 57–81). Stanford, CA: Stanford University Press.

Montemayor, R. (1974). Children's performance in a game and their attraction to it as a function of sex-typed labels. *Child Development, 45,* 152–156. http://dx.doi.org/10.2307/1127761

Olson, K. R., Key, A. C., & Eaton, N. R. (2015). Gender cognition in transgender children. *Psychological Science, 26,* 467–474. http://dx.doi.org/10.1177/0956797614568156

Ruble, D. N., Balaban, T., & Cooper, J. (1981). Gender constancy and the effects of sex-typed televised toy commercials. *Child Development, 52,* 667–673. http://dx.doi.org/10.2307/1129188

Ruble, D. N., & Martin, C. L. (1998). Gender development. In N. Eisenberg (Ed.), *Handbook of child psychology: Vol. 3. Social, emotional, and personality development* (5th ed., pp. 933–1016). Hoboken, NJ: Wiley.

Ruble, D. N., Taylor, L. J., Cyphers, L., Greulich, F. K., Lurye, L. E., & Shrout, P. E. (2007). The role of gender constancy in early gender development. *Child Development, 78*, 1121–1136. http://dx.doi.org/10.1111/j.1467-8624.2007.01056.x

Shutts, K., Banaji, M. R., & Spelke, E. S. (2010). Social categories guide young children's preferences for novel objects. *Developmental Science, 13*, 599–610. http://dx.doi.org/10.1111/j.1467-7687.2009.00913.x

Silvern, L. E., & Katz, P. A. (1986). Gender roles and adjustment in elementary school children: A multidimensional approach. *Sex Roles, 14*, 181–202. http://dx.doi.org/10.1007/BF00288248

Slaby, R. G., & Frey, K. S. (1975). Development of gender constancy and selective attention to same-sex models. *Child Development, 46*, 849–856. http://dx.doi.org/10.2307/1128389

Smetana, J. G., & Letourneau, K. J. (1984). Development of gender constancy and selective attention to same-sex models. *Developmental Psychology, 20*, 691–696. http://dx.doi.org/10.1037/0012-1649.20.4.691

Stangor, C., & Ruble, D. N. (1987). Development of gender role knowledge and gender constancy. In L. S. Liben & M. L. Signorella (Eds.), *Children's gender schemata* (pp. 5–22). San Francisco, CA: Jossey-Bass. http://dx.doi.org/10.1002/cd.23219873803

Stangor, C., & Ruble, D. N. (1989). Differential influences of gender schemata and gender constancy on children's information processing and behavior. *Social Cognition, 7*, 353–372. http://dx.doi.org/10.1521/soco.1989.7.4.353

Stein, A. H., Pohly, S. R., & Mueller, E. (1971). The influence of masculine, feminine, and neutral tasks on children's achievement behavior, expectancies of success, and attainment values. *Child Development, 42*, 195–207. http://dx.doi.org/10.2307/1127075

Szkrybalo, J. (1998). *The motivational consequences of gender constancy: A test of competing interpretations of Lawrence Kohlberg's cognitive-developmental theory* (Unpublished doctoral dissertation). New York University, New York, NY.

Taylor, M. G., & Gelman, S. A. (1993). Children's gender- and age-based categorization in similarity and induction tasks. *Social Development, 2*, 104–121. http://dx.doi.org/10.1111/j.1467-9507.1993.tb00006.x

Urberg, K. A. (1982). The development of concepts of masculinity and femininity in young children. *Sex Roles, 8*, 659–668. http://dx.doi.org/10.1007/BF00289899

Warin, J. (2000). The attainment of self-consistency through gender in young children. *Sex Roles, 42*, 209–231. http://dx.doi.org/10.1023/A:1007039222998

Weisgram, E. S. (2016). The cognitive construction of gender stereotypes: Evidence for the dual pathways model of gender differentiation. *Sex Roles, 75*, 301–313. http://dx.doi.org/10.1007/s11199-016-0624-z

Weisgram, E. S., Fulcher, M., & Dinella, L. (2014). Pink gives girls permission: Exploring the roles of explicit gender labels and gender-typed colors on preschool children's toy preferences. *Journal of Applied Developmental Psychology, 35*, 401–409. http://dx.doi.org/10.1016/j.appdev.2014.06.004

Yee, M., & Brown, R. (1994). The development of gender differentiation in young children. *British Journal of Social Psychology, 33*, 183–196. http://dx.doi.org/10.1111/j.2044-8309.1994.tb01017.x

Zosuls, K. M., Ruble, D. N., Tamis-Lemonda, C. S., Shrout, P. E., Bornstein, M. H., & Greulich, F. K. (2009). The acquisition of gender labels in infancy: Implications for gender-typed play. *Developmental Psychology, 45*, 688–701. http://dx.doi.org/10.1037/a0014053

III

CONSEQUENCES OF GENDER-TYPED TOY PLAY

8

IMPACT OF GENDER-TYPED TOYS ON CHILDREN'S NEUROLOGICAL DEVELOPMENT

LISE ELIOT

In April 2016, the White House held a multidisciplinary conference on the seemingly superficial topic of gender-stereotyped toys. Why is the government interested in toys? The conclusions of the conference were succinctly summarized in a Fact Sheet titled "Breaking Down Gender Stereotypes in Media and Toys So That Our Children Can Explore, Learn, and Dream Without Limits" (The White House, Office of the Press Secretary, 2016). According to the proceedings, addressing early gender messaging through toys and media is anticipated to help expand career opportunities across the nation and specifically, to enhance women's entry into the science, technology, engineering, and mathematics (STEM) workforce and men's entry into caregiving professions. If gender labeling and partitioning of toys really does limit girls' and boys' exploration and skill development, then researchers should be able to measure the neurological impact of gender-specific play and its ramifications for children's career choices and advancement.

http://dx.doi.org/10.1037/0000077-009
Gender Typing of Children's Toys: How Early Play Experiences Impact Development, E. S. Weisgram and L. M. Dinella (Editors)

The purpose of this chapter is to examine the proximal steps of this equation—that is, to evaluate the evidence that children's experience with gender-stereotyped toys, games, books, and other media actually tilts their brain development in permanent, career-altering ways. Phrased bluntly, I can cut to the chase and state straight off that currently no evidence indicates that gender-stereotyped play changes human brain structure or circuitry. To my knowledge, no research has directly assessed the brain as children interact with gender-stereotyped toys. Nonetheless, researchers understand enough about the mechanisms of brain development to be confident that variations in play have long-lasting impacts. Moreover, neuroscience has now amassed a sizeable arsenal of tools that can be used to seek such evidence. One such tool is high-density EEG measurement (Saby & Marshall, 2012), which is the least invasive and least-restrictive method for monitoring high-speed activity from across the forebrain. Another promising method is functional near-infrared spectroscopy (fNIRS), which is as equally nonrestrictive and noninvasive as EEG but provides better spatial resolution by using hemodynamic responses to estimate neuronal activation in the superficial 1 cm of the cerebral cortex (Wilcox & Biondi, 2015). Other noninvasive imaging methods, such as functional magnetic resonance imaging (fMRI; Raschle et al., 2012) and magneto-encephalography (Imada et al., 2006), provide even better spatial resolution of brain activity but are more challenging to use in play studies because of the need to physically restrain and minimize movement in child participants.

The truth is that for something as complex as toy play, researchers are still at a stage where much more can be learned from careful observation of children's behavior than of brain activity. The good news is that such fine-grained analysis of behavior is becoming common in developmental research and, at this point, is actually a better readout of brain function than anything that can be done with neuroimaging or EEG measures. For example, Kretch, Franchak, and Adolph (2014) used head-mounted eye tracking to compare the visual experience of infants at the crawling versus walking stages of loco-motor development and documented dramatic sensory differences that are of likely importance for spatial cognition. Using the same technology, C. Yu and Smith (2013) found that infants look more to their parents' hands than to their faces during bouts of joint toy play, suggesting a more direct pathway for skill learning than the traditional understanding of joint attention (gaze-matching) would allow. Measured at this level of detail, children's behavior is a more precise reflection of brain function and learning mechanisms than any existing noninvasive brain measure, which at this point provides the equivalent of a 30,000-foot view of neural circuit organization.

I therefore defer to the rest of this book for demonstrating how gender-stereotyped playthings foster different types of sensory stimulation, physical activity, social–emotional engagement, and skill advancement in specific areas such as verbal and spatial cognition (see Chapters 9, 10, and 11, this volume). I also forgo any speculation about the ways in which boys' and girls' brains may be innately disposed toward interest in different types of toys, although I hasten to assert that currently no evidence indicates sex differences in particular brain structures that could explain the divergence in toy choice that begins around 12 months of age and grows to be one of the largest behavioral sex differences. As described in Chapter 5, studies in both animals (Meaney & Stewart, 1981) and human clinical populations (Hines, Constantinescu, & Spencer, 2015) have suggested that early androgen exposure somehow drives boys' neural circuitry toward more active, spatially oriented play. However, the actual evidence linking prenatal testosterone to specific features of human brain anatomy remains conflicted (e.g., compare Friederici et al., 2008, with Lust et al., 2010), with the largest study (Knickmeyer et al., 2014) failing to identify any clear relationship between testosterone levels and specific brain structures. Such findings suggest that any effect of early androgens on neuronal development is modest, acting merely to bias, rather than to fix, children's later interest in gender-typed toys. Moreover, levels of testosterone actually overlap substantially between boys and girls during the "minipuberty" of neonatal development (Kung, Browne, Constantinescu, Noorderhaven, & Hines, 2016). Rather than testosterone acting directly to drive divergent brain development, it is likely the actual experience of playing for hundreds of hours with different types of toys and with predominantly same-gender peers that fuels divergent brain development, giving rise to the gender differences in leisure interests and cognitive abilities of adolescents and adults (Berenbaum, Bryk, & Beltz, 2012).

The effects of gender-typed play on the brain are thus largely unknown at present. Nonetheless, it is possible to extrapolate from a broader understanding of brain development to the likely divergence of brain and skill maturation through gender-differentiated play. To build this argument, I first discuss the general principles of neocortical development, including its fundamental dependence on experience and neuronal activity during early ("critical") periods of development. I then turn to the mechanisms of brain adaptation, or plasticity, that are known to underlie learning and other behavioral change and are especially potent in early life. Last, I focus on the importance of play in mammalian development and evidence from animal studies of enriched environments to suggest mechanisms by which brain structure and behavior are molded by the different properties of gender-typed toys. My goal is to stimulate future research that can evaluate more directly the proximal mechanisms of gender-differentiated brain development.

PRINCIPLES OF BRAIN DEVELOPMENT AND PLASTICITY

Human brain development is a long, protracted process. It begins in the first trimester of gestation and continues until early adulthood, with certain neuronal properties maturing well into the third decade of life (Houston, Herting, & Sowell, 2014; Stiles, Brown, Haist, & Jernigan, 2015). The long and multiphased process of brain development allows ample time for learning and neuroplasticity to adapt a young person's neural circuits to the specific demands of his or her physical and social environment. However, similar to all development (picture a tree sapling putting out its first branches), early choice points have a decisive effect on later possibilities, limiting the potential circuits and skills that a young brain can later exhibit.

The central nervous system (CNS) emerges in the fifth week of embryonic development, when the primordial neural tube starts specializing into a brain and spinal cord (de Graaf-Peters & Hadders-Algra, 2006). Neurons—which are the information-carrying cells of the nervous system—are formed from the inner wall of the neural tube and migrate outward, away from the fluid-filled core that will become the ventricles of the brain and spinal cord. As they migrate up and out, new neurons form the bricks that build up the mass of the voluminous cerebral cortex and smaller subcortical structures of the human brain (basal ganglia, thalamus, brainstem, and cerebellum) and spinal cord. Neuronal birth, migration, and differentiation into specific types (e.g., excitatory or inhibitory neurons) take place largely before birth and are mostly determined by genetic factors (Custo Greig, Woodworth, Galazo, Padmanabhan, & Macklis, 2013). By contrast, the connections between neurons, or synapses, that determine the ultimate direction and form of information flow, develop largely postnatally (Huttenlocher & Dabholkar, 1997) and are critically shaped by neural activity—that is, by children's and adolescents' precise experiences and environment (Greenough, Black, & Wallace, 1987).

Another key developmental event, myelination, also takes place largely postnatally, continuing in some areas (especially the frontal and temporal lobes) as late as age 28 (Miller et al., 2012). Myelin is the white matter coating on neuronal axons and is essential to the clear and rapid information flow between brain nodes that permits smooth action and mature thought. The basic sequence of myelination across different brain areas appears to be genetically programmed and follows a Piagetian order: sensorimotor areas of the brain, followed by language and emotion areas, followed by multimodal association areas capable of abstract reasoning and planning (Brody, Kinney, Kloman, & Gilles, 1987; Eliot, 2000; Konner, 1991). Nonetheless, the thickness and relative efficacy of this myelin coating is shaped by repeated practice, experience and other environmental influences that are a growing focus of research interest (Fields, 2015).

Turning to the role of toy play in development, such experience activates all parts of the nervous system: sensory circuits that relay touch, vision, hearing, and vestibular sensation; motor circuits that control both fine oral–tactile and gross postural–locomotor skills; and cognitive circuits that process spatial–mechanical awareness, cause-and-effect relationships, sociolinguistic understanding, memory, attention, and other executive functions. Each of these circuits traverses both higher and lower brain regions, but generally speaking, it is the higher levels of the CNS that are more subject to modification as a result of experience and learning (Fox, Levitt, & Nelson, 2010). When researchers talk about behaviors being hard-wired, meaning fixed and innate, this applies only to the most basic reflexes, such as breathing, blinking, rooting, sucking, swallowing, sneezing, and gagging, along with the postural and eye movement reflexes that are controlled by the vestibular system (Eliot, 2000). The purpose of such fixed, lower-brain responses is to protect survival. Located in the brainstem and spinal cord, reflex circuits are largely mature before birth (Konner, 1991), in contrast to circuits involving the cerebral cortex and basal ganglia that depend on experience and practice for their maturation (Tau & Peterson, 2010). Toy play may look instinctive in children—as when we see toddlers cuddling a doll or pushing a toy truck across the floor—but every piece of such actions requires learning and tuning of neural circuits to the specific sensory, motor, spatial, social, cultural, and motivational demands of both object and environment (Thelen & Smith, 1994).

The so-called neocortex is the most recently evolved part of the brain, present only in mammals and especially expanded in higher primates. In humans, it comprises the vast majority of the cerebral cortex. Although the basic wiring plan of the neocortex is laid out genetically, the final, precise circuitry depends critically on children's experience for its development. Picture the establishment of a huge shipping company, like FedEx: Its major truck lines, connecting central distribution in places like New York City and Chicago, can be laid out by preplanning (genes), but the finest, local routes are worked out only after the business starts operating (after birth), as customer demands evolve and daily experience allows drivers to hone their most efficient routes through trial-and-error iteration. This iterative tuning keeps development flexible, which is precisely what a command-and-control system needs to be in a highly intelligent, highly nimble corporation (or animal).

Synaptic plasticity occurs throughout the nervous system, but neocortical circuits are absolutely dependent on it for normal development. This is reflected in the protracted maturation of cortical gray matter, which includes neuronal cell bodies, synapses, and the massive receptive branches, or dendrites, that extend and remodel to accommodate new synapses throughout development (de Graaf-Peters & Hadders-Algra, 2006; Stiles et al., 2015).

Importantly, gray matter volume and synapse number do not merely increase during development; both expand through childhood but then actually retract or "prune" during adolescence, a turning point that coincides with the end of various developmental critical periods (Huttenlocher & Dabholkar, 1997; Shaw et al., 2008). Thus, the mammalian brain overproduces synapses (and gray matter) during children's most experimental, exploratory phase, setting up the conditions for a Darwinian-like selection of the most useful, ecologically relevant connections and pruning away of the inefficient, least useful pathways. Considering that the human cerebral cortex contains some 10 billion neurons and each neuron typically receives about 10,000 synaptic connections, this adds up to some 100 trillion synapses that need to be sorted out during development, a number far too high for genes ("nature") alone to specify. The problem is solved by letting "nurture," or experience, do the work of synapse selection, which for children comes largely in the context of play.

Research over the past 30 years has identified one cellular mechanism in particular, long-term potentiation (LTP), that appears crucial for the neuronal remodeling that stores the memory for both skills and knowledge (Sweatt, 2016). First hypothesized by Canadian psychologist Donald Hebb in the 1950s, so-called Hebbian LTP was proven to exist in the 1980s and 1990s by neurophysiologists studying neurons in the key memory-storing structure, the hippocampus. Buried deep in our two temporal lobes, the hippocampus is a gateway for conscious memory, with its synaptic plasticity determining which few of one's ongoing sea of experiences will be shipped out to the cerebral cortex for permanent storage. LTP was later found to occur outside the hippocampus and is now known to play a key role in information storage throughout the brain, consolidating both conscious (or autobiographical) memories and the unconscious skills, habits, and perceptual biases that actually constitute the majority of learned behavior.

Familiar to nonscientists through the slogan "Cells that fire together, wire together," LTP is triggered by the repeated, simultaneous electrical activity of pre- and postsynaptic neurons. It is this cellular process that essentially explains why "practice makes perfect." The basic idea is that, compared with the background electrical chatter produced by moment-to-moment experience, highly salient or repeated experiences exceed a biochemical threshold that triggers actual physical change in the size and strength of the synapse. Going back to our FedEx analogy, it is as if the roadway automatically widens on any route a driver reliably takes day after day.

Since its discovery in the hippocampus, LTP has been found to underlie every possible form of learning—including developmental changes that are not necessarily thought of as learning. Take visual development: Researchers and clinicians have long known that visual experience is critical for properly wiring circuits in the occipital lobe, or visual cortex. Children who are deprived of clear vision in early life—for example, if they are born with a congenital cataract or persistent strabismus ("lazy eye")—can permanently lose fine acuity and depth perception if the problem is not fixed within the first 2 years of life. Beginning with the Nobel Prize–winning work of David Hubel and Torsten Wiesel in the 1960s, occipital circuits were found to depend critically on normal early vision to properly wire into a high-acuity, depth-perceiving visual apparatus. More recent work has confirmed that LTP is integral to the process of turning visual experience into the precise, efficient network that allows fine vision (Hensch, 2005).

As best we can tell, similar principles apply throughout the cerebral cortex, and explain the existence of critical periods for other sensory (Erzurumlu & Gaspar, 2012), motor (Reid, Rose, & Boyd, 2015), linguistic (Werker & Hensch, 2015), social–emotional (McLaughlin et al., 2015), and cognitive abilities (Fox et al., 2010). The fact that even something as simple as vision depends on experience and neuroplasticity for normal development makes it inescapable that higher order interests and abilities—which grow from, and are in many ways entrenched by, these sensorimotor and linguistic building blocks—are also critically shaped by developmental divergences that begin in the first months and years of life.

THE BIOLOGY OF PLAY

Play is deeply integral to this activity-dependent development. Most placental mammals, marsupials, and birds engage in some form of play as juveniles; it is an intrinsically motivated, biologically based behavior that evolved to promote adaptive brain and body development (Pellis & Pellis, 2009). Play appears to have emerged multiple times in evolution, whenever the juveniles of a species found themselves with "surplus resources"—large brains, a prolonged childhood, sustained parental care, and a high resting metabolic rate (Graham & Burghardt, 2010). Such conditions afford the leisure for young ones to explore, follow their curiosity, and expand their behavioral and cognitive repertoire with obvious later adaptive value. An extended period of juvenile play enables practice of physical skills (strength, coordination), social skills (give-and-take, bonding, sharing, reciprocity, fairness, altruism), and adult behaviors (courtship, sexuality, aggression, foraging) that are critical for survival, reproductive success, and evolutionary innovation (Pellegrini, Dupuis, & Smith, 2007). More generally, the creative, low-stakes tenor of play behavior is thought to promote cognitive facility and flexibility in the face of unknown future demands, especially when it motivates young animals to test skills at the brink of their physical and mental prowess (Špinka, Newberry, & Bekoff, 2001).

By definition, play is motivated in the absence of extrinsic reward, punishment, or consequence for immediate survival. It is voluntary, self-orchestrated, and occurs spontaneously, as long as juveniles are safe, well-fed, and healthy (Vanderschuren & Trezza, 2014). Children do not need to be taught how to play or shown how to use toys. Their flexible brains seek out novelty, which drives exploration and then discovery about the physical and social world. Play thus provides seemingly optimal stimulation for learning and neural plasticity, a fact that researchers are beginning to capitalize on as they seek to better understand the experiential roots of mature brain architecture.

New research has focused on the temporal features of play as a way to better understand its impact on brain development (Hedges et al., 2013). Most forms of play involve lots of repetition, which cellular studies have shown to be the best way to alter developing neural circuits. Young children seek out predictable events they can control—picture a baby dropping items off a high chair—and then endlessly repeat them, honing their sense of predictive timing. It is important to note that this playful repetition is not rote or stereotyped; it is "repetition without repetition"—that is, a repeated movement, action or strategy amidst ever-changing circumstances, evolving motivation, and growing skill. This flexible context helps generalize skill development and mastery. When a child asks to hear the same bedtime story every night, it is presumably because she or he finds pleasure in predicting the words and pictures with greater accuracy each time until finally, the child can "read" it as well as a beloved grown-up. Predictive timing builds sustained attention and skill mastery and is built into the rules of synaptic plasticity that underlie most learning and behavioral change (Feldman, 2012). Such timing is also crucially dependent on the cerebellum, one of the slowest parts of the brain to complete its neuronal migration and synaptogenesis, perhaps not coincidentally during this period of peak play in children.

Most research on the neurobiology of play has been conducted in laboratory rats. When they are isolated and unable to wrestle with peers during the peak of their juvenile play period, rats develop social deficits, depressive-like behavior, and cognitive impairments that persist into later life (Vanderschuren & Trezza, 2014). Rough-and-tumble play in rats (which both sexes partake of, though males more than females; Argue & McCarthy, 2015) depends on key parts of the limbic brain, including the amygdala, nucleus accumbens, and orbital prefrontal cortex. The behavioral deficits caused by social isolation during the peak play period have been linked to alterations in this cortico-limbic circuitry and in neurochemical arousal systems involving dopamine, opioid, and cannabinoid transmitters. According to Vanderschuren and Trezza (2014), sex differences in play appear specifically tied to alterations in amygdala neurochemistry. Because normal amygdala development is also dependent on the opportunity for social play, such neurochemical differentiation could be a product as much as a cause of sex difference in play behaviors.

ENVIRONMENTAL ENRICHMENT AND THE BRAIN

Researchers' best understanding of how play and exploration affect brain development comes from a long history of research on "enriched environments." About 150 years ago, Charles Darwin (1868) observed in *The Variation of Animals and Plants Under Domestication* that rabbits raised in captivity have smaller heads than their wild counterparts and speculated the following:

> When we remember that rabbits, from having been domesticated and closely confined during many generations, cannot have exerted their intellect, instincts, senses, and voluntary movements, either in escaping from various dangers or in searching for food, we many conclude that their brains will have been feebly exercised, and consequently have suffered in development. (p. 129)

Fast-forward nearly one century, to research by Mark Rosenzweig and his colleagues at University of California, Berkeley, in the 1960s. Their studies were the first to experimentally examine the impact of enriched environments on the brains and behavior of laboratory animals. They took the standard rat cage, enlarged its volume severalfold, and then added multiple cage-mates and a rotating menagerie of toys, tunnels, platforms, and ladders to dramatically enhance animals' opportunity for exploration and physical and social stimulation. As Darwin predicted, such changes were sufficient to increase the animals' brain mass and cortical thickness, compared with rats raised in standard cages without toys or companions. Subsequent research demonstrated that the cortical expansion is due to increases in dendritic length and branching and to increases in synaptic size and density (Nithianantharajah & Hannan, 2006). Similar findings have been extended to mice, gerbils, squirrels, cats, and monkeys (Benefiel & Greenough, 1998), indicating that environmental enrichment has comparable effects on all mammalian brains. Rosenzweig (1996) also examined how animals' age affects this plasticity and found that although enriched environments produce qualitatively similar cerebral enhancements across the lifespan, the changes are larger and develop more quickly in young, compared with older, animals.

A thicker, more synaptically dense cerebral cortex is presumably advantageous to behavior, and indeed, enriched rearing has been found to benefit animals' learning, memory, problem-solving, and emotional behavior. Early studies focused on reverse discrimination learning and showed that animals raised for 1 month in an enriched environment made fewer errors in a task requiring adaptive choice to access a food reward (Krech, Rosenzweig, &

Bennett, 1962). Such flexible problem-solving implicates changes in the prefrontal cortex and enriched environments are associated with changes in levels of prefrontal acetylcholine and dopamine that may contribute to enriched animals' lower anxiety under stressful conditions (Segovia, del Arco, & Mora, 2009). Considerable further research has found other benefits for animals raised in enriched environments, include improved learning and memory in spatial mazes, better recognition of novel objects, greater exploratory behavior, and reduced anxiety and depressive-type behavior (Brenes et al., 2016; reviewed in Nithianantharajah & Hannan, 2006).

Given its role in memory and spatial cognition, the hippocampus has been a major focus for understanding the effects of environmental enrichment on the brain. Various studies have found that animals housed in enriched environments show increased synaptic strength and easier induction of hippocampal LTP (Artola et al., 2006; Foster & Dumas, 2001). Moreover, the hippocampus is one of the few brain areas that continues to produce new neurons ("neurogenesis") into adulthood. Kempermann, Kuhn, and Gage (1997) first showed that environmental enrichment dramatically enhances hippocampal neurogenesis. Further research has demonstrated that these new neurons are integrated into functional circuits and may be especially important for transferring memories from the hippocampus to more permanent storage in the cerebral cortex. Such transfer is more efficient in young, compared with old, brains and is thought to be crucial for freeing up hippocampal capacity so that new learning can continue unimpeded (Inokuchi, 2011).

Hippocampal neurogenesis has also been implicated in the control of mood and buffering of stress responses. The hippocampus is well known to undergo atrophy in people experiencing depression (McKinnon, Yucel, Nazarov, & MacQueen, 2009), and the enhancement of hippocampal neurogenesis appears to be a key mechanism by which antidepressant drugs, such as fluoxetine (Prozac), exert their therapeutic effect (Sahay & Hen, 2007). Through its connections to both the prefrontal cortex and the hypothalamus, the hippocampus helps link emotion to cognition and to modulate emotional responses. Thus, enriched environments have as important an effect on mood and motivation as they do on learning memory, presumably serving—much like toy play—to stimulate the positive emotions and absorption that lead to skill building and cognitive advancement. Because of these multifaceted benefits, enriched environments are being studied as a way of ameliorating a wide range of neurologic and developmental disorders, including Alzheimer's disease, Parkinson's disease, epilepsy, stroke, traumatic brain injury, Fragile X, and Down syndrome (Alwis & Rajan, 2014; Nithianantharajah & Hannan, 2006).

Enriched environments are complex and so many studies have attempted to dissect the different components of enrichment—for instance, social versus sensory versus motor opportunities—to determine which features are responsible for specific brain and behavioral benefits. Is it the added visual stimulation, as suggested by early studies that noted the largest amount of growth in the occipital lobe (Rosenzweig, 1996)? Is it the social stimulation—arguably the most complex type of stimulation a young animal encounters? Or is it the increased physical activity of having a larger space and (in later experiments) the opportunity to run on a wheel and engage in voluntary physical exercise?

Surprisingly, it is the latter intervention that has the most dramatic effect, at least on the many neuroplastic changes that take place in the rodent hippocampus. Voluntary exercise alone was found to enhance learning, neurogenesis, growth factor release, neurotransmitter levels and synaptic transmission, much like the full-blown enriched environment experience (van Praag, Kempermann, & Gage, 2000). At the same time, complex environments (that include lots of physical exercise) trigger other changes, including lowered levels of circulating stress hormone, likely to help foster circuits underlying learning and emotional regulation (Grégoire, Bonenfant, Le Nguyen, Aumont, & Fernandes, 2014). Other studies have isolated very specific forms of stimulation, such as a multitextural training or exposure to an enhanced acoustic environment, and report changes in corresponding somatosensory and auditory areas of the cerebral cortex (Alwis & Rajan, 2014). Thus, it is likely that every brain area that is robustly activated by a certain form of enrichment (or play) will undergo plastic changes, altering its future processing and strengthening abilities that utilize those circuits.

GENDER-STEREOTYPICAL PLAY AND THE BRAIN

What does all this mean for studies of gender-typed toys? The simple message is that the properties of toys and type of play a child engages with must steer the trajectory of his or her brain and skill development. Considering the distinct affordances of different types of toys and play (see Chapter 4), one can expect that feminine toys—such as dolls, dress-up, arts-and-crafts materials, and homemaker gear (e.g., cooking and cleaning toys)—will engage close-distance, fine motor, verbal, preliteracy, and social–relational abilities geared toward domestic roles and self-objectification, along with academic success. Masculine toys—such as vehicles, balls, and other sports gear; weapons and other targeting toys; superhero props; and construction toys (e.g., tools, building blocks)—will engage more gross motor, visual–spatial, mechanical, and social–relational skills geared toward competition and control over other people and the physical environment. Many of these skills have lasting value (excluding self-objectification and aggression), so the problem lies in the early gender labeling and segregation of toys that literally limit children's occupations and, thus, the brain-building exploration and practice that open the door toward a wider range of adult occupations.

In a few studies, researchers have used toys to study brain activity during cognitive processing in infants and young children (e.g., Bell & Wolfe, 2007). However, no one has yet compared brain activity as children engage with contrasting gender-typed playthings, such as dolls versus trucks. It would be interesting to do so, as well as to compare boys' and girls' brain activity while engaged with identical toys. fMRI studies (e.g., Hugdahl, Thomsen, & Ersland, 2006) have provided some evidence that men and women activate different brain areas while performing mental rotation, the classic visual–spatial problem that represents one of the largest cognitive sex differences in adults. It is interesting that this neural processing does not yet differ between 8- to 10-year-old girls and boys (Kucian et al., 2007; Roberts & Bell, 2000), raising the possibility that gender differences in adult brain activation are shaped by cumulative time-on-task with divergent activities that differentially exercise visual–spatial circuits.

Studies of video game play support this hypothesis. Most video games demand considerable visual–spatial cognition, including navigating, turning, dodging, targeting, evading, and observing stimuli from all directions and moving at all speeds. A 2003 study in *Nature* first demonstrated a causal relationship between action video games and spatial ability by asking inexperienced college students (male and female) to learn and play 10 hours of the game *Medal of Honor*. Compared with control students (who learned the less complex, 2D game *Tetris*), the action gamers exhibited greater improvement in attention to visual space (Green & Bavelier, 2003). Since then, many other studies of video game training have shown both behavioral and brain changes attributable to this fast-paced visual–spatial play, including one that found the sex difference in spatial test scores was actually eliminated by video game training (Feng, Spence, & Pratt, 2007). Of note, another recent study imaged brain changes in a group of young adult men and women after playing the 3D pursuit game, *Super Mario 64*, for 30 minutes per day over a period of 2 months. Compared with a matched but untrained control group, the *Super Mario* players showed increased gray matter density in several brain areas that participate in spatial attention, movement, and navigation (right hippocampus, right dorsolateral prefrontal cortex, and bilateral cerebellum; Kühn, Gleich, Lorenz, Lindenberger, & Gallinat, 2014). These findings are reminiscent of those of many other recent studies demonstrating practice-induced changes in brain structure with activities ranging from juggling, balancing, deciphering Morse code, and studying for a high-stakes medical licensing exam (Thomas & Baker, 2013).

Boys are 4 times more likely to play video games than girls, and typically spend an hour or more per day playing them throughout adolescence

(Cummings & Vandewater, 2007). This is a lot more practice than in any of the neuroimaging studies, and it also begins at a much younger age than the participants in extant experimental studies—mostly young adults whose brains are less plastic than children's. Thus, it is reasonable to assume that the divergence in children's experience due to gender-specific play has an even more potent effect on brain structure and function than has been observed in adulthood.

In addition to playing video games, boys are much likelier to play with building toys and to play sports than are girls; both types of activities involve intensive visual–spatial experience that likely benefits the brain as much as fast-paced video games. Although the enactment of Title IX has led to many more girls playing sports than 40 years ago, the number is still considerably lower than boys, and girls tend to start a sport at a later age and quit at younger ages than boys (Kelley & Carchia, 2013). The gender gap is even greater for playing with construction toys, which provides some of the best practice for mental rotation, spatial visualization, and the 2D-to-3D translation that are critical for physics, engineering, architecture, and similar fields. A mere 10% of LEGO sets were originally purchased for girls, according to the company's own findings in 2008 (LaFrance, 2016).

These stark differences in playtime activities mean that boys enter and progress through school with a lot more visual–spatial experience than girls. When combined with persistent gender stereotypes about many professions, these play differences likely contribute to differences in interest and achievement in various STEM-related careers. In an attempt to reduce the achievement gap in spatially intense fields like physics and engineering, some schools have implemented crash courses in spatial cognition; a recent summary of research on such programs involving students from elementary school to college suggests they are indeed beneficial at boosting math and physical reasoning skills. More research is needed to see if such programs boost long-term retention in STEM fields, but the results thus far are promising (Stieff & Uttal, 2015).

There is, of course, a downside to many boys' obsession with video games and sports, and here we can consider the net advantage conferred by activities that girls are more likely to engage with, such as doll play, dress-up, drawing, and reading. Cross-culturally, girls hold a small advantage in early verbal development (Kovas et al., 2005; Zhang, Jin, Shen, Zhang, & Hoff, 2008) and a larger advantage in reading and writing that grows progressively through primary and secondary education (National Center for Education Statistics, 2012; Organisation for Economic Co-operation and Development [OECD], 2009). Verbal skill is the gateway to literacy; parents both talk (Leaper, Anderson, & Sanders, 1998) and read (Westerlund & Lagerberg, 2008) more to young girls than boys; by high school, girls are nearly twice as likely to read for pleasure than boys (OECD, 2009). Literacy itself has profound effects on the developing brain, creating circuits that link visual perception to linguistic processing and strengthen verbal memory, rewiring that appear to be most efficient during childhood (Dehaene, Cohen, Morais, & Kolinsky, 2015). It is therefore entirely feasible to design brain imaging studies that will test for a dose-dependent effect of the more verbal, preliteracy, and fine motor skills that typical "girl play" with dolls, drawing, books, and penmanship engage. In fact, neuroimaging studies of children's reading development are generally consistent with girls' earlier maturation and boys' eventual catch-up, as opposed to any qualitative gender difference in brain circuitry used to process written language (Burman, Bitan, & Booth, 2008; Plante, Schmithorst, Holland, & Byars, 2006; V. Y. Yu et al., 2014). In other words, the potential is the same among both genders, but time-on-task may be the limiting factor that controls the maturation and fine-tuning of neural circuits for reading, writing, and social cognition.

CONCLUSION

Mammalian brain development depends critically on early experience to lay down the circuits for all but the most reflexive of mental tasks. This development is highly dynamic, involving constant feedback and integration between sensory, motor, and higher neural systems as skill levels progressively evolve and adapt to the child's growing body (Byrge, Sporns, & Smith, 2014). Considering the amount of time children spend in play, and the greater plasticity of their synaptic, dendritic, and myelin development during early life, it is inescapable that gender differences in toy choice and the physical and cognitive processes these toys engage profoundly impact their brain development. Like that first branch point on a young tree, early divergences lead to a greater distance and more complete differentiation of mature neural circuits and behavioral capabilities than later, distal branches.

In recent decades, girls' greater involvement in traditional male pursuits such as sports and STEM competitions has demonstrated the potency of this plasticity, resulting in more sustained female achievement across athletic and academic pursuits. There is further to go for girls and women, ground that may be partially gained through reduced gender stereotyping and labeling of toys and early childhood pursuits. For boys, the needle has barely budged, in spite of an evolving global economy that will require men to branch into more verbally and socially intensive fields, such as education, health care, and service industries. Neuroscientists have yet to broach the impact of gender-differentiated toys on early brain development, but the experiments are feasible and likely to yield important insights into the processes of gender development, with important implications for maximizing human potential.

REFERENCES

Alwis, D. S., & Rajan, R. (2014). Environmental enrichment and the sensory brain: The role of enrichment in remediating brain injury. *Frontiers in Systems Neuroscience, 8*, 156. http://dx.doi.org/10.3389/fnsys.2014.00156

Argue, K. J., & McCarthy, M. M. (2015). Characterization of juvenile play in rats: Importance of sex of self and sex of partner. *Biology of Sex Differences, 6*. http://dx.doi.org/10.1186/s13293-015-0034-x

Artola, A., von Frijtag, J. C., Fermont, P. C., Gispen, W. H., Schrama, L. H., Kamal, A., & Spruijt, B. M. (2006). Long-lasting modulation of the induction of LTD and LTP in rat hippocampal CA1 by behavioural stress and environmental enrichment. *European Journal of Neuroscience, 23*, 261–272. http://dx.doi.org/10.1111/j.1460-9568.2005.04552.x

Bell, M. A., & Wolfe, C. D. (2007). Changes in brain functioning from infancy to early childhood: Evidence from EEG power and coherence working memory tasks. *Developmental Neuropsychology, 31*, 21–38. Retrieved from http://www.tandfonline.com/doi/full/10.1080/87565640709336885

Benefiel, A. C., & Greenough, W. T. (1998). Effects of experience and environment on the developing and mature brain: Implications for laboratory animal housing. *ILAR Journal, 39*, 5–11. http://dx.doi.org/10.1093/ilar.39.1.5

Berenbaum, S. A., Bryk, K. L., & Beltz, A. M. (2012). Early androgen effects on spatial and mechanical abilities: Evidence from congenital adrenal hyperplasia. *Behavioral Neuroscience, 126*, 86–96. http://dx.doi.org/10.1037/a0026652

Brenes, J. C., Lackinger, M., Höglinger, G. U., Schratt, G., Schwarting, R. K., & Wöhr, M. (2016). Differential effects of social and physical environmental enrichment on brain plasticity, cognition, and ultrasonic communication in rats. *The Journal of Comparative Neurology, 524*, 1586–1607. http://dx.doi.org/10.1002/cne.23842

Brody, B. A., Kinney, H. C., Kloman, A. S., & Gilles, F. H. (1987). Sequence of central nervous system myelination in human infancy. I. An autopsy study of myelination. *Journal of Neuropathology and Experimental Neurology, 46*, 283–301. http://dx.doi.org/10.1097/00005072-198705000-00005

Burman, D. D., Bitan, T., & Booth, J. R. (2008). Sex differences in neural processing of language among children. *Neuropsychologia, 46*, 1349–1362. http://dx.doi.org/10.1016/j.neuropsychologia.2007.12.021

Byrge, L., Sporns, O., & Smith, L. B. (2014). Developmental process emerges from extended brain-body-behavior networks. *Trends in Cognitive Sciences, 18*, 395–403. http://dx.doi.org/10.1016/j.tics.2014.04.010

Cummings, H. M., & Vandewater, E. A. (2007). Relation of adolescent video game play to time spent in other activities. *Archives of Pediatrics & Adolescent Medicine, 161*, 684–689. http://dx.doi.org/10.1001/archpedi.161.7.684

Custo Greig, L. F., Woodworth, M. B., Galazo, M. J., Padmanabhan, H., & Macklis, J. D. (2013). Molecular logic of neocortical projection neuron specification, development and diversity. *Nature Reviews Neuroscience, 14,* 755–769. http://dx.doi.org/10.1038/nrn3586

Darwin, C. (1868). *The variations of animals and plants under domestication* (Vol. 1). London, England: Charles Murray.

de Graaf-Peters, V. B., & Hadders-Algra, M. (2006). Ontogeny of the human central nervous system: What is happening when? *Early Human Development, 82,* 257–266. http://dx.doi.org/10.1016/j.earlhumdev.2005.10.013

Dehaene, S., Cohen, L., Morais, J., & Kolinsky, R. (2015). Illiterate to literate: Behavioural and cerebral changes induced by reading acquisition. *Nature Reviews Neuroscience, 16,* 234–244. http://dx.doi.org/10.1038/nrn3924

Eliot, L. (2000). *What's going on in there? How the brain and mind develop in the first five years of life.* New York, NY: Bantam.

Erzurumlu, R. S., & Gaspar, P. (2012). Development and critical period plasticity of the barrel cortex. *European Journal of Neuroscience, 35,* 1540–1553. http://dx.doi.org/10.1111/j.1460-9568.2012.08075.x

Feldman, D. E. (2012). The spike-timing dependence of plasticity. *Neuron, 75,* 556–571. http://dx.doi.org/10.1016/j.neuron.2012.08.001

Feng, J., Spence, I., & Pratt, J. (2007). Playing an action video game reduces gender differences in spatial cognition. *Psychological Science, 18,* 850–855. http://dx.doi.org/10.1111/j.1467-9280.2007.01990.x

Fields, R. D. (2015). A new mechanism of nervous system plasticity: Activity-dependent myelination. *Nature Reviews Neuroscience, 16,* 756–767. http://dx.doi.org/10.1038/nrn4023

Foster, T. C., & Dumas, T. C. (2001). Mechanism for increased hippocampal synaptic strength following differential experience. *Journal of Neurophysiology, 85,* 1377–1383.

Fox, S. E., Levitt, P., & Nelson, C. A., III. (2010). How the timing and quality of early experiences influence the development of brain architecture. *Child Development, 81,* 28–40. http://dx.doi.org/10.1111/j.1467-8624.2009.01380.x

Friederici, A. D., Pannekamp, A., Partsch, C. J., Ulmen, U., Oehler, K., Schmutzler, R., & Hesse, V. (2008). Sex hormone testosterone affects language organization in the infant brain. *NeuroReport, 19,* 283–286. http://dx.doi.org/10.1097/WNR.0b013e3282f5105a

Graham, K. L., & Burghardt, G. M. (2010). Current perspectives on the biological study of play: Signs of progress. *The Quarterly Review of Biology, 85,* 393–418. http://dx.doi.org/10.1086/656903

Green, C. S., & Bavelier, D. (2003). Action video game modifies visual selective attention. *Nature, 423,* 534–537. http://dx.doi.org/10.1038/nature01647

Greenough, W. T., Black, J. E., & Wallace, C. S. (1987). Experience and brain development. *Child Development, 58,* 539–559. http://dx.doi.org/10.2307/1130197

Grégoire, C. A., Bonenfant, D., Le Nguyen, A., Aumont, A., & Fernandes, K. J. (2014). Untangling the influences of voluntary running, environmental complexity, social housing and stress on adult hippocampal neurogenesis. *PLOS ONE, 9*, e86237. http://dx.doi.org/10.1371/journal.pone.0086237

Hedges, J. H., Adolph, K. E., Amso, D., Bavelier, D., Fiez, J. A., Krubitzer, L., . . . Ghajar, J. (2013). Play, attention, and learning: How do play and timing shape the development of attention and influence classroom learning? *Annals of the New York Academy of Sciences, 1292*, 1–20. http://dx.doi.org/10.1111/nyas.12154

Hensch, T. K. (2005). Critical period mechanisms in developing visual cortex. *Current Topics in Developmental Biology, 69*, 215–237. http://dx.doi.org/ 10.1016/S0070-2153(05)69008-4

Hines, M., Constantinescu, M., & Spencer, D. (2015). Early androgen exposure and human gender development. *Biology of Sex Differences, 6*. http://dx.doi. org/10.1186/s13293-015-0022-1

Houston, S. M., Herting, M. M., & Sowell, E. R. (2014). The neurobiology of childhood structural brain development: Conception through adulthood. *Current Topics in Behavioral Neurosciences, 16*, 3–17. http://dx.doi.org/10.1007/ 7854_2013_265

Hugdahl, K., Thomsen, T., & Ersland, L. (2006). Sex differences in visuo-spatial processing: An fMRI study of mental rotation. *Neuropsychologia, 44*, 1575–1583. http://dx.doi.org/10.1016/j.neuropsychologia.2006.01.026

Huttenlocher, P. R., & Dabholkar, A. S. (1997). Regional differences in synaptogenesis in human cerebral cortex. *The Journal of Comparative Neurology, 387*, 167–178. http://dx.doi.org/10.1002/(SICI)1096-9861(19971020)387:2<167:: AID-CNE1>3.0.CO;2-Z

Imada, T., Zhang, Y., Cheour, M., Taulu, S., Ahonen, A., & Kuhl, P. K. (2006). Infant speech perception activates Broca's area: A developmental magnetoencephalography study. *NeuroReport, 17*, 957–962. http://dx.doi.org/10.1097/ 01.wnr.0000223387.51704.89

Inokuchi, K. (2011). Adult neurogenesis and modulation of neural circuit function. *Current Opinion in Neurobiology, 21*, 360–364. http://dx.doi.org/10.1016/ j.conb.2011.02.006

Kelley, B., & Carchia, C. (2013, July 11). "Hey data data—swing!" *ESPN*. Retrieved from http://www.espn.com/espn/story/_/id/9469252/hidden-demographicsyouth-sports-espn-magazine

Kempermann, G., Kuhn, H. G., & Gage, F. H. (1997). More hippocampal neurons in adult mice living in an enriched environment. *Nature, 386*, 493–495. http:// dx.doi.org/10.1038/386493a0

Knickmeyer, R. C., Wang, J., Zhu, H., Geng, X., Woolson, S., Hamer, R. M., . . . Gilmore, J. H. (2014). Impact of sex and gonadal steroids on neonatal brain structure. *Cerebral Cortex, 24*, 2721–2731. http://dx.doi.org/10.1093/cercor/bht125

Konner, M. (1991). Universals of behavioral development in relation to brain myelination. In K. R. Gibson & A. C. Petersen (Eds.), *Brain maturation and cognitive development: Comparative and cross-cultural perspectives* (pp. 181–223). New York, NY: Aldine de Gruyter.

Kovas, Y., Hayiou-Thomas, M. E., Oliver, B., Dale, P. S., Bishop, D. V., & Plomin, R. (2005). Genetic influences in different aspects of language development: The etiology of language skills in 4.5-year-old twins. *Child Development, 76,* 632–651. http://dx.doi.org/10.1111/j.1467-8624.2005.00868.x

Krech, D., Rosenzweig, M. R., & Bennett, E. L. (1962). Relations between brain chemistry and problem-solving among rats raised in enriched and impoverished environments. *Journal of Comparative and Physiological Psychology, 55,* 801–807. http://dx.doi.org/10.1037/h0044220

Kretch, K. S., Franchak, J. M., & Adolph, K. E. (2014). Crawling and walking infants see the world differently. *Child Development, 85,* 1503–1518. http://dx.doi.org/10.1111/cdev.12206

Kucian, K., von Aster, M., Loenneker, T., Dietrich, T., Mast, F. W., & Martin, E. (2007). Brain activation during mental rotation in school children and adults. *Journal of Neural Transmission, 114,* 675–686. http://dx.doi.org/10.1007/s00702-006-0604-5

Kühn, S., Gleich, T., Lorenz, R. C., Lindenberger, U., & Gallinat, J. (2014). Playing Super Mario induces structural brain plasticity: Gray matter changes resulting from training with a commercial video game. *Molecular Psychiatry, 19,* 265–271. http://dx.doi.org/10.1038/mp.2013.120

Kung, K. T., Browne, W. V., Constantinescu, M., Noorderhaven, R. M., & Hines, M. (2016). Early postnatal testosterone predicts sex-related differences in early expressive vocabulary. *Psychoneuroendocrinology, 68,* 111–116. http://dx.doi.org/10.1016/j.psyneuen.2016.03.001

LaFrance, A. (2016, May 25). How to play like a girl. *The Atlantic.* Retrieved from http://www.theatlantic.com/entertainment/archive/2016/05/legos/484115/

Leaper, C., Anderson, K. J., & Sanders, P. (1998). Moderators of gender effects on parents' talk to their children: A meta-analysis. *Developmental Psychology, 34,* 3–27. http://dx.doi.org/10.1037/0012-1649.34.1.3

Lust, J. M., Geuze, R. H., Van de Beek, C., Cohen-Kettenis, P. T., Groothuis, A. G., & Bouma, A. (2010). Sex specific effect of prenatal testosterone on language lateralization in children. *Neuropsychologia, 48,* 536–540. http://dx.doi.org/10.1016/j.neuropsychologia.2009.10.014

McKinnon, M. C., Yucel, K., Nazarov, A., & MacQueen, G. M. (2009). A meta-analysis examining clinical predictors of hippocampal volume in patients with major depressive disorder. *Journal of Psychiatry & Neuroscience, 34,* 41–54.

McLaughlin, K. A., Sheridan, M. A., Tibu, F., Fox, N. A., Zeanah, C. H., & Nelson, C. A., III. (2015). Causal effects of the early caregiving environment on development of stress response systems in children. *Proceedings of the National Academy of Sciences of the United States of America, 112,* 5637–5642. http://dx.doi.org/10.1073/pnas.1423363112

Meaney, M. J., & Stewart, J. (1981). Neonatal-androgens influence the social play of prepubescent rats. *Hormones and Behavior, 15,* 197–213. http://dx.doi.org/10.1016/0018-506X(81)90028-3

Miller, D. J., Duka, T., Stimpson, C. D., Schapiro, S. J., Baze, W. B., McArthur, M. J., . . . Sherwood, C. C. (2012). Prolonged myelination in human neocortical evolution. *Proceedings of the National Academy of Sciences of the United States of America, 109*, 16480–16485. http://dx.doi.org/10.1073/pnas.1117943109

National Center for Education Statistics. (2012). *The nation's report card: Writing 2011 (NCES 2012–470)* (Publication No. NCES 2012–470). Washington, DC: National Center for Education Statistics, U.S. Department of Education. Retrieved from https://nces.ed.gov/nationsreportcard/pdf/main2011/2012470.pdf

Nithiananatharajah, J., & Hannan, A. J. (2006). Enriched environments, experience-dependent plasticity and disorders of the nervous system. *Nature Reviews Neuroscience, 7*, 697–709. http://dx.doi.org/10.1038/nrn1970

Organisation for Economic Co-operation and Development. (2009). *PISA: Equally prepared for life? How 15-year-old boys and girls perform in school.* Paris, France: Author. Retrieved from https://www.oecd.org/pisa/pisaproducts/42843625.pdf

Pellegrini, A. D., Dupuis, D., & Smith, P. K. (2007). Play in evolution and development. *Developmental Review, 27*, 261–276. http://dx.doi.org/10.1016/j.dr.2006.09.001

Pellis, S., & Pellis, V. (2009). *The playful brain: Ventures to the limits of neuroscience.* Oxford, England: Oneworld Press.

Plante, E., Schmithorst, V. J., Holland, S. K., & Byars, A. W. (2006). Sex differences in the activation of language cortex during childhood. *Neuropsychologia, 44*, 1210–1221. http://dx.doi.org/10.1016/j.neuropsychologia.2005.08.016

Raschle, N., Zuk, J., Ortiz-Mantilla, S., Sliva, D. D., Franceschi, A., Grant, P. E., . . . Gaab, N. (2012). Pediatric neuroimaging in early childhood and infancy: Challenges and practical guidelines. *Annals of the New York Academy of Sciences, 1252*, 43–50. http://dx.doi.org/10.1111/j.1749-6632.2012.06457.x

Reid, L. B., Rose, S. E., & Boyd, R. N. (2015). Rehabilitation and neuroplasticity in children with unilateral cerebral palsy. *Nature Reviews Neurology, 11*, 390–400. http://dx.doi.org/10.1038/nrneurol.2015.97

Roberts, J. E., & Bell, M. A. (2000). Sex differences on a mental rotation task: Variations in electroencephalogram hemispheric activation between children and college students. *Developmental Neuropsychology, 17*, 199–223. http://dx.doi.org/10.1207/S15326942DN1702_04

Rosenzweig, M. R. (1996). Aspects of the search for neural mechanisms of memory. *Annual Review of Psychology, 47*, 1–32. http://dx.doi.org/10.1146/annurev.psych.47.1.1

Saby, J. N., & Marshall, P. J. (2012). The utility of EEG band power analysis in the study of infancy and early childhood. *Developmental Neuropsychology, 37*, 253–273. http://dx.doi.org/10.1080/87565641.2011.614663

Sahay, A., & Hen, R. (2007). Adult hippocampal neurogenesis in depression. *Nature Neuroscience, 10*, 1110–1115. http://dx.doi.org/10.1038/nn1969

Segovia, G., del Arco, A., & Mora, F. (2009). Environmental enrichment, prefrontal cortex, stress, and aging of the brain. *Journal of Neural Transmission, 116*, 1007–1016. http://dx.doi.org/10.1007/s00702-009-0214-0

Shaw, P., Kabani, N. J., Lerch, J. P., Eckstrand, K., Lenroot, R., Gogtay, N., . . . Wise, S. P. (2008). Neurodevelopmental trajectories of the human cerebral cortex. *The Journal of Neuroscience, 28,* 3586–3594. http://dx.doi.org/10.1523/JNEUROSCI.5309-07.2008

Špinka, M., Newberry, R. C., & Bekoff, M. (2001). Mammalian play: Training for the unexpected. *The Quarterly Review of Biology, 76,* 141–168. http://dx.doi.org/10.1086/393866

Stieff, M., & Uttal, D. (2015). How much can spatial training improve STEM achievement? *Educational Psychology Review, 27,* 607–615. http://dx.doi.org/10.1007/s10648-015-9304-8

Stiles, J., Brown, T. T., Haist, F., & Jernigan, T. L. (2015). Brain and cognitive development. In R. M. Lerner (Ed.), *Handbook of child psychology and developmental science* (7th ed., pp. 9–62). Bingley, England: Emerald.

Sweatt, J. D. (2016). Neural plasticity and behavior—Sixty years of conceptual advances. *Journal of Neurochemistry, 139*(Suppl. 2), 179–199. http://dx.doi.org/10.1111/jnc.13580

Tau, G. Z., & Peterson, B. S. (2010). Normal development of brain circuits. *Neuropsychopharmacology, 35,* 147–168. http://dx.doi.org/10.1038/npp.2009.115

Thelen, E., & Smith, L. B. (1994). *A dynamic systems approach to development: Applications.* Cambridge, MA: MIT Press.

Thomas, C., & Baker, C. I. (2013). Teaching an adult brain new tricks: A critical review of evidence for training-dependent structural plasticity in humans. *NeuroImage, 73,* 225–236. http://dx.doi.org/10.1016/j.neuroimage.2012.03.069

Vanderschuren, L. J., & Trezza, V. (2014). What the laboratory rat has taught us about social play behavior: Role in behavioral development and neural mechanisms. *Current Topics in Behavioral Neurosciences, 16,* 189–212. http://dx.doi.org/10.1007/7854_2013_268

van Praag, H., Kempermann, G., & Gage, F. H. (2000). Neural consequences of environmental enrichment. *Nature Reviews Neuroscience, 1,* 191–198. http://dx.doi.org/10.1038/35044558

Werker, J. F., & Hensch, T. K. (2015). Critical periods in speech perception: New directions. *Annual Review of Psychology, 66,* 173–196. http://dx.doi.org/10.1146/annurev-psych-010814-015104

Westerlund, M., & Lagerberg, D. (2008). Expressive vocabulary in 18-month-old children in relation to demographic factors, mother and child characteristics, communication style and shared reading. *Child: Care, Health and Development, 34,* 257–266. http://dx.doi.org/10.1111/j.1365-2214.2007.00801.x

The White House, Office of the Press Secretary. (2016, April 6). *Breaking down gender stereotypes in media and toys so that our children can explore, learn, and dream without limits* [Fact sheet]. Retrieved from https://obamawhitehouse.archives.gov/the-press-office/2016/04/06/factsheet-breaking-down-gender-stereotypes-media-and-toys-so-our

Wilcox, T., & Biondi, M. (2015). fNIRS in the developmental sciences. *Wiley Interdisciplinary Reviews: Cognitive Science, 6,* 263–283. http://dx.doi.org/10.1002/wcs.1343

Yu, C., & Smith, L. B. (2013). Joint attention without gaze following: Human infants and their parents coordinate visual attention to objects through eye-hand coordination. *PLOS ONE, 8,* e79659. http://dx.doi.org/10.1371/journal.pone.0079659

Yu, V. Y., MacDonald, M. J., Oh, A., Hua, G. N., De Nil, L. F., & Pang, E. W. (2014). Age-related sex differences in language lateralization: A magnetoencephalography study in children. *Developmental Psychology, 50,* 2276–2284. http://dx.doi.org/10.1037/a0037470

Zhang, Y., Jin, X., Shen, X., Zhang, J., & Hoff, E. (2008). Correlates of early language development in Chinese children. *International Journal of Behavioral Development, 32,* 145–151. http://dx.doi.org/10.1177/0165025407087213

9

FASHION OR ACTION? GENDER-STEREOTYPED TOYS AND SOCIAL BEHAVIOR

SARAH K. MURNEN

Although the average American adult might not know these specific toys from the Toys "R" Us website (http://www.toysrus.com), they could probably guess that one of them is intended for girls and the other for boys. Contemporary toys are very gender stereotyped, even more so than was true in years past (Sweet, 2012). Feminine-stereotyped toys promote domesticity, nurturance, and a focus on appearance, and masculine stereotyped toys encourage riskiness, assertiveness, and a focus on action (Blakemore & Centers, 2005; see also Chapter 4, this volume). Most children play with toys that are stereotyped for their gender, so it is important to understand how stereotyped toys affect children's social development. In this chapter, I review research on the characteristics of gender-stereotyped toys that might influence children's social development. I propose that gendered toys help train children for gendered social roles. It is still the case that women are more associated with caretaking roles in the home and men are more associated with risk-taking

http://dx.doi.org/10.1037/0000077-010
Gender Typing of Children's Toys: How Early Play Experiences Impact Development, E. S. Weisgram and L. M. Dinella (Editors)

roles outside the home (Wood & Eagly, 2013). The research on the influence of toys on social behavior is limited; however, theory supports the idea that gendered toys perpetuate gendered roles and a gender unequal society. Some research links play with feminine-stereotyped toys to nurturing behavior and to a focus on appearance and play with masculine-stereotyped toys to aggression. I review these data, discuss their implications, and make suggestions for future research.

GENDER-STEREOTYPED TOYS

Much research supports the idea that toys are gender stereotyped. In an early study of 50 toys, it was determined that 41 of them were associated with a particular gender (Miller, 1987). The toys judged more appropriate for girls were rated higher in creativity, nurturance, and attractiveness, and those judged more appropriate for boys were evaluated as higher in constructiveness, competition, and aggressiveness. A more recent study of 100 toys yielded similar results (Blakemore & Centers, 2005). The most feminine-stereotyped toys, such as a baby doll, tea set, and a Barbie doll, were linked with nurturance, domesticity, and a focus on appearance, and the most masculine-stereotyped toys, such as a superhero costume, a tool bench, and a toy gun, were rated as more exciting, risky, and aggressive.

Comparing the same types of toys dichotomized by gender—dolls and action figures—shows a magnification of gender-polarized stereotypes. Klugman (1999) contrasted Barbie dolls and action figures, finding that action figures were more mobile with joints in several places. Further, the packaging of action figures tended to depict them in motion with words like "kill" and "destroy," whereas the packaging of Barbie typically showed girls gazing at the dolls. It is clear that action figures are aptly named, as they promote an assertive (even aggressive) focus on action. In contrast, Barbie promotes a somewhat passive focus on appearance. In a more recent study, Internet depictions of popular female dolls and popular male action figures were compared (Murnen, Greenfield, Younger, & Boyd, 2016). Dolls were usually portrayed with decorative (often sexualized) clothing, and action figures wore functional clothing like uniforms. Facial expressions also distinguished the characters such that dolls were much more likely to appear friendly, whereas action figures were much more likely to appear stoic or angry.

Thus, clear gender stereotypes are associated with toys, and much research shows that on average, children prefer to play with toys that are stereotyped for their gender. In fact, Hines and Davis (Chapter 5, this volume) have found that these differences are large, $d = -1.21$ to $d = 3.48$. Cherney and London (2006) asked 60 girls and 60 boys about their favorite toys, and girls' top toys were dolls, stuffed animals, and educational toys; boys' top toys were manipulative toys, vehicles, and action figures. These choices reveal clear gender stereotypes.

Why do children choose such gender-stereotyped toys? First, it is likely that a large number of stereotyped toys have entered the marketplace because of the increased commercialization of toys. Changes in Federal Communications Commission (FCC) rules in the 1980s made it legal to provide product-based programming to children. This is associated with the marketing of commercial products to children (Linn, 2008). For example, the television show *Power Rangers* was developed in the 1990s, and the sale of the accompanying Power Ranger characters set a record in 1994. In the examples of toys given at the beginning of this chapter, the Disney Descendants are represented in a movie by that name, and the Power Rangers characters come from cartoons with that name that can be accessed from a website, along with other materials.

In the mid-1970s the toy market in the United States was a $2 billion industry, but by 1986 it was worth $12 billion (Kline, 1998, p. 140), and in 2015 it was worth $19.48 billion (Toy Industry Association, 2016). It is argued that toy manufacturers can profit by placing stereotyped toys in the marketplace in that they can sell one version of a toy for girls and a different version for boys (Sweet, 2012). Groups of children are also divided by age, creating many different groups to which to market, leading to more sales (Orenstein, 2011). LEGO developed its LEGO Friends line in 2011, which was aimed at girls who had previously made up a small proportion of LEGO customers (C. Allen, 2014). LEGO Friends are depicted in pastel rather than primary colors, contain female figures, and domestic and retail settings, which likely signals that the toys are intended for girls. By 2012, this line was the fourth best-selling line (C. Allen, 2014).

The continued existence of gender-stereotyped toys might represent a backlash against feminism (Sweet, 2012), and proponents of gender stereotyping inappropriately use neuroscience research on gender to make essentialist claims that there are immutable, biologically based gender differences that support stereotyped toys (Fine, 2010). Adults buying toys for children often want to buy gender-stereotyped toys, as that helps make their choice easier (Williams, 2006). Nevertheless, in a recent review of the research on gendered toy marketing, Fine and Rush (2016) argued that gendered toys are "old fashioned and offensively out of touch with twenty-first century values of gendered equality" (p. 12).

It is not difficult for children to learn which toys are stereotyped for their gender, as they are color-coded in advertisements. For example, 85% of toys advertised on the Disney website with pink as a predominant color were advertised for girls, and 85% of toys with red, black, gray, and brown were advertised for boys (Auster & Mansbach, 2012). Even on the somewhat gender-progressive children's network Nickelodeon, toy commercials were often found to be color-coded, with almost all of the pastel-colored commercials depicting only girls (Kahlenberg & Hein, 2010).

Depictions on commercial television also can make it clear who is supposed to play with a particular toy. Kahlenberg and Hein's (2010) study of 455 television commercials on Nickelodeon found that toy dolls and animals were in commercials that typically featured only girls, and action figures, sports toys, and transportation/construction toy commercials often featured only boys. Girls were frequently depicted in cooperative play, and in settings inside the home. If girls were outside the home, they were usually engaged in stereotypic behavior, such as gossiping at the mall. Boys-only commercials had locations that were more diverse.

Although manufacturers and advertisers might make the gender stereotypes associated with toys quite clear, children are also motivated to choose gendered toys because of cognitive readiness to organize their world by gender, and environmental reinforcement for making gendered choices (e.g., Green, Bigler, & Catherwood, 2004). According to cognitive developmental perspectives (see Chapter 7, this volume), when children start labeling their own gender around the age of 2, they become aware of gender distinctions and use gender as an organizing framework for understanding the world (e.g., Martin & Ruble, 2004). Further, children can learn gender stereotypes from role models and from direct experience; for example, children might be rewarded by peer and/or parent approval for making a stereotyped choice (Bussey & Bandura, 2004).

Much research offers support for social–cognitive explanations for gendered toy choices. Research shows that children will use color cues to help them choose stereotyped toys, as well as labels provided by adults (Cherney & Dempsey, 2010; LoBue & DeLoache, 2011; Weisgram, Fulcher, & Dinella, 2014; Wong & Hines, 2015). Children might also be influenced in their gendered toy choice by their perceptions of parent and peer approval for such choices (Raag, 1999). Boys' toy choices are usually more stereotyped than girls' (Cherney & London, 2006), perhaps because of great social repercussions for males engaging in feminine-stereotyped behavior. In one study, boys ages 5 to 7 reported more stereotyped toy choices in front of peers, an effect that did not occur for older boys or for girls (Banerjee & Lintern, 2000). Among a group of very gender-stereotyped children, girls were found to change their toy choice in response to counterstereotypic stories to a greater extent than did boys (Green et al., 2004; see Chapter 6, this volume, for a thorough review of environmental contributions to gender-typed toy play).

TOYS AND SOCIAL BEHAVIOR

Given a strong likelihood of gendered toy choice, what are the implications for social behavior? Child development experts agree that play is not purposeless, but functional. Linn (2009) argued that "play is the foundation of intellectual exploration" (p. 11) and helps children develop social skills. Sometimes play with humanlike objects, such as puppets, is even used in therapy for children as it is argued to help children process difficult emotions (Linn, 2008). Playing make-believe allows children to express fears and fantasies (Linn, 2008).

Thus, gendered toy play represents an important behavior. Cognitive developmental and social learning theories suggest that gendered toy choice will influence gendered behavior. Liben and Bigler (2002) proposed that children's behavior is likely restricted by gender-appropriate toys. Feminine-stereotyped toys, such as baby dolls, tea sets, and Barbie dolls, might promote nurturance, domesticity, and focus on appearance. In contrast, masculine-stereotyped toys, such as superhero costumes, construction toys, and action figures, might promote assertive activity, and perhaps aggression (Blakemore & Centers, 2005).

It is believed that the commercialization of children's toys limits children's ability to play with toys creatively (Linn, 2008). If a child plays with a doll or action figure character that is associated with a cartoon, the cartoon depiction might limit the child's imagination about what the character might do. Support for this idea comes from a study by Greenfield et al. (1990) of first- and second-grade children in which the most imitative and least creative play occurred among children who watched a cartoon and subsequently played with cartoon-related characters.

Commercial culture would not have much to gain by producing toys that would encourage children's imagination, because toys such as a set of generic blocks with no instruction manual could be used over and over again, and no new toy would need to be purchased. Thus, commercialized toys that are advertised in a stereotyped manner might be likely to be used in that way, perpetuating stereotyped behavior.

Further, stereotyped toys exist in a culture in which gender-stereotyped roles still exist. Feminine-stereotyped traits encompass characteristics of communality and expressiveness, whereas masculine-stereotyped traits are associated with agency and industriousness (Wood & Eagly, 2013). According to social role theory, gender-stereotyped traits likely developed from biological differences between women and men, such as women's ability to bear children and men's upper body strength, that historically placed women and men into gender-segregated roles, including women's care of children and men's role in securing food away from the home (Wood & Eagly, 2013). With the development of agriculture and industry, resources accrued that needed to be defended, and patriarchy developed through men's roles as defenders/ warriors. Further, according to this theory, gendered behavior is elicited that allows people to perform their roles successfully, resulting in actual gender differences in behavior. Gender stereotypes develop consistent with the roles and accompanying behaviors. For women, some societal prescriptions are to be emotional, warm, interested in children, friendly, and attentive to appearance, whereas men are prescribed career-orientation, leadership, aggression, assertiveness, and independence, among other traits (Rudman, Moss-Racusin, Phelan, & Nauts, 2012). In addition, gender-related proscriptions might prevent people from engaging in counterstereotypic behavior. Proscribed traits for men include being emotional, naive, and weak. Some proscriptions for women include being aggressive, intimidating, dominating, and angry.

Although aspects of gendered roles can be positive and important to society, such as female nurturance and male assertiveness, the polarized nature of the roles promotes inequality. Masculine-prescribed traits are associated with higher status persons, but feminine traits are not (Rudman et al., 2012). Women's roles have changed to some extent, with the second wave of the women's movement, but men's roles have not changed to the same degree (Twenge, 2009), leading to the idea of a "half-changed" world (Fine, 2010). Some believe that a backlash against women's accomplishments in the workplace is leading to increased pressure on women to retain their role as sexual objects (Douglas, 2010). Further, sexualized portrayals of women in the culture have increased (e.g., Hatton & Trautner, 2011; Mager & Helgeson, 2011), as have sexualized portrayals of girls (Graff, Murnen, & Krause, 2013). K. J. Anderson (2015) argued that the events of 9/11 led people to want to return to gender-traditional values, for example, through a focus on male heroism in the media. An emphasis on very gender-stereotyped toys promotes a patriarchal society. Masculine-stereotyped toys that encourage assertive action can promote dominance in boys, and feminine-stereotyped toys that encourage nurturance and a focus on appearance can promote domestic and sex-object roles for girls, which can be subordinating.

Further, some actual gender differences in behavior are consistent with traditional gender roles. Although Hyde (2005) found in her review of meta-analyses of gender differences that most are small or not significant (leading her to conclude gender similarity), a moderate-size gender difference in levels of physical aggression, d around .60, was found, with boys showing more aggression than girls. Another moderate-size difference was found in body esteem ($d = .58$), with males scoring higher than females. Feingold (1994) examined personality differences and found that for "tender-mindedness" (measured by empathy, nurturance, and tender-mindedness scales from various personality inventories), the effect size was large ($d = -.97$), with females showing more.

Of course, toy play is not the only behavior that reinforces gendered social roles, but it is worth examining the extent to which it might have an influence. Not much research has directly tested the causal relationship between toy play and social behavior, and some of it is dated, but the research that does exist supports some associations between toy play and social behaviors.

FEMININE-STEREOTYPED TOYS

Baby Dolls and Nurturing Behavior

Baby dolls are one of the most gender-stereotyped toys, and the toy most likely to encourage the practice of nurturing behaviors. The production of dolls was encouraged by President Teddy Roosevelt in the late 19th century when the birthrate was dropping (Orenstein, 2011). Some research shows that doll play encourages nurturing behavior. For example, Li and Wong (2016) observed first-grade children in Hong Kong and found that girls' play with feminine-stereotyped toys, such as dolls, was associated with a greater ability to think of comforting solutions to a crying infant. The researchers found that toy play predicted comforting more strongly than the other way around, so that a causal effect of play on comforting was considered likely. Among boys in the study, play with gender-neutral toys, such as a puzzle and chess set, was positively associated with comforting, and play with masculine-stereotyped toys, such as a toy gun and a fire truck, was negatively related. Overall, girls generated more comforting strategies than did boys. The authors determined that boys should be encouraged to play with nurturing toys. As indicated previously, the particular stigma associated with boys playing with feminine-stereotyped toys needs to be considered.

Playing with dolls also likely encourages children's ability to share attention with others, which is believed to promote social competence (Gavrilov, Rotem, Ofek, & Geva, 2012). Gavrilov et al. (2012) studied 5-year-old children in Israel from families of different cultural backgrounds. Children, observed with a parent, were presented with toys that varied in how much they encouraged social interaction including a high-interaction toy (Mr. Potato Head), a medium-interaction toy (LEGO blocks with miniature figures), and a low-interaction toy (a construction game). The dependent variable was the number of times that the child directed or redirected parent attention to an aspect of the toy—called *joint attentional bids* (JABS). The frequency of JABS was 3 times higher when children engaged with the most social stimuli compared with the least, and it was most pronounced for girls from gender traditional societies. Thus, already by age 5, more feminine-stereotyped behavior was clearly associated with feminine toys and more gender-stereotypic parenting.

Appearance-Focused Dolls and Toys

Not all dolls are likely to promote the positive aspects of feminine stereotypes, though. In 1959, the fashion doll Barbie was developed to help maturing girls understand their changing bodies. Some researchers have been concerned with the values that Barbie promotes. One major issue is her unrealistic body proportions (Dittmar, 2012); and although she has had a variety of careers in her history, she probably is more associated with appearance than career. In January 2016, Mattel introduced new versions of Barbie with varying body shapes (e.g., curvy, tall, petite), as well as varied skin tones and hairstyles that more accurately represent ethnic minority women. The sale of the doll has increased since that time (Reuters, 2016). This might suggest that consumers are eager for fashion dolls that do not present extremely unrealistic standards of attractiveness.

On the other hand, in recent years other fashion dolls have been produced that are much more sexualized than any version of Barbie. Bratz dolls have been singled out for their sexualized appearance (e.g., low-cut dresses, extreme high heels, heavy make-up) and open promotion of materialism. Bratz dolls were released in 2001 and initially outsold the more "old-fashioned" Barbie (Orenstein, 2011). Other dolls have followed suit. Murnen et al. (2016) found that the more recently developed Monster High dolls were the most sexualized of the dolls they studied. Sales of Monster High dolls have surpassed those of Barbie since their 2010 release (S. Allen, 2014).

Fashion dolls seem not to encourage nurturing behavior but instead encourage a focus on appearance and material consumption. One study found that looking at images of Barbie lowered body esteem in 5- to 8-year-old girls (Dittmar, Halliwell, & Ive, 2006), but Anschutz and Engels (2010) did not find that playing with the doll had this effect in their study of 6- to 10-year-old girls. Girls are likely interested in sexualized dolls because they represent attractive girls who are knowledgeable about commercial culture. Starr and Ferguson (2012) asked girls ages 6 to 9 about their interest in sexualized versus nonsexualized doll portrayals and found that girls were most likely to choose a sexualized doll for their "ideal self," and predicted that the sexualized doll would be more popular among their peers. Girls who choose sexualized dolls might be identifying with a sex-object role, which might limit their opportunities. In a study of perceptions of a fifth-grade girl dressed in childlike versus sexualized clothing (using images found on the Internet), the sexualized girl was judged less intelligent and less moral by college student participants (Graff, Murnen, & Smolak, 2012).

In addition to fashion dolls, many products in girls' culture likely encourage a focus on appearance, such as toy makeup kits and dress-up clothing, but little direct research has been conducted on the influence of these products. In one study of children's products, mothers of 4- to 10-year-old daughters were asked to report on their girls' interest in sexualized products (Tiggemann & Slater, 2014). Most young girls did not use very sexualized products (e.g., high heels), but many of them used beauty products. A third of 4- to 5-year-olds used at least one beauty product, such as nail polish, and the percentages increased across the ages. Mothers whose girls used these products also were more likely to report that their daughter was concerned with appearance. Malik and Wojdynski (2014) studied toy websites for girls and boys, analyzing messages associated with materialism. Websites for girls focused heavily on shopping and buying.

Fashion doll play and other appearance-related items could encourage a focus on appearance that is not healthy for girls. Objectification theory (Fredrickson & Roberts, 1997) proposes that the ubiquitous objectification of women (and girls) in the culture leads one to focus attention on how their body appears to others, to engage in self-objectification. Self-objectification is linked with body shame and depression through a large body of research (Tiggemann, 2011). Self-objectification deprives girls of "peak" emotional experiences and can diminish cognitive resources. Girls as young as 11 have been found to engage in debilitating amounts of self-objectification (Lindberg, Hyde, & McKinley, 2006).

Princess Toys

Perhaps perceived as an antidote to sexualized dolls are princess dolls. Disney Princess products started to be marketed in 2000 and were quickly very successful (Orenstein, 2011). Since then, other doll companies have produced princesses, and some familiar characters (e.g., Dora the Explorer) were turned into princesses. Princess characters might seem more palatable than sexualized fashion dolls (Orenstein, 2011), but do they promote positive values? An analysis of the gender role characteristics of princesses in nine Disney movies revealed a somewhat androgynous portrayal in that where they were frequently shown as fearful and attentive to appearance but also as assertive and athletic (England, Descartes, & Collier-Meek, 2011). Portrayals were found to be less stereotyped across time, but in most of the movies the resolution still centered on the stereotyped idea that the princess wins the love of the prince (England et al., 2011). In another analysis of Disney movies (not just princess movies, $n = 61$), the researchers found that the characters engaged in much prosocial behavior—an average of 1 action per minute (Padilla-Walker, Coyne, Fraser, & Stockdale, 2013).

Thus, identifying with a Disney Princess might have some positive and negative benefits. Coyne, Linder, Rasmussen, Nelson, and Birkbeck (2016) conducted a longitudinal study of just that topic with young children ages 3 to 6. Princess engagement (identification with princesses, play with princess products, viewing princess media) was high among the girls in the study with 50% viewing a film at least once a month and 61% playing with a toy at least once a week. For both girls and boys, princess engagement at Time 1 predicted feminine-gender-stereotyped behavior (engaging in quiet play, playing dress-up) 1 year later (Time 2). Princess engagement did not predict prosocial behavior in girls, but it did in boys if there was also a high level of parental mediation. Similarly, princess engagement did not relate longitudinally to body esteem in girls, perhaps because body esteem decreased for all girls. Among boys, engagement with princesses at Time 1, along with high parental mediation, was associated with better body esteem at Time 2. These results suggest it might be beneficial for parents to actively encourage boys to play with princess products, but it is unclear whether it is helpful for girls. In an experiment with 3- to 6-year-old girls, exposure to appearance-related video clips from animated films (including Disney) did not affect girls' appearance-related play or body image of the girls compared with the control group (Hayes & Tantleff-Dunn, 2010), lending further support to the idea that princess products might not induce appearance problems in young girls.

Thus, research on dolls suggests both positive and negative effects, likely depending on the type of doll and the type of play. Playing with dolls can encourage nurturance and fantasy role-play. Cherney, Kelly-Vance, Glover, Ruane, and Ryalls (2003) found that play with feminine-stereotyped toys, including a doll and a kitchen set, was associated with greater play complexity in both preschool girls and boys. More research should examine the effects of sexualized dolls and products on the body image and self-concept of girls, as these products do not seem to promote powerful behavior on the part of girls. These products in children's culture may influence boys' attitudes about girls' roles: An increase in sexualized products suggests an increased emphasis on the sex-object role for girls, which can reinforce gender traditional roles in both girls and boys.

MASCULINE-STEREOTYPED TOYS

Action-Oriented Toys and Positive Behaviors?

Toys stereotyped for boys are associated with action, risk, adventure, and sport. Boys report spending more time in sports play than girls (Cherney & London, 2006) and are more likely to participate in organized sports

(Fredricks & Eccles, 2005). Further, outdoor and sports toys represented the largest selling division of toys in 2015 (Toy Industry Association, 2016). Sports games are heavily commercialized, and they are stereotyped male in that 95% of sports programming contains depictions of men (Brown, Lamb, & Tappan, 2009). Not much direct research has examined the influence of such toys on behavior, but because sports participation has been linked to many positive outcomes, some positive relationships are likely. For example, longitudinal studies have found that team sports participation is linked with lowering social isolation and anxiety, and improving self-concept and self-esteem (reviewed by Eime, Young, Harvey, Charity, & Payne, 2013).

Not all of sports culture is positive, though (Brown et al., 2009). Messner, Dunbar, and Hunt (2000) analyzed the messages gleaned from analyzing text from 23 hours of televised sport and found themes associated with glorifying violence, sexualizing women, and treating White men as the voice of authority. More research on the effects of sport and action toy play on boys (and girls) is warranted.

"War Toys" and Aggression

Contemporary commercialized toys might be likely to promote extreme masculinity that includes aggression. For example, even the company that makes Nerf has made many of their soft toys into weapons, which was not the case when the company was founded (Brown et al., 2009). Bartneck, Min Ser, Moltchanova, Smithies, and Harrington (2016) found an increase in the presence of weapons in LEGO sets from 1978 (when the first weapon brick was created) to 2014, when about 30% of LEGO sets had a weapon brick. Raters also perceived LEGO to be more violent across time. It has been found that boys are particularly interested in toys that are aggressive (Benenson, Carder, & Geib-Cole, 2008).

Some are concerned that toys associated with "war," such as toy guns, encourage aggression. This issue has been studied empirically since at least the 1970s. In a 1988 review of eight studies, Sutton-Smith determined that the studies on this topic were not well-controlled. For example, studies did not always distinguish between real and pretend aggression. He concluded, though, that any aggression that did result in these studies was short term and occurred mostly among boys (Sutton-Smith, 1988).

In a more recent review that included studies that were more controlled, Malloy and McMurray-Schwarz (2004) concluded that violent toys sometimes serve as cues for real-life aggression, consistent with the Berkowitz (1993) aggressive cue hypothesis (1993). At least two studies reviewed supported this idea. Watson and Peng (1992) found that children ages 3 to 5 who played with toy guns were more likely to exhibit real aggression, and less likely to engage in nonaggressive play than when they played with nonaggressive toys. However, parents' use of physical punishment was a better predictor of aggression than toy gun play. Goff (1995) found that children ages 3 to 5 engaged in more real aggression and play aggression when playing with violent toys than nonviolent toys, but family factors helped predict aggression in this study, too. Thus, toy gun play might be a cue to aggression, but other factors in the child's environment need to be taken into consideration.

As indicated earlier, play can serve important functions and children who have experienced violence might need to engage in war play to try to understand their experiences (Levin, 2003). However, war play probably does not need to be encouraged with the provision of aggressive cues. Research has not supported the catharsis hypothesis that exposure to violence decreases the need to be violent. Further, the more commercialized the war toy, the less creative might be its use. It is believed that toys that are highly structured "channel children into replicating the violent stories they see on screen" (Levin, 2003, p. 61).

Action figures and superheroes are likely to be attractive to children because they are displayed as powerful and heroic (Coyne, Linder, Rasmussen, Nelson, & Collier, 2014). Enacting the role of a superhero might allow a child to feel powerful. Coyne et al. (2014) indicated that superhero characters should be particularly important in the United States, where masculinity values are important. The researchers cited statistics confirming the popularity of these characters, and an increase in films with superheroes since 2000 (Coyne et al., 2014). Action figures and superheroes tend to be male and exhibit masculine-stereotyped behavior (Baker & Raney, 2007). In a longitudinal study, boys and girls who were exposed to superheroes on television were more likely to subsequently engage in weapon play, although effects were stronger for boys (Coyne et al., 2014).

Video Games and Aggression

Turning to a more recent type of toy associated with aggression, much research has now amassed concerning the association between violent video games and aggression. More than 90% of American children report playing video games, and 85% of video games on the market contain some kind of violence (APA Task Force on Violent Media, 2015). More than one third of the top 20 video games in 2013 were labeled for a "mature audience," including *Battlefield 4* and *Assassin's Creed IV: Black Flag* (Entertainment Software Association, 2014). The Entertainment Software Association (2016) also reported that 41% of 2015 video game users were female, but females report less play with violent games.

Enough research has accumulated on the topic of violent video games and aggression that meta-analyses have been conducted. In one such analysis of 381 effect sizes, significant effects were found for aggressive behavior: $r = .262$ in cross-sectional studies, $r = .203$ in longitudinal studies, and $r = .210$ in experimental studies (C. A. Anderson et al., 2010). Effects were larger among more valid studies. Some other researchers have not found effects this large, though (e.g., Ferguson & Kilburn, 2009). Nevertheless, APA Task Force on Violent Media (2015) recently reviewed the meta-analyses on this issue, along with more recent research, and concluded that violent video game use does have an effect on aggression: "This effect is manifested both as an increase in negative outcomes such as aggressive behavior, cognitions, and affect and as a decrease in positive outcomes such as prosocial behavior, empathy, and sensitivity to aggression" (p. 16). The APA report also pointed out, though, that "no single risk factor consistently leads a person to act aggressively or violently. Rather, it is the accumulation of risk factors that tends to lead to aggressive or violent behavior" (p. 16).

Thus, the relationship between exposure to violent video games and subsequent aggressive acts is likely not simple. C. A. Anderson et al. (2010) concluded that violent video games likely have both short-term and long-term effects. Short-term effects might be due to priming such that a video game triggers an aggressive script that already exists, making it more accessible. Long-term effects are believed to include changes in beliefs about violence, densensitization to violence, and lowered empathy.

Of course, not all video games are violent. Less research has examined prosocial games (C. A. Anderson et al., 2010), but such games do exist. Among the other top 20 video games in 2013 were some labeled appropriate for all audiences, such as *Pokemon X* and *NBA2K13* (Entertainment Software Association, 2014), which are not obviously associated with violence. The context in which one plays a game likely matters. Greitemeyer (2013) found that playing video games cooperatively increased empathic concern. More than half of frequent video game players in 2015 reported playing games with others (Entertainment Software Association, 2016). More research should examine the possible prosocial effects of video games. In a recent meta-analysis, Ferguson (2015) found that the effect size for the association between violent video games and aggression was similar in size to that relating violent games to prosocial behavior (in a positive direction). Both effect sizes were small, and it is notable that Ferguson had stricter inclusion criteria for the studies in his analysis compared with C. A. Anderson et al. (2010).

Video Games and Female Sexual Objectification

In addition to being violent, many video games sexually objectify female characters. The top-selling video game in 2013 was *Grand Theft Auto V*, in which the player can pick up a prostitute, have sex with her, and kill her. In the game *RapeLay*, developed by a Japanese company, rape is the goal of the game. This game was quickly taken off the market because of protests—but not until after it went viral (Hunt, 2009). Although these games are extreme, it is not unusual to portray female characters in a sexualized way. Dill and Thill (2007) conducted a content analysis of male and female characters in popular video game magazines (males represented 75% of the characters found). They found that 82.6% of male characters were shown as aggressive (e.g., portrayed with a weapon); among female characters, 59.9% were portrayed as sexualized (e.g., in a sexually provocative pose) and 38.7% were scantily clad. Stermer and Burkley (2012) found that sexualized portrayals of women were found at every stage of the production and use of many video games, from advertising the game through rewards for playing the game.

Several studies of adult men have found links between experimental exposure to video games with sexually objectified portrayals of women (e.g., *Grand Theft Auto*) and increased likelihood to view women as sexual objects, to indicate willingness to sexually harass them (Yao, Mahood, & Linz, 2010), and to accept myths about rape (Beck, Boys, Rose, & Beck, 2012). The treatment of women as sexual objects makes them vulnerable to being treated as "legitimate" targets of sexual violence.

Links between sexist video games and acceptance of violence against women support the cognitive neoassociationistic model of media effects, according to J. R. Anderson and Bower (1973; as cited by Yao et al., 2010). According to this model, media can prime existing knowledge structures, making them more likely to be accessed in the future. Further, through spreading activation, ideas can be paired together, such as sex and violence, and the activation of one thought primes the other. A recent correlational study of adult participants found that video game consumption across the lifetime was correlated with acceptance of interpersonal aggression, hostile sexism, and belief in rape myths (Fox & Potocki, 2016). Studies on this subject have not been conducted with boys, but in a longitudinal study conducted in the Netherlands, researchers found that adolescents' viewing of media depictions of sexualized women predicted the development of attitudes that legitimize the sexual objectification of women (Vandenbosch & Eggermont, 2015). More research on this subject should be conducted, and with younger boys, if it can be done in an ethical manner.

CONCLUSIONS AND IMPLICATIONS

Theory suggests that gender-stereotyped toys encourage gendered roles, but the research on this issue is still limited. Although sufficient research on violent video games has been conducted to make some firm conclusions about relationships, less research has been conducted in other areas. It can be ethically and practically difficult to test children, but more research is needed with children as participants. In addition, very few studies are longitudinal, so few studies have examined long-term effects. More longitudinal research should be done, and toy play should be examined along with other important aspects of children's environments, such as their media use and relevant parent and peer attitudes and behaviors.

It is also important to conduct more cross-cultural research. Some countries, such as New Zealand, do not advertise to children on television to the extent that this occurs in the United States (Linn, 2008). Are the toys different in these countries? Is children's toy play different? Are gender stereotypes similarly rigid? Researchers could also examine different environments within one culture. Some schools are more likely to promote gender integration than others, and preschools likely vary in the toys they select for children. One study found less gender stereotyping in play among children at a school that had a more gender-progressive curriculum (Bianchi & Bakeman, 1983).

Thus, some limited evidence indicates that gender-stereotyped toys promote behaviors that are consistent with gender-stereotyped roles. Some of these behaviors are likely positive, such that play with certain kinds of dolls might encourage nurturing behavior in girls, and play with sports and action toys might encourage physical competence and other positive qualities in boys. The fact that these positive behaviors are polarized by gender, though, is problematic. More boys should be nurturing, and more girls should be feeling physically competent. Because male roles are associated with greater status (Rudman et al., 2012), gender-polarized roles perpetuate a gendered power imbalance (see Chapter 12 for further discussion).

Like many other areas of gender development, extremely stereotyped toys promote unhealthy behaviors. Fashion dolls for girls likely promote a focus on appearance that encourages self-objectification, which is a risk factor for mental health problems (Tiggemann, 2011). War toys and violent video games for boys likely encourage aggression. These extreme gender role behaviors are problematic on their own, but they also discourage friendship among girls and boys, where much gender segregation in childhood social groups, fueled by gender-stereotyped activity (Martin, Fabes, Hanish, Leonard, & Dinella, 2011), already exists.

Extreme gender roles also promote unhealthy heterosexual relationships. The "heterosexual script" in American culture portrays women as sexual objects and men as sexual actors with different goals for heterosexual relationships (Kim et al., 2007). The existence of sexualized fashion dolls and aggressive action figures illustrates the existence of this script in children's toys. The existence of high levels of sexual objectification of women in video games is extremely problematic. This pattern promotes adversarial heterosexual relationships between women and men, and reinforces females' sexually subordinate position.

The commercialization of toys is believed to have led to a magnification of gender stereotypes, and less encouragement of imaginative play (Linn, 2008). Groups in various countries are speaking out against gender-stereotyped toys and initiating action, such as the Campaign for a Commercial-Free Childhood in the United States, Let Toys be Toys in the United Kingdom, and Play Unlimited in Australia. The U.S. toy retailer Target stopped separating their toys into a labeled "girls" aisle and "boys" aisle (Armitage, 2015), and in the United Kingdom Toys "R" Us quit labeling toys by gender on their website (Christodoulou, 2015).

Psychologists should support these efforts to contest the commercial culture that promotes rigid gender stereotyping. Individual efforts among parents might include limiting children's screen time and trying to choose toys that encourage imagination and outdoor play (Linn, 2008). Play in mixed-gender groups at young ages and with gender-neutral toys should also be encouraged. Brown et al. (2009) advocated that parents get to know the products in children's culture to engage in "reality-based parenting." They advocated trying to see products in children's culture from the child's point of view, and also sharing parental views with children. They also advocated saying no when needed (and when justified) and indicated that children have more respect for parents setting limits than most parents believe. We should aim toward the goal of Play Unlimited (2016): "Eliminating the segregation of toys along gender lines and promoting the idea that children should be encouraged to learn through the widest possible range of play experiences."

REFERENCES

Allen, C. (2014, March 9). LEGO wars: A report from the front lines: How LEGO earned the wrath of the "gender-neutral toys" crowd. *Pittsburgh Post-Gazette.* Retrieved from http://www.post-gazette.com/

Allen, S. (2014, October 21). *Barbie is out, Monster High is in.* Retrieved from http://www.thedailybeast.com/articles/2014/10/21/barbie-is-out-monster-high-is-in.html

Anderson, C. A., Shibuya, A., Ihori, N., Swing, E. L., Bushman, B. J., Sakamoto, A., . . . Saleem, M. (2010). Violent video game effects on aggression, empathy, and prosocial behavior in Eastern and Western countries: A meta-analytic review. *Psychological Bulletin, 136,* 151–173. http://dx.doi.org/10.1037/a0018251

Anderson, K. J. (2015). *Modern misogyny: Anti-feminism in a post-feminist era.* New York, NY: Oxford University Press.

Anschutz, D. J., & Engels, R. C. M. E. (2010). The effects of playing with thin dolls on body image and food intake in young girls. *Sex Roles, 63*, 621–630. http://dx.doi.org/10.1007/s11199-010-9871-6

APA Task Force on Violent Media. (2015). *Technical report on the review of the violent video game literature.* Retrieved from http://www.apa.org/pi/families/violent-media.aspx

Armitage, C. (2015, August 22). Pink on blue: Stereotypes hit their shelf life. *Sydney Morning Herald*, p. 37.

Auster, C. J., & Mansbach, C. S. (2012). The gender marketing of toys: An analysis of color and type of toy on the Disney Store website. *Sex Roles, 67*, 375–388. http://dx.doi.org/10.1007/s11199-012-0177-8

Baker, K., & Raney, A. A. (2007). Equally super? gender-role stereotyping of superheroes in children's animated programs. *Mass Communication & Society, 10*, 25–41. http://dx.doi.org/10.1080/15205430709337003

Banerjee, R., & Lintern, V. (2000). Boys will be boys: The effect of social evaluation concerns on gender-typing. *Social Development, 9*, 397–408. http://dx.doi.org/10.1111/1467-9507.00133

Bartneck, C., Min Ser, Q., Moltchanova, E., Smithies, J., & Harrington, E. (2016). Have LEGO products become more violent? *PLOS ONE, 11*, e0155401. http://dx.doi.org/10.1371/journal.pone.0155401

Beck, V. S., Boys, S., Rose, C., & Beck, E. (2012). Violence against women in video games: A prequel or sequel to rape myth acceptance? *Journal of Interpersonal Violence, 27*, 3016–3031. http://dx.doi.org/10.1177/0886260512441078

Benenson, J. F., Carder, H. P., & Geib-Cole, S. J. (2008). The development of boys' preferential pleasure in physical aggression. *Aggressive Behavior, 34*, 154–166. http://dx.doi.org/10.1002/ab.20223

Berkowitz, L. (1993). *Aggression: Its causes, consequences, and control.* New York, NY: McGraw-Hill.

Bianchi, B. D., & Bakeman, R. (1983). Patterns of sex typing in an open school. In M. B. Liss (Ed.), *Social and cognitive skills: Sex roles and children's play* (pp. 219–233). New York, NY: Academic Press.

Blakemore, J. E. O., & Centers, R. E. (2005). Characteristics of boys' and girls' toys. *Sex Roles, 53*, 619–633. http://dx.doi.org/10.1007/s11199-005-7729-0

Brown, L. M., Lamb, S., & Tappan, M. (2009). *Packaging boyhood: Saving our sons from superheroes, slackers, and other media stereotypes.* New York, NY: St. Martin's Press. http://dx.doi.org/10.1037/e572032009-006

Bussey, K., & Bandura, A. (2004). Social cognitive theory of gender development and functioning. In A. H. Eagly, A. E. Beall, & R. J. Sternberg (Eds.), *The psychology of gender* (pp. 92–119). New York, NY: Guilford Press.

Cherney, I. D., & Dempsey, J. (2010). Young children's classification, stereotyping and play behavior for gender neutral and ambiguous toys. *Educational Psychology, 30*, 651–669. http://dx.doi.org/10.1080/01443410.2010.498416

Cherney, I. D., Kelly-Vance, L., Glover, K. G., Ruane, A., & Ryalls, B. O. (2003). The effects of stereotyped toys and gender on play assessment in children aged 18–47 months. *Educational Psychology, 23,* 95–106. http://dx.doi.org/10.1080/01443410303222

Cherney, I. D., & London, K. (2006). Gender-linked differences in the toys, television shows, computer games, and outdoor activities of 5- to 13-year old children. *Sex Roles, 54,* 717–726. http://dx.doi.org/10.1007/s11199-006-9037-8

Christodoulou, H. (2015, November 23). Toys "R" Us ditches boy or girl labels. *The Sun,* p. 26. Retrieved from https://www.thesun.co.uk

Coyne, S. M., Linder, J. R., Rasmussen, E. E., Nelson, D. A., & Birkbeck, V. (2016). Pretty as a princess: Longitudinal effects of engagement with Disney Princesses on gender stereotypes, body esteem, and prosocial behavior in children. *Child Development, 87,* 1909–1925. http://dx.doi.org/10.1111/cdev.12569

Coyne, S. M., Linder, J. R., Rasmussen, E. E., Nelson, D. A., & Collier, K. M. (2014). It's a bird! It's a plane! It's a gender stereotype! Longitudinal associations between superhero viewing and gender stereotyped play. *Sex Roles, 70,* 416–430. http://dx.doi.org/10.1007/s11199-014-0374-8

Dill, K. E., & Thill, K. P. (2007). Video game characters and the socialization of gender roles: Young people's perceptions mirror sexist media depictions. *Sex Roles, 57,* 851–864. http://dx.doi.org/10.1007/s11199-007-9278-1

Dittmar, H. (2012). Dolls and action figures. In T. F. Cash (Ed.), *Encyclopedia of body image and human appearance* (Vol. 1, pp. 386–391). San Diego, CA: Elsevier Academic Press. http://dx.doi.org/10.1016/B978-0-12-384925-0.00061-4

Dittmar, H., Halliwell, E., & Ive, S. (2006). Does Barbie make girls want to be thin? The effect of experimental exposure to images of dolls on the body image of 5- to 8-year-old girls. *Developmental Psychology, 42,* 283–292. http://dx.doi.org/10.1037/0012-1649.42.2.283

Douglas, S. J. (2010). *Enlightened sexism: The seductive message that feminism's work is done.* New York, NY: Times Books.

Eime, R. M., Young, J. A., Harvey, J. T., Charity, M. J., & Payne, W. R. (2013). A systematic review of the psychological and social benefits of participation in sport for children and adolescents: Informing development of a conceptual model of health through sport. *International Journal Behavior Nutrition and Physical Activity, 10.* http://dx.doi.org/10.1186/1479-5868-10-98

England, D. E., Descartes, L., & Collier-Meek, M. A. (2011). Gender role portrayal and the Disney Princess. *Sex Roles, 64,* 555–567. http://dx.doi.org/10.1007/s11199-011-9930-7

Entertainment Software Association. (2014). *Essential facts about the computer and video game industry: 2014.* Retrieved from http://www.theesa.com/wp-content/uploads/2014/10/ESA_EF_2014.pdf

Entertainment Software Association. (2016). *Essential facts about the computer and video game industry: 2016.* Retrieved from http://www.theesa.com/wp-content/uploads/2016/04/Essential-Facts-2016.pdf

Feingold, A. (1994). Gender differences in personality: A meta-analysis. *Psychological Bulletin, 116,* 429–456. http://dx.doi.org/10.1037/0033-2909.116.3.429

Ferguson, C. J. (2015). Do angry birds make for angry children? A meta-analysis of video game influences on children's and adolescents' aggression, mental health, prosocial behavior, and academic performance. *Perspectives on Psychological Science, 10,* 646–666. http://dx.doi.org/10.1177/1745691615592234

Ferguson, C. J., & Kilburn, J. (2009). The public health risks of media violence: A meta-analytic review. *The Journal of Pediatrics, 154,* 759–763. http://dx.doi.org/10.1016/j.jpeds.2008.11.033

Fine, C. (2010). *Delusions of gender: How our minds, society, and neurosexism create difference.* New York, NY: Norton.

Fine, C., & Rush, E. (2016). "Why does all the girls have to buy pink stuff?" The ethics and science of the gendered toy marketing debate. *Journal of Business Ethics.* Advance online publication. http://dx.doi.org/10.1007/s10551-016-3080-3

Fox, J., & Potocki, B. (2016). Lifetime video game consumption, interpersonal aggression, hostile sexism, and rape myth acceptance: A cultivation perspective. *Journal of Interpersonal Violence, 31,* 1912–1931. http://dx.doi.org/10.1177/0886260515570747

Fredricks, J. A., & Eccles, J. S. (2005). Family socialization, gender, and sport motivation and involvement. *Journal of Sport & Exercise Psychology, 27,* 3–31. http://dx.doi.org/10.1123/jsep.27.1.3

Fredrickson, B. L., & Roberts, T. (1997). Objectification theory: Toward understanding women's lived experiences and mental health risks. *Psychology of Women Quarterly, 21,* 173–206. http://dx.doi.org/10.1111/j.1471-6402.1997.tb00108.x

Gavrilov, Y., Rotem, S., Ofek, R., & Geva, R. (2012). Socio-cultural effects on children's initiation of joint attention. *Frontiers in Human Neuroscience, 6,* 1–10.

Goff, K. E. (1995). *The relation of violent and nonviolent toys to play behavior in preschoolers.* (Unpublished dissertation). Iowa State University, Ames.

Graff, K., Murnen, S. K., & Krause, A. (2013). Low-cut shirts and high-heeled shoes: Increased sexualization across time in magazine depictions of girls. *Sex Roles, 69,* 571–582. http://dx.doi.org/10.1007/s11199-013-0321-0

Graff, K., Murnen, S. K., & Smolak, L. (2012). Too sexualized to be taken seriously? Perceptions of a girl in childlike vs. sexualizing clothing. *Sex Roles, 66,* 764–775. http://dx.doi.org/10.1007/s11199-012-0145-3

Green, V. A., Bigler, R., & Catherwood, D. (2004). The variability and flexibility of gender-typed toy play: A close look at children's behavioral responses to counterstereotypic models. *Sex Roles, 51,* 371–386. http://dx.doi.org/10.1023/B:SERS.0000049227.05170.aa

Greenfield, P., Yut, E., Chung, M., Land, D., Kreider, H., Pantoja, M., & Horsley, K. (1990). The program-length commercial: A study of the effects of television/toy tie-ins on imaginative play. *Psychology & Marketing, 7,* 237–255. http://dx.doi.org/10.1002/mar.4220070402

Greitemeyer, T. (2013). Playing video games cooperatively increases empathic concern. *Social Psychology, 44*, 408–413. http://dx.doi.org/10.1027/1864-9335/a000154

Hatton, E., & Trautner, M. N. (2011). Equal opportunity objectification? The sexualization of men and women on the cover of *Rolling Stone. Sexuality and Culture, 15*, 256–278. http://dx.doi.org/10.1007/s12119-011-9093-2

Hayes, S., & Tantleff-Dunn, S. (2010). Am I too fat to be a princess? Examining the effects of popular children's media on young girls' body image. *British Journal of Developmental Psychology, 28*, 413–426. http://dx.doi.org/10.1348/026151009X424240

Hunt, J. (2009, December 19). Response: These videogames are not art. They're extreme pornography: Has imagery of violence against women become so normal that we no longer notice? *The Guardian*, p. 33. Retrieved from https://www.theguardian.com/commentisfree/2009/dec/16/adult-videogames-sexual-violence-women

Hyde, J. S. (2005). The gender similarities hypothesis. *American Psychologist, 60*, 581–592. http://dx.doi.org/10.1037/0003-066X.60.6.581

Kahlenberg, S. G., & Hein, M. M. (2010). Progression on Nickelodeon? Gender-role stereotypes in toy commercials. *Sex Roles, 62*, 830–847. http://dx.doi.org/10.1007/s11199-009-9653-1

Kim, J. L., Sorsoli, C. L., Collins, K., Zylbergold, B. A., Schooler, D., & Tolman, D. L. (2007). From sex to sexuality: Exposing the heterosexual script on prime-time network television. *Journal of Sex Research, 44*, 145–157. http://dx.doi.org/10.1080/00224490701263660

Kline, S. (1998). The making of children's culture. In H. Jenkins (Ed.), *The children's culture reader* (pp. 95–109). New York: New York University Press.

Klugman, K. (1999). A bad hair day for G. I. Joe. In B. L. Clark & M. R. Higonnet (Eds.), *Girls, boys, books, toys* (pp. 169–182). Baltimore, MD: Johns Hopkins University Press.

Levin, D. (2003, May). Beyond banning war and superhero play: Meeting children's needs in violent times. *Young Children, 58*, 60–63.

Li, R. Y. H., & Wong, W. I. (2016). Gender-typed play and social abilities in boys and girls: Are they related? *Sex Roles, 74*, 399–410. http://dx.doi.org/10.1007/s11199-016-0580-7

Liben, L. S., & Bigler, R. S. (2002). The developmental course of gender differentiation: Conceptualizing, measuring, and evaluating constructs and pathways. *Monographs of the Society for Research in Child Development, 67*, vii–147. http://dx.doi.org/10.1111/1540-5834.t01-1-00187

Lindberg, S. M., Hyde, J. S., & McKinley, N. M. (2006). A measure of objectified body consciousness for preadolescent and adolescent youth. *Psychology of Women Quarterly, 30*, 65–76. http://dx.doi.org/10.1111/j.1471-6402.2006.00263.x

Linn, S. (2008). Commercializing childhood: The corporate takeover of kids' lives. *Multinational Monitor, 30,* 32–38. Retrieved from http://www.multinational monitor.org/mm2008/072008/interview-linn.html

Linn, S. (2009). *The case for make-believe: Saving play in a commercialized world.* New York, NY: The New York Press.

LoBue, V., & DeLoache, J. S. (2011). Pretty in pink: The early development of gender-stereotyped colour preferences. *British Journal of Developmental Psychology, 29,* 656–667. http://dx.doi.org/10.1111/j.2044-835X.2011.02027.x

Mager, J., & Helgeson, J. G. (2011). Fifty years of advertising images: Some changing perspectives on role portrayals along with enduring consistencies. *Sex Roles, 64,* 238–252. http://dx.doi.org/10.1007/s11199-010-9782-6

Malik, C., & Wojdynski, B. W. (2014). Boys earn, girls buy: Depictions of materialism on U.S. children's branded-entertainment websites. *Journal of Children and Media, 8,* 404–422. http://dx.doi.org/10.1080/17482798.2013.852986

Malloy, H. L., & McMurray-Schwarz, P. (2004). War play, aggression, and peer culture: A review of the research examining the relationship between war play and aggression. In S. Reifel & M. Brown (Eds.), *Advances in early education and day care* (Vol. 13, pp. 235–265). Bingley, England: Emerald. http://dx.doi.org/10.1016/S0270-4021(04)13009-7

Martin, C. L., Fabes, R. A., Hanish, L., Leonard, S., & Dinella, L. M. (2011). Experienced and expected similarity to same-gender peers: Moving toward a comprehensive model. *Sex Roles, 65,* 421–434. http://dx.doi.org/10.1007/s11199-011-0029-y

Martin, C. L., & Ruble, D. (2004). Children's search for gender cues: Cognitive perspectives on gender development. *Current Directions in Psychological Science, 13,* 67–70. http://dx.doi.org/10.1111/j.0963-7214.2004.00276.x

Messner, M. A., Dunbar, M., & Hunt, D. (2000). The televised sports manhood formula. *Journal of Sport & Social Issues, 24,* 380–394. http://dx.doi.org/10.1177/0193723500244006

Miller, C. L. (1987). Qualitative differences among gender-stereotyped toys: Implications for cognitive and social development in girls and boys. *Sex Roles, 16,* 473–487. http://dx.doi.org/10.1007/BF00292482

Murnen, S. K., Greenfield, C., Younger, A., & Boyd, H. (2016). Boys act and girls appear: A content analysis of gender stereotypes associated with characters in children's popular culture. *Sex Roles, 74,* 78–91. http://dx.doi.org/10.1007/s11199-015-0558-x

Orenstein, P. (2011). *Cinderella ate my daughter: Dispatches from the front lines of the new girlie-girl culture.* New York, NY: HarperCollins.

Padilla-Walker, L. M., Coyne, S. M., Fraser, A. M., & Stockdale, L. A. (2013). Is Disney the nicest place on earth? A content analysis of prosocial behavior in animated Disney films. *Journal of Communication, 63,* 393–412. http://dx.doi.org/10.1111/jcom.12022

Play Unlimited. (2016). *Our aim*. Retrieved from: http://www.playunlimited.org.au/about-the-campaign/our-aim/

Raag, T. (1999). Influences of social expectations of gender, gender stereotyped, and situational constraints on children's toy choices. *Sex Roles, 41*, 809–831. http://dx.doi.org/10.1023/A:1018828328713

Reuters. (2016, October 20). Mattel shares soar after booming Barbie sales boost revenues. *Fortune*. Retrieved from http://fortune.com/2016/10/20/mattel-shares-soar-booming-barbie-sales-boost-revenues/

Rudman, L. A., Moss-Racusin, C. A., Phelan, J. E., & Nauts, S. (2012). Status incongruity and backlash effects: Defending the gender hierarchy motivates prejudice toward female leaders. *Journal of Experimental Social Psychology, 48*, 165–179. http://dx.doi.org/10.1016/j.jesp.2011.10.008

Starr, C. R., & Ferguson, G. M. (2012). Sexy dolls, sexy grade schoolers? Media and maternal influences on young girls' self-sexualization. *Sex Roles, 67*, 463–476. http://dx.doi.org/10.1007/s11199-012-0183-x

Stermer, S. P., & Burkley, M. (2012). Xbox or SeXbox? An examination of sexualized content in video games. *Social and Personality Psychology Compass, 6*, 525–535. http://dx.doi.org/10.1111/j.1751-9004.2012.00442.x

Sutton-Smith, B. (1988). War toys and childhood aggression. *Play & Culture, 1*, 57–69.

Sweet, E. (2012, December 21). Guys and dolls no more? *New York Times*. Retrieved from http://www.nytimes.com/2012/12/23/opinion/sunday/gender-based-toy-marketing-returns.html

Tiggemann, M. (2011). Mental health risks of self-objectification: A review of the empirical evidence for disordered eating, depressed mood, and sexual dysfunction. In R. M. Calogero, S. Tantleff-Dunn, & J. K. Thompson (Eds.), *Self-objectification in women: Causes, consequences, and counteractions* (pp. 139–159). Washington, DC: American Psychological Association. http://dx.doi.org/10.1037/12304-007

Tiggemann, M., & Slater, A. (2014). Contemporary girlhood: Maternal reports on sexualized behaviour and appearance concern in 4–10-year-old girls. *Body Image, 11*, 396–403. http://dx.doi.org/10.1016/j.bodyim.2014.06.007

Toy Industry Association. (2016). *The Toy Association*. Retrieved from https://www.toyassociation.org/

Twenge, J. M. (2009). Status and gender: The paradox of progress in an age of narcissism. *Sex Roles, 61*, 338–340. http://dx.doi.org/10.1007/s11199-009-9617-5

Vandenbosch, L., & Eggermont, S. (2015). The role of mass media in adolescents' sexual behaviors: Exploring the explanatory value of the three-step self-objectification process. *Archives of Sexual Behavior, 44*, 729–742. http://dx.doi.org/10.1007/s10508-014-0292-4

Watson, M. W., & Peng, Y. (1992). The relation between toy gun play and children's aggressive behavior. *Early Education and Development, 3*, 370–389. http://dx.doi.org/10.1207/s15566935eed0304_7

Weisgram, E. S., Fulcher, M., & Dinella, L. M. (2014). Pink gives girls permission: Exploring the roles of explicit gender labels and gender-typed colors on pre-school children's toy preferences. *Journal of Applied Developmental Psychology, 35*, 401–409. http://dx.doi.org/10.1016/j.appdev.2014.06.004

Williams, C. L. (2006). *Inside toyland: Working, shopping, and social inequality.* Berkeley, CA: University of California Press.

Wong, W. I., & Hines, M. (2015). Effects of gender color-coding on toddlers' gender-typical toy play. *Archives of Sexual Behavior, 44*, 1233–1242. http://dx.doi.org/10.1007/s10508-014-0400-5

Wood, W., & Eagly, A. H. (2013). Biology or culture alone cannot account for human sex differences and similarities. *Psychological Inquiry, 24*, 241–247. http://dx.doi.org/10.1080/1047840X.2013.815034

Yao, M. Z., Mahood, C., & Linz, D. (2010). Sexual priming, gender stereotyping, and likelihood to sexually harass: Examining the cognitive effects of playing a sexually-explicit video game. *Sex Roles, 62*, 77–88. http://dx.doi.org/10.1007/s11199-009-9695-4

10

COGNITIVE CONSEQUENCES OF GENDERED TOY PLAY

LYNN S. LIBEN, KINGSLEY M. SCHROEDER, GIULIA A. BORRIELLO, AND ERICA S. WEISGRAM

A sister and brother play side by side in their home, each using different toys and each enacting different play styles. The girl engages quietly in gentle, pretend play. She cradles a doll in her arms while she shifts plastic food around in the toy pan that sits on the stove of her child-sized kitchen set. Her brother plays in another part of the room, having just built towers from blocks to support a ramp for his toy cars. He races two toy cars down the ramp with accompanying, high-volume vrooming and honking sound effects. He smashes the second car into the first, which then flies dramatically off the ramp.

Despite many reductions in societal gender constraints over the last century (Liben, 2016), gender-stereotypical play patterns like these remain common, particularly during toddlerhood and the preschool years (Blakemore, Berenbaum, & Liben, 2009). These patterns are of interest not only because they demonstrate that girls and boys engage in different kinds of play during their childhoods but also because these different behaviors may have long-term

http://dx.doi.org/10.1037/0000077-011
Gender Typing of Children's Toys: How Early Play Experiences Impact Development, E. S. Weisgram and L. M. Dinella (Editors)

effects on the development of cognitive skills, in turn affecting individuals' educational, occupational, and daily lives. In the sibling pair just described, the girl may be fostering skills in nurturance, caretaking, and multitasking that attract her to and support her success in a career in nursing; the boy may be fostering his interests and skills in structural design, construction, and physics in ways that eventually lead him to a successful career in architecture or engineering.

This chapter is designed to address links between gendered toy play and cognitive development. In the sections that follow, we (a) explain how we conceptualize key constructs related to gendered toy play and specify which we emphasize here; (b) define cognitive development and outline strategies for examining gendered toy play in the context of gendered play; and (c) review empirical research that examines links between cognition and gendered play in two illustrative domains: spatial cognition and mathematics; (d) in the concluding section, we provide recommendations for directions for future research and action at the intersection of cognition, toy play, and gender.

GENDERED TOYS AND TOY PLAY

The key goal of the current chapter is to explore the links between gendered toy play and cognitive development. Both components are multifaceted, and neither can be covered fully. In this section, we provide our interpretations of the constructs entailed in gendered toy play and identify which ones we emphasize in our chapter.

What Are Toys?

We begin with the seemingly simple definitional question, *What are toys?* The first definition for *toy* given by the online Merriam-Webster dictionary is: "something for a child to play with" ("Toy," n.d.-a). The Oxford dictionary defines a toy as "an object for a child to play with, typically a model or miniature replica of something" ("Toy," n.d.-b). Wikipedia defines a toy as "an item that is used in play. . . . Many items are designed to serve as toys, but goods produced for other purposes can also be used. For instance, a small child may fold an ordinary piece of paper into an airplane shape and 'fly it'" ("Toy," n.d.-c).

These dictionary definitions thus encompass two types of toys: objects that are explicitly designed to be play objects (hereinafter referred to as *designed* toys) or objects and materials that are appropriated for, or transformed into play objects (hereinafter, *appropriated* toys). Sometimes the functional distinction between designed toys and appropriated toys is minimal or even nonexistent. As just one example, entering the words "toy" and "geology" into a Google search returns advertisements for boxed toy sets that contain little more than some rocks, most of which could be collected by children on independent walks through outdoor environments. Designed toys nevertheless provide convenient (if more expensive) access to relevant materials; they allow manufacturers to convey messages about appropriate ages, educational benefits, and safety; and, of most importance here, they offer opportunities to signal toy gender. For example, although samples of limestone, mica, and quartz convey no information about gender, a box of rocks that is decorated with images of geologist Marie Tharp versus geologist James Hutton might do so.

Our focus is primarily on designed toys—that is, on objects or collections of objects that are explicitly created as children's toys, packaged as toys, marketed as toys, and purchased (or otherwise acquired) as toys. Reasons for this focus are largely practical. First, the range of appropriated toys is virtually limitless (e.g., how many ways might a piece of paper or a rock be used?) and thus they cannot be covered within a single chapter. Second, scholarship on designed toys is likely to be more useful for policy and educational recommendations: It is far easier to imagine convincing manufacturers to change the packaging or advertising of particular toys or encouraging adults to change their toy-buying habits than it is to imagine convincing children, their playmates, and their caretakers to identify and implement new strategies for creating and employing found objects (like pieces of paper or rocks) in gender-neutral ways. Thus, we next turn to a more detailed consideration of how we conceptualize the gender typing of toys and play.

What Are Gender-Typed Toys?

A second key construct for this chapter is *gender-typed toys*. What makes a toy gender typed? One humorous but pointed answer to this question is captured by decision tree images that were widely circulated on social media and other online sources. Illustrative is one produced by Myers (2013) entitled "How to tell if a toy is for boys or girls: A guide." The question posed is: "Do you operate the toy with your genitalia?" If the answer is yes, the conclusion is: "This toy is not for children." If the answer is no, the conclusion is: "It is for either girls or boys." Although this decision rule is one we embrace for a future world, it is not the rule that operates in most of society. Instead, from an early age, individuals are highly knowledgeable about which toys are for which gender (Signorella, Bigler, & Liben, 1993). As a first approximation, then, we take the term *gender-typed toys* to denote toys that in contemporary society are tagged as differentially appropriate for or relevant to girls versus boys.

Before unpacking the bases on which one might so tag a particular toy, we interject a comment about two ways in which our discussions are constrained. First, the "contemporary society" on which we focus is almost entirely limited to the United States. Most of the studies we cite were conducted in the United States, and even these are further restricted insofar as they disproportionately focus on White, middle-class families. Second, we use the terms *girls* and *boys* in traditional ways, as if their meanings were obvious, yet within both academia and society more generally, there is increasing rethinking about traditional binary divisions and assumptions about the permanence and constraints of natal gender. Discussions of gender in the context of culture may be found in Best and Williams (2001); discussions of identification and implications of nonbinary and fluid conceptualizations of gender may be found in Tate, Ledbetter, and Youssef (2013). Although it is beyond the scope of this chapter to address these issues here, we urge readers to interpret our discussions with awareness of these constraints.

Having offered these caveats about definitional complexities, we return to gender-typed toys and ask, on what bases may toys be said to be differentially associated with girls or boys? We identify five means by which toys may be gendered: (a) labeled categorization, (b) cultural marking, (c) social partner messaging, (d) observed or expressed preferences, and (e) stereotypic beliefs.

Labeled Categorization

One way in which toys may be identified as gendered is through explicit labels that define them as being for girls or boys (rather than for children in general). In brick-and-mortar stores, for example, such categories are established and communicated by placing toys in separate aisles and labeling one "girls' toys" and the other "boys' toys" (e.g., see Fine & Rush, 2016; see also Chapter 1, this volume). Many online toy catalogs and websites are similarly organized and labeled. For example, on the Disney Store website, 208 toys are listed under a tab for girls and 410 are listed under a tab for boys; only 91 toys are listed under both tabs (see Auster & Mansbach, 2012).

Experimental studies in both laboratories and classrooms have demonstrated that explicit labels and organizational structures like these affect children's interests, behaviors, and stereotypes. For example, Martin, Eisenbud, and Rose (1995) showed unfamiliar toys to preschool children and labeled some as toys for boys and others for girls. Children liked toys less if they had been said to be for the other gender, even when those toys were inherently more appealing. In a later study conducted in children's preschool classrooms, Hilliard and Liben (2010) asked experimental-group preschool teachers to organize their classrooms by gender (e.g., creating separate girls' and boys' bulletin boards for children's work). Control-group teachers maintained their usual gender-neutral classroom structures. After just 2 weeks, children in experimental (but not control) classes showed significant increases in endorsements of gender stereotypes and dramatic reductions in play with children of the other gender. These and related studies have demonstrated that gender labeling and organization affect children's attitudes and behaviors (Bigler, 1995; Bigler & Liben, 2007; Liben & Coyle, 2017; Weisgram, Fulcher, & Dinella, 2014; see also Chapter 12, this volume).

Cultural Marking

A second way that toys can be gendered is by designing or advertising them with cultural markers of femininity or masculinity. If the viewer is knowledgeable about the meaning of those cultural markers, the impact of gender marking is likely to be roughly equivalent to verbal gender labeling just discussed. One particularly effective marker is toy color. In contemporary U.S. society, pink and pastels are associated with femininity and blue and dark colors with masculinity (although gendered colors have changed over history; see Paoletti, 2012). Illustratively, a Google search for boys' and girls' toys returns toy images that are disproportionately pink or pastel for girls and blue or dark for boys. Children understand color marking early in life, and this marking affects their toy preferences (Cherney & Dempsey, 2010; Weisgram et al., 2014; Wong & Hines, 2015).

Gender may also be culturally marked in advertisements by sound and pacing. Television commercials, for example, advertise toys meant for girls with slow transitions, gentle music, and quieter play while toys targeted to boys are shown in rapidly changing, loud, highly active scenes (Kahlenberg & Hein, 2010; Rovinelli & Whissell, 1998; Welch, Huston-Stein, Wright, & Plehal, 1979). By about 6 years, children recognize the intended gender of advertised products from nonlinguistic cues like these (Huston, Greer, Wright, Welch, & Ross, 1984; see also Chapter 4, this volume).

Social Partner Messaging

A third avenue by which toys may be tagged as gendered is through messages children receive during social interactions with adults or peers (see Chapter 6). Parents may provide explicit messages to children about the gendered nature of toys by selecting only gender "appropriate" toys for their own children or when buying gifts for their children's friends. Parents also behave differently in response to play overtures or engagement with "appropriate" versus "inappropriate" toys. Illustratively, Caldera, Huston, and O'Brien (1989) invited parents and their toddlers to play with six toys (one at a time) drawn from traditionally feminine, traditionally masculine, and neutral categories. Parents' initial nonverbal reactions were significantly more positive when the toy was matched to their child's gender than when it was not. On the basis of a meta-analysis that included observational studies in natural settings, Lytton and Romney (1991) concluded that although parents do not reinforce behaviors differently in relation to gender in all arenas, they do so during toy play. Similar conclusions come from parental responses to questionnaires. For example, Blakemore and Hill (2008) found that parents reported more positive attitudes about their children playing with toys culturally matched (rather than mismatched) to their child's gender.

Social interactions with peers similarly tag toys as gendered. For example, children receive more favorable responses from peers when they play with toys preferred by others of their gender (e.g., Langlois & Downs, 1980; see also Chapter 6, this volume). Likewise, children are more likely to be rejected when they play with toys typically favored by children of the other gender, a pattern particularly strong for boys (Shell & Eisenberg, 1990). Peers may also teach other children these classifications directly by bullying or taunting children who defy traditional gender preferences (e.g., see Lamb, Bigler, Liben, & Green, 2009; Liben, 2016).

Observed or Expressed Preferences

A fourth basis that can be used to categorize toys as gender typed is via actual differences in toy use. The most direct indices of differential use come from contexts in which both feminine and masculine toys are within reach (e.g., in laboratory playrooms or classrooms), and children are observed to see which toys they choose to play with, and how long they play with each. Investigators have routinely reported gendered play patterns with actual toys (e.g., Connor & Serbin, 1977; Dinella, Weisgram, & Fulcher, 2017; O'Brien & Huston, 1985). Other data on gendered toy preferences and use come from self-report measures, in which children are asked how much they would like to play with toys represented in photographs, pictures, or labels (e.g., Blakemore, LaRue, & Olejnik, 1979; Liben & Bigler, 2002; Weisgram et al., 2014); from toy requests made in letters to Santa Claus, in which girls more often ask for doll houses, clothing, jewelry, and dolls, while boys more commonly request sports equipment, vehicles, and machines (Bradbard & Parkman, 1984); and from sales on differential buying patterns by and for boys and girls (e.g., Fisher-Thompson, 1993).

Stereotypic Beliefs

A fifth way to classify toys as gender typed is by cultural stereotypes. The most straightforward evidence that a toy is viewed as gender stereotyped comes from responses to questions that ask directly about whether the culture views the toy as differentially appropriate for girls or boys. For example, as a first step in selecting items for gender-typing measures, Liben and Bigler (2002) asked college students to use a 7-point scale to rate various items—including children's toys—on the degree to which the items "are stereotyped in American culture" (p. 113). Irrespective of their own gender, raters generally showed strong agreement about which toys were culturally masculine, feminine, or neutral. Research using the resulting and related scales has shown that even by preschool, children almost universally know these cultural stereotypes even though they vary in their personal endorsements of those stereotypes (see Signorella et al., 1993).

What Is Gender-Typed Play?

In addition to evidence that there are gender-typed toys, there is also evidence of gender-typed play, that is, of differences between how girls and boys play with given toys. Compelling demonstrations of this phenomenon come from early observational studies of children's play in childcare settings. For example, Schau, Kahn, Diepold, and Cherry (1980) reported that most of the time that preschool boys spent playing with a dollhouse, they incorporated a second available toy—a kitchen mixer. However, rather than using it as a food appliance, they turned it into a drill or a machine gun. In an observational study of children's play, O'Brien, Huston, and Risley (1983) reported that of the total time 3-year-old boys spent playing with gendered toys, about as much time was spent playing with one of the available feminine toys—a toy house (23%)—as playing with each of two masculine toys—a train (22%) and tools (22%). However, and paralleling the observation by Schau et al. (1980), they found that about 80% of the time that boys played with the toy house, they used it in conjunction with tools, for example, using a hammer to pretend to fix the roof.

Recent research that examined preschoolers' play behaviors with gender-marked toys in controlled laboratory settings has also shown gender-differentiated play with functionally identical toys. In a recent study by Coyle and Liben (2015), for example, mother–child dyads were invited to play both independently and jointly with a toy that was focused on the masculine domain of mechanics (assembling belt drives) and incorporated the feminine domain of reading (instructions were embedded in a storybook narrative). Dyads were randomly assigned to play with a version of the toy that had been packaged as either masculine or feminine by using gendered colors, protagonists, and language. Data revealed gender-differentiated play styles in children, mothers, and dyads. To give just one example, among children given the masculine version, boys spent more of their time assembling pieces without consulting the toy's book; girls spent more of their building time in conjunction with the book (see Chapter 11).

In addition to using identical toys differently, boys and girls play differently in situations that do not involve toys at all. For example, without props, boys may enact roles of Superman or of an army general; girls may enact roles of Princess Ariel or of an elementary school teacher (e.g., see the review of pretend play by Lillard, 2015). Play may also be gender differentiated with respect to overarching styles. For example, boys have been observed to spend relatively more time than do girls in unstructured play, that is, in play that is neither highly rule-bound nor closely monitored by adults, a gender difference that has been hypothesized to encourage boys' generation of independent and novel solutions to intellectual problems (Carpenter, 1983; Carpenter & Huston-Stein, 1980).

COGNITIVE DEVELOPMENT

Having established how we conceptualize gendered play and which components we emphasize, we turn to a brief discussion of the other side of the chapter's focus, cognitive development, and then to strategies for examining links between the two.

Defining Cognitive Development

In broad terms, *cognitive development* refers to age-linked advances in the skills and products of thought. It includes a vast array of substantive domains. Illustratively, in the introductory chapter to her advanced textbook titled *Cognitive Development*, Galotti (2017) listed key topics as (a) perception; (b) attention; (c) memory; (d) knowledge representation and categorization; (e) language; (f) thinking, reasoning, and decision making; (g) academic skills; and (h) social cognition. Similar topics are addressed in the 23 chapters that compose the cognitive–developmental volume of the seventh edition of the *Handbook of Child Psychology and Developmental Science* (Liben & Müller, 2015). For example, in the *Handbook*, coverage of what Galotti labeled "knowledge representation and categorization" comes via separate chapters on symbolic representation and conceptual development; coverage of "academic skills" comes from separate chapters on mathematical reasoning, literacy, artistic accomplishments, and scientific thinking. What is clear from these or other examples we could have picked is that cognitive development is not some monolithic construct that can be assessed by a single test such as a measure of general intelligence. Indeed, even general intelligence tests have subcomponents that tap distinct cognitive skills (Guilford, 1959). We thus conceptualize cognitive development as age-linked progressions in a variety of specific cognitive skills (e.g., spatial, linguistic, mathematical).

Strategies for Linking Cognitive Development and Gendered Play

How might we approach the study of cognitive development in relation to gendered play? One strategy would be to begin by using one or more of the means discussed earlier to identify which toys are gendered, analyze those toys' demands and affordances to formulate hypotheses about the cognitive skills they might foster, and then examine empirical associations between gendered toy play and cognitive skills. A serious difficulty of this approach is that there are huge numbers of specific gendered toys, and it is easy to imagine generating an impossibly long and unwieldy list of potential skills that might be fostered by play with each.

An alternative strategy would be to begin with a list of cognitive domains such as the ones from the textbook and handbook described above, draw from cognitive science to identify subskills or processes entailed in each, hypothesize ways that those cognitive skills and processes might be fostered through play, and then review empirical evidence of links between the cognitive domain and play, particularly play that is in some way gendered. This second approach faces a similar difficulty of scope given the long list of cognitive domains.

To identify a reasonable scope for the current chapter—one that allows us to describe empirical studies in some detail—we have thus focused our review on two illustrative cognitive domains that have themselves been identified as gender differentiated. Paralleling our earlier discussion of the identification of gendered toys, we next consider the identification of gendered cognitive domains.

Gendered Cognition

What cognitive domains are gender differentiated? The answer to this question is more contentious than might be presumed, and the varied positions have been discussed in publications written for both academic (e.g., Halpern, 2012) and general audiences (e.g., L. Eliot, 2010; Fine, 2010). As reviewed earlier (Liben, 2015, 2016), at one end of the continuum are those claiming that boys' and girls' brains are biologically, pervasively, and perhaps immutably different, so much so that they are best served by gender-segregated classrooms and different curricula (e.g., Gurian, Stevens, & Daniel, 2009). At the other end are those who argue that gender differences of all kinds are few and far between, and can be explained almost entirely as the result of gender socialization (e.g., Bem, 1983, 1998).

In a seminal summary of scientific research on a broad range of psychological gender differences, Hyde (2005) included a table of effect sizes from prior meta-analyses. Of the 39 cognitive effect sizes listed, only seven showed even moderate effects of gender and of these, only two were large. Of the seven, four were observed on spatial skills (a male advantage on tests of the same spatial skill included in two of the meta-analyses), one on mechanical skills (a male advantage on a test of mechanical reasoning), and two on literacy skills (female advantage on tests tapping spelling, grammar, punctuation, and capitalization skills). Reilly (2012) identified similar gender-differentiated areas in a review focused exclusively on cognitive abilities. Within the U.S., boys outperformed girls on mathematics and on science; girls outperformed boys on reading literacy. Consistent with Hyde's argument that cognitive gender differences are neither pervasive nor dramatic, none of these effect sizes was large and only one was even moderate.

As acknowledged in almost all contemporary scholarship on gender-related differences of any kind (e.g., Blakemore et al., 2009; Halpern, 2012; Hines, 2015; Ruble, Martin, & Berenbaum, 2006), the existence of gender differences in no way implies that the differences are biologically determined or impervious to experience. On the contrary, there is much evidence that experience matters for genetic processes, during gestation, and throughout life after birth. At the macro level, for example, the importance of experience is demonstrated by data showing variations in patterns of gendered cognition across nations (e.g., Else-Quest, Hyde, & Linn, 2010; Reilly, 2012).

In short, there is not complete agreement among researchers and educators about either the size or explanations of cognitive gender differences, but the available data support the conclusion that there are reasonably consistent gender differences in some arenas of children's and adults' cognitive functioning. From among these gendered cognitive domains, and for several reasons explained next, we have selected two as the focus of our empirical review: spatial cognition and mathematics.

First, both are areas in which gender differences are apparent not only to academicians and educators who explicitly study cognitive skills, but also to members of the general public who see imbalanced gender distributions in outcomes assumed to draw on cognitive abilities. For example, gender differences are apparent in the distributions of males and females in mathematics- and science-oriented jobs, recipients of various kinds of honors, and contestants and winners of certain kinds of competitions. Second, both domains are increasingly viewed as core parts of education. Mathematics has long been identified as one of the essential components of education, illustrated by the inclusion of mathematics tests in achievement tests given at all educational levels. For example, mathematics achievement is assessed biennially as part of the federally funded National Assessment of Educational Progress of elementary-, middle-, and high-school students (see National Assessment Governing Board, 2017); and quantitative thinking is included in tests used to select students into undergraduate and graduate school programs such as the Scholastic Aptitude Test and the Graduate Record Examination (see, respectively, The College Board, 2017; Educational Testing Service, 2017). Spatial thinking has been recognized as a key educational focus more recently, but as documented in additional detail later, there is growing attention to the importance of the domain (e.g., see Clements, 2004; Liben, 2006; National Research Council, 2006; Newcombe, 2010; Wai, Lubinski, & Benbow, 2009). Third, both domains are ones in which toy play has been hypothesized to have a major role, and, relatedly, both domains have inspired much empirical research on the contribution of play. As a result, these domains offer a large and diverse corpus of relevant empirical work from which to draw in the current chapter.

EMPIRICAL LINKS BETWEEN TOY PLAY AND COGNITIVE DEVELOPMENT

In this section, we review empirical work linking gendered cognition and toy play in the selected domains of spatial cognition and mathematics. Given that spatial skills appear to provide important support for mathematical thinking, we discuss the spatial domain first.

Spatial Development

Spatial skills have been receiving growing attention in part because of increasing recognition that they are foundational for success in STEM fields (science, technology, engineering, and mathematics) that are themselves highly valued and highly gendered (Liben & Coyle, 2014). It is especially appropriate to examine the current or potential contribution of play to these spatial skills because there has traditionally been no explicit spatial curriculum in formal education, thus making out-of-school experiences—including play—particularly important. Despite its importance, spatial cognition is typically less well known than other cognitive domains such as mathematics and language. Thus, before turning to research addressing links among spatial skills, gender, and toy play, we offer a brief orientation to spatial thinking and the assessment of spatial skills.

Definitions and Assessments

There is no single, accepted definition of spatial thinking, spatial development, or even space (Liben, 1981, 2006). Here we use the term *spatial thinking* to refer to encoding, storing, and manipulating knowledge about or representations of spaces and objects. The spaces and objects may be smaller than one's body, visible from a single glance (e.g., a desk top and the individual objects resting upon it); somewhat larger than one's body but still visually accessible from a single location within the space (e.g., a room that can be seen by swiveling one's head); considerably larger than one's body but accessible to direct experience via human locomotion (e.g., a campus or town); or so large and distant that understanding and manipulating the space is possible only with representational aids such as photographs or maps (e.g., an entire continent).

The spatial skills involved in conceptualizing, representing, and mentally manipulating spaces and objects are diverse and have been assessed by a myriad of paper-and-pencil tests (e.g., J. Eliot & Smith, 1983; Hegarty & Waller, 2005; Linn & Petersen, 1985). Illustrative are two- or three-dimensional *mental rotation* tasks, in which respondents are asked how a letter-like figure (or a block construction) would look after being rotated through the plane or in three-dimensional space); *paper folding* tasks, in which respondents are shown how a piece of paper is folded, shown where the folded paper is punched, and then asked to select which of several drawings shows the pattern of holes that would be seen when the paper is again unfolded; *perspective taking* tasks, in which respondents are asked what a vista (e.g., a mountainous landscape) looks like to an observer located at a position different from the respondent's own; and *horizontality* or *verticality* tasks, in which respondents are asked to produce or identify horizontal or vertical lines within surrounding, nonorthogonal frames (e.g., the *water level* task, in which respondents are asked to draw a horizontal water line within a tipped glass; or the *rod and frame* task, in which respondents are shown an oblique rod embedded within a similarly oblique rectangular frame and asked to adjust the rod to the true vertical). Spatial skills have also been measured by tests in the larger environment as illustrated by *navigation* or *wayfinding* tasks, in which respondents are asked to travel to locations in real environments or to mark maps to show their own location or the location of other objects in the surrounding environment.

Gender Differences

As noted earlier, gender differences on spatial tests are well established in children and adults (e.g., Halpern, 2012; Liben, 2006; Linn & Petersen, 1985), and are especially strong on tests that assess skill in mental rotation (e.g., Hyde, 2005; Voyer, Voyer, & Bryden, 1995) and the use of Cartesian horizontal and vertical axes (e.g., Linn & Petersen, 1985; Vasta & Liben, 1996). Research has also commonly shown gender differences in navigation tasks, especially when the tasks involve maps or other graphic representations of space (e.g., Lawton, 2010; Liben, Myers, Christensen, & Bower, 2013).

Some data suggest that biological processes play a role in these gender differences. For example, higher spatial skills have been reported for girls with congenital adrenal hyperplasia, who are exposed to dramatically higher levels of prenatal testosterone than are typically developing genetic females (Berenbaum & Resnick, 1997), although evidence for this association has been inconsistent (see Hines et al., 2003). There is ample evidence that spatial skills are affected by experience, a conclusion supported, for example, by variations in gender differences across national contexts (e.g., Lippa, Collaer, & Peters, 2010) and by meta-analyses demonstrating significant improvement in spatial functioning as a consequence of experimentally assigned experiences (Baenninger & Newcombe, 1989; Uttal et al., 2013).

Salutary effects of interventions need not wipe out gender differences to demonstrate the impact of experience. Indeed, it would be unreasonable to expect that experimentally assigned participation in minutes, hours, weeks, or even months of spatial interventions would completely erase differences that have emerged from years or even decades of gender-differentiated spatial experiences. From the perspective of education, what is important is identifying ways to maximize the chance that all children will acquire the foundational competencies needed to pursue desirable educational or occupational goals, not that all individual and group differences in spatial skills are eliminated. The key question guiding this section is, thus, whether research findings are consistent with the hypothesis that certain kinds of toy play—especially play that is commonly favored by boys—fosters children's spatial development. An affirmative answer to this question helps to illuminate developmental mechanisms, and contributes to efforts intended to develop, implement, and evaluate play-based interventions to foster spatial thinking.

Early Studies of Gendered Play and Spatial Outcomes

At least by the middle of the 20th century, gender researchers suggested that gendered play might help to account for gender differences in spatial performance (Sherman, 1967). Findings from an early observational study of preschoolers' classroom play by Connor and Serbin (1977), for example, provided data that were partially consistent with this hypothesis. Based on observations collected over a 12-week period, the proportions of time that children spent playing with masculine and feminine toys were calculated. For boys (but not girls), amount of masculine play was significantly correlated with scores on the Preschool Embedded Figures Test (Witkin, Oltman, Raskin, & Karp, 1971), which—like horizontality and verticality tests—assesses skill in spatial disembedding. In this study, masculine play was not similarly predictive of children's scores on a second spatial task (the Wechsler Preschool and Primary Scale of Intelligence [WPPSI] block design; Wechsler, 1967), but in a similar study conducted later with a larger sample (Serbin & Connor, 1979), masculine play did predict block design scores as well.

Most discussions of the study by Connor and Serbin (1977) emphasize the associations they observed between gendered play and spatial performance, but we note that their data also revealed significant correlations between gendered play and social behaviors. Among boys, greater masculine play was correlated with more parallel and cooperative play with other boys; among girls, greater feminine play was correlated with more cooperative play with boys. There were also significant positive correlations in both boys and girls between play with activities deemed culturally "appropriate" for their own gender and their performance on a test of verbal intelligence.

Although there is no immediately obvious explanation of this particular pattern of results taken as a whole, the various significant associations do serve as a reminder that many factors are likely to covary with the variable of interest (i.e., gendered play). As a consequence, correlational studies like these cannot yield definitive conclusions about causal connections. Correlational studies are especially suspect when the play behavior is reported retrospectively by informants (e.g., parents) who may show selective memory or confirmation bias. For example, knowing that one's child became an architect may lead a parent to selectively recall their child's earlier interest in constructing buildings from blocks; parents' own gender-stereotyped attitudes may lead them to selectively forget or underreport their children's gender "inappropriate" play. One obvious response to methodological issues like these is to employ designs that manipulate toy play experimentally (see Chapter 2). In the following sections, we sample from both correlational and experimental research on the connections between spatial outcomes and play with three types of toys: blocks and construction toys, jigsaw puzzles, and computer and video games.

Play With Blocks and Construction Toys

Blocks and other toys used to construct structures and objects (e.g., Tinker Toys, Lincoln Logs, model building kits) are culturally stereotyped as masculine (e.g., Liben & Bigler, 2002) and are disproportionately preferred and used by boys during free play (e.g., Connor & Serbin, 1977; Edens & Potter, 2013). Several investigators (e.g., Caldera et al., 1999; Nath & Szücs, 2014) have found that children's skill in building a specified object (e.g., assembling blocks to create a physical structure that matches one shown in a picture) is positively correlated with performance on standardized spatial tests such as the block design tasks from intelligence tests such as the WPPSI and the Stanford–Binet. However, success in using blocks and construction toys in response to a researcher's explicit requests to build something is arguably different from children's experience in using blocks in the context of play, and thus it is also important to consider evidence of free-choice play in relation to spatial skills.

In one recent and relevant study, Jirout and Newcombe (2015) asked parents whose children had participated in a standardization of the fourth edition of the WPPSI (Wechsler, 2012) to provide reports of how frequently their children played with various toys, including those the investigators categorized as spatial (viz., blocks, puzzles, and board games, grouped into a single category). Parents reported more of this spatial play for sons than daughters. In addition, there was a significant association between reported spatial play and children's scores on the WPPSI block design test. These findings are compelling in light of the diversity and size of the sample ($N > 800$). At the same time, and as the authors themselves explicitly noted, parental reports must be interpreted with caution in light of concerns about informant data just discussed, and in light of the correlational nature of the design, which leaves open the possibilities that covariates of spatial play account for the association, or that higher spatial skills lead to more spatial play rather than the inverse.

Some studies have failed to find even correlational evidence for associations between children's play with blocks and puzzles and spatial performance. Caldera et al. (1999), for example, conducted an observational study of the amount of time children spent playing with various toys in their preschool classrooms and examined the relation between play patterns and performance on various spatial tests. They found no links between children's preferential engagement with blocks, LEGOs, and puzzles (i.e., what they categorized as manipulative toy play) and scores on any of several spatial tasks they administered (including the WPPSI block design test). They did, however, report associations between other kinds of play and scores on the spatial tests they administered. In particular, they found that preference for play with art materials was associated with higher performance on the block design test, and marginally associated with scores on a block copying task. This finding, too, contrasts with findings from the study by Jirout and Newcombe (2015) in which no links were found between reported children's play with drawing materials and performance on the block design measure.

It is important to note that the findings we report above from individual studies are necessarily only a small selection of the results reported in the original sources, and thus these alone cannot provide a complete picture. We urge interested readers to consult the original sources for more detail. What can be gleaned even from brief reviews, however, is a sense of the considerable variability in methodologies and participant samples across studies. For example, Jirout and Newcombe (2015) used data from questionnaires and standardized tests drawn from over 800 families recruited from a nationally representative sample that had participated in test standardization; Caldera et al. (1999) used intensive observational data but from a smaller and more homogeneous sample ($N = 60$; children attended university-affiliated preschool classrooms serving predominantly White, Midwestern, middle-class families). Investigators examine different kinds of play and merge toys into single categories differently; they use different measures of spatial skills. Some studies provide data consistent with the general statement that block play is correlated with better spatial skills (e.g., see the review in Levine, Foley, Lourenco, Ehrlich, & Ratliff, 2016), but not all well-designed individual studies show a direct contribution of spatial activities in particular to the tested spatial skills (e.g., see Dearing et al., 2012, for a good example of such a study). Given these and many other kinds of differences across studies in both methodologies and findings, it is difficult to reach firm conclusions even about descriptive associations.

Given the limitations of correlational designs, experimental research is particularly valuable for testing whether experiences with the kinds of activities entailed in block or construction toy play can have a direct impact on measured spatial skills. Several investigators have developed and evaluated the impact of interventions that involve block play in particular. In one early study, Sprafkin, Serbin, Denier, and Connor (1983) randomly assigned some preschoolers to participate in an intervention in which children were encouraged and instructed to use constructive play materials like blocks in their play. Children in this experimental group showed significantly greater gains on spatial visualization tasks than did children in the control group.

In later work, Casey et al. (2008) studied the effects of providing about 2 months of weekly, structured, block-building activities in the kindergarten curriculum. Children were shown photographs of block structures (e.g., walls, bridges, houses) and were asked to create similar structures with the instructional support of the teacher. Two experimental conditions were used: (a) teachers gave directions on how to build the figures and (b) teachers preceded the directions with a fictional story about the structures to be built. Children in a control condition were given identical materials and time to engage with the blocks, but were not given the structured tasks. After controlling for pretest spatial scores, data showed that children in both intervention conditions performed better than control children on the WPPSI Block Design task (but not on a mental rotation task).

A similar block-building intervention with older (middle school) children revealed spatial gains in both boys and girls that were evident a year later (Ben-Chaim, Lappan, & Houang, 1988). Another study with 9- to 14-year-old children showed beneficial effects of intensive, structured LEGO training, but for boys only (Coxon, 2012). Perhaps the training was less effective for girls because it simulated LEGO robotics competitions and may thereby have been perceived as computer science, a field that has traditionally been relatively less appealing to girls (e.g., see Liben & Coyle, 2014). Overall, the positive results from intervention studies have led researchers to call incorporating block play into school classrooms as a means of facilitating children's spatial thinking (e.g., Kersh, Casey, & Young, 2008).

Jigsaw Puzzles

Jigsaw puzzles are also toys that are commonly found in children's homes and schools, and these, too, involve spatial rotations and translations of individual pieces. They also provide opportunities during play to observe and verbally label spatial features such as contrasts between pieces' straight and curvy edges (e.g., Borriello & Liben, 2017). However, unlike construction toys and blocks, jigsaw puzzles are not typically identified as masculine. For example, children's and adults' answers to explicit questions about how jigsaw puzzles are viewed in the culture lead puzzles to be categorized as gender neutral (Blakemore & Centers, 2005; Liben & Bigler, 2002). Observations in home and classroom settings show that preschool boys and girls are equally likely to play with puzzles and spend similar amounts of time engaged in puzzle play (Connor & Serbin, 1977; Levine, Ratliff, Huttenlocher, & Cannon, 2012).

Some investigators have combined jigsaw puzzles with blocks and other construction toys into a single category. For example, as noted earlier, Caldera et al. (1999) included both puzzles and blocks within the category of "manipulative toys" in their observational study of children's play, while Jirout and Newcombe (2015) grouped blocks, puzzles, and board games into a single category of "spatial play" when they asked parents to report on their children's play. Interestingly, the former study revealed no association between this play category and children's spatial skills, whereas the latter study reported a positive association. A 2-year longitudinal, correlational study by Levine et al. (2012) examined play during six home visits that had been recorded beginning when children were about 2 years old, and ending when children reached 4 years. At 4.5 years, children were given a spatial transformation task. After controlling for parent variables such as education and income, the data showed that children who had been observed playing with puzzles during the home visits performed better on the laboratory spatial task than did children who had not been observed to play with puzzles at home. Although the investigators did not observe significant gender differences in frequency of puzzle play, they did observe higher quality play in dyads with sons than daughters. Note, though, that because the quality measure was based on dyadic play, the gender difference may have been initiated or strengthened by parent, child, or both. Interestingly, for girls but not for boys, higher quality puzzle play predicted higher spatial transformation scores.

In comparison with the relatively rich experimental research literature in developmental science designed to test the impact of block play on spatial skills, there is relatively little experimental research designed to test the impact of jigsaw puzzle experiences on spatial skills. One related effort by

Chabani and Hommel (2014) involved tangrams, a Chinese puzzle in which various geometric shapes are assembled to make figures of various kinds. Dutch and French elementary-school children were assigned to one of three groups. One group received verbal and visual training with tangrams, the second received only visual training, and the third (control) received no training but was instead "engaged in discussion and drawing tasks" (p. 1000).

Compared with children in the control group, both instructional groups showed significantly greater improvement from pretest to posttest as measured by the number and accuracy of completed puzzles. In all but the youngest age group (6–7.5 years), girls showed significantly greater improvement than boys. However, given that both training and assessments were focused exclusively on tangram problems (i.e., no other spatial tests were given at pretest or post-test), and given that apparently children in the control group did not play at all with tangrams during the intervening period, it is difficult to judge whether the intervention experience simply provided practice with tangrams in particular, or if it had a generalizable impact on spatial skills. Additional research using puzzle interventions would be valuable, particularly because such toys would not require confronting gender stereotypes.

Play With Video (Electronic) Games

Computer or video games comprise another play category that is culturally stereotyped as masculine and that involves activities that appear to be poised to encourage spatial skills (e.g., Cherney, 2008; Subrahmanyam & Greenfield, 1994). Games of particular interest are games that are interactive, fast paced, and spatially challenging. Such games involve, for example, eye–hand coordination, map use, and inferring configurational arrangements among multiple locations that had been encountered during separate forays into fantasy environments. Although relevant games are often labeled with the modifier "computer" or "video," the games of interest are more appropriately defined not by the platform on which they appear but by their first-person, fast-paced, interactive, qualities.

On average, and particularly during adolescence, boys spend more time than girls engaging with these kinds of action games (e.g., Cherney & London, 2006; Dominick, 1984; Greenberg, Sherry, Lachlan, Lucas, & Holmstrom, 2010; Homer, Hayward, Frye, & Plass, 2012). College men report more computer use than women, and reports of computer use predict students' mental rotation skills (e.g., De Lisi & Cammarano, 1996; Terlecki & Newcombe, 2005). Experience with computer games is positively associated with selected spatial skills in childhood and adulthood (see Spence & Feng, 2010, for a review). As was true for research on block play, correlational studies such as these demonstrate statistical associations between electronic engagement and spatial skills, but they cannot alone prove that it is engagement (rather than factors that covary with engagement) that accounts for the correlation. Likewise, these correlational studies cannot establish direction of effects. It may be that people with better spatial skills are attracted to games of these kinds. Again, experimental designs are needed to test causal predictions about the effects of play on spatial skills.

In one such experimental study, for example, McClurg and Chaillé (1987) assigned children in Grades 5, 7, and 9 to one of two experimental groups or to a no-treatment control condition. (Children in the United States typically begin Grade 1 at about 6 years of age; thus, chronological age may be approximated by adding 6 to Grade level.) Experimental-group children received 6 weeks of biweekly play with either of two video games (*Factory* or *Stellar 7*) that involved complex mental rotation. In comparison with control-group children, those in both experimental groups showed significantly greater improvement on mental rotation tests at posttest, an effect evident across grades and in both genders.

Another game that has been popular in experimental research is *Tetris* in which players must rotate shapes that fall from the top of the computer screen so that by the time a shape arrives at the bottom, it will slide into the available opening. Illustrative is a study by De Lisi and Wolford (2002) in which 8- to 9-year-old children played computer games for 11 half-hour sessions distributed over a month. Those in the experimental group played Tetris; those in the control group played *Where in the USA Is Carmen Sandiego?*, a game that involves geography-related problem solving but not mental rotation. All children were given mental rotation tests both before and after the game sessions. Compared with children in the control group, and controlling for pretest scores, children who had played *Tetris* performed significantly better on the mental rotation posttest. In this study, the training eliminated pretest gender differences in mental rotation scores entirely. Similar findings have been reported in studies with adolescents (e.g., Okagaki & Frensch, 1994) and college students (Cherney, 2008; De Lisi & Cammarano, 1996; Terlecki & Newcombe, 2005).

Other studies have used both correlational and experimental approaches to examine connections between play with complex action video games and spatial performance. Correlational studies have found that people who report more experience playing three-dimensional, first-person shooter games display better performance on spatial tasks (e.g., Dorval & Pépin, 1986; Feng, Spence, & Pratt, 2007, Study 1). Experimental studies demonstrate that randomly assigned play experiences influence spatial outcomes as expected. For example, Feng et al. (2007, Study 2) randomly assigned college men and college women who were not already video gamers to participate in play with either a 3D, first-person shooter game (*Medal of Honor: Pacific Assault*) or a

3D puzzle game (*Balance*) that requires players to steer a ball through mazes of paths and rails, avoiding obstacles. Tests of spatial attention and mental rotation were given immediately before and after 10 hours of play (1- to 2-hour sessions distributed over a 4-week period) and again 5 months later. Data showed that those who played the action video game improved on both spatial measures; those who played the puzzle game improved on neither.

The lack of improvement from playing the "control" puzzle game might appear surprising insofar as *Balance* also appears to exercise spatial skills (e.g., judging directions, sizes, angles). In accounting for these findings, Feng et al. (2007) argued that a key contributor to higher level spatial skills (e.g., mental rotation) are lower level skills (e.g., directing attention appropriately across the visual field), and that only the action game would be expected to facilitate the latter. Data also showed that women benefitted from training more than did men. Women's posttest spatial scores did, however, remain lower than men's on both kinds of tasks, significantly so for only the mental rotation task.

Although there are some correlational studies of the association between action gaming and spatial skills in youth (e.g., Dye & Bavelier, 2004), there appears to be little comparable experimental work with children. We surmise that this lacuna exists because of ethical concerns about intentionally exposing children to commercially available first-person shooter video games that are aggressive and violent. Perhaps it will be possible to develop more benign first-person action games for research (and, ultimately, intervention) purposes. Ideally, future developmental research in this arena should also avoid methodological pitfalls that have plagued most gaming research with adults (see Boot, Blakely, & Simons, 2011).

The use of educational and entertainment applications for mobile devices such as tablets and smartphones is rapidly increasing among young children and even infants (Hirsh-Pasek et al., 2015). These applications share many properties of computer and video games but may also allow children to manipulate the device as a whole (e.g., tilting a smartphone to steer a car on a racetrack). Illustrative of research evaluating effects of educational electronic games is a recent study conducted in an all-girls' school (Al-Balushi, Al-Musawi, Ambusaidi, & Al-Hajri, 2017). Students in 12th-grade chemistry classes were given instruction using either an interactive tablet or a standard textbook. Following instruction, students in the former group displayed better mental rotation skills. Also available are electronic applications that are marketed explicitly to improve children's spatial skills. For example, an application called *Pictorial* (CloudGears UG, 2015) challenges children to find pictures hidden in images of the night sky and to solve a mystery presented by a pirate's map. The application is explicitly said to be geared to enhancing spatial reasoning, itself described as important because spatial skills are measured on tests used to select individuals for educational and job opportunities.

What remains far more difficult to find is scientific work evaluating the impact of educational applications like these, particularly in relation to gender. Interestingly, even individuals who explicitly draw on scientific research to develop recommendations for parents and educators find it difficult to identify relevant evaluation literature. For example, in a web page for parents entitled *Smart Toys and Educational Games for Kids: An Evidence-Based Guide*, Dewar (2015) posed the question "Which toys and games offer the most effective educational experiences?" and answered it, "Unfortunately, we have very little research to guide us. For example, the vast majority of supposedly instructional electronic games have not been rigorously tested for their educational effects." Evaluation work is sorely needed given the ever-growing pervasiveness of electronic games and instructional applications and the persistent gender differences in the use of computers and electronics. It will be important to consider if, and under what circumstances, electronic "games" cross from the realm of free-choice play and into the realm of formal education. Experiences with "games" may well have a different impact on children's interests and skills depending on whether they are perceived as play or drudgery.

Mathematics

Mathematics is a second cognitive domain that is commonly stereotyped as masculine (Cvencek, Meltzoff, & Greenwald, 2011; Nosek et al., 2009). Conclusions about actual gender-differentiated performance in mathematics are not always consistent with this stereotype, however. For example, on the basis of an extensive meta-analysis, Else-Quest and colleagues (2010) concluded that effect sizes of gender differences in mathematics range between nonexistent and moderate. In keeping with her 2005 argument that cognitive gender differences are generally nonexistent or trivial, Hyde (2016) recently summarized findings related to mathematics by stating, "Overall, then, findings from meta-analyses indicate that females have reached parity with males in math performance today, although there are variations in this pattern as a function of factors such as nation and culture" (p. 54).

Despite this general conclusion, there remain visible associations between gender and performance in the domain of mathematics. For example, girls are dramatically underrepresented in highly selective math competitions. As one specific example, the winning U.S. team in the 2016 International Math Olympiad was composed entirely of boys, a characterization that applies to about 90% of the U.S. teams that have competed since 1974 when American participation began (Antonick, 2016). An analysis of high-achievement contests like this led Ellison and Swanson (2009) to paint a still-gendered picture of the contemporary state of mathematics, ending their analysis by writing "The AMC [American Mathematics Competitions] data reveal a very large and widespread gender gap at the high achievement levels. The gender gap at these levels is more striking and significant than gaps in average scores[,] and calls out for further study" (p. 29). Importantly, Ellison and Swanson offered a range of potential experiential explanations—rather than intrinsic (essentialist) differences—that might account for these data patterns.

In this section, we thus consider empirical work bearing on the links between mathematical skills and several kinds of play-based experiences. Given the considerable evidence that spatial skills contribute to success in mathematics (e.g., Kersh et al., 2008; Wai et al., 2009), some of the same kinds of play discussed in the prior section on spatial skills are relevant here as well.

Block and Puzzle Play

Playing with blocks and puzzles has been proposed as a means of supporting not only spatial thinking but also mathematical thinking. For example, Wolfgang, Stannard, and Jones (2001) suggested that "construction play with blocks offers the preschool child the opportunity to classify, measure, order, count, use fractions, and become more aware of depth, width, length, symmetry, shape, and space" (p. 174). The National Association for the Education of Young Children (NAEYC) and the National Council for Teachers of Mathematics (NCTM) have recommended block programs for young children as a way to support the development of mathematical skills (National Governors Association Center for Best Practices & Council of Chief State School Officers, 2010), and educational researchers have developed and evaluated various classroom block play programs for both younger and older children (e.g., Kersh et al., 2008; Tepylo, Moss, & Stephenson, 2015).

Empirical work has provided correlational evidence that links mathematical achievement and children's block-building skills and experiences. Illustratively, Nath and Szücs (2014) examined the concurrent association between how well 7-year-old children could build a series of requested LEGO constructions and their scores on a standardized test of mathematics skills. Performance on the LEGO task and math scores were positively related, with visuospatial memory fully mediating this association. Verdine et al. (2014a) examined the concurrent association between children's block constructions and mathematical skills. Young children (age 3 years) were asked to assemble a series of LEGO structures by copying model structures. Performance on this Test of Spatial Abilities (TOSA) did not differ by gender, but TOSA performance was significantly linked to concurrent mathematical performance as measured on an assessment of early mathematical skills (Ginsburg, Lee, Pappas, Hartman, & Rosenfeld, 2010). Similar associations between block building skills and mathematics skills have also been seen in adolescents' classrooms (e.g., Casey, Pezaris, & Bassi, 2012).

There have also been longitudinal studies examining the connection between early block construction skill and later mathematics skills. For example, using data from a longitudinal study that began in 1982, Stannard, Wolfgang, Jones, and Phelps (2001) examined the associations between levels of block constructions produced at age 4 to levels of mathematics achievement during elementary-, middle-, and high-school years. The initial block construction assessments, given in three contexts (blocks, LEGOs, and carpentry), were a cross between free-play and standardized assessment. Children were given standard sets of materials and relatively open-ended requests (e.g., "Build whatever you would like, use as many blocks as you like, and spend as much time as you need" [p. 119]). The data showed no link between quality of pre-schoolers' block constructions and standardized math test scores in Grades 3 or 5. However, performance on the early building measures did predict scores on standardized math tests in Grade 7, and course-related measures of math-ematical achievements in high school (e.g., the number of advanced mathe-matics courses taken; course grades). In a recent shorter term longitudinal study, Verdine, Irwin, Golinkoff, and Hirsh-Pasek (2014b) retested the chil-dren first studied at the age of 3 (Verdine et al., 2014a; see above). The follow-up data showed that children's scores on the spatial assembly task (TOSA) at age 3 predicted scores on the math problem-solving test of the Wechsler Individual Achievement Test (WIAT; Wechsler, 2009) at age 4.

Data from these studies are consistent with the possibility that early spa-tial play has a positive impact on later mathematical skills, but the data do not allow conclusions about a causal effect of toy play given that these studies were correlational. Additionally, the block measures used in the research just described were based on ratings of children's success in responding to explicit requests from researchers to build block structures; they were not assessments of the quantity and quality of children's self-generated block play. Some sug-gestion that block-play contexts matter is suggested by findings from a study by Casey et al. (2008) described earlier. Their work showed that spatial-skill gains from a block-building intervention differed depending on whether the intervention was, or was not, embedded in a storytelling context. Perhaps pat-terns of findings concerning mathematical outcomes differ similarly depend-ing on whether measures of the quality of block constructions are drawn from children's spontaneous block play or from their responses to explicit requests to build a specific block structure.

In contrast to the considerable body of correlational research address-ing the link between mathematical skills and block activities, there is as yet relatively little published research reporting how mathematical outcomes are affected by randomly assigned block-activity interventions. The experi-mental studies described earlier that included randomly assigned block-building activities included outcome measures focused on spatial rather than mathematical skills (e.g., Caldera et al., 1999; Casey et al., 2008; Sprafkin et al., 1983).

In summary, investigators have provided correlational evidence of associations between young children's success in building specified block constructions and their concurrent or later mathematical achievements. There is, however, little experimental work testing whether math outcomes are enhanced by encouraging more frequent and complex block play (e.g., via engaging parents to encourage spatial thinking during dyadic block play; see Borriello & Liben, 2017). Thus, the available empirical evidence is consistent with the hypothesis that boys' greater interest and experience in playing with blocks contributes to better spatial skills that, in turn, support mathematical cognition, but additional studies using experimental, longitudinal designs are needed to evaluate whether play with blocks and related construction toys can lead directly to better mathematical outcomes.

Chess

Another play activity that has been examined in relation to children's mathematics achievement is chess, also an activity generally stereotyped as masculine. For example, when college students were given the 7-point scale described earlier to rate the cultural views of various activities (Liben & Bigler, 2002), their responses led chess to be categorized as masculine. Similarly, when elementary school-aged children were asked directly about various gender chess stereotypes (e.g., "Have you heard that good chess players are usually boys?"), their responses revealed masculine stereotypes of both the game and its players (Rothgerber & Wolsiefer, 2014). Actual participation in chess also shows dramatic gender imbalance: Chess tournaments attract mostly male competitors (Chabris & Glickman, 2006) and public-school-sponsored chess clubs and tournaments are disproportionately populated by boys (e.g., see Leland, 2016).

Various experimental studies have been conducted to determine whether cognitive skills, including mathematics, can be enhanced by playing chess. Illustrative is an intervention study in which classes of children in Grades 3, 4, and 5 were randomly assigned to either experimental or control conditions (Sala, Gorini, & Pravettoni, 2015). Experimental-group children were given three months of in-class chess instruction and chess software for optional use at home; control-group children received only their standard school activities. Findings showed that children in the experimental group improved significantly more on problem-based mathematics tests.

To look at effects of chess instruction more broadly, Sala and Gobet (2016) conducted a meta-analysis of studies that had experimentally manipulated chess instruction, and had included measures of later mathematics, reading, or other cognitive outcomes. Of particular interest was whether treatment effects—if found—would be greater for mathematics than for other cognitive outcomes, an expectation based on the argument that chess and mathematics share "their problem-solving nature and the importance of quantitative relationships" (Sala & Gobet, 2016, p. 54). Other cognitive domains were judged to lack specific commonalities with chess. Data from 24 studies involving children from kindergarten to 12th grade showed that, indeed, chess instruction had a positive impact on mathematics skills that was stronger than its impact on other cognitive outcomes. Their analysis also revealed an effect of dosage: intervention gains were limited to those studies that included at least 25 hours of instruction. On the basis of their review, Sala and Gobet also identified a number of serious methodological limitations in the existing literature and thus argued that future investigators should be more careful to assign training randomly, include both pre- and postintervention assessments, systematically vary quantity of training, identify mechanisms that might account for observed associations among variables and, most important, include both "do nothing" and "active" control groups to allow evaluation of placebo effects. Interestingly for the present context, they completely ignored gender in their meta-analysis, thus adding another important element in need of attention in future work on the impact of chess.

Board and Card Games

An additional toy-related experience that has been proposed as relevant to enhancing mathematical skills is play with board and card games. Given that such games are typically viewed as gender neutral by both children and adults (Liben & Bigler, 2002), engagement with these toys is unlikely to play an important role in gender-differentiated mathematical skills. From the perspective of identifying potential avenues for educational programs, however, it is valuable to learn whether board and card games are linked to individual differences in mathematical outcomes because it may be easy to encourage play with these games in all children.

One classic game that has attracted researchers' attention is *Chutes and Ladders*. Its game board has 100 numbered squares, presented in 10 rows. The bottom left cell contains the number 1 and numbers are incremented by 1 in a boustrophedon pattern (i.e., left to right, then right to left, then left to right, and so on, in ascending rows). Players move their markers along numbered spaces as determined by numbers on a spinner. Landing on squares with chutes (or ladders) requires players to drop their pieces down (or ascend) the board. Researchers of children's developing understanding of mathematics have suggested that play with games like these helps children understand order and magnitude of numbers, one-to-one correspondence, and number line representations (e.g., Case & Griffin, 1990; Laski & Siegler, 2014; Siegler & Booth, 2005).

Consistent with this suggestion, LeFevre et al. (2009) found a positive correlation between parents' reports of children's play with board and card games and young children's mathematical knowledge and fluency in Grades 1 and 2. Similarly, Ramani and Siegler (2008, Study 2) found that children who reported more play with number-related board, card, and video games at home, showed better performance on tests of numerical understanding.

These studies rely on self- or parent-report of children's play and use correlational designs, but there has also been experimental work that provides evidence of the facilitative role of board-game play. For example, Ramani and Siegler (2008, Study 1) studied effects of game play using an experimental design in which preschool children were randomly assigned to play with one of two versions of a board game. Both games involved a board with 10 horizontally arranged spaces, but in one game the spaces were marked by numbers and in the other, by colors. Moves along the spaces were determined by spinners that were marked, respectively, with numbers or colors. Children who played the number rather than the color version of the game showed significantly greater increases in performance on several numerical tasks, an advantage that remained nine weeks later.

Whyte and Bull (2008) also conducted research to explore the association between children's experience with games and their mathematical understanding and use of linear number lines. Preschoolers were randomly assigned to play with one of three games. In the linear number group, children played a game with a linear number board that visually linked numbers and space (as in the bottom row of the *Chutes and Ladders* board described above). In the nonlinear number group, the game also involved numerical quantities, but without a game board linking numbers to space. Instead, the game used a deck of cards, each card having some number of apple drawings. At each turn, two cards were shown and children were asked to pick the one with more apples. To check their answers, children inverted the cards where words and Arabic numerals indicated the number of apples. Finally, in the linear color group, the game involved neither numbers nor quantities. In this game, the board layout was like that used in the linear number game, but here the spaces were distinguished by colors in repeating five-color sequences rather than by incremental numbers. A color spinner rather than a number spinner was used to determine players' movements along the board, and children were asked to name the colors (rather than numbers) as they traversed across spaces.

The games were played in four 25-minute play sessions held about 1 week apart. One week before and again 1 week after the game sessions, children were tested for their counting skills, number comprehension and numerical estimation (asked to mark a target number on a horizontal line labeled 0 at the left and 10 at the right). Among the results was the finding that children in the linear number group significantly improved on all posttest measures, offering evidence of having progressed from a logarithmic to a linear representation of numerical magnitude. The nonlinear number group also showed gains in basic number skills, but the group did not show increased skill in locating numbers along a number line. Although these studies do not speak explicitly to gender with respect to initial skills or with respect to responses to interventions (gender was mentioned as balanced within each group, but gender was not addressed in analyses), they are useful in demonstrating that certain kinds of game play can have a demonstrably positive effect on children's mathematical understanding.

Reflecting on and Beyond Spatial and Mathematical Domains

As explained earlier, we chose to focus on spatial and mathematical domains in our review of empirical work relating gendered toy play and cognitive development not only because of their particular importance to STEM but also because these are the domains that have attracted the greatest amount of empirical work. Even in these domains, though, the available data do not permit definitive conclusions about the role of gendered toy play. Some of the reasons that conclusions remain tentative have been threaded throughout our earlier discussions. For example, many of the studies are correlational, and only a small proportion of studies assess and attempt to account for potentially powerful factors that may covary with toy play, for example, important individual differences (e.g., children's general intellectual functioning, strength of gender identity) and contextual variables (e.g., parental responses to gendered play, economic resources or other familial attributes).

In addition, there are few if any direct procedural replications across studies, thus providing little opportunity to evaluate reproducibility of results (see Goodman, Fanelli, & Ioannidis, 2016). Instead, studies vary dramatically along many dimensions. Among the important variations are methods used to collect data on children's play (e.g., direct observations vs. informant reports, some concurrent and some retrospective), demographic characteristics of participants (e.g., age, socioeconomic status, nationality, ethnicity), data-collection settings (e.g., homes, schools, or laboratories), and presence or types of play partners (e.g., solitary play, peer play, parent–child play). Studies also vary with respect to how a given toy is conceptualized, and as a consequence, which toys are merged into a single category. For example, blocks may be construed as "spatial toys" or "manipulative toys," and which construal is used affects which other toys are assigned to the category. Cognitive measures also differ markedly across studies. Within the spatial domain, for example, skills may be assessed by block design, mental rotation, or spatial disembedding tests; within mathematics, skills may be assessed by shape, number-line, or quantity-estimation tasks.

For the current focus on gender, it is also important to note that in some of the best-designed studies that examine spatial or mathematical skills in relation to play (e.g., Dearing et al., 2012; LeFevre et al., 2009), toys and activities are assigned to given categories without regard to whether they are in any way gendered. Although these categorization systems are fully appropriate for the original investigators' research goals (e.g., studying links between spatial activities and mathematical skills), they are not ideal for researchers whose focus is explicitly on gendered toy play.

While discussing limitations, we also note again the relatively small research literature addressed to the role of toy play in other cognitive domains. There are many interesting questions related to gender in those domains. For example, might gender-differentiated play with language toys or word games (e.g., *LeapReader*, *Scrabble*, *Boggle*) be linked to female advantages in literacy skills reported in meta-analyses described earlier? Similarly, are there gender differences in play with strategy or logic games (e.g., *Battleship*, *Tower of Hanoi*), and are these related to male advantages in science that have been reported in some meta-analyses? Although there have been some studies addressed to these and related questions, the relevant research in many cognitive domains remains sparse. Thus, it will be important for future researchers to examine a greater range of cognitive domains at the same time that that they expand the already extensive corpus of empirical work linking play to spatial and mathematical skills.

FUTURE DIRECTIONS FOR RESEARCH AND APPLICATION

As just acknowledged, much remains unknown about how gendered toy play influences cognitive development. Nevertheless, the work already in hand provides a useful foundation for making recommendations for future research and for the design, implementation, and evaluation of new or modified toys. We thus conclude by offering suggestions relevant to both academic research and toy design.

Research Approaches

Many links between gendered toy play and cognitive outcomes have been demonstrated in the empirical work reviewed in this chapter. However, the correlational and concurrent designs of many studies limit conclusions that can be reached about the direct, causal, and long-lasting impact of gendered toy play on cognitive development as it proceeds in the natural ecology. One important way to extend past work is to conduct longitudinal research that includes assessments of distal outcomes. For example, investigators might study links between early toy play and later occupational outcomes such as those suggested in the chapter's opening vignette.

Furthermore, studies using correlational designs would benefit by consistently assessing multiple factors—apart from toy play—that might also (or instead) account for observed variability in the cognitive variables of interest. The unique contribution of gendered toy play will be clearer if it can be examined in the context of reliable assessments of other potentially important predictors such as those related to family context (e.g., parental attitudes about gender socialization, familial financial resources; see Dearing et al., 2012; LeFevre et al., 2009) and child qualities (e.g., children's personal gender identities, gender stereotypes, and gender-schematicity; see Coyle & Liben, 2016; Weisgram, 2016).

Another important way to extend past work is by using experimental methods within the natural ecology. For example, random assignment could be used to test the effectiveness of interventions that vary the kinds of toys provided to children in home or school, or that vary the kinds of programs offered to caregivers in a position to scaffold children's toy play. Although experimental designs in real-world settings are difficult, they are possible, as demonstrated by successful real-world experimental manipulations of other established contextual factors such as family income (e.g., see Duncan, Huston, & Weisner, 2007).

Toy Design and Marketing

Irrespective of the timeframes and research designs used to structure future studies, we urge investigators to routinely examine quality as well as quantity of gendered toy play. As noted earlier, there is evidence from naturalistic free-play school settings (e.g., Caldera et al., 1999; Schau et al., 1980) and from controlled laboratory play sessions (e.g., Coyle & Liben, 2015) that identical toys are used differently by boys and girls. Greater knowledge about stylistic differences is especially important for designing toy-play interventions meant to inspire children of one gender to play with toys typically associated with the other gender. If children manage to impose play styles typical of their own gender on play with toys linked to children of the other gender, their play experience may not be as diversified as intended. For example, given a pile of LEGO blocks, the young girl in the opening vignette of this chapter might treat them as vegetables and stir them around in the pan on her pretend stove. Playing with blocks in this way is unlikely to have much impact on her spatial prowess.

It is not only children who may impose gender-traditional play styles on gender-nontraditional toys. Toy designers and marketers may do so as well. For example, in an effort to make traditionally masculine toys more appealing to girls, the LEGO Group has produced feminized block pieces (e.g., the *Pink Brick Box*) and construction sets with feminine themes (e.g., the *Butterfly Beauty Shop*). Although such toys afford construction activities of the kind thought to foster spatial skills, marketers have stressed these toys' symbolic, role-playing affordances rather than their building affordances (Liben, 2016). An online advertisement for the recently retired *Butterfly Beauty Shop* (LEGO, 2016) provides a striking example. Its opening "Product Details" section reads, "Get primped and pretty at the Butterfly Beauty Shop!" The next section, "Features," points out that "Emma and all of her friends will look fabulous with bows, sunglasses, a hairbrush, mirror, lipsticks, and new hair styles." Images of these accessories appear in an accompanying photograph. The bulleted list of play suggestions that follows includes exciting activities such as: "Gossip out on the bench by the scenic fountain!" "Shop for makeup and hair accessories!" and "Give all of the LEGO® Friends makeovers." Only one comment alludes to an action that is in any way spatial (viz., that objects can be placed in new locations): "Get the girls ready for any event with the salon where you can rearrange the interior!" There is no mention at all of the process or joy of constructing the shop itself.

Toy designers and marketers could do more to encourage girls to use the toys for building. For example, the beauty shop set might include several different base platforms on which alternative beauty shops could be constructed, or might include game cards that pose challenges that call for spatial thinking. One such card could announce a new building code that requires wheelchair accessibility, thus leading players to plan and build an exterior ramp and to renovate the interior to widen halls and doorways.

The preceding comments address research and action focused on enticing children to play with toys that are not traditionally linked to their own gender, and, further, to use those toys in ways that are also gender nontraditional. Another tack is to encourage children to engage in nontraditional activities in the context of playing with gender traditional toys. For example, given that traditionally masculine toys already appear to exercise spatial thinking, the challenge is to find ways for traditionally feminine toys to do likewise. Illustratively, a jewelry-making toy could include activities that require tying different kinds of knots, designing new clasp styles, or figuring out sequences of wire bends and bead placements needed to create a pendant or hair ornament displayed in a photograph or drawing. Some instructions might include diagrams of step-by-step sequences, perhaps drawn from varying vantage points and in varying spatial projections (orthographic, oblique, or perspective; see Forseth, 1980). In addition to fostering girls' spatial skills, such experiences may also expand girls' motivation and self-confidence for pursuing educational and career opportunities (e.g., drafting; engineering) that draw on these skills (e.g., see Eccles, 2014).

Diverse Influences and Consequences

Whatever attempts are made to expand children's cognitive skills through play (e.g., via modifications in toys, marketing, or parenting), careful research is needed to monitor effects broadly, including those that lie beyond the intended, targeted cognitive domain. To illustrate, we return to an intervention study by Borriello and Liben (2017) cited earlier. Prior to playing with their preschool children, mothers in the experimental condition were told about spatial thinking and ways to foster it; mothers in the control condition were simply asked to play with their children as they normally would. During subsequent play with blocks, experimental-group mothers produced higher proportions of spatial language and other kinds of spatial guidance than did control-group mothers. Interestingly, mothers and children in the experimental group also engaged in less pretend play.

How one interprets this pattern of effects (more spatial play but less pretend play) is likely to differ depending on one's relative valuing of cognitive domains (e.g., spatial thinking, theory of mind). Our goal here is not to address the absolute or relative value of pretend play (but see Lillard et al., 2013). Instead, our goal is to draw attention to the systemic and relational nature of human development in general and of gender development in particular (Liben & Coyle, 2017). An intervention intended to affect one cognitive outcome may have important consequences for another.

Given the complexity of the child's constructivist–ecological system (Liben, 2017; see also Chapter 12, this volume), it is important for researchers to cast a wide net not only—as already argued—with respect to inputs (i.e., examining a wide range of specific experiences, environmental contexts, and individual human qualities), but also with respect to consequences (i.e., examining a wide range of cognitive and motivational outcomes). For example, does focusing children's, parents' and teachers' attention on one cognitive domain (e.g., spatial) diminish their attentiveness to another (e.g., pretend play)? When toys such as LEGOs, *Tetris*, or *Chutes and Ladders* are taken from the context of free-choice play and moved into classrooms, didactic parent–child play activities, or monitored practice sessions, do the toys lose their playful appeal? Are cognitive outcomes affected as a result?

Goals and Values

Although our discussion thus far has focused explicitly on ways that gendered toy play affects cognitive development, gendered toy play—and interventions intended to modify that toy play—may simultaneously affect gender development more broadly. It is, therefore, also important to identify how interventions intended to diminish gender differences in cognitive outcomes may simultaneously affect gender differences in other arenas.

If the goal is to reduce or eradicate behavioral gender differences, best practices with respect to toys are arguably those that minimize gendered labeling, aisle divisions, and cultural markers like pink and blue. Avoiding masculine and feminine markers entirely (rather than including markers of both) is especially appropriate if the goal is also to dispel the notion of gender as a stable binary concept. However, as argued in detail in the context of discussing single-sex schooling (Liben, 2015), not all people wish to eradicate or even diminish the use of gender as an organizing framework for human development and behavior. Some people explicitly value gender differences and believe that gender differences should be treasured and even strengthened (e.g., see Gilbert, 2006; Gurian et al., 2009; Sommers, 2013).

Much as we earlier observed that not all people would embrace the genitalia-based decision rule concerning toy gender described earlier (Myers, 2013), we close by observing that some people are likely to rebuff actions that diminish gender-role differences in general, even while welcoming actions that expand cognitive skills in particular. Given this societal actuality, we recommend the simultaneous use of two major strategies. One is to expand the availability of toys that appeal to all children, irrespective of children's gender identities. The second is to recognize the continued reality of gendered toys, and to find ways—via toy design and instructions, or via parent- and educator-targeted interventions—to expand the range of cognitively rich experiences that these toys afford.

REFERENCES

Al-Balushi, S., Al-Musawi, A., Ambusaidi, A. K., & Al-Hajri, F. (2017). The effectiveness of interacting with scientific animations in chemistry using mobile devices on Grade 12 students' spatial ability and scientific reasoning skills. *Journal of Science Education and Technology, 26,* 70–81.

Antonick, G. (2016, July 18). U.S. team wins first place at International Math Olympiad. *The New York Times.* Retrieved from http://wordplay.blogs.nytimes.com/2016/07/18/imo-2016/?_r=0

Auster, C. J., & Mansbach, C. S. (2012). The gender marketing of toys: An analysis of color and type of toy on the Disney store website. *Sex Roles, 67,* 375–388. http://dx.doi.org/10.1007/s11199-012-0177-8

Baenninger, M., & Newcombe, N. (1989). The role of experience in spatial test performance: A meta-analysis. *Sex Roles, 20,* 327–344. http://dx.doi.org/10.1007/BF00287729

Bem, S. L. (1983). Gender schema theory and its implications for child development: Raising gender-aschematic children in a gender-schematic society. *Signs: Journal of Women in Culture and Society, 8,* 598–616. http://dx.doi.org/10.1086/493998

Bem, S. L. (1998). *An unconventional family.* New Haven, CT: Yale University Press.

Ben-Chaim, D., Lappan, G., & Houang, R. T. (1988). The effect of instruction on spatial visualization skills of middle school boys and girls. *American Educational Research Journal, 25,* 51–71. http://dx.doi.org/10.3102/00028312025001051

Berenbaum, S. A., & Resnick, S. M. (1997). Early androgen effects on aggression in children and adults with congenital adrenal hyperplasia. *Psychoneuroendocrinology, 22,* 505–515. http://dx.doi.org/10.1016/S0306-4530(97)00049-8

Best, D. L., & Williams, J. E. (2001). Gender and culture. In D. Matsumoto (Ed.), *The handbook of culture and psychology* (pp. 195–219). New York, NY: Oxford University Press.

Bigler, R. S. (1995). The role of classification skill in moderating environmental influences on children's gender stereotyping: A study of the functional use of gender in the classroom. *Child Development, 66,* 1072–1087. http://dx.doi.org/10.2307/1131799

Bigler, R. S., & Liben, L. S. (2007). Developmental intergroup theory: Explaining and reducing children's social stereotyping and prejudice. *Current Directions in Psychological Science, 16,* 162–166. http://dx.doi.org/10.1111/j.1467-8721.2007.00496.x

Blakemore, J. E. O., Berenbaum, S. A., & Liben, L. S. (2009). *Gender development.* New York, NY: Psychology Press.

Blakemore, J. E. O., & Centers, R. E. (2005). Characteristics of boys' and girls' toys. *Sex Roles, 53,* 619–633. http://dx.doi.org/10.1007/s11199-005-7729-0

Blakemore, J. E. O., & Hill, C. A. (2008). The child gender socialization scale: A measure to compare traditional and feminist parents. *Sex Roles, 58,* 192–207. http://dx.doi.org/10.1007/s11199-007-9333-y

Blakemore, J. E. O., LaRue, A. A., & Olejnik, A. B. (1979). Sex-appropriate toy preference and the ability to conceptualize toys as sex-role related. *Developmental Psychology, 15,* 339–340. http://dx.doi.org/10.1037/0012-1649.15.3.339

Boot, W. R., Blakely, D. P., & Simons, D. J. (2011). Do action video games improve perception and cognition? *Frontiers in Psychology, 2,* 1–6. http://dx.doi.org/10.3389/fpsyg.2011.00226

Borriello, G. A., & Liben, L. S. (2017). Encouraging maternal guidance of preschoolers' spatial thinking during block play. *Child Development.* Advance online publication. http://dx.doi.org/10.1111/cdev.12779

Bradbard, M. R., & Parkman, S. A. (1984). Gender differences in preschool children's toy requests. *The Journal of Genetic Psychology, 145,* 283–284. http://dx.doi.org/10.1080/00221325.1984.10532277

Caldera, Y. M., Huston, A. C., & O'Brien, M. (1989). Social interactions and play patterns of parents and toddlers with feminine, masculine, and neutral toys. *Child Development, 60,* 70–76. http://dx.doi.org/10.2307/1131072

Caldera, Y. M., McDonald Culp, A., O'Brien, M., Truglio, R. T., Alvarez, M., & Huston, A. C. (1999). Children's play preferences, construction play with blocks, and visual–spatial skills: Are they related? *International Journal of Behavioral Development, 23,* 855–872. http://dx.doi.org/10.1080/016502599383577

Carpenter, C. J. (1983). Activity structure and play: Implications for socialization. In M. B. Liss (Ed.), *Social and cognitive skills: Sex roles and children's play* (pp. 117–145). New York, NY: Academic Press.

Carpenter, C. J., & Huston-Stein, A. (1980). Activity structure and sex-typed behavior in preschool children. *Child Development, 51,* 862–872. http://dx.doi.org/10.2307/1129475

Case, R., & Griffin, S. (1990). Child cognitive development: The role of central conceptual structures in the development of scientific and social thought. In C. Hauert (Ed.), *Developmental psychology: Cognitive, perceptuo-motor and neuropsychological perspectives* (pp. 193–230). New York, NY: Elsevier Science.

Casey, B. M., Andrews, N., Schindler, H., Kersh, J. E., Samper, A., & Copley, J. (2008). The development of spatial skills through interventions involving block building activities. *Cognition and Instruction, 26,* 269–309. http://dx.doi.org/10.1080/07370000802177177

Casey, B. M., Pezaris, E., & Bassi, J. (2012). Adolescent boys' and girls' block constructions differ in structural balance: A block-building characteristic related to math achievement. *Learning and Individual Differences, 22,* 25–36. http://dx.doi.org/10.1016/j.lindif.2011.11.008

Chabani, E., & Hommel, B. (2014). Effectiveness of visual and verbal prompts in training visuospatial processing skills in school age children. *Instructional Science, 42,* 995–1012. http://dx.doi.org/10.1007/s11251-014-9316-7

Chabris, C. F., & Glickman, M. E. (2006). Sex differences in intellectual performance: Analysis of a large cohort of competitive chess players. *Psychological Science, 17,* 1040–1046. http://dx.doi.org/10.1111/j.1467-9280.2006.01828.x

Cherney, I. D. (2008). Mom, let me play more computer games: They improve my mental rotation skills. *Sex Roles, 59,* 776–786. http://dx.doi.org/10.1007/s11199-008-9498-z

Cherney, I. D., & Dempsey, J. (2010). Young children's classification, stereotyping and play behavior for gender neutral and ambiguous toys. *Educational Psychology, 30,* 651–669. http://dx.doi.org/10.1080/01443410.2010.498416

Cherney, I. D., & London, K. (2006). Gender-linked differences in the toys, television shows, computer games, and outdoor activities of 5- to 13-year-old children. *Sex Roles, 54,* 717–726. http://dx.doi.org/10.1007/s11199-006-9037-8

Clements, D. H. (2004). Major themes and recommendations. In D. H. Clements & J. Sarama (Eds.), *Engaging young children in mathematics: Standards for early childhood mathematics education* (pp. 7–72). Mahwah, NJ: Lawrence Erlbaum.

CloudGears UG. (2015). *Pictorial* (Version 2.9.1) [Mobile application software]. Retrieved from http://appcrawlr.com/ios/pictorial#authors-description

The College Board. (2017). *SAT suite of assessments: Key content features*. Retrieved from https://collegereadiness.collegeboard.org/about/key-features

Connor, J. M., & Serbin, L. A. (1977). Behaviorally based masculine- and feminine-activity-preference scales for preschoolers: Correlates with other classroom behaviors and cognitive tests. *Child Development, 48*, 1411–1416. http://dx.doi.org/10.2307/1128500

Coxon, S. V. (2012). The malleability of spatial ability under treatment of a FIRST LEGO League-based robotics unit. *Journal for the Education of the Gifted, 35*, 291–316. http://dx.doi.org/10.1177/0162353212451788

Coyle, E. F., & Liben, L. S. (2015, March). *Toys marketed to girls: A path to STEM engagement?* Symposium conducted at the biennial meeting of the Society for Research in Child Development, Philadelphia, PA.

Coyle, E. F., & Liben, L. S. (2016). Affecting girls' activity and job interests through play: The moderating roles of personal gender salience and game characteristics. *Child Development, 87*, 414–428. http://dx.doi.org/10.1111/cdev.12463

Cvencek, D., Meltzoff, A. N., & Greenwald, A. G. (2011). Math–gender stereotypes in elementary school children. *Child Development, 82*, 766–779. http://dx.doi.org/10.1111/j.1467-8624.2010.01529.x

Dearing, E., Casey, B. M., Ganley, C. M., Tillinger, M., Laski, E., & Montecillo, C. (2012). Young girls' arithmetic and spatial skills: The distal and proximal roles of family socioeconomics and home learning experiences. *Early Childhood Research Quarterly, 27*, 458–470. http://dx.doi.org/10.1016/j.ecresq.2012.01.002

De Lisi, R., & Cammarano, D. M. (1996). Computer experience and gender differences in undergraduate mental rotation performance. *Computers in Human Behavior, 12*, 351–361. http://dx.doi.org/10.1016/0747-5632(96)00013-1

De Lisi, R., & Wolford, J. L. (2002). Improving children's mental rotation accuracy with computer game playing. *The Journal of Genetic Psychology: Research and Theory on Human Development, 163*, 272–282. http://dx.doi.org/10.1080/00221320209598683

Dewar, G. (2015). *Smart toys and educational games for kids: An evidence-based guide*. Retrieved from http://www.parentingscience.com/educational-games-for-kids.html

Dinella, L. M., Weisgram, E. S., & Fulcher, M. (2017). Children's gender-typed toy interests: Does propulsion matter? *Archives of Sexual Behavior, 46*, 1295–1305. Advance online publication. http://dx.doi.org/10.1007/s10508-016-0901-5

Dominick, J. R. (1984). Videogames, television violence, and aggression in teenagers. *Journal of Communication, 34*, 136–147. http://dx.doi.org/10.1111/j.1460-2466.1984.tb02165.x

Dorval, M., & Pépin, M. (1986). Effect of playing a video game on a measure of spatial visualization. *Perceptual and Motor Skills, 62*, 159–162. http://dx.doi.org/10.2466/pms.1986.62.1.159

Duncan, G. J., Huston, A. C., & Weisner, T. S. (2007). *Higher ground: New hope for the working poor and their children*. New York, NY: Russell Sage Foundation.

Dye, M. W. G., & Bavelier, D. (2004). Playing video games enhances visual attention in children [Abstract]. *Journal of Vision, 4*, 40, 40a. http://dx.doi.org/10.1167/4.11.40

Eccles, J. S. (2014). Gender and achievement choices. In E. T. Gershoff, R. S. Mistry, & D. A. Crosby (Eds.), *Societal contexts of child development: Pathways of influence and implications for practice and policy* (pp. 19–34). New York, NY: Oxford University Press.

Edens, K. M., & Potter, E. F. (2013). An exploratory look at the relationships among math skills, motivational factors and activity choice. *Early Childhood Education Journal, 41*, 235–243. http://dx.doi.org/10.1007/s10643-012-0540-y

Educational Testing Service. (2017). *About the GRE general test.* Retrieved from https://www.ets.org/gre/revised_general/about

Eliot, J., & Smith, I. M. (1983). *International directory of spatial tests.* Nelson, England: National Foundation for Educational Research.

Eliot, L. (2010). *Pink brain, blue brain: How small differences grow into troublesome gaps—and what we can do about it.* London, England: Oneworld.

Ellison, G., & Swanson, A. (2009). The gender gap in secondary school mathematics at high achievement levels: Evidence from the American Mathematics Competitions (Working Paper 15238). *The NBER Working Paper Series.* Cambridge, MA: National Bureau of Economic Research. Retrieved from http://www.nber.org/papers/w15238

Else-Quest, N. M., Hyde, J. S., & Linn, M. C. (2010). Cross-national patterns of gender differences in mathematics: A meta-analysis. *Psychological Bulletin, 136*, 103–127. http://dx.doi.org/10.1037/a0018053

Feng, J., Spence, I., & Pratt, J. (2007). Playing an action video game reduces gender differences in spatial cognition. *Psychological Science, 18*, 850–855. http://dx.doi.org/10.1111/j.1467-9280.2007.01990.x

Fine, C. (2010). *Delusions of gender: How our minds, society, and neurosexism create difference.* New York, NY: W. W. Norton.

Fine, C., & Rush, E. (2016). "Why does all the girls have to buy pink stuff?" The ethics and science of the gendered toy marketing debate. *Journal of Business Ethics.* Advance online publication. http://dx.doi.org/10.1007/s10551-016-3080-3

Fisher-Thompson, D. (1993). Adult toy purchases for children: Factors affecting sex-typed toy selection. *Journal of Applied Developmental Psychology, 14*, 385–406. http://dx.doi.org/10.1016/0193-3973(93)90016-O

Forseth, K. (1980). *Graphics for architecture.* New York, NY: John Wiley & Sons.

Galotti, K. M. (2017). *Cognitive development: Infancy through adolescence* (2nd ed.). Thousand Oaks, CA: Sage.

Gilbert, M. (2006). *The disposable male: Sex, love, and money—Your world through Darwin's eyes.* East Calder, Scotland: The Hunter Press.

Ginsburg, H. P., Lee, Y. S., Pappas, S., Hartman, G., & Rosenfeld, D. (2010, June). *A comprehensive mathematics assessment for preschool-age children.* Poster presented at the biennial meeting of the Head Start's National Research Conference, Washington, DC.

Goodman, S. N., Fanelli, D., & Ioannidis, J. P. A. (2016). What does research reproducibility mean? *Science Translational Medicine, 8,* 341ps12. http://dx.doi.org/10.1126/scitranslmed.aaf5027

Greenberg, B. S., Sherry, J., Lachlan, K., Lucas, K., & Holmstrom, A. (2010). Orientations to video games among gender and age groups. *Simulation & Gaming, 41,* 238–259. http://dx.doi.org/10.1177/1046878108319930

Guilford, J. P. (1959). Three faces of intellect. *American Psychologist, 14,* 469–479. http://dx.doi.org/10.1037/h0046827

Gurian, M., Stevens, K., & Daniel, P. (2009). *Successful single-sex classrooms: A practical guide to teaching boys and girls separately.* San Francisco, CA: Jossey–Bass.

Halpern, D. F. (2012). *Sex differences in cognitive abilities* (4th ed.). New York, NY: Psychology Press.

Hegarty, M., & Waller, D. (2005). Individual differences in spatial abilities. In P. Shah & A. Miyake (Eds.), *The Cambridge handbook of visuospatial thinking* (pp. 121–169). Cambridge, England: Cambridge University Press. http://dx.doi.org/10.1017/CBO9780511610448.005

Hilliard, L. J., & Liben, L. S. (2010). Differing levels of gender salience in preschool classrooms: Effects on children's gender attitudes and intergroup bias. *Child Development, 81,* 1787–1798. http://dx.doi.org/10.1111/j.1467-8624.2010.01510.x

Hines, M. (2015). Gendered development. In M. E. Lamb & R. M. Lerner (Eds.), *Handbook of child psychology and developmental science: Socioemotional processes* (Vol. 3, 7th ed., pp. 842–887). Hoboken, NJ: John Wiley & Sons. http://dx.doi.org/10.1002/9781118963418.childpsy320

Hines, M., Fane, B. A., Pasterski, V. L., Mathews, G. A., Conway, G. S., & Brook, C. (2003). Spatial abilities following prenatal androgen abnormality: Targeting and mental rotations performance in individuals with congenital adrenal hyperplasia. *Psychoneuroendocrinology, 28,* 1010–1026. http://dx.doi.org/10.1016/S0306-4530(02)00121-X

Hirsh-Pasek, K., Zosh, J. M., Golinkoff, R. M., Gray, J. H., Robb, M. B., & Kaufman, J. (2015). Putting education in "educational" apps: Lessons from the science of learning. *Psychological Science in the Public Interest, 16,* 3–34. http://dx.doi.org/10.1177/1529100615569721

Homer, B. D., Hayward, E. O., Frye, J., & Plass, J. L. (2012). Gender and player characteristics in video game play of preadolescents. *Computers in Human Behavior, 28,* 1782–1789. http://dx.doi.org/10.1016/j.chb.2012.04.018

Huston, A. C., Greer, D., Wright, J. C., Welch, R., & Ross, R. (1984). Children's comprehension of televised formal features with masculine and feminine connotations. *Developmental Psychology, 20,* 707–716. http://dx.doi.org/10.1037/0012-1649.20.4.707

Hyde, J. S. (2005). The gender similarities hypothesis. *American Psychologist, 60,* 581–592. http://dx.doi.org/10.1037/0003-066X.60.6.581

Hyde, J. S. (2016). Sex and cognition: Gender and cognitive functions. *Current Opinion in Neurobiology, 38*, 53–56. http://dx.doi.org/10.1016/j.conb.2016.02.007

Jirout, J. J., & Newcombe, N. S. (2015). Building blocks for developing spatial skills: Evidence from a large, representative U.S. sample. *Psychological Science, 26,* 302–310. http://dx.doi.org/10.1177/0956797614563338

Kahlenberg, S. G., & Hein, M. M. (2010). Progression on Nickelodeon? Gender-role stereotypes in toy commercials. *Sex Roles, 62,* 830–847. http://dx.doi.org/10.1007/s11199-009-9653-1

Kersh, J. E., Casey, B. M., & Young, J. M. (2008). Research on spatial skills and block building in girls and boys: The relationship to later mathematics learning. In O. N. Saracho & B. Spodek (Eds.), *Contemporary perspectives on mathematics in early childhood education* (pp. 233–251). Charlotte, NC: Information Age.

Lamb, L. M., Bigler, R. S., Liben, L. S., & Green, V. A. (2009). Teaching children to confront peers' sexist remarks: Implications for theories of gender development and educational practice. *Sex Roles, 61,* 361–382. http://dx.doi.org/10.1007/s11199-009-9634-4

Langlois, J. H., & Downs, A. C. (1980). Mothers, fathers, and peers as socialization agents of sex-typed play behaviors in young children. *Child Development, 51,* 1237–1247. http://dx.doi.org/10.2307/1129566

Laski, E. V., & Siegler, R. S. (2014). Learning from number board games: You learn what you encode. *Developmental Psychology, 50,* 853–864. http://dx.doi.org/10.1037/a0034321

Lawton, C. A. (2010). Gender, spatial abilities, and wayfinding. In J. C. Chrisler & D. R. McCreary (Eds.), *Handbook of gender research in psychology: Vol. 1. Gender research in general and experimental psychology* (pp. 317–341). New York, NY: Springer. http://dx.doi.org/10.1007/978-1-4419-1465-1_16

LeFevre, J., Skwarchuk, S., Smith-Chant, B., Fast, L., Kamawar, D., & Bisanz, J. (2009). Home numeracy experiences and children's math performance in the early school years. *Canadian Journal of Behavioural Science, 41,* 55–66. http://dx.doi.org/10.1037/a0014532

LEGO. (2016). Butterfly beauty shop. In *LEGO Shop.* Retrieved from https://shop.lego.com/en-US/Butterfly-Beauty-Shop-3187

Leland, J. (2016, April 22). The littlest chess champions. *The New York Times,* MB1. Retrieved from https://www.nytimes.com/2016/04/24/nyregion/the-littlest-chess-champions.html?mcubz=0

Levine, S. C., Foley, A., Lourenco, S., Ehrlich, S., & Ratliff, K. (2016). Sex differences in spatial cognition: Advancing the conversation. *WIREs: Cognitive Science, 7,* 127–155. http://dx.doi.org/10.1002/wcs.1380

Levine, S. C., Ratliff, K. R., Huttenlocher, J., & Cannon, J. (2012). Early puzzle play: A predictor of preschoolers' spatial transformation skill. *Developmental Psychology, 48,* 530–542. http://dx.doi.org/10.1037/a0025913

Liben, L. S. (1981). Copying and reproducing pictures in relation to subjects' operative levels. *Developmental Psychology, 17*, 357–365. http://dx.doi.org/10.1037/0012-1649.17.3.357

Liben, L. S. (2006). Education for spatial thinking. In K. A. Renninger & I. E. Sigel (Eds.), *Handbook of child psychology: Child psychology in practice* (Vol. 4, 6th ed., pp. 197–247). Hoboken, NJ: John Wiley & Sons.

Liben, L. S. (2015). Probability values and human values in evaluating single-sex education. *Sex Roles, 72*, 401–426. http://dx.doi.org/10.1007/s11199-014-0438-9

Liben, L. S. (2016). We've come a long way, baby (but we're not there yet): Gender past, present, and future. *Child Development, 87*, 5–28. http://dx.doi.org/10.1111/cdev.12490

Liben, L. S. (2017). Gender development: A constructivist–ecological perspective. In N. Budwig, E. Turiel, & P. Zelazo (Eds.), *New perspectives on human development* (pp. 143–144). Cambridge, England: Cambridge University Press. http://dx.doi.org/10.1017/CBO9781316282755.010

Liben, L. S., & Bigler, R. S. (2002). The developmental course of gender differentiation: Conceptualizing, measuring, and evaluating constructs and pathways. *Monographs of the Society for Research in Child Development, 67*, i–viii. Retrieved from https://www.ncbi.nlm.nih.gov/pubmed/12465575

Liben, L. S., & Coyle, E. F. (2014). Developmental interventions to address the STEM gender gap: Exploring intended and unintended consequences [Abstract]. In L. S. Liben & R. S. Bigler (Eds.), *Advances in child development and behavior: Vol. 47. The role of gender in educational contexts and outcomes* (pp. 77–115). San Diego, CA: Elsevier. Retrieved from https://www.ncbi.nlm.nih.gov/pubmed/25344994

Liben, L. S., & Coyle, E. F. (2017). Gender development: A relational approach. In A. S. Dick & U. Müller (Eds.), *Advancing developmental science: Philosophy, theory, and method* (pp. 170–184). London, England: Routledge; Taylor and Francis.

Liben, L. S., & Müller, U. (Eds.). (2015). *Handbook of child psychology and developmental science: Vol. 2. Cognitive processes* (7th ed.). Hoboken, NJ: John Wiley & Sons.

Liben, L. S., Myers, L. J., Christensen, A. E., & Bower, C. A. (2013). Environmental-scale map use in middle childhood: Links to spatial skills, strategies, and gender. *Child Development, 84*, 2047–2063. http://dx.doi.org/10.1111/cdev.12090

Lillard, A. S. (2015). The development of play. In L. S. Liben & U. Müller (Eds.), *Handbook of child psychology and developmental science: Vol. 2. Cognitive processes* (7th ed., pp. 425–468). Hoboken, NJ: John Wiley & Sons. http://dx.doi.org/10.1002/9781118963418.childpsy211

Lillard, A. S., Lerner, M. D., Hopkins, E. J., Dore, R. A., Smith, E. D., & Palmquist, C. M. (2013). The impact of pretend play on children's development: A review of the evidence. *Psychological Bulletin, 139*, 1–34. http://dx.doi.org/10.1037/a0029321

Linn, M. C., & Petersen, A. C. (1985). Emergence and characterization of sex differences in spatial ability: A meta-analysis. *Child Development, 56,* 1479–1498. http://dx.doi.org/10.2307/1130467

Lippa, R. A., Collaer, M. L., & Peters, M. (2010). Sex differences in mental rotation and line angle judgments are positively associated with gender equality and economic development across 53 nations. *Archives of Sexual Behavior, 39,* 990–997. http://dx.doi.org/10.1007/s10508-008-9460-8

Lytton, H., & Romney, D. M. (1991). Parents' differential socialization of boys and girls: A meta-analysis. *Psychological Bulletin, 109,* 267–296. http://dx.doi.org/10.1037/0033-2909.109.2.267

Martin, C. L., Eisenbud, L., & Rose, H. (1995). Children's gender-based reasoning about toys. *Child Development, 66,* 1453–1471. http://dx.doi.org/10.2307/1131657

McClurg, P. A., & Chaillé, C. (1987). Computer games: Environments for developing spatial cognition? *Journal of Educational Computing Research, 3,* 95–111. http://dx.doi.org/10.2190/9N5U-P3E9-R1X8-0RQM

Myers, K. (2013, December 2). How to tell if a toy is for boys or girls in one easy step. *The Huffington Post.* Retrieved from http://www.huffingtonpost.com/2013/12/02/how-to-tell-if-a-toy-is-for-boys-or-girls_n_4372629.html

Nath, S., & Szücs, D. (2014). Construction play and cognitive skills associated with the development of mathematical abilities in 7-year-old children. *Learning and Instruction, 32,* 73–80. http://dx.doi.org/10.1016/j.learninstruc.2014.01.006

National Assessment Governing Board. (2017). *What is NAEP?* Retrieved from https://www.nagb.org/about-naep/what-is-naep.html

National Governors Association Center for Best Practices & Council of Chief State School Officers. (2010). *Common Core State Standards for Mathematics.* Washington, DC: NGA; CCSSO. Retrieved from: http://www.corestandards.org/assets/CCSSI_Math%20Standards.pdf

National Research Council. (2006). *Learning to think spatially.* Washington, DC: The National Academies Press. Retrieved from https://nces.ed.gov/nationsreport card/pdf/parents/2009490rev.pdf

Newcombe, N. S. (2010). On tending to our scientific knitting: Thinking about gender in the context of evolution. In J. C. Chrisler & D. R. McCreary (Eds.), *Handbook of gender research in psychology: Gender research in general and experimental psychology* (Vol. 1, pp. 259–274). New York, NY: Springer. http://dx.doi.org/10.1007/978-1-4419-1465-1_13

Nosek, B. A., Smyth, F. L., Sriram, N., Lindner, N. M., Devos, T., Ayala, A., . . . Greenwald, A. G. (2009). National differences in gender-science stereotypes predict national sex differences in science and math achievement. *PNAS Proceedings of the National Academy of Sciences of the United States of America, 106,* 10593–10597. http://dx.doi.org/10.1073/pnas.0809921106

O'Brien, M., & Huston, A. C. (1985). Development of sex-typed play behavior in toddlers. *Developmental Psychology, 21,* 866–871. http://dx.doi.org/10.1037/0012-1649.21.5.866

O'Brien, M., Huston, A. C., & Risley, T. R. (1983). Sex-typed play of toddlers in a day care center. *Journal of Applied Developmental Psychology, 4,* 1–9. http://dx.doi.org/10.1016/0193-3973(83)90054-0

Okagaki, L., & Frensch, P. A. (1994). Effects of video game playing on measures of spatial performance: Gender effects in late adolescence. *Journal of Applied Developmental Psychology, 15,* 33–58. http://dx.doi.org/10.1016/0193-3973(94)90005-1

Paoletti, J. B. (2012). *Pink and blue: Telling the boys from the girls in America.* Bloomington: Indiana University Press.

Ramani, G. B., & Siegler, R. S. (2008). Promoting broad and stable improvements in low-income children's numerical knowledge through playing number board games. *Child Development, 79,* 375–394. http://dx.doi.org/10.1111/j.1467-8624.2007.01131.x

Reilly, D. (2012). Gender, culture, and sex-typed cognitive abilities. *PLoS ONE, 7,* e39904. http://dx.doi.org/10.1371/journal.pone.0039904

Rothgerber, H., & Wolsiefer, K. (2014). A naturalistic study of stereotype threat in young female chess players. *Group Processes & Intergroup Relations, 17,* 79–90. http://dx.doi.org/10.1177/1368430213490212

Rovinelli, L., & Whissell, C. (1998). Emotion and style in 30-second television advertisements targeted at men, women, boys, and girls. *Perceptual and Motor Skills, 86,* 1048–1050. http://dx.doi.org/10.2466/pms.1998.86.3.1048

Ruble, D. N., Martin, C. L., & Berenbaum, S. A. (2006). Gender development. In N. Eisenberg (Ed.), *Handbook of child psychology: Social, emotional, and personality development* (Vol. 3, 6th ed., pp. 858–932). Hoboken, NJ: John Wiley & Sons.

Sala, G., & Gobet, F. (2016). Do the benefits of chess instruction transfer to academic and cognitive skills? A meta-analysis. *Educational Research Review, 18,* 46–57. http://dx.doi.org/10.1016/j.edurev.2016.02.002

Sala, G., Gorini, A., & Pravettoni, G. (2015). Mathematical problem-solving abilities and chess: An experimental study on young pupils. *SAGE Open, 5,* 1–9. http://dx.doi.org/10.1177/2158244015596050

Schau, C. G., Kahn, L., Diepold, J. H., & Cherry, F. (1980). The relationships of parental expectations and preschool children's verbal sex typing to their sex-typed toy play behavior. *Child Development, 51,* 266–270. http://dx.doi.org/10.2307/1129620

Serbin, L. A., & Connor, J. M. (1979). Sex-typing of children's play preferences and patterns of cognitive performance. *The Journal of Genetic Psychology: Research and Theory on Human Development, 134,* 315–316. http://dx.doi.org/10.1080/00221325.1979.10534065

Shell, R., & Eisenberg, N. (1990). The role of peers' gender in children's naturally occurring interest in toys. *International Journal of Behavioral Development, 13,* 373–388. http://dx.doi.org/10.1177/016502549001300309

Sherman, J. A. (1967). Problem of sex differences in space perception and aspects of intellectual functioning. *Psychological Review, 74,* 290–299. http://dx.doi.org/10.1037/h0024723

Siegler, R. S., & Booth, J. L. (2005). Development of numerical estimation: A review. In J. I. D. Campbell (Ed.), *Handbook of mathematical cognition* (pp. 197–212). New York, NY: Psychology Press.

Signorella, M. L., Bigler, R. S., & Liben, L. S. (1993). Developmental differences in children's gender schemata about others: A meta-analytic review. *Developmental Review, 13*, 147–183. http://dx.doi.org/10.1006/drev.1993.1007

Sommers, C. H. (2013, August 28). *Should single-sex schooling be eliminated?* [Debate between Christina Hoff Sommers and Lise Eliot]. Washington, DC: American Enterprise Institute. Retrieved from http://live.aei.org/Event/Should_single-sex_schooling_be_eliminated

Spence, I., & Feng, J. (2010). Video games and spatial cognition. *Review of General Psychology, 14*, 92–104. http://dx.doi.org/10.1037/a0019491

Sprafkin, C., Serbin, L. A., Denier, C., & Connor, J. M. (1983). Gender-differentiated play: Cognitive consequences and early interventions. In M. B. Liss (Ed.), *Social and cognitive skills: Gender roles and children's play* (pp. 167–192). New York, NY: Academic Press.

Stannard, L., Wolfgang, C. H., Jones, I., & Phelps, P. (2001). A longitudinal study of the predictive relations among construction play and mathematical achievement. *Early Child Development and Care, 167*, 115–125. http://dx.doi.org/10.1080/0300443011670110

Subrahmanyam, K., & Greenfield, P. M. (1994). Effect of video game practice on spatial skills in girls and boys. *Journal of Applied Developmental Psychology, 15*, 13–32. http://dx.doi.org/10.1016/0193-3973(94)90004-3

Tate, C. C., Ledbetter, J. N., & Youssef, C. P. (2013). A two-question method for assessing gender categories in the social and medical sciences. *The Journal of Sex Research, 50*, 767–776. http://dx.doi.org/10.1080/00224499.2012.690110

Tepylo, D. H., Moss, J., & Stephenson, C. (2015). A developmental look at a rigorous block play program. *Young Children, 70*, 18–25.

Terlecki, M. S., & Newcombe, N. S. (2005). How important is the digital divide? The relation of computer and videogame usage to gender differences in mental rotation ability. *Sex Roles, 53*, 433–441. http://dx.doi.org/10.1007/s11199-005-6765-0

Toy. (n.d.-a). In *Merriam-Webster's online dictionary*. Retrieved from https://www.merriam-webster.com/dictionary/toy

Toy. (n.d.-b). In *Oxford dictionaries*. Retrieved from https://en.oxforddictionaries.com/definition/toy

Toy. (n.d.-c). In *Wikipedia*. Retrieved September 21, 2017, from https://en.wikipedia.org/wiki/Toy

Uttal, D. H., Meadow, N. G., Tipton, E., Hand, L. L., Alden, A. R., Warren, C., & Newcombe, N. S. (2013). The malleability of spatial skills: A meta-analysis of training studies. *Psychological Bulletin, 139*, 352–402. http://dx.doi.org/10.1037/a0028446

Vasta, R., & Liben, L. S. (1996). The water-level task: An intriguing puzzle. *Current Directions in Psychological Science, 5*, 171–177. http://dx.doi.org/10.1111/1467-8721.ep11512379

Verdine, B. N., Golinkoff, R. M., Hirsh-Pasek, K., Newcombe, N. S., Filipowicz, A. T., & Chang, A. (2014a). Deconstructing building blocks: Preschoolers' spatial assembly performance relates to early mathematical skills. *Child Development, 85,* 1062–1076. http://dx.doi.org/10.1111/cdev.12165

Verdine, B. N., Irwin, C. M., Golinkoff, R. M., & Hirsh-Pasek, K. (2014b). Contributions of executive function and spatial skills to preschool mathematics achievement. *Journal of Experimental Child Psychology, 126,* 37–51. http://dx.doi.org/10.1016/j.jecp.2014.02.012

Voyer, D., Voyer, S., & Bryden, M. P. (1995). Magnitude of sex differences in spatial abilities: A meta-analysis and consideration of critical variables. *Psychological Bulletin, 117,* 250–270. http://dx.doi.org/10.1037/0033-2909.117.2.250

Wai, J., Lubinski, D., & Benbow, C. P. (2009). Spatial ability for STEM domains: Aligning over 50 years of cumulative psychological knowledge solidifies its importance. *Journal of Educational Psychology, 101,* 817–835. http://dx.doi.org/10.1037/a0016127

Wechsler, D. (1967). *Manual for the Wechsler Preschool and Primary Scale of Intelligence.* New York, NY: Psychological Corporation.

Wechsler, D. (2009). *Wechsler Individual Achievement Test* (3rd ed.). San Antonio, TX: NCS Pearson.

Wechsler, D. (2012). *Wechsler Preschool and Primary Scale of Intelligence—Fourth edition technical and interpretative manual.* San Antonio, TX: Psychological Corporation.

Weisgram, E. S. (2016). The cognitive construction of gender stereotypes: Evidence for the dual pathways model of gender differentiation. *Sex Roles, 75,* 301–313. http://dx.doi.org/10.1007/s11199-016-0624-z

Weisgram, E. S., Fulcher, M., & Dinella, L. M. (2014). Pink gives girls permission: Exploring the roles of explicit gender labels and gender-typed colors on preschool children's toy preferences. *Journal of Applied Developmental Psychology, 35,* 401–409. http://dx.doi.org/10.1016/j.appdev.2014.06.004

Welch, R. L., Huston-Stein, A., Wright, J. C., & Plehal, R. (1979). Subtle sex-role cues in children's commercials. *Journal of Communication, 29,* 202–209. http://dx.doi.org/10.1111/j.1460-2466.1979.tb01733.x

Whyte, J. C., & Bull, R. (2008). Number games, magnitude representation, and basic number skills in preschoolers. *Developmental Psychology, 44,* 588–596. http://dx.doi.org/10.1037/0012-1649.44.2.588

Witkin, H. A., Oltman, P. K., Raskin, E., & Karp, S. A. (1971). *A manual for the embedded figures tests.* Palo Alto, CA: Consulting Psychologists Press.

Wolfgang, C. H., Stannard, L. L., & Jones, I. (2001). Block play performance among preschoolers as a predictor of later school achievement in mathematics. *Journal of Research in Childhood Education, 15,* 173–180. http://dx.doi.org/10.1080/02568540109594958

Wong, W. I., & Hines, M. (2015). Effects of gender color-coding on toddlers' gender-typical toy play. *Archives of Sexual Behavior, 44,* 1233–1242. http://dx.doi.org/10.1007/s10508-014-0400-5

11

WORKING AT PLAY: GENDER-TYPED PLAY AND CHILDREN'S VISIONS OF FUTURE WORK AND FAMILY ROLES

MEGAN FULCHER AND EMILY F. COYLE

Play is the work of childhood.

—Jean Piaget

When children play, alone or with one another, they learn roles, build skills, and create visions of their future selves. When play is gendered, these roles, skills, and visions may become constrained by the types of toys available to boys versus to girls, adult and peer support for gender-traditional toy play, and cultural messages about the appropriateness of toys for boys versus for girls. In this chapter, we review the development of children's visions of future work and family roles, and consider how empirical evidence and developmental theories indicate the process by which play works to shape, inspire, and constrain such visions. We also describe the cultural breadwinner/ caregiver ideal and consider how the current segregation of many children's toys by gender appears to prepare children to envision a gender-traditional future as either a caregiver or a breadwinner.

In preschool, children begin to think about their future work and family roles (Fulcher, Sutfin, & Patterson, 2008). Although their early aspirations

http://dx.doi.org/10.1037/0000077-012
Gender Typing of Children's Toys: How Early Play Experiences Impact Development, E. S. Weisgram and L. M. Dinella (Editors)

are often fantastical, they also usually are gender traditional. Children at a young age understand gender segregation and stereotypes surrounding occupations (Liben & Bigler, 2002; Liben, Bigler, & Krogh, 2001). By preschool, they anticipate gendered future labor, both paid and unpaid (Fulcher et al., 2008). Children may build efficacy for occupational skills while playing with toys. Those toys they play with most frequently may influence the children's visions of their future selves. Additionally, children may eliminate some jobs from the slate of possibilities because those jobs are deemed gender inappropriate (Gottfredson & Lapan, 1997). For example, girls may eliminate science, technology, engineering, and mathematics (STEM) careers from their list of possible careers because they have not had the opportunity to build efficacy through scientific play. Interventions to increase the presence of women in STEM should include toys that encourage interest in those domains in a gender-minimized way. Instead, many toys highlight gender and reinforce stereotypes. Girls build efficacy for nurturing and boys, for agency. Children may use the breadwinner/caregiver ideal as a template to envision future families in which women are primarily responsible for the care and nurturance of family, whereas men are primarily responsible for paid labor (Fulcher & Coyle, 2011). The marketing of domestic role toys (e.g., baby dolls, kitchen sets) to girls and the strong prohibition against boys' playing with such toys may explain differences in feelings of competencies for domestic tasks and for gendered visions of future roles. Different toys encourage boys versus girls to envision different, gendered futures.

PLAY AND TOYS

It is during play that children learn most efficiently (Bandura, 1978; Piaget, 1932; Vygotski, 1929). When engaged in play with peers, children use more advanced language than in typical conversation. Children remember objects better if they have played with them than if they simply have seen them. Indeed, when more play materials and toys are available in preschool, children show improved cognitive performance by age 7 (Montie, Xiang, & Schweinhart, 2006). Many preschool programs are designed so that children experience *playful learning*, that is, learning through interactions with toys and materials (Lillard et al., 2013). Several types of play are important for children's constructions of their visions of their future selves, including motor play, mastery play, sociodramatic play, and construction play. Children build feelings of efficacy for future roles through practice and enactment of future roles (Burghardt, 2011). Additionally, children may use playmates or the toys themselves as models to emulate when envisioning their future. Children spend their time with peers and adults interacting with toys. It is during these times that play also can serve to communicate and instruct children about social and cultural norms and expectations (Goncu & Gaskins, 2011, Kavanaugh, 2011; Vygotsky, 1933/1967). Toys deliver clear cultural dictums in the messages presented during play to children by peers, the media, parents, and teachers.

Sociodramatic play is seen as more interesting and more appropriate for girls (Lynch, 2015). Increased pretend or fantastical play is associated with improved executive function in preschool children. Interestingly, it is not just that especially imaginative children show increased executive function. Fantasy play interventions may improve some children's executive function (Thibodeau, Gilpin, Brown, & Meyer, 2016), which suggests that toys that elicit pretend play could improve children's cognition (see Chapter 10, this volume). With increased executive functioning, children are ready to learn, even in more academic contexts. Girls' early pretend play also predicts later math achievement (Wallace & Russ, 2015). However, the toys designed to encourage pretend play are different for boys versus for girls. Teachers have reported that girls are more interested in house and nurturing pretend play, whereas boys are more interested in superhero and fighting pretend play (Logue & Harvey, 2009). Playing house may activate girls' stereotypes about math, thereby potentially negating the positive influence of pretend play on math achievement. Although symbolic thinking may help children achieve number sense and number concept, feminine play may wash out these effects.

Children's toys are designed to promote either primary or secondary activities. *Primary activities* are those performed to fulfill needs; they most closely resemble adult roles. *Secondary activities* are those that simply involve play or learning with no emphasis on future roles (Nelson, 2005). Although toys that represent secondary activities are more likely to be gender neutral (e.g., art supplies, stuffed animals, board games), primary activity toys can be divided into roles that take place in the public sphere (e.g., tools, vehicles, machines) and in the private sphere (e.g., dolls, kitchen sets, clothing), and clear gender differences emerge (Blakemore & Centers, 2005). This toy segregation sends a message to girls that their adult roles take place in the home, whereas boys' futures are outside the home (Nelson, 2005). A small study of children's favorite toys (Francis, 2010) found that masculine toys, although not intentionally educational, included significant amounts of information about the mechanics and technology of vehicles, weaponry, and robotics. Such embedded information that may lead boys to feel competent in a technological world and build efficacy for engineering and mechanical skills (Klugman, 2000). These hidden skill-builders were available across masculine toys with little information-building packaged with feminine toys (outside of child care and domestic skills).

In addition to the aforementioned differences, masculine and feminine have other defining characteristics (see Chapter 4). Masculine toys are rated as more violent and competitive than neutral or feminine toys, and as more exciting and dangerous, and calling for adult supervision than are feminine toys (Blakemore & Centers, 2005). Masculine toys also are rated as more realistic, including having more information and details, while feminine toys are reported to be more fantastical and simple. Additionally, masculine toys are more likely to reward action and movement, while feminine toys do not (Pennell, 1994). As children play with these different toys, they are building different efficacies and skills that they will continue to draw on as they develop.

OCCUPATIONAL ASPIRATIONS

Children think about their future in terms of future work and family. By preschool, their occupational aspirations are tied to gender (e.g., Fulcher et al., 2008; Gottfredson, 1981; Helwig, 1998). Among school-age children, gender is the most powerful predictor of their vision of future work (Fulcher, 2011; Stockard & McGee, 1990; Teig & Susskind, 2008). Children's gender-nontraditional occupational aspirations, although less studied, are associated with flexible parental gender attitudes, children's gender flexibility, parents' equitable division of paid and unpaid labor, and the prestige and traditionality of parents' occupations (Fulcher, 2011; Fulcher & Coyle, 2011; Fulcher et al., 2008; O'Brien & Fassinger, 1993).

Children's experiences with play and toys may impact their traditional or nontraditional occupational aspirations. It is especially important to investigate the toys and play patterns associated with children's occupational aspirations because of growing demands and employee shortages in several traditionally gendered occupational domains, such as in STEM—given the ongoing gender imbalance in STEM education and employment (see Ceci & Williams, 2010, for a review) and the growing number of U.S. jobs in that sector (U.S. Department of Labor, Bureau of Labor Statistics, 2013). Additionally, there is growing demand as well as a shortage of new nurses (American Association of Colleges of Nursing, 2014) and teachers (Aragon, 2016). If such occupations seemed available for both boys and girls, perhaps such shortages would decrease. Thus, it is important to examine theoretical underpinnings of how toy play may impact occupational aspirations.

Social-Cognitive Theory

According to the social-cognitive theory (SCT) of gender development (Bussey & Bandura, 1999), people build efficacy for tasks through practice, direct tuition, and modeling. When people hold efficacy for tasks, they spend more time engaged in such tasks, enjoy the tasks more, and persist longer when working on the task. Bandura and his colleagues similarly have argued that children's occupational choices stem directly from feelings of efficacy for occupational skills (Bandura, Barbaranelli, Caprara, & Pastorelli, 2001). Thus, boys and girls may have different, gendered occupational aspirations because they have efficacies in different, gendered domains. Children with gender-nontraditional occupational aspirations must have feelings of efficacy for nontraditional skills (Fulcher, 2011). If boys and girls receive different messages about toys and thus play with different toys, they will build feelings of efficacy in different domains. Children also may use dolls, action figures, or media characters as models when considering the possibilities of their future roles. Similarly, children's play in gender-segregated peer groups implies exposure to single-gender peer models, further prompting the development of gendered visions of future selves.

Building of STEM Skills

According to SCT, if children feel efficacy for skills associated with STEM occupations, they will practice these skills more, enjoy time spent practicing, and persevere through failure and frustration in associated activities. Domains typically associated with STEM careers include spatial skills, science, math, and technology. Unfortunately, by preschool, both boys and girls predict that girls will find math to be more difficult than language arts but do not predict a similar gap for boys (del Rio & Strasser, 2013).

STEM jobs in particular draw on well-developed spatial skills (Wai, Lubinski, & Benbow, 2009). Toys that encourage such efficacies include construction sets, building sets, vehicles, and video games. Masculine toys and neutral toys are perceived to offer more spatial skill-building opportunities, especially construction-based toys (e.g., Blakemore & Centers, 2005). Adults who recall engaging in more spatial play (e.g., LEGOs, block building, vehicle play, sports) in childhood have better spatial skills and higher math grades than those who recall less spatial play, regardless of gender (Doyle, Voyer, & Cherney, 2012; Wolfgang, Stannard, & Jones, 2003). Similar associations have been found between children's LEGO and puzzle play and their spatial skill and math achievement (Levine, Ratliff, Huttenlocher, & Cannon, 2012; Wolfgang et al., 2003). Interestingly, doll play (e.g., baby, Barbie) has been negatively associated with adult spatial skills (Doyle et al., 2012). Boys are more likely to own a video gaming system than are girls and spend more time playing video games each day (Cotten, Shank, & Anderson, 2014; Kaiser Family Foundation, 2010). Even short (e.g., 1-hour) experiences with video games can decrease the gender gap in spatial skills, which appear to be highly trainable (e.g., Cherney, Bersted, & Smetter, 2014; Wai, Cacchio, Putallaz,

& Makel, 2010). Boys engage with these spatial skill-building toys more often than do girls (Auster & Mansbach, 2012; Jirout & Newcombe, 2015), thus potentially contributing to the observed spatial skills gap favoring boys and men (e.g., Linn & Petersen, 1985; Wai et al., 2010).

One aspect of envisioning a career in STEM includes comfort with and efficacy for technology and computers. Currently, one of the most gender-segregated careers is computer science, although this is not true historically or cross culturally (National Science Foundation, 2013; Varma & Kapur, 2015). The use of technology toys, computer software, and video games could build efficacy for technology-related tasks. Yet, boys have reported spending more time playing computer games than do girls (Cherney & London, 2006; Kaiser Family Foundation, 2010). When girls do play computer games, the games are less masculine than those that boys play (Cherney & London, 2006). Computer games, such as competitive and timed games, can be used enhance math skills. Because masculine toys are rated as being more competitive in nature (Blakemore & Centers, 2005), these games may seem more conducive for boys. However, research on learning from computer games suggests that such games may be more effective in teaching math skills when framed as noncompetitive (Wei & Hendrix, 2009). Toys and games could serve to untangle gender and skills by offering the best method of increasing skills that is attractive to boys and girls.

Obstacles to Efficacy Building

In theory, if boys and girls played with a variety of toys, they could build efficacy in both gender-traditional and nontraditional domains. Yet, we know that on average, boys and girls play with different toys (e.g., Cherney, Kelly-Vance, Glover, Ruane, & Ryalls, 2003; Maccoby & Jacklin, 1974). Gender-based marketing appears to have a powerful effect on gender-typed play and related learning outcomes that ultimately are relevant for career interests. In a recent laboratory study (Coyle & Liben, 2015), preschool and kinder-garten boys and girls played with the same engineering toy marketed either to girls (GoldieBlox) or to boys (BobbyBlox). Children played longer when assigned to play with the same-gender toy (i.e., girls with GoldieBlox, boys with BobbyBlox) than with the cross-gender toy (girls with BobbyBlox, boys with GoldieBlox). Interestingly, despite differences in the length of play, chil-dren actually learned more about engineering (i.e., belt-drive concept) when playing with the cross-gender toy than with the same-gender toy. Coding of children's play suggested that children engaged in more free play with a toy labeled as "for their gender," for example, making novel (but not mechani-cal) constructions, rather than following along with an associated storybook that contained instructions for the belt-drive. In the cross-gender condition, children used the storybook to a greater extent, resulting in mechanical learning gains in that condition over the same-gender condition (Coyle & Liben, 2015). Efforts to increase girls' interest in STEM by making the context more feminine (e.g., the *LEGO Friends* line) may backfire because simply highlighting gender may amplify, rather than wash away, its effects.

In addition to the barrier created by explicitly gendered marketing is the barrier created by implicit stereotyping of a domain such as STEM through the ambient environment in which it is conducted or taught. One theory about the underrepresentation of women in some STEM careers is that the occupations and the course work associated with preparing for such occupations does not seem welcoming, regardless of girls' and women's personal interest or feelings of efficacy. Finding techniques to decrease stereotypes surrounding such occupations has been shown to increase adolescent girls' interest in computer science, a particularly stereotyped and gender-segregated domain (Master, Cheryan, & Meltzoff, 2016). It seems that the key to encouraging all children to explore STEM, build efficacy, and consider it as part of their vision of the future is to minimize gender and work to remove stereotypes.

Modeling and Nontraditional Careers

Research indicates that children use models as templates for their visions of their future selves. Preschoolers observe their parents' division of child care when thinking about their own future (Fulcher et al., 2008). Daughters of women with nontraditional jobs are themselves more interested in nontraditional careers (Castellino, Lerner, Lerner, & von Eye, 1998). It is clear that children observe the adults around them, particularly parents, as models for future selves. Peers, playmates, and toy characters also may serve as models for children's construction of gendered future selves.

Peers as Models

Peers are a powerful influence in many aspects of child development (e.g., Degner & Dalege, 2013; Harris, 1995, 2009; Rubin, Bukowski, & Parker, 2006). In the domain of play, peers influence how, what, and with whom children play. Thus, peers are a primary source of information about social roles and skills, and may offer opportunities for more variety in play and play materials. However, from early in life, children's peer groups are predominantly same gender (e.g., Maccoby & Jacklin, 1974; C. L. Martin, Fabes, Hanish, & Hollenstein, 2005). Moreover, play with same-gender peers appears to promote increased play in gender-segregated peer groups (C. L. Martin et al., 2013). Martin and colleagues observed preschoolers' play over the course of a year. They observed, as expected, that single-gender play-groups were more common than mixed-gender groups. They also found that children with a greater number of same-gender friends played with same-gender peers more often over time. Children also played more over time with peers with similar activity preferences (C. L. Martin et al., 2013). In other research, C. L. Martin and colleagues found children's playmate preferences were best predicted by perceived similarity to peers (C. L. Martin, Fabes, Hanish, Leonard, & Dinella, 2011). Children reported expected peer interest in toys based on perceived similarly, such that girls expected other girls to like the same toys they did, and vice versa for boys. Perceived similarity to the gender group also increased with age (C. L. Martin et al., 2011). Taken together, these findings suggest that single-gender peer groups may be self-perpetuating, thus encouraging increasingly gender-typed play. As children play with same-gender peers in gendered activities, they are building efficacies only for such activities. Using only same-gender peers for information about appropriate behavior may begin to limit children's ideas about their future roles.

Other research suggests that in addition to encouraging gender-typed play, children discourage cross-gender play (Blakemore, 2003; Smetana, 1986). Blakemore (2003) found that children reported less interest in being friends with girls who engaged in cross-gender play styles and boys with cross-gender-typed appearance or interest. Still, other research illustrates how peers have the potential to encourage cross-gendered play (Goble, Martin, Hanish, & Fabes, 2012). Goble and colleagues examined gender-typing of play across social contexts. They found that both boys and girls engaged in gender-typed play when playing alone and in same-gender peer groups. Indeed, girls playing with other girls engaged in similar levels of feminine play and less masculine play than girls playing alone, whereas boys playing with other boys engaged in similar levels of masculine play and less feminine play than boys playing alone. But, when girls played with boys, they engaged in more masculine play than girls alone or girls playing with girls. Boys playing with female teachers showed a similar pattern, engaging in more feminine play than boys playing alone or with other boys (Goble et al., 2012). Thus, although single-gender peer groups model and encourage gender-typed play over cross-gendered play, mixed-gender social contexts may facilitate some cross-gendered play. Strict gender-typed play may promote the development of gendered skills and interests to the exclusion of other skills, thus encouraging career development in traditionally gendered domains. Children potentially may benefit in the breadth of their interest and skill development from playing in mixed-gender groups.

Dolls as Models

Broadly classified, toys that represent the human figure are equally likely to be owned by boys versus girls. However, girls are more likely to have female human forms (e.g., baby or adult dolls) and boys are more likely to have male human forms (usually adult action figures; Nelson, 2005). When boys and girls play with dolls, they show more complex play than when they play with masculine or neutral toys (Cherney et al., 2003). Doll play also encourages pretend play, which has many cognitive benefits. Indeed, some dolls are designed to promote occupational play. Mattel has promoted Barbie dolls as an example to girls of all the careers they can pursue. By some estimates, Barbie dolls representing more than 130 careers have been sold (Goudreau, 2012). Reflecting on their play with Barbie, some girls reported that Barbie's career roles influenced aspects of play (Kuther & McDonald, 2004). After playing with Barbie for a short time, girls reported fewer possible career options for themselves and more options for boys than did girls who played with Mrs. Potato Head (Sherman & Zurbriggen, 2014). Career Barbie presents a quandary: She may serve as model of ideal physical femininity similar to typical, noncareer Barbies or she may encourage girls to consider nontraditional careers. Some evidence suggests that feminized models may not work (or may even backfire) in encouraging girls to consider nontraditional careers (Betz & Sekaquaptewa, 2012).

When young girls play with career Barbies, do they simply retain the femininity of the model or do they become more flexible about career roles? Coyle and Liben (2016) suggested that dolls may serve as important models for young girls—and in nuanced ways. Preschool and kindergarten girls played a computer game about various occupations, including STEM jobs. The jobs were enacted by a doll character, either Barbie (highly feminized condition) or a Playmobil doll called "Jane" (less feminized condition). Girls were assessed for their interest in various occupations and play activities at pretest and again at posttest. Girls also were assessed in a pretest for their attentiveness to gender (i.e., personal gender salience; Liben & Bigler, 2002). Several outcomes were possible: Girls might become more interested in the depicted jobs, perhaps differentially by model, and girls might become more interested in related play activities, perhaps differentially by gender and model. Coyle and Liben (2016) found that girls were no more interested in masculine jobs after playing either version of the game. Rather, girls were more interested in other feminine activities after playing the highly feminized Barbie game but showed no change in interests after playing the less feminized Jane game. This finding interacted with gender salience, such that girls who were more gender salient were especially interested in other feminine activities after playing with Barbie (Coyle & Liben, 2016). Barbie, a highly gender-typed model, appears to have reinforced and even enhanced girls' interest in gender-typed play. In some ways, this outcome operates contrary to the hope that feminized models will increase girls' interest in gender-nontraditional domains, such as in STEM jobs or masculine-typed play that could support building relevant skills (e.g., spatial skills). Rather, aspects of the model itself reinforce gender traditionality (i.e., stereotypic femininity). More research of this type is needed to link doll play with aspirations, particularly research that examines what characteristics of dolls might encourage nontraditional aspirations in girls. Although this study looked at how dolls (i.e., Barbie or Playmobil) could serve as a model, the task itself was embedded in a video game. Video games may be associated with improved spatial skills and comfort with technology, although more research is needed to determine whether feminized versions also lead to the expected skills associated with STEM success.

Dolls can serve as models for children as they construct visions of their future work and family roles. For African American girls in particular, it may be valuable to play with dolls of their own racial minority. In a study of preschool girls, African American girls were more likely to identify with Barbies on the basis of skin color than were White girls (Coyle & Fulcher, 2017). Playing with Barbies may be informing girls about the expectations and roles associated with their racial group along with their gender. Black dolls (including Barbie) are less accessible and available than are White dolls (Montford, 2014; Rochman, 2013), leaving Black girls with fewer potential models. Exposure to information about other racial groups also builds children's knowledge about their own racial group as different (Kowalski, 1998, 2003). Thus, as Black girls play with White dolls, they may be creating visions of their future that are limited by what they cannot do instead of building efficacies for what they can do. This may be particularly important for occupational aspirations in elementary school, where Black children have reported that Black adults are less likely to hold high-status occupational positions (Bigler, Averhart, & Liben, 2003). Therefore, Black career dolls may help African American girls build skills for jobs that they had only observed being performed by White adults and increase the number of occupations these girls see as accessible.

Self-Socialization Theories

In addition to the socializing effects within the framework of SCT, a variety of cognitive theories suggest that rather than simply being influenced by the environment, children actively glean information from that environment to build cognitive structures to organize, think about, and perform gender. This idea of self-socialization (Maccoby & Jacklin, 1974; C. L. Martin, Ruble, & Szkrybalo, 2002; Zosuls et al., 2009) presents the child as actively searching, performing, and maintaining gendered behaviors. Interestingly, toddlers in homes where gender is a particularly salient organizing tool learn to label gender significantly earlier than those in more egalitarian homes (Fagot, Leinbach, & O'Boyle, 1992). One way that gender can become salient to children is by the decor and toys provided in their rooms (Sutfin, Fulcher, Bowles, & Patterson, 2008). Children who wake up in pink or blue bedrooms surrounded by dolls or trucks may be constantly reminded of the importance of their gender. As children understand and think about gender, they begin to imagine a future that includes only occupations included in their gender schema (Stockard & McGee, 1990). According to the circumscription and compromise theory of vocational aspirations (Gottfredson & Lapan, 1997), jobs considered inconsistent with one's self-image are not considered. Thus, children may not consider a gender-incongruent occupation regardless of personal interest or competence. Toys offer children information about occupations and roles that children incorporate into their ideas about what is right or not right for adults of their gender.

Gender Schema Theory

Gender schema theory (GST; Bem, 1981; C. L. Martin & Halverson, 1981; see also Chapter 7, this volume, for a review) is one such self-socialization lens for understanding how gendered play influences occupational development. According to this framework, boys and girls seek out information about their own group. Children approach what they perceive as culturally appropriate for their own gender and avoid what they perceive as inappropriate, or appropriate for the other gender only. They then consolidate this information into gender schemas, which operate to guide a child's own behavior and to predict that of others. According to GST, presented with a feminine-typed toy, a girl would judge the toy to be consistent with her gender and thus approach the toy, play with it, and learn the skills it affords. In contrast, a boy would judge the toy to be inconsistent with his own gender, avoid it, and miss the opportunity to learn from the particular toy. Because toys in the United States are marketed by gender now more than ever (Sweet, 2014), children encounter ample cues about what toys are *for* them. Given that different kinds of toys are marketed to girls versus to boys (e.g., dolls for girls and construction toys for boys; Auster & Mansbach, 2012), boys and girls may develop different skill sets and interests through play with gender-typed toys, missing out on skills afforded by the other gender's toys. For example, because LEGOs are primarily marketed toward boys, girls may think they are not for them and miss an opportunity to build spatial skills that are important for STEM careers.

Additionally, consistent with GST, children make assumptions about how to play with the toys they perceive to be gender appropriate, which might further constrain skill and interest development to gendered domains. In the case of the earlier laboratory example by Coyle and Liben (2015), children's assumptions about how to use the gender-congruent toy (i.e., girls with GoldieBlox and boys with BobbyBlox) seem to have interfered with mechanical learning. Research needs to be conducted about toys that are inviting to all children and encourage playful learning.

Of course, children are differentially attentive to gender and may care more or less about whether a toy is for them. Liben and Bigler's (2002) dual pathways model extends GST to account for individual differences, such as attention to gender (i.e., gender salience) and personal interest in a toy. According to their model, a girl will approach a feminine toy if she perceives gender to be relevant (e.g., "I am a girl and this is a toy for girls") or if she is personally interested in the toy. Children who pay a great deal of attention to gender may be especially attracted to gender-typed toys and thus particularly affected by their affordances (e.g., Coyle & Liben, 2016). Ultimately, strict gender-typed play may constrain children's developing interests and skills to domains that set them up for more traditionally gendered occupations. Especially when gender-typed toys build occupational skills or encourage occupational play, children may begin to limit the careers they feel are appropriate for themselves.

Developmental Media Persuasion Model

Another framework in which to understand children's self-socialization with toys is through the developmental media persuasion model (DMPM; Buijzen, Van Reijmersdal, & Owen, 2010). According to DMPM, media, including toys, are influential at three levels of children's processing. *Systematic-persuasion processing* occurs when a child deliberately considers and elaborates on a message. This deepest level of processing is least likely to occur among younger children but is more likely among older children. *Heuristic-persuasion processing* involves moderate attention to persuasive messages guided by heuristic cues, such as toy attractiveness or desirable packaging. The most surface-level processing and the processing level most used by younger children is *automatic-persuasion processing*, which is driven by cues unrelated to persuasive facets of the toy itself but, rather, how a child feels while playing with it (Buijzen et al., 2010). Fun and attractive toys, therefore, may be most likely to impact children's developing interests and attitudes. Children may play more often with fun versus boring toys, thus internalizing their associated messages and skills more so than with toys they use less often. If those toys themselves are gender typed, children's trajectory to developing gender-typed skills and interests relevant for future careers is encouraged.

FUTURE FAMILY ROLES

Of course, when children envision their future, they consider occupations in paid labor or what they are "going to be when they grow up," but they also are thinking about future family roles. Boys and girls have reported that they plan to both parent and hold a job as adults (Fulcher, 2011; Fulcher & Coyle, 2011; Fulcher et al., 2008). Girls and boys plan differently, however, for how to manage work and family simultaneously, and these plans become more divergent across development (Coyle, Van Leer, Schroeder, & Fulcher, 2015; Fulcher & Coyle, 2011). Throughout development, heteronormative images of families permeate children's environment. In children's homes, in their books, on the television and computer screens, and in their toys, families are represented almost exclusively as heterosexual and with a breadwinner/caregiver division of paid and unpaid labor. Under the breadwinner/caregiver model of family organization, men primarily are responsible for providing financially for their family, whereas women primarily are responsible for caring for children and other domestic tasks. Although few families actually enact this strict division of labor (Pew Research Center, 2013), the ideal of the model seeps into the roles of every member of the family. Mothers' paid work is seen as supplemental and helpful (or simply important to a mother's own identity), while fathers' domestic work is seen as helpful and under the organizational control of mothers (as when fathers complete domestic tasks on a list created by mothers or when fathers "babysit"). This management/helper arrangement also may serve to stunt men's growth in feelings of efficacy for child care tasks. When mothers are perceived as family managers, fathers may have difficulty constructing a caregiving role; thus, children may define mothers' roles as caregiver and fathers' as breadwinners (Meteyer & Perry-Jenkins, 2010).

Women have reported more efficacy and competence for child care tasks than have men, even before becoming parents themselves. Even young children (Sinno & Killen, 2009) have reported women to be more competent caregivers. Thus, boys and girls must be developing different efficacies and perceptions of their roles in the family before becoming parents, and their behaviors within the family subsequently are tied to their gender. Daughters are given dolls and domestic toys that encourage the development of social and language skills. Conversely, sons are encouraged to play more independently and are given toys that encourage large motor skill and spatial relation skills (Leaper & Gleason, 1996). Children take these skills to preschool and form different types of friendships: Girls use the social and language skills built at home to make intense, intimate friendships that revolve around talking; boys form larger groups of friends that revolve around activities they enjoy doing as group (Zarbatany, McDougall, & Hymel, 2000). Parents encourage boys and girls to develop different skills that prepare them for different futures, either as breadwinner or caregiver.

Although mothers spend little time talking to children about sex and sexual relationships, they do spend time talking about marriage and heterosexual romance (K. Martin, 2009). Mothers present love and marriage to preschool daughters as being like Disney movies, where love is magical and transformative, and includes the heterosexual pursuit of a woman by a man. Many companies designate in stores and online which toys are appropriate for boys versus for girls. For example, the online Disney Store designates 60% of toys as only for boys, 22% as only for girls, and 17% as for both boys and girls (although it should be noted that Disney did not designate a "both boys and girls" section; rather, the researchers counted toys that appeared on both lists). Toys for both boys and girls included stuffed animals, action figures, and other figures and vehicles, but nothing domestic (Auster & Mansbach, 2012). Of the toys that were dolls, domestic, or related to beauty, Disney designated 95% as for girls only, which suggests to children and to toy buyers that girls' focus should be on practicing for heterosexual marriage and family formation.

K. Martin (2009) found that 33% of mothers of preschoolers are parenting in a way they believe will prevent nonheterosexuality, in part by encouraging gendered play and activities. Men have reported more homophobic attitudes than have women (Loftus, 2001). Fathers see themselves as responsible for their sons' future sexual orientation and are especially invested in helping them be more masculine (Solebello & Elliott, 2011). Thus, fathers spend energy ensuring that their children, particularly their sons, are behaving in a gender-typed and heterosexual manner. Fathers typically have more traditional gender role attitudes and encourage more traditional play than do mothers (Langlois & Downs, 1980). Fathers will engage in masculine play with daughters and sons but will only engage in feminine play with daughters (Fagot & Hagan, 1991). Fathers also give direct information to sons about gendered attitudes and behaviors (Caldera, Huston, & O'Brien, 1989). When presented with feminine toys, sons reported knowing that those toys were ones their fathers would not like them to play with (Raag & Rackliff, 1998). In the face of counterstereotypical information, fathers are likely to make stereotype-confirming comments (Endendijk et al., 2014). As children create visions of their future selves, they incorporate notions of the breadwinner/caregiver ideal. It is clear by preschool that girls indeed envision caring for children as an import aspect of the future selves, whereas boys do not. As girls' occupational aspirations mature and narrow, they seem to have double vision—aspiring to demanding and prestigious careers while also planning to be primary caregivers to several children (Fulcher, 2011; Fulcher & Coyle, 2011). By college, these double visions seem to collide, and young women begin to scale back the occupational prestige of their aspirations to make room for their future family role. It may be here that intervention needs to occur to not only encourage girls in nontraditional occupations such as STEM but also talk with them about nontraditional family roles. It also may be important to encourage boys and men to envision a future that includes family care.

Although many interventions have been aimed at increasing girls' interest in and pursuit of STEM and other prestigious and demanding careers, there have not been analogous interventions to decrease the primacy of caregiving in girls' future selves. Such interventions could be aimed at girls' play (e.g., doll houses that come with nearby daycare centers, baby accessories that include notes for the nanny, a Ken doll that comes with children). However it may be even more effective to aim such interventions at boys because little research has examined the barriers to men's nurturing roles (Croft, Schmader, & Block, 2015). Men are capable of caregiving and nurturance, and when given opportunities for primary child care responsibilities, they behave similarly to mothers. When, instead, mothers are viewed as experts and fathers as helpers, fathers are not given the opportunity to build efficacy for child care tasks. Boys and college-age men report feeling less competent at child care tasks. However, college men who remember their fathers' being more responsible for child care feel both more competence for child care tasks and plan on being more caregiving with their own future children (Fulcher, Dinella, & Weisgram, 2015). Fathers who take paternity leave or extended time off at the birth of a child are perceived to be a coparent as opposed to a helper. Coparenting fathers show the same nurturing behaviors as do mothers (Rehel, 2014). Men who engage in child care tasks indeed build efficacy for child care and are capable caregivers. Moreover, increased parental involvement is associated with more psychological health in men (Schindler, 2010) and in children.

The more time fathers spend with children, the more competent they feel for child care tasks, especially if they observe male caregiving models (Magill-Evans, Harrison, Benzies, Gierl, & Kimak, 2007). Interactional quality between fathers and toddlers is of the same quality of mothers' interaction, especially if fathers are caring for the children alone (de Mendonça, Cossette, Strayer, & Gravel, 2011). Married fathers increase their engagement with children when alone rather than when mothers are present, which suggests that their helper role simply is culturally constructed (Meteyer & Perry-Jenkins, 2010). It seems that nurturing skills are learned, not innate or gendered. Providing boys with more male caregiving models of all types may help alleviate the breadwinner/caregiver pressure on women. In addition to models, practice and play with domestic toys and dolls also could increase boys' efficacy for caregiving tasks and thereby increase the likelihood that boys will include a caregiving role in their vision of their future.

Although toys designed to increase girls' interest in masculine domains and roles are more available and culturally acceptable (although perhaps not effective; e.g., Coyle & Liben, 2015, 2016), few toys exist to increase boys' interest in caregiving and domestic tasks. Indeed, when boys do show interest in feminine activities, adults are likely to worry about them and to encourage them to participate in more masculine activities (Coyle, Fulcher, & Trübutschek, 2016). Parents have reported supporting and encouraging girls' more masculine interests and play, yet reported more concern for boys' cross-gender play (Kane, 2006). Fathers, in particular, have reported being concerned when sons play with domestic toys and work to convince boys to play with more masculine toys (Fagot & Hagan, 1991). Parents and other adults are more rigid about stereotypical feminine toys, such as domestic toys and dolls, than stereotypical masculine toys, such as vehicles (Campenni, 1999). When playing with children, parents and other adults are likely to engage in masculine play with boys but are less stereotyped in their play with girls (Wood, Desmarais, & Gugula, 2002). Kindergarten teachers also are likely to shift boys' attention away from feminine toys and encourage play with more masculine toys (Lynch, 2015). Adults' stereotyped beliefs about toys (Campenni, 1999) and their provision of gender-typed toys for children (Nelson, 2005) increase as children enter preschool. Girls' toy preferences are most gender typed in preschool and become less gender typed across middle childhood (although across ages, girls prefer more feminine toys more than do boys; Cherney & London, 2006). Thus, boys are removed from the opportunity to build skills associated with feminine toys, but perhaps more important, they received the message that domestic and nurturing roles are inappropriate for them. So, whereas girls may have permission to play with masculine toys that build efficacy for certain masculine tasks, boys do not have permission to play with toys that promote nurturance and relational skills.

In addition to parental influences, children are actively selecting toys that are culturally appropriate for their gender when they play alone. This gendered selection begins at the onset of children's labeling of their and others' gender shortly before their second birthday (Todd, Barry, & Thommessen, 2016; Zosuls et al., 2009). This gendered selection suggests that children not only understand their gender in toddlerhood but are actively searching for ways to behave in support of gendered identity. Very young children then are selecting out toys that prepare them for nontraditional careers and future family roles.

Action Figures and Dolls

Building efficacy for caregiving, nurturance, and relational skills is achieved through play with human figures, typically dolls. One important nurturing and caregiving skill is comforting. Some evidence has suggested that girls are able to generate more comforting strategies than boys when faced with an upset infant (Catherine & Schonert-Reichl, 2011; Li & Wong, 2016). Girls who play more with feminine toys and boys who play less with masculine toys are more socially skilled when it comes to comforting infants

(Li & Wong, 2016). Regardless of children's gender, play with feminine toys predicts greater comforting skills and play with masculine toys predicts decreased comforting skills (Li & Wong, 2016). Indeed, type of toy play mediated the relationship between gender and comforting skills, thus suggesting that it is the toys that children play with that increase or decrease children's competence at comforting an infant, an important component of child care.

When boys do play with human figures, it is usually with male action figures. Parents and children view action figures as distinct from dolls. They are more likely to associate action figures than dolls with an existing storyline from television or movies (Klugman, 2000), so boys have less opportunity to use imagination or relational skills to create stories of their own. Action figures are almost solely adult men with exaggerated masculinity, large muscles, aggressive storylines, weapons, and angry faces (e.g., Baghurst, Carlston, Wood, & Wyatt, 2007; Klugman, 2000), thus limiting boys' play with human figures to aggressive and violent scripted play. It presents masculinity to boys as unemotional strength (Francis, 2010) and individualized, and, importantly, relegates play of human relationships, family storylines, and play with child dolls to girls, thereby feminizing those activities.

Although doll sets often include dolls of both genders (e.g., boyfriend, father, baby boy), action figures targeted at boys rarely include female characters. The exclusion of female characters suggests that although the feminine world includes men and women, women are invisible or absent from the masculine world. When women are included in action figure sets, they often are hypersexualized and presented as the villain counterpart to the male hero (Francis, 2010). Boys have little practice with feminine activities or with thinking about or imagining the lives of women.

Heteronormativity of Dolls

When girls play with dolls, the script invokes for them a *heteronormative script:* They are caregivers when playing with baby dolls, and they are focused on the promotion of beauty when playing with fashion or princess dolls. In both scenarios, girls are maintaining the heteronormative script of being beautiful to find romance with a man who will provide for the family that they will care for and nurture. Blakemore and Centers (2005) found that toys rated as being only for girls were primarily associated with appearance. Indeed, a popular character doll for girls to play with is Disney Princess. The dolls come with scripts, and even imaginative play with character dolls tends to be limited to appearance and romance (Wohlwend, 2012). Recent longitudinal work showed that girls who played with Disney Princesses engaged in more stereotypically feminine behavior (including prosocial behavior) concurrently and after 1 year (Coyne, Linder, Rasmussen, Nelson, & Birkbeck, 2016). Interestingly, the researchers found similar effects for boys who played with Disney Princesses, suggesting that feminine toys have the potential to induce positive, prosocial behavior in boys who are interested in playing with them.

Similarly, girls who owned more fashion dolls (e.g., Barbies, Bratz) reported feeling more feminine than girls with fewer fashion dolls. As girls get older, even masculine girls show more interest in Bratz dolls than in Barbie dolls (Karniol, Stuemler-Cohen, & Lahav-Gur, 2012). Bratz dolls are considered to be even more sexualized than Barbie dolls (American Psychological Association, 2007). The set of experiences of playing with such toys emphasizes to girls that their value and future lie in being attractive and in caregiving, perhaps to the exclusion of occupational achievements. Even if girls are building skills that could advance them in STEM and in other occupations, girls may not see the importance or salience of these skills (and interests) to their future.

Segregation of Toys Parallels the Breadwinner/Caregiver Model

The gender segregation of toys not only limits children's experiences and learning opportunities but also serves as a template for children envisioning their future as one that has distinct objects and roles for men versus for women. When children are provided different toys or different versions of the same toy, not only do they build skills in divergent domains and create gendered versions of their future selves, they also come to understand or endorse distinct, important differences between boys and girls (Francis, 2010). Children come to believe that the genders are so different that they cannot even play with the same types of toys (Hilton, 1996). For children, the world is divided clearly into two important social groups, men and women, and such strong categories fit neatly with the breadwinner/caregiver ideal. One of the most powerful ways that toys are designed to segregate the genders is through the use of the color pink.

Feminine toys are presented in pastels, particularly pinks and purples, and are similar to infant toys in color and soft, rounded shapes (Pennell, 1994). By preschool, almost all children understand that pink and purple are considered girl colors (Cherney, Harper, & Winter, 2006). However, a parallel strong color marker doesn't seem to exist for masculine toys. The preference for the color pink by girls and women is not universal or biologically driven (e.g., Taylor, Clifford, & Franklin, 2013); therefore, it must be socially constructed as a cultural marker for what is gender appropriate for women and girls. Such a clear signal is readily included in children's constructions of gender schemas of what is for girls and what is not for boys (Weisgram, Fulcher, & Dinella, 2014). For boys, pink seems to indicate "do not touch" regardless of the object presented. Interestingly, boys did not use pink when coloring stereotypically feminine pictures (i.e., fairy), suggesting that not only do boys know the color pink is for girls—showing strong avoidance around age 3 (LoBue & DeLoache, 2011)—boys do not even use it to signal girls (Karniol, 2011). The color blue is not as clear of a gender marker as is pink, and other gendered signals can override the masculine color. For example, Cherney et al. (2006) found that children reported a blue car to be a toy for girls because it had a woman driver and a baby in the backseat. Boys may be more concerned with not appearing feminine than girls are with not appearing masculine; hence, pink is a more powerful signal than blue. Pink, however, has been used as a marketing technique to get girls interested in masculine toys. Evidence suggests that girls are more interested in masculine toys that are pink than masculine toys in traditional colors (Weisgram et al., 2014). Yet, the result still is a segregation of toys such that girls may play with pink science, construction, or active toys and may perceive those toys may as somehow different than "real" masculine toys. Moreover, in light of experimental findings by Coyle and Liben (2015, 2016) that showed diminished effect of the feminine toys (Barbie or GoldieBlox) on girls' occupational cognitions, it cannot be assumed that simply making a masculine toy pink would result in similar outcomes for girls that the toy produces for boys.

Interestingly, when neutral toys were rated by adults, a primary characteristic of such toys were that they encouraged occupational skills (Blakemore & Centers, 2005). However, toys that encourage enacting future family roles are strictly segregated. That the LEGO Friends line has been nominated for Worst Toy Award by the Campaign for a Commercial-Free Childhood (Dell'Antonia, 2012) indicates that a substantial number of consumers and interest groups are upset about stereotypically feminine toys that reflect a narrow definition of girlhood (Knudsen & Kuever, 2015). Yet, toys that promote hypermasculinity or even a limited version of boys' future roles have not received the same negative attention.

CONCLUSION AND FUTURE DIRECTIONS

It is clear that the types of toys that children play with impact their vision of their future selves. The gender segregation of children's toys serves as persistent reminder of a cultural endorsement of the breadwinner/caregiver model of work and family roles. Masculine toys help boys build the skills needed for success and confidence in STEM classes and careers. Toys designed for boys' imaginative play do not include children or women. Conversely, toys designed primarily for girls focus on appearance and domestic tasks. Although crossover into masculine toys occurs for girls, a prohibition against domestic and doll play for boys still exists, suggesting that family nurturance is the primary responsibility of women. This belief constrains the visions of the future for boys and girls.

More research is needed to understand how toys can be used to encourage nontraditional visions of future occupations and family roles. Experimental research that directly ties children's play with gender-amplified toys to visions of future selves is needed. Similarly, can playing with domestic toys enhance boys' views of future coparenting roles? Additionally, further examination is needed of the role gender-neutral toys may serve in desegregating boys' and girls' play experiences. Coyle and Liben (2015) found that although mothers were most interested in purchasing neutral STEM toys for sons or daughters, children themselves were most interested in gendered toys, followed by neutral, and boys did not perceive a category difference between masculine and neutral STEM toys. Perhaps most fundamentally, longitudinal research is needed that examines children's toy play across development and its link to course selection, college majors, and occupations in young adulthood.

During play, children build skills and efficacies they may later draw on when imagining future work and family roles. If these play experiences are limited to gender-typed toys and activities, children's ideas about their future roles may be limited. Indeed, children may bring building skills into play that will change their experiences of work in adulthood. As girls build nurturing skills and envision a nurturing future, they cater their expectations for work around this family role. Women are more likely to report valuing flexibility for family responsibilities when choosing jobs (Weisgram, Bigler, & Liben, 2010). Thus, the ability to prioritize nurturing roles while working may be seen as benefit of a particular job. This benefit paired with the family view of women's salary as supplemental may encourage women to accept lower wages for their work than do men.

To encourage flexibility in future occupational and family roles, children should play with a variety of toys. Although some toys are marketed for both boys and girls, a domain of toys is still for girls alone—pink, appearance, and domestic-typed toys. This division reminds girls (and boys) that girls can do anything, but they should expect do the housework alone. All the pink microscopes in the world are not going to increase the number of women in prestigious and demanding STEM jobs until they can envision a parenting partner who can and will competently collaborate to rear children and run a household.

REFERENCES

American Association of Colleges of Nursing. (2014). *Nursing shortage fact sheet.* Retrieved from http://www.aacn.nche.edu/media-relations/fact-sheets/nursing-shortage

American Psychological Association. (2007). *Report of the APA Task Force on the Sexualization of Girls.* Washington, DC: American Psychological Association.

Aragon, S. (2016). *Teacher shortages: What we know.* Retrieved from http://www.ecs.org/ec-content/uploads/Teacher-Shortages-What-We-Know.pdf

Auster, C. J., & Mansbach, C. S. (2012). The gender marketing of toys: An analysis of color and type of toy on the Disney store website. *Sex Roles, 67,* 375–388. http://dx.doi.org/10.1007/s11199-012-0177-8

Baghurst, T., Carlston, D., Wood, J., & Wyatt, F. B. (2007). Preadolescent male perceptions of action figure physiques. *Journal of Adolescent Health, 41,* 613–615. http://dx.doi.org/10.1016/j.jadohealth.2007.07.013

Bandura, A. (1978). The self system in reciprocal determinism. *American Psychologist, 33,* 344–358. http://dx.doi.org/10.1037/0003-066X.33.4.344

Bandura, A., Barbaranelli, C., Caprara, G. V., & Pastorelli, C. (2001). Self-efficacy beliefs as shapers of children's aspirations and career trajectories. *Child Development, 72,* 187–206. http://dx.doi.org/10.1111/1467-8624.00273

Bem, S. L. (1981). Gender schema theory: A cognitive account of sex typing. *Psychological Review, 88,* 354–364. http://dx.doi.org/10.1037/0033-295X.88.4.354

Betz, D. E., & Sekaquaptewa, D. (2012). My fair physicist? Feminine math and science role models demotivate young girls. *Social Psychological and Personality Science, 3,* 738–746. http://dx.doi.org/10.1177/1948550612440735

Bigler, R. S., Averhart, C. J., & Liben, L. S. (2003). Race and the workforce: Occupational status, aspirations, and stereotyping among African American children. *Developmental Psychology, 39,* 572–580. http://dx.doi.org/10.1037/0012-1649.39.3.572

Blakemore, J. E. O. (2003). Children's beliefs about violating gender norms: Boys shouldn't look like girls, and girls shouldn't act like boys. *Sex Roles, 48,* 411–419. http://dx.doi.org/10.1023/A:1023574427720

Blakemore, J. E. O., & Centers, R. E. (2005). Characteristics of boys' and girls' toys. *Sex Roles, 53,* 619–633. http://dx.doi.org/10.1007/s11199-005-7729-0

Buijzen, M., Van Reijmersdal, E. A., & Owen, L. H. (2010). Introducing the PCMC model: An investigative framework for young people's processing of commercialized media content. *Communication Theory, 20,* 427–450. http://dx.doi.org/10.1111/j.1468-2885.2010.01370.x

Burghardt, G. M. (2011). Defining and recognizing play. In A. Pellegrini (Ed.), *The Oxford handbook of the development of play* (pp. 9–18). New York, NY: Oxford University Press.

Bussey, K., & Bandura, A. (1999). Social cognitive theory of gender development and differentiation. *Psychological Review, 106,* 676–713. http://dx.doi.org/10.1037/0033-295X.106.4.676

Caldera, Y. M., Huston, A. C., & O'Brien, M. (1989). Social interactions and play patterns of parents and toddlers with feminine, masculine, and neutral toys. *Child Development, 60,* 70–76. http://dx.doi.org/10.2307/1131072

Campenni, C. E. (1999). Gender stereotyping of children's toys: A comparison of parents and nonparents. *Sex Roles, 40,* 121–138. http://dx.doi.org/10.1023/A:1018886518834

Castellino, D. R., Lerner, J. V., Lerner, R. M., & von Eye, A. (1998). Maternal employment and education: Predictors of young adolescent career trajectories. *Applied Developmental Science, 2,* 114–126. http://dx.doi.org/10.1207/s1532480xads0203_1

Catherine, N. L. A., & Schonert-Reichl, K. A. (2011). Children's perceptions and comforting strategies to infant crying: Relations to age, sex, and empathy-related responding. *British Journal of Developmental Psychology, 29,* 524–551. http://dx.doi.org/10.1348/026151010X521475

Ceci, S. J., & Williams, W. M. (2010). *The mathematics of sex: How biology and society conspire to limit talented women and girls.* New York, NY: Oxford University Press.

Cherney, I. D., Bersted, K., & Smetter, J. (2014). Training spatial skills in men and women. *Perceptual and Motor Skills, 119,* 82–99. http://dx.doi.org/10.2466/23.25.PMS.119c12z0

Cherney, I. D., Harper, H. J., & Winter, J. A. (2006). Nouveaux jouets: Ce que les enfants identifient comme "jouets de garcons" et "jouets de filles" [New toys for tots: What preschoolers identify as "boy toys" and "girl toys"]. *Enfance, 58,* 266–282. http://dx.doi.org/10.3917/enf.583.0266

Cherney, I. D., Kelly-Vance, L., Glover, K. G., Ruane, A., & Ryalls, B. O. (2003). The effects of stereotyped toys and gender on play assessment in children aged 18–47 months. *Educational Psychology, 23,* 95–106. http://dx.doi.org/10.1080/01443410303222

Cherney, I. D., & London, K. (2006). Gender-linked differences in the toys, television shows, computer games, and outdoor activities of 5- to 13-year-old children. *Sex Roles, 54,* 717–726. http://dx.doi.org/10.1007/s11199-006-9037-8

Cotten, S. R., Shank, D. B., & Anderson, W. A. (2014). Gender, technology use, and ownership and media-based multitasking among middle school students. *Computers in Human Behavior, 35,* 99–106. http://dx.doi.org/10.1016/j.chb.2014.02.041

Coyle, E. F., & Fulcher, M. (2017, April). *Possible selves are not necessarily similar selves: Preschool girls' reasoning about future jobs using Barbie career dolls.* Poster session at the biennial meeting of the Society for Research on Child Development, Austin, TX.

Coyle, E. F., Fulcher, M., & Trübutschek, D. (2016). Sissies, mama's boys, and tomboys: Is children's gender nonconformity more acceptable when nonconforming traits are positive? *Archives of Sexual Behavior, 45,* 1827–1838. http://dx.doi.org/10.1007/s10508-016-0695-5

Coyle, E. F., & Liben, L. S. (2015, March). Toys marketed to girls: A path to STEM engagement? In E. Weisgram (Chair), *Gender typing of toys: Causes, correlates, and consequences.* Symposium conducted at the meeting of the Society for Research in Child Development, Philadelphia, PA.

Coyle, E. F., & Liben, L. S. (2016). Affecting girls' activity and job interests through play: The moderating roles of personal gender salience and game characteristics. *Child Development, 87*, 414–428. http://dx.doi.org/10.1111/cdev.12463

Coyle, E. F., Van Leer, E., Schroeder, K. M., & Fulcher, M. (2015). Planning to have it all: Emerging adults' expectations of future work–family conflict. *Sex Roles, 72*, 547–557. http://dx.doi.org/10.1007/s11199-015-0492-y

Coyne, S. M., Linder, J. R., Rasmussen, E. E., Nelson, D. A., & Birkbeck, V. (2016). Pretty as a princess: Longitudinal effects of engagement with Disney Princesses on gender stereotypes, body esteem, and prosocial behavior in children. *Child Development, 87*, 1909–1925. http://dx.doi.org/10.1111/cdev.12569

Croft, A., Schmader, T., & Block, K. (2015). An underexamined inequality: Cultural and psychological barriers to men's engagement with communal roles. *Personality and Social Psychology Review, 19*, 343–370. http://dx.doi.org/10.1177/1088868314564789

Degner, J., & Dalege, J. (2013). The apple does not fall far from the tree, or does it? A meta-analysis of parent–child similarity in intergroup attitudes. *Psychological Bulletin, 139*, 1270–1304. http://dx.doi.org/10.1037/a0031436

Dell'Antonia, K. J. (2012, November 29). "Worst toy awards" target LEGO Friends [Web log post]. Retrieved from https://parenting.blogs.nytimes.com/2012/11/29/worst-toy-awards-target-lego-friends/

del Rio, M. F., & Strasser, K. (2013). Preschool children's beliefs about gender differences in academic skills. *Sex Roles, 68*, 231–238. http://dx.doi.org/10.1007/s11199-012-0195-6

de Mendonça, J. S., Cossette, L., Strayer, F. F., & Gravel, F. (2011). Mother–child and father–child interactional synchrony in dyadic and triadic interactions. *Sex Roles, 64*, 132–142. http://dx.doi.org/10.1007/s11199-010-9875-2

Doyle, R. A., Voyer, D., & Cherney, I. D. (2012). The relation between childhood spatial activities and spatial abilities in adulthood. *Journal of Applied Developmental Psychology, 33*, 112–120. http://dx.doi.org/10.1016/j.appdev.2012.01.002

Endendijk, J. J., Groeneveld, M. G., van der Pol, L. D., van Berkel, S. R., Hallers-Haalboom, E. T., Mesman, J., & Bakermans-Kranenburg, M. J. (2014). Boys don't play with dolls: Mothers' and fathers' gender talk during picture book reading. *Parenting: Science and Practice, 14*, 141–161. http://dx.doi.org/10.1080/15295192.2014.972753

Fagot, B. I., & Hagan, R. (1991). Observations of parent reactions to sex-stereotyped behaviors: Age and sex effects. *Child Development, 62*, 617–628. http://dx.doi.org/10.2307/1131135

Fagot, B. I., Leinbach, M. D., & O'Boyle, C. (1992). Gender labeling, gender stereotyping, and parenting behaviors. *Developmental Psychology, 28*, 225–230. http://dx.doi.org/10.1037/0012-1649.28.2.225

Francis, B. (2010). Gender, toys, and learning. *Oxford Review of Education, 36*, 325–344. http://dx.doi.org/10.1080/03054981003732278

Fulcher, M. (2011). Individual differences in children's occupational aspirations as a function of parental traditionality. *Sex Roles, 64,* 117–131. http://dx.doi.org/10.1007/s11199-010-9854-7

Fulcher, M., & Coyle, E. F. (2011). Breadwinner and caregiver: A cross-sectional analysis of children's and emerging adults' visions of their future family roles. *British Journal of Developmental Psychology, 29,* 330–346. http://dx.doi.org/10.1111/j.2044-835X.2011.02026.x

Fulcher, M., Dinella, L. M., & Weisgram, E. S. (2015). Constructing a feminist reorganization of the heterosexual breadwinner/caregiver family model: College students' plans for their own future families. *Sex Roles, 73,* 174–186. http://dx.doi.org/10.1007/s11199-015-0487-8

Fulcher, M., Sutfin, E. L., & Patterson, C. J. (2008). Individual differences in gender development: Associations with parental sexual orientation, attitudes and division of labor. *Sex Roles, 58,* 330–341. http://dx.doi.org/10.1007/s11199-007-9348-4

Goble, P., Martin, C. L., Hanish, L. D., & Fabes, R. A. (2012). Children's gender-typed activity choices across preschool social contexts. *Sex Roles, 67,* 435–451. http://dx.doi.org/10.1007/s11199-012-0176-9

Goncu, A., & Gaskins, S. (2011). Comparing and extending Piaget's and Vygotsky's understanding of play: Symbolic play as individual, sociocultural and educational interpretation. In A. D. Pellegrini (Ed.), *The Oxford handbook of the development of play* (pp. 48–57). New York, NY: Oxford University Press.

Gottfredson, L. S. (1981). Circumscription and compromise: A developmental theory of occupational aspirations. *Journal of Vocational Behavior, 29,* 545–579.

Gottfredson, L. S., & Lapan, R. T. (1997). Assessing gender-based circumscription of occupational aspirations. *Journal of Career Assessment, 5,* 419–441. http://dx.doi.org/10.1177/106907279700500404

Goudreau, J. (2012, April 4). Serial career changer Barbie now running for president [Web log post]. Retrieved from http://www.forbes.com/sites/jennagoudreau/2012/04/04/barbie-is-running-for-president/

Harris, J. R. (1995). Where is the child's environment? A group socialization theory of development. *Psychological Review, 102,* 458–489. http://dx.doi.org/10.1037/0033-295X.102.3.458

Harris, J. R. (2009). *The nurture assumption: Why children turn out the way they do.* New York, NY: Free Press.

Helwig, A. A. (1998). Gender-role stereotyping: Testing theory with a longitudinal sample. *Sex Roles, 38,* 403–423. http://dx.doi.org/10.1023/A:1018757821850

Hilton, M. (1996). Manufacturing make-believe: Notes on the toy and media industry for children. In M. Hilton (Ed.), *Potent fictions: Children's literacy and the challenge of popular culture* (pp. 19–46). London, England: Routledge.

Jirout, J. J., & Newcombe, N. S. (2015). Building blocks for developing spatial skills: Evidence from a large, representative U.S. sample. *Psychological Science, 26,* 302–310. http://dx.doi.org/10.1177/0956797614563338

Kaiser Family Foundation. (2010). *Generation M²: Media in the lives of 8- to 18-year-olds.* Retrieved from https://kaiserfamilyfoundation.files.wordpress. com/2013/04/8010.pdf

Kane, E. W. (2006). "No way my boys are going to be like that!" Parents' responses to children's gender nonconformity. *Gender & Society, 20,* 149–176. http://dx.doi.org/ 10.1177/0891243205284276

Karniol, R. (2011). The color of children's gender stereotypes. *Sex Roles, 65,* 119–132. http://dx.doi.org/10.1007/s11199-011-9989-1

Karniol, R., Stuemler-Cohen, T., & Lahav-Gur, Y. (2012). Who likes Bratz? The impact of girls' age and gender role orientation on preferences for Barbie versus Bratz. *Psychology & Marketing, 29,* 897–906. http://dx.doi.org/10.1002/ mar.20572

Kavanaugh, R. D. (2011). Origins and consequences of social pretend play. In A. D. Pellegrini (Ed.), *The Oxford handbook of the development of play* (pp. 296–307). New York, NY: Oxford University Press.

Klugman, K. (2000). A bad hair day for G. I. Joe. In B. L. Clark & M. R. Higonnet (Eds.), *Girls, boys, books, toys: Gender in children's literature and culture* (pp. 169–182). Baltimore, MD: Johns Hopkins University Press.

Knudsen, G. H., & Kuever, E. (2015). The peril of pink bricks: Gender ideology and LEGO Friends. In A. E. Thyroff, J. B. Murray, & R. W. Belk (Series Eds.), *Research in Consumer Behavior Series: Vol. 17. Consumer culture theory* (pp. 171–188). http://dx.doi.org/10.1108/S0885-211120150000017009

Kowalski, K. (1998). The impact of vicarious exposure to diversity on preschooler's emerging ethnic/racial attitudes. *Early Child Development and Care, 146,* 41–51. http://dx.doi.org/10.1080/0300443981460105

Kowalski, K. (2003). The emergence of ethnic and racial attitudes in preschool-aged children. *Journal of Social Psychology, 143,* 677–690. http://dx.doi.org/ 10.1080/00224540309600424

Kuther, T. L., & McDonald, E. (2004). Early adolescents' experiences with, and views of, Barbie. *Adolescence, 39,* 39–51.

Langlois, J. H., & Downs, A. C. (1980). Mothers, fathers, and peers as socialization agents of sex-typed play behaviors in young children. *Child Development, 51,* 1237–1247. http://dx.doi.org/10.2307/1129566

Leaper, C., & Gleason, J. B. (1996). The relationship of play activity and gender to parent and child sex-typed communication. *International Journal of Behavioral Development, 19,* 689–703. http://dx.doi.org/10.1177/016502549601900401

Levine, S. C., Ratliff, K. R., Huttenlocher, J., & Cannon, J. (2012). Early puzzle play: A predictor of preschoolers' spatial transformation skill. *Developmental Psychology, 48,* 530–542. http://dx.doi.org/10.1037/a0025913

Li, R. Y. H., & Wong, W. I. (2016). Gender-typed play and social abilities in boys and girls: Are they related? *Sex Roles, 74,* 399–410. http://dx.doi.org/10.1007/ s11199-016-0580-7

Liben, L. S., & Bigler, R. S. (2002). The developmental course of gender differentiation: Conceptualizing, measuring, and evaluating constructs and pathways. *Monographs of the Society for Research in Child Development, 67*, i–viii.

Liben, L. S., Bigler, R. S., & Krogh, H. R. (2001). Pink and blue collar jobs: Children's judgments of job status and job aspirations in relation to sex of worker. *Journal of Experimental Child Psychology, 79*, 346–363. http://dx.doi.org/10.1006/jecp.2000.2611

Lillard, A. S., Lerner, M. D., Hopkins, E. J., Dore, R. A., Smith, E. D., & Palmquist, C. M. (2013). The impact of pretend play on children's development: A review of the evidence. *Psychological Bulletin, 139*, 1–34. http://dx.doi.org/10.1037/a0029321

Linn, M. C., & Petersen, A. C. (1985). Emergence and characterization of sex differences in spatial ability: A meta-analysis. *Child Development, 56*, 1479–1498. http://dx.doi.org/10.2307/1130467

LoBue, V., & DeLoache, J. S. (2011). Pretty in pink: The early development of gender-stereotyped colour preferences. *British Journal of Developmental Psychology, 29*, 656–667. http://dx.doi.org/10.1111/j.2044-835X.2011.02027.x

Loftus, J. (2001). America's liberalization in attitudes toward homosexuality, 1973 to 1998. *American Sociological Review, 66*, 762–782. http://dx.doi.org/10.2307/3088957

Logue, M. E., & Harvey, H. (2009). Preschool teachers' view of active play. *Journal of Research in Childhood Education, 24*, 32–49. http://dx.doi.org/10.1080/02568540903439375

Lynch, M. (2015). Guys and dolls: A qualitative study of teachers' views of gendered play in kindergarten. *Early Child Development and Care, 185*, 679–693. http://dx.doi.org/10.1080/03004430.2014.950260

Maccoby, E. E., & Jacklin, C. N. (1974). *The psychology of sex differences*. Stanford, CA: Stanford University Press.

Magill-Evans, J., Harrison, M. J., Benzies, K., Gierl, M., & Kimak, C. (2007). Effects of parenting education on first-time fathers' skills in interactions with their infants. *Fathering: A Journal of Theory, Research, and Practice About Men as Fathers, 5*, 42–57. http://dx.doi.org/10.3149/fth.0501.42

Martin, C. L., Fabes, R. A., Hanish, L. D., & Hollenstein, T. (2005). Social dynamics in the preschool. *Developmental Review, 25*, 299–327. http://dx.doi.org/10.1016/j.dr.2005.10.001

Martin, C. L., Fabes, R. A., Hanish, L., Leonard, S., & Dinella, L. M. (2011). Experienced and expected similarity to same-gender peers: Moving toward a comprehensive model of gender segregation. *Sex Roles, 65*, 421–434. http://dx.doi.org/10.1007/s11199-011-0029-y

Martin, C. L., & Halverson, C. F. (1981). A schematic processing model of sex typing and stereotyping in children. *Child Development, 52*, 1119–1134. http://dx.doi.org/10.2307/1129498

Martin, C. L., Kornienko, O., Schaefer, D. R., Hanish, L. D., Fabes, R. A., & Goble, P. (2013). The role of sex of peers and gender-typed activities in young children's peer affiliative networks: A longitudinal analysis of selection and influence. *Child Development, 84,* 921–937. http://dx.doi.org/10.1111/cdev.12032

Martin, C. L., Ruble, D. N., & Szkrybalo, J. (2002). Cognitive theories of early gender development. *Psychological Bulletin, 128,* 903–933. http://dx.doi.org/10.1037/0033-2909.128.6.903

Martin, K. (2009). Normalizing heterosexuality: Mothers' assumptions, talk, and strategies with young children. *American Sociological Review, 74,* 190–207. http://dx.doi.org/10.1177/000312240907400202

Master, A., Cheryan, S., & Meltzoff, A. N. (2016). Computing whether she belongs: Stereotypes undermine girls' interest and sense of belonging in computer science. *Journal of Educational Psychology, 108,* 424–437. http://dx.doi.org/10.1037/edu0000061

Meteyer, K., & Perry-Jenkins, M. (2010). Father involvement among working-class, dual-earner couples. *Fathering: A Journal of Theory, Research, and Practice About Men as Fathers, 8,* 379–403. http://dx.doi.org/10.3149/fth.0803.379

Montford, C. (2014, December 20). Where did the Black dolls go?: Why you couldn't find a Black Barbie for your daughter this Christmas. *Atlanta Black Star.* Retrieved from http://atlantablackstar.com/2014/12/20/last-doll-shelf-wont-getting-child-black-barbie-christmas/

Montie, J. E., Xiang, Z., & Schweinhart, L. J. (2006). Preschool experience in 10 countries: Cognitive language performance at age 7. *Early Childhood Research Quarterly, 21,* 313–331. http://dx.doi.org/10.1016/j.ecresq.2006.07.007

National Science Foundation. (2013). *Women, minorities, and persons with disabilities in science and engineering.* Retrieved from http://www.nsf.gov/statistics/wmpd/2013/start.cfm?CFID=14614984&CFTOKEN=56461309&jsessionid=f0306d628c00285dc6a71c511a3461f5b7a7

Nelson, A. (2005). Children's toy collections in Sweden: A less gender-typed country? *Sex Roles, 52,* 93–102. http://dx.doi.org/10.1007/s11199-005-1196-5

O'Brien, K. M., & Fassinger, R. E. (1993). A causal model of the career orientation and career choice of adolescent women. *Journal of Counseling Psychology, 40,* 456–469. http://dx.doi.org/10.1037/0022-0167.40.4.456

Pennell, G. E. (1994). Babes in toyland: Learning an ideology of gender. In C. T. Allen & D. R. John (Eds.), *Advances in consumer research* (Vol. 21, pp. 359–364). Provo, UT: Association for Consumer Research.

Pew Research Center. (2013). *Modern parenthood: Roles of moms and dads converge as they balance work and family.* Retrieved from http://www.pewsocialtrends.org/2013/03/14/modern-parenthood-roles-of-moms-and-dads-converge-as-they-balance-work-and-family/

Piaget, J. (1932). *The language and thought of the child.* New York, NY: Harcourt, Brace.

Raag, T., & Rackliff, C. L. (1998). Preschoolers' awareness of social expectations of gender: Relationships to toy preferences. *Sex Roles, 38*, 685–700. http://dx.doi.org/10.1023/A:1018890728636

Rehel, E. M. (2014). When dad stays home too: Paternity leave, gender, and parenting. *Gender & Society, 28*, 110–132. http://dx.doi.org/10.1177/0891243213503900

Rochman, B. (2013, April 3). A mom asks Mattel to make party supplies featuring "Barbies of Color." *Time*. Retrieved from http://healthland.time.com/2013/04/03/a-mom-asks-mattel-to-make-party-supplies-featuring-barbies-of-color/

Rubin, K. H., Bukowski, W. M., & Parker, J. G. (2006). Peer interactions, relationships, and groups. In W. Damon & R. M. Lerner (Eds.), *Handbook of child psychology* (Vol. 3, pp. 571–645). Hoboken, NJ: Wiley.

Schindler, H. S. (2010). The importance of parenting and financial contributions in promoting fathers' psychological health. *Journal of Marriage and Family, 72*, 318–332. http://dx.doi.org/10.1111/j.1741-3737.2010.00702.x

Sherman, A. M., & Zurbriggen, E. L. (2014). "Boys can be anything": Effect of Barbie play on girls' career cognitions. *Sex Roles, 70*, 195–208. http://dx.doi.org/10.1007/s11199-014-0347-y

Sinno, S. M., & Killen, M. (2009). Moms at work and dads at home: Children's evaluations of parental roles. *Applied Developmental Science, 13*, 16–29. http://dx.doi.org/10.1080/10888690802606735

Smetana, J. G. (1986). Preschool children's conceptions of sex-role transgressions. *Child Development, 57*, 862–871. http://dx.doi.org/10.2307/1130363

Solebello, N., & Elliott, S. (2011). "We want them to be as heterosexual as possible": Fathers talk about their teen children's sexuality. *Gender & Society, 25*, 293–315. http://dx.doi.org/10.1177/0891243211403926

Stockard, J., & McGee, J. (1990). Children's occupational preference: The influence of sex and perceptions of occupational characteristics. *Journal of Vocational Behavior, 36*, 287–303. http://dx.doi.org/10.1016/0001-8791(90)90033-X

Sutfin, E. L., Fulcher, M., Bowles, R. P., & Patterson, C. J. (2008). How lesbian and heterosexual parents convey attitudes about gender to their children: The role of gendered environments. *Sex Roles, 58*, 501–513. http://dx.doi.org/10.1007/s11199-007-9368-0

Sweet, E. (2014, December). Toys are more divided by gender now than they were 50 years ago. *The Atlantic*. Retrieved from https://www.theatlantic.com/business/archive/2014/12/toys-are-more-divided-by-gender-now-than-they-were-50-years-ago/383556/

Taylor, C., Clifford, A., & Franklin, A. (2013). Color preferences are not universal. *Journal of Experimental Psychology: General, 142*, 1015–1027. http://dx.doi.org/10.1037/a0030273

Teig, S., & Susskind, J. E. (2008). Truck driver or nurse? The impact of gender roles and occupational status on children's occupational preferences. *Sex Roles, 58*, 848–863. http://dx.doi.org/10.1007/s11199-008-9410-x

Thibodeau, R. B., Gilpin, A. T., Brown, M. M., & Meyer, B. A. (2016). The effects of fantastical pretend-play on the development of executive functions: An intervention study. *Journal of Experimental Child Psychology, 145*, 120–138. http://dx.doi.org/10.1016/j.jecp.2016.01.001

Todd, B. K., Barry, J. A., & Thommessen, S. A. O. (2016). Preferences for "gender-typed" toys in boys and girls aged 9 to 36 months. *Infant and Child Development, 26*(3). Advance online publication. http://dx.doi.org/10.1002/icd.1986

U.S. Department of Labor, Bureau of Labor Statistics. (2013). *Occupational employment projections to 2022* [Monthly Labor Review]. Retrieved from http://www.bls.gov/opub/mlr/2013/article/occupational-employment-projections-to-2022.htm

Varma, R., & Kapur, D. (2015). Decoding femininity in computer science in India. *Communications of the ACM, 58*, 56–62.

Vygotsky, L. S. (1929). The problem of the cultural development of the child. *Journal of Genetic Psychology: Research and Theory on Human Development, 36*(3), 415–434.

Vygotsky, L. S. (1967). Play and its role in the mental development of the child. *Soviet Psychology, 5*(3), 6–18. (Original work published 1933)

Wai, J., Cacchio, M., Putallaz, M., & Makel, M. C. (2010). Sex differences in the right tail of cognitive abilities: A 30 year examination. *Intelligence, 38*, 412–423. http://dx.doi.org/10.1016/j.intell.2010.04.006

Wai, J., Lubinski, D., & Benbow, C. P. (2009). Spatial ability for STEM domains: Aligning over 50 years of cumulative psychological knowledge solidifies its importance. *Journal of Educational Psychology, 101*, 817–835. http://dx.doi.org/10.1037/a0016127

Wallace, C. E., & Russ, S. W. (2015). Pretend play, divergent thinking and math achievement in girls: A longitudinal study. *Psychology of Aesthetics, Creativity, and the Arts, 9*, 296–305. http://dx.doi.org/10.1037/a0039006

Wei, F. Y. F., & Hendrix, K. G. (2009). Gender differences in preschool children's recall of competitive and noncompetitive computer mathematics games. *Learning, Media and Technology, 34*, 27–43. http://dx.doi.org/10.1080/17439880902759893

Weisgram, E. S., Bigler, R. S., & Liben, L. S. (2010). Gender, values, and occupational interests among children, adolescents, and adults. *Child Development, 81*, 778–796. http://dx.doi.org/10.1111/j.1467-8624.2010.01433.x

Weisgram, E. S., Fulcher, M., & Dinella, L. M. (2014). Pink gives girls permission: Exploring the roles of explicit gender labels and gender-typed colors on preschool children's toy preferences. *Journal of Applied Developmental Psychology, 35*, 401–409. http://dx.doi.org/10.1016/j.appdev.2014.06.004

Wohlwend, K. E. (2012). "Are you guys girls?": Boys, identity texts, and Disney Princess play. *Journal of Early Childhood Literacy, 12*, 3–23. http://dx.doi.org/10.1177/1468798411416787

Wolfgang, C., Stannard, L., & Jones, I. (2003). Advanced constructional play with LEGOs among preschoolers as a predictor of later school achievement in mathematics. *Early Child Development and Care, 173,* 467–475. http://dx.doi.org/10.1080/0300443032000088212

Wood, E., Desmarais, S., & Gugula, S. (2002). The impact of parenting experience on gender stereotyped toy play of children. *Sex Roles, 47,* 39–49. http://dx.doi.org/10.1023/A:1020679619728

Zarbatany, L., McDougall, P., & Hymel, S. (2000). Gender-differentiated experience in the peer culture: Links to intimacy in preadolescence. *Social Development, 9,* 62–79. http://dx.doi.org/10.1111/1467-9507.00111

Zosuls, K. M., Ruble, D. N., Tamis-Lemonda, C. S., Shrout, P. E., Bornstein, M. H., & Greulich, F. K. (2009). The acquisition of gender labels in infancy: Implications for gender-typed play. *Developmental Psychology, 45,* 688–701. http://dx.doi.org/10.1037/a0014053

12

SOCIETAL CAUSES AND CONSEQUENCES OF GENDER TYPING OF CHILDREN'S TOYS

CAMPBELL LEAPER AND REBECCA S. BIGLER

Children universally exhibit a drive to engage in activities that have no clear instrumental purpose but instead appear to be pursued for their inherent enjoyment. These activities reflect children's unique personal cognitive and social proclivities, and they shape their future cognitive and social development (Lillard, 2015). Play is especially interesting to those who study gender development because it is both strongly *gender differentiated* (i.e., characterized by average differences across groups of girls and boys) and *gender typed* (i.e., characterized by beliefs that prescribe and proscribe particular forms of play as appropriate for only one gender).

As described in the prior chapters of this book, boys and girls, on average, prefer different toys (see Chapter 4, this volume). Girls are more likely than boys to prefer dolls, cooking toys, and dress-up sets. In contrast, boys are more likely than girls to favor vehicles, construction toys, action-adventure toys, and sports-related toys. Although most average differences between girls

http://dx.doi.org/10.1037/0000077-013
Gender Typing of Children's Toys: How Early Play Experiences Impact Development, E. S. Weisgram and L. M. Dinella (Editors)

and boys in behavior are associated with small effect sizes, differences in toy preferences are large in magnitude (see Leaper, 2015). Moreover, these average differences in toy preferences are seen early in development—often as young as 18 months of age—even in relatively gender-egalitarian societies such as Sweden (Nelson, 2005; Servin & Bohlin, 1999). At the same time that toy play is gender differentiated, it is associated with strong prescriptive and proscriptive beliefs, which also emerge early in development. Thus, the domain of toy play is useful as one in which to test theoretical tenets about the causes and consequences of both gender differentiation and gender typing across domains (work, academics, relationships). Furthermore, research on play has important implications for social, educational, and legal policies. If gender differentiation and gender typing of toys is associated with dysfunctional or nonoptimal developmental outcomes, as some of the research reviewed in this volume suggests (see Chapters 8–11), one might, for example, design and test interventions aimed at reducing the phenomena, with implications for parenting and schooling.

Other chapters in this volume have addressed biological and social–cognitive processes that contribute to the emergence of gender-typed play preferences (see Chapters 5–7). In our chapter, we consider toy play within broad cultural contexts. Bronfenbrenner (1979) argued that individual development occurs within nested ecologies. At the center is the *microsystem*, which represents the child's direct interactions with others in the immediate context (e.g., children's interactions with their parents and peers). The majority of theoretical and empirical work on toy play is focused on the microsystem. The microsystem itself is embedded within the *mesosystem*, representing transactions among those in the environment that exclude the child (e.g., interactions among adults that lead to the purchasing of a particular toy for a target child). The *exosystem* represents distal influences that affect the child indirectly (e.g., a day care center whose policies lead staff to purchase and make available particular toys for children in the center). The *macrosystem* represents the broad cultural qualities and values that infuse all nested layers within it (e.g., the mass production of toys by commercial enterprises for profit). Our focus is predominately (albeit not exclusively) on the collective effect of the mesosystem, the exosystem, and the macrosystem on children's gender-typed toy play—as well as the reciprocal effect of children's gender-typed toy play on these systems. Because much of the relevant empirical work, including our own, is focused on cisgender children (i.e., those who identify with their gender assigned at birth) from predominately White and middle-class families within the U.S. and other Western, industrialized countries (Henrich, Heine, & Norenzayan, 2010), we focus primarily on these contexts in the present chapter.

The subsequent sections of our chapter address the following topics. First, we review a theoretical framework for understanding the gender differentiation and gender typing of toys. In the second section, we consider the consequences of gender differentiation and gender typing of toys, focusing on children's developing expectations and abilities—and by extension how these developments affect gender divisions among adults in society. In the third section, we consider empirical evidence for the role of societal context (e.g., socialization) of gender-typed toy play and argue that the gender typing of toys and play can be seen as forms of gender discrimination. Finally, we speculate about whether and how reductions in the gender differentiation of play behaviors might alter broad societal characteristics and review possible interventions that parents, educators, and others might employ to encourage more flexible toy and play experiences among children.

A CONSTRUCTIVIST–ECOLOGICAL
PERSPECTIVE ON TOY PLAY

Our explanatory perspective on toy play is rooted in a constructivist–ecological approach to gender development (e.g., Liben, 2017; Liben & Coyle, 2017). According to this account, gender differences, including those in toy play, emerge as the result of a dynamic, relational interplay of children's characteristics and their social contexts—and it emphasizes the role of children's creation and construal of their own environments in shaping developmental outcomes (see also Liben, 2014; Leaper, 2000b). That is, children are not viewed as passive recipients of messages that are conveyed by socializing agents but rather as active creators of meaning. Children are active in the process of constructing knowledge and beliefs about social groups and the self (thereby constructing group and *self schemas*) and in the process of applying those schemas to new environmental encounters. The active nature of children's role is reflected in the term *self-socialization*. Such models are also interactionist in the sense that children's qualities and environmental contexts act in dynamic, nonadditive ways to produce outcomes. These models assume that children's personal qualities (e.g., their traits, knowledge, skills) shape the salience, value, and meaning of social groups and identities, including gender, and thus exposure to the same environments can produce differing developmental outcomes among different children (see Leaper, 2000b; Liben, 2014).

Consistent with this perspective, children differ considerably in how rigidly they engage in gender-typed play and avoid cross-gender-typed play (Green, Bigler, & Catherwood, 2004; Leaper, in press). This variation appears within cultures, regions, communities, and even among siblings within the same family. Researchers have identified many factors that may influence gender-related variations in children's play activities. These factors include the child's unique biological characteristics, including sex-related hormonal and genetic variations (Hines, 2013; see also Chapter 5, this volume). For example, girls with congenital adrenal hyperplasia (CAH) who are exposed to high androgen levels during prenatal development are more likely than other girls to favor physically active play and dislike sedentary play—such as preferring sports games over doll play (Hines, 2013; see also Chapter 5, this volume). Despite these strong dispositions that are common among girls with CAH, researchers find their play preferences are partly influenced by socialization (Wong, Pasterski, Hindmarsh, Geffner, & Hines, 2013).

At the same time that children's unique personal characteristics contribute to their play, their cognitive beliefs and values also affect their toy selection and play activities. For example, children who endorse proscriptive attitudes that gender should constrain one's play are more likely to show gender-typed play preferences than their peers (Weisgram, 2016). That is, children appear, as Bussey and Bandura (1999) argued, to constrain their own behavior:

> In the course of development, the regulation of behavior shifts from predominately external sanctions and mandates to gradual substitution of self-sanctions and self-direction grounded in personal standards (Bandura, 1986, 1991b). After self-regulatory functions are developed, children guide their conduct by sanctions they apply to themselves. They do things that give them self-satisfaction and a sense of self-worth. They refrain from behaving in ways that violate their standards to avoid self-censure. The standards provide the guidance; the anticipatory self-sanctions provide the motivators. Self-sanctions thus keep conduct in line with personal standards. (p. 690)

In turn, variations in children's beliefs are often linked to variations in children's contexts. We now turn to a discussion of societal factors that appear to affect the gender differentiation and gender typing of toy play.

ANTECEDENTS OF GENDER-DIFFERENTIATED AND GENDER-TYPED TOY PLAY

When laypeople are asked to identify factors in children's environments likely to shape their toy play, a common reply is to point to "parents." The encouragement of gender-typed play activities is, indeed, a common means by which parents treat sons and daughters differently (Lytton & Romney, 1991). In addition to reinforcing gender-typed play, parents sometime punish gender nonconforming play preferences and styles (Freeman, 2007; Kane, 2006; Langlois & Downs, 1980). However, evidence indicates that many parents in Western cultures are becoming more flexible in their attitudes about the kinds of play they deem acceptable for their children (e.g., Grinberg, 2014;

Wood, Desmarais, & Gugula, 2002). Greater flexibility appears more likely among mothers (vs. fathers), parents with daughters (vs. sons), and lesbian and gay (vs. heterosexual) parents (Goldberg, Kashy, & Smith, 2012; Lytton & Romney, 1991; Wood et al., 2002). It is important to note that parent behavior is not a powerful predictor of children's gender-typed play; only weak associations are seen between parent reinforcement and child play preferences in the preschool years, and little pertinent research is available in middle childhood (see Leaper, 2015, for a review).

One possible reason for the limited effect of parental socialization on children's play preferences may be the strong effect of factors collectively operating beyond the microsystem—within the mesosystem, the exosystem, and the macrosystem—on children's beliefs about gender (see Bigler & Liben, 2006, 2007). Specifically, we argue that these collective factors strongly channel children to attend to gender and to develop gender stereotypic attitudes about toys; as a consequence, they become active agents in the gender socialization of their own and their peers' toy play. That is, children simultaneously are products of the gender socialization of their cultures and agents in the socialization of gender-typed toy play.

Consider, for example, the very early onset of gender stereotyping of toys and play activities. Between the ages of 2 and 3 years, children construct and personally endorse gender stereotypes about toys (see Leaper, 2015). For example, the activity subscale of the Preschool Occupation, Activity, and Traits scale asks children whether "only boys," "only girls," or "both boys and girls" should play with items such as toy doll cribs, stoves and ovens, robots, and basketballs (Liben & Bigler, 2002). Between the ages of 3 and 6 years, the majority of children assign at least some of these toys to only one gender (Arthur, Bigler, & Ruble, 2009; Friedman, Leaper, & Bigler, 2007; Lamb, Bigler, Liben, & Green, 2009; Pahlke, Bigler, & Martin, 2014).

Rather than being inevitable, however, recent theoretical and empirical work suggests that societal factors lead children to attend to and categorize others by gender. Bigler and Liben's (2006) theoretical account of the formation of social stereotypes and prejudices—known as developmental intergroup theory—posits that humans vary along myriad dimensions (height, hair color, handedness, gender, etc.), which offer children many possible bases for social categorization. They argued that children look to adults for cues about which attributes to use as a basis for classification. Labeling and sorting individuals by gender are especially powerful cues and both practices are exceedingly common within U.S. children's environments. For example, speakers routinely use gendered noun labels (e.g., boys, girls, men, women) to refer to individuals, even when unnecessary (e.g., teachers often greet their classrooms with "Good morning, boys and girls" rather than "Good morning, students"). In educational settings, gender is also used to sort children into seats (e.g., sitting "boy-girl-boy-girl"), lines (e.g., "Girls can line up first; now boys can line up"), and even classes and entire schools as a result of a movement toward single-sex public schooling (see Liben, 2015; Signorella & Bigler, 2013). These practices make gender salient and lead children to categorize themselves and others on that basis. As a consequence of such categorization, children tend to endorse gender-essentialist views; that is, they believe members of same gender to share deep, meaningful, and innate characteristics. In addition, children attend to and learn the attributes (including toys) that are linked with gender in their environment (see Bigler & Leaper, 2015; Bigler & Liben, 2006; Liben, 2016).

Importantly, children in the United States are embedded in a broad cultural context that both makes gender psychologically salient and links gender to particular toys. Analyses of toy marketing have found that toys are commonly presented as for boys or for girls through explicit labeling and implicit use. Explicit labeling includes signage that marks some store aisles as "girls' toys" and others as "boys' toys" (Auster & Mansbach, 2012). A form of implicit use occurs in the placement of toys in gender-typed clusters; for example, this is seen in classrooms in which feminine-stereotyped and masculine-stereotyped toys are clustered in differing corners of play spaces (e.g., Pellegrini, 1985). Implicit use also includes demonstrating toy play with models of only one gender, as well as producing and packaging toys in a color associated with only one gender (e.g., Auster & Mansbach, 2012; Kahlenberg & Hein, 2010). Research supports the idea that young children are aware of the meaning of gendered color-coding of toys (Cunningham & Macrae, 2011; Weisgram, Fulcher, & Dinella, 2014) and that this implicit labeling affects their preferences.

The tendency for toys to be marked and marketed (explicitly and implicitly) by adults as "for boys" or "for girls" varies across time and cultures. In the United States, gender-targeted marketing was common between the 1920s and 1960s and then it declined in the 1970s in response to the second wave of the feminist movement. It has seen a strong resurgence in the last two decades, largely as a result of profit motives associated with the commercial enterprise within capitalist economies (Orenstein, 2011). For example, a toy painted in a gender-neutral color (a yellow drum) could be purchased for a daughter and passed onto a younger brother without violating cultural gender norm. In contrast, the production of only two highly gendered drums (e.g., pink and blue) would require parents of boys and girls either to purchase two versions of the same toy or to violate gender conventions. In 2015, the toy industry in the United States made nearly $20 billion in sales (Toy Association, 2016). The deregulation of children's television programming in the mid-1980s freed toy companies to create program-length advertisements for their products, and implicit and explicit gender marking of toys became an increasingly common characteristic of these shows and the toys that they advertised (Sweet, 2014).

The wider cultural context does not, however, operate alone to affect children's interests but instead interacts with the cognitive characteristics of children to produce gender differentiation of toy play. Although children as young as 3 years of age endorse gender stereotypes concerning traits, activities, and occupations, they are also generally very rigid in their use of gender categories to interpret their social worlds. Hence, during early childhood (approximately 3–6 years), girls and boys are often resistant to counterstereotypical messages—especially if they view them as anomalies in their perceived environments. Thus, for example, young boys are often quite unwilling to accept toys, even items that they desire, if those toys are implicitly or explicitly marked as for girl (e.g., pink or flowered). However, increases in cognitive development during middle childhood (approximately 6–10 years) are associated with more variability among children in gender schematicity (i.e., degree of gender labeling and stereotyping; Martin, Ruble, & Szkrybalo, 2002). Children who are relatively gender-aschematic are less likely to use gender categories to infer information; therefore, they may be more likely to engage in a wider range of play activities.

In addition to socializing themselves, children socialize the playmates with whom they interact. Throughout childhood, most girls and boys affiliate primarily with same-gender peer groups (Maccoby, 1998). In these interactions, children often pressure each other to assimilate to the group's peer norms regarding play and other behaviors (see Leaper, 1994). These pressures may mitigate the likelihood that children will express a wider range of play interests. In a revealing longitudinal study of children at a preschool, Martin and Fabes (2001) observed that the amount of time spent with same-gender peers predicted increases in gender-typed play and decreases in cross-gender-typed play from fall to spring. They referred to this phenomenon as the "social dosage effect," whereby exposure to same-gender peers leads to increased conformity in play and other gender-typed behaviors. Thus, same-gender peer groups may have one of the strongest socializing influences on children's opportunities to practice particular play behaviors (see Leaper, 2000b).

EFFECTS OF GENDER-DIFFERENTIATED AND GENDER-TYPED TOY PLAY

Play activities are important in children's development because they provide opportunities to practice particular cognitive and social skills (Lillard, 2015). Feminine- and masculine-stereotyped toys appear to afford practice with differing sets of skills; thus, to the extent that children play exclusively or predominately with toys stereotypically associated with their gender, their opportunities to practice particular skills reduce correspondingly (Cherney

& London, 2006; Etaugh & Liss, 1992; Leaper, 2000b; Pellegrini, 1985). In turn, these gender-differentiated experiences may contribute to girls and boys developing different interests and skills (Blakemore & Centers, 2005; Cherney & London, 2006; Etaugh & Liss, 1992; Huston, 1985; Leaper, 2000b; Miller, 1987).

Cognitive Skills

Masculine- and feminine-stereotyped toys may differentially foster the development of certain cognitive competencies, such as spatial skills, symbolic and representational thinking, and particular academic interests. Over time, these experiences may contribute to average gender differences in occupational motivation and achievement.

Spatial skills are utilized in many of the toys associated more strongly with boys than girls (see Chapter 10). For example, play with puzzles, building blocks, and other construction toys develop children's spatial skills (e.g., Jirout & Newcombe, 2015). Similarly, video game play is also tied to gains in spatial skill (e.g., Spence & Feng, 2010). Some research suggests that play with toys emphasizing spatial skills may further benefit children's developing mathematical skills (Pirrone & Di Nuovo, 2014).

Feminine-stereotyped toys may help to develop particular cognitive abilities. In one study (Cherney, Kelly-Vance, Glover, Ruane, & Ryalls, 2003), researchers compared the cognitive complexity associated with feminine-stereotyped, masculine-stereotyped, or neutral toys among young children between 18 to 47 months. Cognitive complexity was based on the extent that symbolic and representational skills were elicited during play with particular toys. On average, the highest levels of complexity were seen when either girls or boys played with certain feminine-stereotyped toys including the kitchen set and dolls.

Some studies suggest that gender typing in children's toy play may sow the beginnings of later gender gaps in academic achievement (e.g., Serbin, Zelkowitz, Doyle, Gold, & Wheaton, 1990). In turn, early recreational activity interests, such as toy play, may shape children's developing aspirations for particular occupations (e.g., Lee, Lawson, & McHale, 2015; Polnick et al., 2007). Notably, longitudinal research offers support for these patterns of influence over time (Lee et al., 2015; Serbin et al., 1990).

Socioemotional Skills and Adjustment

Masculine- and feminine-stereotyped toys and play activities generally present opportunities to practice different socioemotional skills (see Chapter 9). Among masculine-stereotyped toys, play with construction toys tends to emphasize instrumental speech aimed at solving impersonal tasks, such as solving a puzzle or constructing a building (e.g., Leaper & Gleason, 1996; Leaper et al., 1995). Play with sports-related toys (e.g., balls) can help foster children's physical self-efficacy (King, Ogletree, Fetro, Brown, & Partridge, 2011), and it can bolster positive body image (Hausenblas & Symons Downs, 2001). In many respects, the experiences gained in these forms of repeated play may give boys an edge later in life when they enter the competitive work world outside of the home (Etaugh & Liss, 1992; Lever, 1976).

Feminine-stereotyped toys and games offer their own set of advantages for socioemotional development. Many of the toys and games that are more common among girls foster conversational competence. For example, playing with dolls and other domestic toys ("playing house") typically involves high levels of affiliative speech (e.g., Leaper, 2000a; Leaper & Gleason, 1996). Also, interactions during this kind of play typically have a collaborative conversational structure whereby partners listen and build upon one another's speech acts. This collaborative pattern appears somewhat more likely among girls than boys (see Leaper & Smith, 2004). Furthermore, the focus on the care of baby dolls emphasizes nurturing behaviors. Hence, these play experiences may foster the socioemotional skills necessary for effective functioning later in close friendships and romantic relationships (Blakemore & Centers, 2005; Leaper & Anderson, 1997; Li & Wong, 2016; Sprafkin, Serbin, & Elman, 1982). Moreover, these play experiences can be interpreted as preparing girls to anticipate adult roles as caregivers and homemakers (Etaugh & Liss, 1992; Lever, 1976).

Thus far, we have highlighted the potential benefits of masculine- and feminine-stereotyped toys for all children. However, some aspects of gender-typed toy play may not be beneficial for the socioemotional development of either girls or boys (see Chapter 9). One example concerns the consequences for girls of play with toys that sexualize girls and women, such as female dolls dressed in mini-skirts, midriff-baring shirts, and high heels (e.g., Bratz, Monster High Dolls). Play with sexualized fashion dolls and other dress-up toys may contribute to girls' concerns with physical attractiveness and undermine body image (McKenney & Bigler, 2016b; Murnen & Don, 2012). Moreover, repeated play with fashion-oriented dolls may interfere with many girls' willingness to invest their resources into intellectual domains (see McKenney & Bigler, 2016a) and to develop interests in traditionally masculine jobs, such as scientists, which might not be viewed as glamorous (Coyle & Liben, 2016; Sherman & Zurbriggen, 2014).

Conversely, play with certain types of masculine-stereotyped toys may have potential negative consequences. Many contemporary action figures that are popular among boys tend to emphasize excessive muscularity and may undermine boys' body image (Murnen & Don, 2012). Also, excessive play with violent video games appears to increase aggressive behavior in some (but not most) boys (e.g., Markey & Markey, 2010).

Conclusion

In summary, toys have affordances or functions that tend to elicit and practice particular behaviors. Many gender-typed behaviors during childhood are mediated via the kinds of toys and play activities in which children engage. Indeed, when children or parents were assigned to play with the same set of toys, the type of toy better predicted variations in behavior than did the person's gender (e.g., Caldera, Huston, & O'Brien, 1989; Leaper, 2000a; Leaper & Gleason, 1996; Leaper, Leve, Strasser, & Schwartz, 1995). That is, girls and boys tended to demonstrate similar behaviors when placed in similar situations. Of course, most girls and boys generally are not provided similar opportunities to practice the same sets of behaviors. Instead, the gender-typing process prescribes different kinds of toys and play activities for girls and for boys and, as a consequence, is likely to contribute to the gender-differentiated academic, occupational, and leisure pursuits that characterize the United States and similar societies.

GENDER TYPING OF TOYS AS GENDER DISCRIMINATION

Children learn cultural norms in the context of their social interactions and daily activities (e.g., Bussey & Bandura, 1999; Rogoff, 1990). For example, Rogoff (1990) posited that "the particular skills and orientations that children develop are rooted in the specific historical and cultural activities of the community in which children and their companions interact" (p. vii). Lott and Maluso (1993) also observed that "different situations provide differential opportunities to practice particular behaviors and also present demand characteristics that make some responses more probable than others" (pp. 102–103). Applying this framework, play activities with toys can be construed as cultural practices that integrate children into the larger society (see Chapter 1, this volume).

When certain opportunities are made available to individuals on the basis of group membership—such as their gender, race, ethnicity, sexual orientation, or religion—it is a form of discrimination. In the United States, the passage of Title IX legislation in 1972 mandated that equal opportunities must be provided to students in schools regardless of their sex or race (National Coalition for Women and Girls in Education, 2012). This led to an increase in athletic programs available to girls—and a corresponding dramatic jump in girls' participation in school sports from approximately 3% in 1972 to about 40% in recent years (National Coalition for Women and Girls in Education, 2012). During the same period, boys' participation rate has remained around 50%. Thus, increases in equal opportunity (access to sports teams) led to increased gender parity in behavior (athletic participation).

By extension, the gender typing of toys during childhood may be viewed as a form of gender discrimination (see Leaper, 2000b). As we previously discussed, particular toys tend to foster unique social and cognitive skills. Societal practices that make gender salient foster gender stereotyping, which commonly links gender identities to particular toys and play activities (described earlier); in turn, internalization of these stereotypes leads most children to play with particular toys on the basis of their gender (Tobin et al., 2010). In this manner, girls and boys are often provided different opportunities to learn particular cognitive and social skills. Moreover, they miss out on experiencing the potential enjoyment of toys and play activities that may not be viewed as desirable for their gender.

We can anticipate potential rebuttals to our proposition that the gender typing of toys is a form of gender discrimination. One could argue that toy choices usually reflect children's personal preferences rather than social pressure. For example, Fine and Rush (2016) described gender-essentialist thinkers as defending the gender-based labeling of toys on the grounds that it merely reflects (rather than causes) the robust gender difference in toy preferences.

Evidence clearly indicates, however, that although some children manifest very strong gender-typed toy and play preferences, toy preferences across children and how strongly they may be inclined to favor particular toys is variable (Green et al., 2004). Furthermore, many children avoid particular toys and play activities because of their expectations of what is considered acceptable for their gender ingroup (e.g., Fisher-Thompson & Burke, 1998). That is, socialization pressures may exaggerate the extent that girls and boys might be willing to choose particular toys. As seen in several studies, parents and peers tend to encourage interest in gender-typed toys and play activities and to discourage cross-gender-typed toy interests (see Leaper, 2015, for a review). Thus, we agree with Fine and Rush's (2016, p. 7) conclusion: "It seems then that [gender-typed marketing] does not, in fact, mirror boys' and girls' categorical preferences, but imposes artificial categories on overlapping interests, particularly in the preschool years and for interest in male-typed toys."

Even if some children are inclined to prefer certain toys, we suggest that this should not preclude encouraging children to play with a variety of toys that can foster a broader repertoire of social and cognitive skills. By way of analogy, children show varying degree of interest in particular academic subjects. Also, some of the average gender differences in these interests include, for example, girls demonstrating somewhat higher average interest in reading than do boys, whereas boys demonstrate somewhat higher average interest in mathematics than do girls (see Leaper, 2015, for a review). Yet, parents and teachers generally seek to foster both reading and math skills in all students regardless of children's initial interest—because both sets of skills are usually seen as important for school success. In an analogous manner, greater breadth and flexibility in toy play among children can potentially be encouraged in some ways (discussed later).

In conclusion, gender differences in childhood opportunities may be viewed as early forms of discrimination that perpetuate the reproduction of gender inequities in adulthood (Leaper, 2000b). Girls' and boys' engagement with different toys and play activities in childhood becomes the training ground for later role and status differences in adulthood (see Huston, 1985; Leaper, 1994, 2000b; Liss, 1983). For example, girls will have relatively greater access to doll play, whereas boys will have relatively greater access to sports games. In turn, access provides opportunities to observe and to practice particular behaviors (as described below). Furthermore, practice enables the formation of particular outcome expectancies, preferences, and skills. When men and women develop differing interests and skills as a result of their experiential histories, subsequent generations of children detect these gender differences and develop gender-stereotype notions about these domains in a reciprocally reinforcing causal cycle.

INTERVENTIONS TO FOSTER PLAY WITH A BROAD REPERTOIRE OF TOYS

Some evidence indicates that parents, other family members, and teachers may be able to foster greater flexibility in toy play in many children. In general, interventions aimed at reducing gender typing have produced small, rather than substantial, changes in children's attitudes and behavior—perhaps in part because they are not sustained over time (e.g., see Bigler, 1999). Furthermore, the general weakness of interventions targeting specific microsystem is to be expected when children's combined contexts (i.e., mesosystem, exosystem, and macrosystem) continue to support the gender typing of toys.

Ideally, interventions should focus on societal change, altering the inputs that make gender a salient psychological dimension for categorizing by gender and linking gender to toy play (e.g., via commercial advertising). Several consumer-led campaigns have sought this type of change, including "Let Toys Be Toys," "Let Books Be Books," "Play Unlimited," and "Pink Stinks." As Fine and Rush (2016) noted, such strategies have been successful in some cases at persuading businesses to shift away from gendered marketing of toys (e.g., Target's decision to move away from gender labeling merchandise; Cunha, 2015). Public pressure also appears to have played an instrumental role in leading The LEGO Group to produce a "Research Institute" play set that included three female scientist figures (Criado, 2014). In support of these kinds of efforts, the Obama Administration's White House Council on Women and Girls held a conference in April 2016 addressing ways that toys shape children's views about possible occupations and roles in society (The White House of Barack Obama, 2016). As a result, many companies and organizations committed to taking new actions to reduce gender stereotyping in toys and media (see Chaker, 2016; The White House of Barack Obama, 2016).

Another possible strategy for promoting greater toy play flexibility is to place children in adult-structured settings, such as classrooms or after-school programs, in which children are assigned to play with the same toys (e.g., see Esposito, 2015). For example, teachers could have a period when everyone plays with construction toys and another session when they all make a meal together. When this occurs, studies indicate that girls and boys generally behave in highly similar ways (Caldera et al., 1989; Huston, 1985; Leaper, 2000a; Pellegrini & Perlmutter, 1989). That is, for boys as well as girls, play with toy foods and cooking sets led to more affiliative behaviors, whereas play with construction toys led to more instrumental behaviors (Leaper, 2000a; Leaper & Gleason, 1996). Moreover, it may even help in these situations for the teachers to highlight the value of the skills that are being practiced in each type of activity. When adults (women as well men) and peers openly express their approval of play with cross-gender-typed toys, children may increase their motivation to pursue these activities (e.g., Katz & Walsh, 1991; Serbin, Tonick, & Sternglanz, 1977).

In addition to proactive efforts to promote engagement with both feminine- and masculine-stereotyped toys, adults can intervene to reduce the likelihood that children will apply gender stereotypes to particular toys (see Bigler & Liben, 2007). For example, adults might explicitly contradict the implicit messages presented in toy commercials (i.e., "It's silly that only boys are playing with trucks in that commercial! Some girls like trucks, too!"). They might also challenge the organization of toys into "girls" and "boys" sections in stores (Cunha, 2015).

A related strategy is to limit, monitor, and challenge children's exposure to gender stereotyping in advertising and other media. However, most parents cannot completely limit their children's exposure to gender stereotyping in the media. Some research suggests that media literacy can help; that is, noting and discussing gender stereotypes (and other stereotypes) in the media can help children evaluate these images more critically (e.g., Pahlke et al., 2014; Shewmaker, 2015).

Finally, efforts to reduce children's overall gender stereotyping may help them become less gender-schematic and thereby become more open to playing with a greater variety of toys (see Weisgram, 2016). For example, in one study, repeated exposure to counterstereotypic role models in stories subsequently led to increases in preschool-age children's (and especially girls') play with cross-gender-typed toys (Green et al., 2004). Also, gender stereotyping of toys is affected by the uses of gender-typed colors. In one study, decorating neutral toys as either pink or blue was related respectively to greater or less interest among preschool-age girls (Weisgram, Fulcher, & Dinella, 2014). Thus, toy manufacturers need to move away from gender-based marketing of toys and their packaging using pink for girls and blue for boys (e.g., Cunha, 2015).

CONCLUSION

Toy and play activities provide opportunities for children to rehearse behaviors that affect their social, cognitive, and physical development (Leaper, 2000b, 2015). Yet, children's opportunities to acquire, access, and practice particular play behaviors are commonly limited by their gender. As a result of complex interactions between their personal qualities and societal context, boys typically engage in masculine-stereotyped play activities (e.g., construction toys, athletic toys), and they usually avoid feminine-stereotyped play activities (e.g., dolls, cooking sets, dress-up materials). Conversely, girls exhibit the reverse pattern. An increasing body of research suggests that these different toy and play activities shape later social–cognitive competences (see Leaper, 2015; Lillard, 2015; for reviews). These differences may contribute to later gender inequities in academic interests and skills (and occupation achievement), as well as socioemotional competence in intimate relationships (see Leaper, 1994, 2000b, 2015). Moreover, gender-differentiated toy and play activities reinforce traditional adult gender roles whereby women are expected to be primarily responsible for domestic care and men are expected to be economic providers in the competitive work world. In these ways, the socialization of gender-typed play can be interpreted as a form of gender discrimination that perpetuates gender inequities in later adult roles (see Leaper, 2000b).

Although such claims may seem exaggerated, it is worth remembering that society has historically viewed cross-gender-typed toy interests as signs of mental disorder. Until only a few years ago, gender-nonconforming toy preferences were listed among the criteria in the *Diagnostic and Statistical Manual of Mental Disorders* (DSM) for labeling a child with gender identity disorder (American Psychiatric Association, 1994). Gender identity disorder was dropped in the most recent edition of the *DSM* (fifth ed.) and replaced with gender dysphoria (American Psychiatric Association, 2013). Rigid norms about the appropriate behavior for males and female continue to diminish in the United States and some other Western, industrialized countries. Children are growing up within societal contexts that are, in many ways, more egalitarian than in the past. Also, children and adults are increasingly challenging binary conceptualizations of gender. We believe that it is important that the broad cultural context in which children are embedded also support their play with broadest possible array of toys and activities.

An idealized imagining of what it might mean to have maximum flexibility in toy and play activities during childhood was portrayed nearly 40 years ago in Gould's (1978) fictional children's book, *X: A Fabulous Child's Story*. The story is about a child who is raised as gender neutral by its parents (for examples of recent attempts to raise gender-neutral children, see Dowling, 2010; O'Brien, 2015; Poisson, 2011). No other children or adults know "whether X was a boy or a girl." X plays with feminine-stereotyped toys and games with the girls and with masculine-stereotyped toys and games with the boys. The other children come to realize that "X is having twice as much fun" by engaging in both sets of play, and they begin to do the same. We add that besides allowing children greater opportunities to have fun, playing with both "girls' toys" and "boys' toys" increases the likelihood that children will develop a broader repertoire of social, cognitive, and physical skills. They also may be less likely to view adult roles, such as caregivers and particular occupations, as only relevant or appropriate for one gender. Ultimately, perhaps toys and play activities can be seen as human pursuits equally accessible to all children regardless of their gender.

REFERENCES

American Psychiatric Association. (1994). *Diagnostic and statistical manual of mental disorders* (4th ed.). Washington, DC: Author.

American Psychiatric Association. (2013). *Diagnostic and statistical manual of mental disorders* (5th ed.). Arlington, VA: Author.

Arthur, A. E., Bigler, R. S., & Ruble, D. N. (2009). An experimental test of the effects of gender constancy on sex typing. *Journal of Experimental Child Psychology, 104,* 427–446. http://dx.doi.org/10.1016/j.jecp.2009.08.002

Auster, C. J., & Mansbach, C. S. (2012). The gender marketing of toys: An analysis of color and type of toy on the Disney store website. *Sex Roles, 67,* 375–388. http://dx.doi.org/10.1007/s11199-012-0177-8

Bigler, R. S. (1999). Psychological interventions designed to counter sexism in children: Empirical limitations and theoretical foundations. In W. B. Swann, Jr., J. H. Langlois, & L. A. Gilbert (Eds.), *Sexism and stereotypes in modern society: The gender science of Janet Taylor Spence* (pp. 129–151). Washington, DC: American Psychological Association. http://dx.doi.org/10.1037/10277-006

Bigler, R. S., & Leaper, C. (2015). Gendered language: Psychological principles, evolving practices, and inclusive policies. *Policy Insights from Behavioral and Brain Sciences, 2*, 187–194. http://dx.doi.org/10.1177/2372732215600452

Bigler, R. S., & Liben, L. S. (2006). A developmental intergroup theory of social stereotypes and prejudice. In R. V. Kail (Ed.), *Advances in child development and behavior* (Vol. 34, pp. 39–89). San Diego, CA: Elsevier. http://dx.doi.org/10.1016/S0065-2407(06)80004-2

Bigler, R. S., & Liben, L. S. (2007). Developmental intergroup theory: Explaining and reducing children's social stereotyping and prejudice. *Current Directions in Psychological Science, 16*, 162–166. http://dx.doi.org/10.1111/j.1467-8721.2007.00496.x

Blakemore, J. E. O., & Centers, R. E. (2005). Characteristics of boys' and girls' toys. *Sex Roles, 53*, 619–633. http://dx.doi.org/10.1007/s11199-005-7729-0

Bronfenbrenner, U. (1979). *The ecology of human development: Experiments by nature and design.* Cambridge, MA: Harvard University Press.

Bussey, K., & Bandura, A. (1999). Social cognitive theory of gender development and differentiation. *Psychological Review, 106*, 676–713. http://dx.doi.org/10.1037/0033-295X.106.4.676

Caldera, Y. M., Huston, A. C., & O'Brien, M. (1989). Social interactions and play patterns of parents and toddlers with feminine, masculine, and neutral toys. *Child Development, 60*, 70–76. http://dx.doi.org/10.2307/1131072

Chaker, A. M. (2016, June 21). Toy companies aim to make toys more gender-neutral. *The Wall Street Journal.* Retrieved from http://www.wsj.com/articles/toy-companies-aim-to-make-toys-more-gender-neutral-1466539435

Cherney, I. D., Kelly-Vance, L., Glover, K. G., Ruane, A., & Ryalls, B. O. (2003). The effects of stereotyped toys and gender on play assessment in children aged 18–47 months. *Educational Psychology: An International Journal of Experimental Educational Psychology, 23*, 95–106. http://dx.doi.org/10.1080/01443410303222

Cherney, I. D., & London, K. (2006). Gender-linked differences in the toys, television shows, computer games, and outdoor activities of 5- to 13-year-old children. *Sex Roles, 54*, 717–726. http://dx.doi.org/10.1007/s11199-006-9037-8

Coyle, E. F., & Liben, L. S. (2016). Affecting girls' activity and job interests through play: The moderating roles of personal gender salience and game characteristics. *Child Development, 87*, 414–428. http://dx.doi.org/10.1111/cdev.12463

Criado, E. (2014, August 5). LEGO launches first-ever female scientist set after girl's plea for company to "make more LEGO girls to go on adventures." *Independent.* Retrieved from http://www.independent.co.uk/life-style/health-and-families/lego-launches-female-scientist-set-months-after-7-year-old-requested-they-make-more-lego-girl-people-9650341.html

Cunha, D. (2015, August 10). Target's decision to remove gender-based signs is just the start. *Time.* Retrieved from http://time.com/3990442/target-gender-based-signs/

Cunningham, S. J., & Macrae, C. N. (2011). The colour of gender stereotyping. *British Journal of Psychology, 102*, 598–614. http://dx.doi.org/10.1111/j.2044-8295.2011.02023.x

Dowling, T. (2010, June 23). The Swedish parents who are keeping their baby's gender a secret. *Guardian*. Retrieved from http://www.theguardian.com/lifeandstyle/2010/jun/22/swedish-parents-baby-gender

Esposito, L. (2015, September 4). Gender-neutral parenting: Letting kids choose. *U.S. News & World Report*. Retrieved from https://health.usnews.com/health-news/health-wellness/articles/2015/09/04/gender-neutral-parenting-letting-kids-choose

Etaugh, C., & Liss, M. B. (1992). Home, school, and playroom: Training grounds for adult gender roles. *Sex Roles, 26*, 129–147. http://dx.doi.org/10.1007/BF00289754

Fine, C., & Rush, E. (2016). "Why does all the girls have to buy pink stuff?" The ethics and science of the gendered toy marketing debate. *Journal of Business Ethics*. Advance online publication. http://dx.doi.org/10.1007/s10551-016-3080-3

Fisher-Thompson, D., & Burke, T. A. (1998). Experimenter influences and children's cross-gender behavior. *Sex Roles, 39*, 669–684. http://dx.doi.org/10.1023/A:1018804016650

Freeman, N. K. (2007). Preschoolers' perceptions of gender appropriate toys and their parents' beliefs about genderized behaviors: Miscommunication, mixed messages, and hidden truths? *Early Childhood Education Journal, 34*, 357–366. http://dx.doi.org/10.1007/s10643-006-0123-x

Friedman, C. K., Leaper, C., & Bigler, R. S. (2007). Do mothers' gender-related attitudes or comments predict young children's gender beliefs? *Parenting: Science and Practice, 7*, 357–366. http://dx.doi.org/10.1080/15295190701665656

Goldberg, A. E., Kashy, D. A., & Smith, J. Z. (2012). Gender-typed play behavior in early childhood: Adopted children with lesbian, gay, and heterosexual parents. *Sex Roles, 67*, 503–515. http://dx.doi.org/10.1007/s11199-012-0198-3

Gould, L. (1978). *X: A fabulous child's story*. New York, NY: Daughters.

Green, V. A., Bigler, R., & Catherwood, D. (2004). The variability and flexibility of gender-typed toy play: A close look at children's behavioral responses to counterstereotypic models. *Sex Roles, 51*, 371–386. http://dx.doi.org/10.1023/B:SERS.0000049227.05170.aa

Grinberg, E. (2014, October 3). Six ways to embrace gender differences at school. *CNN*. Retrieved from http://www.cnn.com/2014/10/03/living/children-gender-inclusive-schools/

Hausenblas, H. A., & Symons Downs, D. (2001). Comparison of body image between athletes and nonathletes: A meta-analytic review. *Journal of Applied Sport Psychology, 13*, 323–339. http://dx.doi.org/10.1080/104132001753144437

Henrich, J., Heine, S. J., & Norenzayan, A. (2010). The weirdest people in the world? *Behavioral and Brain Sciences, 33*, 61–83. http://dx.doi.org/10.1017/S0140525X0999152X

Hines, M. (2013). Sex and sex differences. In P. D. Zelazo (Ed.), *Oxford handbook of developmental psychology* (Vol. 1, pp. 164–201). New York, NY: Oxford University Press.

Huston, A. C. (1985). The development of sex-typing: Themes from recent research. *Developmental Review, 5,* 1–17. http://dx.doi.org/10.1016/0273-2297(85)90028-0

Jirout, J. J., & Newcombe, N. S. (2015). Building blocks for developing spatial skills: Evidence from a large, representative U.S. sample. *Psychological Science, 26,* 302–310. http://dx.doi.org/10.1177/0956797614563338

Kahlenberg, S., & Hein, M. (2010). Progression on Nickelodeon? Gender-role stereotypes in toy commercials. *Sex Roles, 62,* 830–847. http://dx.doi.org/10.1007/s11199-009-9653-1

Kane, E. W. (2006). "No way my boys are going to be like that!" Parents' responses to children's gender nonconformity. *Gender & Society, 20,* 149–176. http://dx.doi.org/10.1177/0891243205284276

Katz, P. A., & Walsh, P. V. (1991). Modification of children's gender-stereotyped behavior. *Child Development, 62,* 338–351. http://dx.doi.org/10.2307/1131007

King, K. M., Ogletree, R. J., Fetro, J. V., Brown, S. L., & Partridge, J. A. (2011). Predisposing, reinforcing and enabling predictors of middle school children's afterschool physical activity participation. *American Journal of Health Education, 42,* 142–153. http://dx.doi.org/10.1080/19325037.2011.10599181

Lamb, L., Bigler, R. S., Liben, L. S., & Green, V. A. (2009). Teaching children to confront peers' sexist remarks: Implications for theories of gender development and educational practice. *Sex Roles, 61,* 361–382. http://dx.doi.org/10.1007/s11199-009-9634-4

Langlois, J. H., & Downs, A. C. (1980). Mothers, fathers, and peers as socialization agents of sex-typed play behaviors in young children. *Child Development, 51,* 1237–1247. http://dx.doi.org/10.2307/1129566

Leaper, C. (1994). Exploring the consequences of gender segregation on social relationships. In C. Leaper (Ed.), *Childhood gender segregation: Causes and consequences* (New directions for child development, No. 65, pp. 67–86). San Francisco, CA: Jossey-Bass. http://dx.doi.org/10.1002/cd.23219946507

Leaper, C. (2000a). Gender, affiliation, assertion, and the interactive context of parent–child play. *Developmental Psychology, 36,* 381–393. http://dx.doi.org/10.1037/0012-1649.36.3.381

Leaper, C. (2000b). The social construction and socialization of gender. In P. H. Miller & E. K. Scholnick (Eds.), *Towards a feminist developmental psychology* (pp. 127–152). New York, NY: Routledge Press.

Leaper, C. (2015). Gender and social-cognitive development. In L. S. Liben & U. Muller (Eds.), *Handbook of child psychology and developmental science* (7th ed., Vol. 2, pp. 806–853). New York, NY: Wiley. http://dx.doi.org/10.1002/9781118963418.childpsy219

Leaper, C. (in press). Gender, dispositions, peer relations, and identity during development: Toward an integrative model. In N. K. Dess, J. Marecek, & L. C. Bell (Eds.), *Gender, sex, and sexualities: Psychological perspectives.* New York, NY: Oxford University Press.

Leaper, C., & Anderson, K. J. (1997). Gender development and heterosexual romantic relationships during adolescence. In W. Damon (Series Ed.), S. Shulman, & W. A. Collins (Issue Eds.), *Romantic relationships in adolescence: Developmental perspectives* (New directions for child development, No. 78, pp. 85–103). San Francisco, CA: Jossey-Bass. http://dx.doi.org/10.1002/cd.23219977808

Leaper, C., & Gleason, J. B. (1996). The relationship of play activity and gender to parent and child sex-typed communication. *International Journal of Behavioral Development, 19*, 689–703. http://dx.doi.org/10.1177/016502549601900401

Leaper, C., Leve, L., Strasser, T., & Schwartz, R. (1995). Mother–child communication sequences: Play activity, child gender, and marital status effects. *Merrill-Palmer Quarterly, 41*, 307–327.

Leaper, C., & Smith, T. E. (2004). A meta-analytic review of gender variations in children's language use: Talkativeness, affiliative speech, and assertive speech. *Developmental Psychology, 40*, 993–1027. http://dx.doi.org/10.1037/0012-1649.40.6.993

Lee, B., Lawson, K. M., & McHale, S. M. (2015). Longitudinal associations between gender-typed skills and interests and their links to occupational outcomes. *Journal of Vocational Behavior, 88*, 121–130. http://dx.doi.org/10.1016/j.jvb.2015.02.011

Lever, J. (1976). Sex differences in the games children play. *Social Problems, 23*, 478–487. http://dx.doi.org/10.2307/799857

Li, R. Y. H., & Wong, W. I. (2016). Gender-typed play and social abilities in boys and girls: Are they related? *Sex Roles, 74*, 399–410. http://dx.doi.org/10.1007/s11199-016-0580-7

Liben, L. S. (2014). The individual↔context nexus in developmental intergroup theory: Within and beyond the ivory tower. *Research in Human Development, 11*, 273–290. http://dx.doi.org/10.1080/15427609.2014.967048

Liben, L. S. (2015). Probability values and human values in evaluating single-sex education. *Sex Roles, 72*, 401–426. http://dx.doi.org/10.1007/s11199-014-0438-9

Liben, L. S. (2016). We've come a long way, baby (but we're not there yet): Gender past, present, and future. *Child Development, 87*, 5–28. http://dx.doi.org/10.1111/cdev.12490

Liben, L. S. (2017). Gender development: A constructivist-ecological perspective. In N. Budwig, E. Turiel, & P. D. Zelazo (Eds.), *New perspectives on human development* (pp. 145–164). Cambridge, England: Cambridge University Press. http://dx.doi.org/10.1017/CBO9781316282755.010

Liben, L. S., & Bigler, R. S. (2002). The developmental course of gender differentiation: Conceptualizing, measuring, and evaluating constructs and pathways. *Monographs of the Society for Research in Child Development, 67*, i–viii.

Liben, L. S., & Coyle, E. F. (2017). Gender development: A relational approach. In A. S. Dick & U. Müller (Eds.), *Advancing developmental science: Philosophy, theory, and method* (pp. 170–184). London, England: Routledge.

Lillard, A. S. (2015). The development of play. In L. S. Liben & U. Muller (Eds.), *Handbook of child psychology and developmental science* (7th ed., Vol. 2, pp. 425–468). New York, NY: Wiley. http://dx.doi.org/10.1002/9781118963418.childpsy211

Liss, M. B. (1983). Learning gender-related skills through play. In M. B. Liss (Ed.), *Social and cognitive skills: Sex roles and children's play* (pp. 147–166). New York, NY: Academic Press.

Lott, B., & Maluso, D. (1993). The social learning of gender. In A. E. Beall & R. J. Sternberg (Eds.), *The psychology of gender* (pp. 99–123). New York, NY: Guilford Press.

Lytton, H., & Romney, D. M. (1991). Parents' differential socialization of boys and girls: A meta-analysis. *Psychological Bulletin, 109,* 267–296. http://dx.doi.org/10.1037/0033-2909.109.2.267

Maccoby, E. E. (1998). *The two sexes: Growing up apart, coming together.* Cambridge, MA: Harvard University Press.

Markey, P. M., & Markey, C. N. (2010). Vulnerability to violent video games: A review and integration of personality research. *Review of General Psychology, 14,* 82–91. http://dx.doi.org/10.1037/a0019000

Martin, C. L., & Fabes, R. A. (2001). The stability and consequences of young children's same-sex peer interactions. *Developmental Psychology, 37,* 431–446. http://dx.doi.org/10.1037/0012-1649.37.3.431

Martin, C. L., Ruble, D. N., & Szkrybalo, J. (2002). Cognitive theories of early gender development. *Psychological Bulletin, 128,* 903–933. http://dx.doi.org/10.1037/0033-2909.128.6.903

McKenney, S., & Bigler, R. S. (2016a). High heels, low grades: Internalized sexualization and academic orientation among adolescent girls. *Journal of Research on Adolescence, 26,* 30–36. http://dx.doi.org/10.1111/jora.12179

McKenney, S., & Bigler, R. S. (2016b). Internalized sexualization and its relation to sexualized appearance, body surveillance, and body shame among early adolescent girls. *The Journal of Early Adolescence, 36,* 171–197. http://dx.doi.org/10.1177/0272431614556889

Miller, C. L. (1987). Qualitative differences among gender-stereotyped toys: Implications for cognitive and social development in girls and boys. *Sex Roles, 16,* 473–487. http://dx.doi.org/10.1007/BF00292482

Murnen, S. K., & Don, B. P. (2012). Body image and gender roles. In T. Cash (Ed.), *Encyclopedia of body image and human appearance* (Vol. 1, pp. 128–134). San Diego, CA: Elsevier Academic Press. http://dx.doi.org/10.1016/B978-0-12-384925-0.00019-5

National Coalition for Women and Girls in Education. (2012). *Title IX at 40.* Retrieved from http://www.ncwge.org/athletics.html

Nelson, A. (2005). Children's toy collections in Sweden: A less gender-typed country? *Sex Roles, 52,* 93–102. Retrieved from http://dx.doi.org/10.1007/s11199-005-1196-5

O'Brien, S. (2015, August 4). No gender on the agenda, boys and girls. *Herald Sun*. Retrieved from http://www.heraldsun.com.au/news/opinion/susie-obrien/no-gender-on-the-agenda-boys-and-girls/news-story/6875ea60b44e8609b5b48e38f873c51b

Orenstein, P. (2011). *Cinderella ate my daughter: Dispatches from the front lines of the new girlie-girl culture*. New York, NY: Harper.

Pahlke, E., Bigler, R. S., & Martin, C. L. (2014). Can fostering children's ability to challenge sexism improve critical analysis, internalization, and enactment of inclusive, egalitarian peer relationships? *Journal of Social Issues, 70*, 115–133. http://dx.doi.org/10.1111/josi.12050

Pellegrini, A. D. (1985). Social-cognitive aspects of children's play: The effects of age, gender, and activity centers. *Journal of Applied Developmental Psychology, 6*, 129–140. http://dx.doi.org/10.1016/0193-3973(85)90055-3

Pellegrini, A. D., & Perlmutter, J. C. (1989). Classroom contextual effects on children's play. *Developmental Psychology, 25*, 289–296. http://dx.doi.org/10.1037/0012-1649.25.2.289

Pirrone, C., & Di Nuovo, S. (2014). Can playing and imagining aid in learning mathematics? An experimental study of the relationships among building-block play, mental imagery, and arithmetic skills. *Applied Psychology Bulletin, 271*, 30–39.

Poisson, J. (2011, May 21). Parents keep child's gender secret. *Toronto Star*. Retrieved from http://www.thestar.com/life/parent/2011/05/21/parents_keep_childs_gender_secret.html

Polnick, B., Dweyer, C. A., Haynie, C. F., Froschl, M., Sprung, B., & Fromberg, D. (2007). Gender equity in early learning environments. In S. S. Klein, B. Richardson, D. A. Grayson, L. H. Fox, & C. Kramarae (Eds.), *Handbook for achieving gender equity through education* (2nd ed., pp. 609–630). Mahwah, NJ: Erlbaum.

Rogoff, B. (1990). *Apprenticeship in thinking: Cognitive development in social context*. New York, NY: Oxford University Press.

Serbin, L. A., Tonick, I. J., & Sternglanz, S. H. (1977). Shaping cooperative cross-sex play. *Child Development, 48*, 924–929. http://dx.doi.org/10.2307/1128342

Serbin, L. A., Zelkowitz, P., Doyle, A., Gold, D., & Wheaton, B. (1990). The socialization of sex-differentiated skills and academic performance: A mediational model. *Sex Roles, 23*, 613–628. http://dx.doi.org/10.1007/BF00289251

Servin, A., & Bohlin, G. (1999). Do Swedish mothers have sex-stereotyped expectations and wishes regarding their own children? *Infant and Child Development, 8*, 197–210. http://dx.doi.org/10.1002/(SICI)1522-7219(199912)8:4<197::AID-ICD198>3.0.CO;2-H

Sherman, A. M., & Zurbriggen, E. L. (2014). "Boys can be anything": Effect of Barbie play on girls' career cognitions. *Sex Roles, 70*, 195–208. http://dx.doi.org/10.1007/s11199-014-0347-y

Shewmaker, J. W. (2015). *Sexualized media messages and our children: Teaching kids to be smart critics and consumers.* Santa Barbara, CA: Praeger.

Signorella, M. L., & Bigler, R. S. (2013). Single-sex schooling: Bridging science and school boards in educational policy. *Sex Roles, 69,* 349–355. http://dx.doi.org/10.1007/s11199-013-0313-0

Spence, I., & Feng, J. (2010). Video games and spatial cognition. *Review of General Psychology, 14,* 92–104. http://dx.doi.org/10.1037/a0019491

Sprafkin, C., Serbin, L. A., & Elman, M. (1982). Sex-typing of play and psychological adjustment in young children: An empirical investigation. *Journal of Abnormal Child Psychology, 10,* 559–567. http://dx.doi.org/10.1007/BF00920754

Sweet, E. (2014). Toys are more divided by gender now than they were 50 years ago. *The Atlantic.* Retrieved from http://www.theatlantic.com/business/archive/2014/12/toys-are-more-divided-by-gender-now-than-they-were-50-years-ago/383556/

Tobin, D. D., Menon, M., Menon, M., Spatta, B. C., Hodges, E. V. E., & Perry, D. G. (2010). The intrapsychics of gender: A model of self-socialization. *Psychological Review, 117,* 601–622. http://dx.doi.org/10.1037/a0018936

Toy Association, Inc. (2016). *Annual U.S. sales data.* Retrieved from https://www.toyassociation.org/ta/research/data/annual/toys/research-and-data/data/annual-us-sales-data.aspx

Weisgram, E. S. (2016). The cognitive construction of gender stereotypes: Evidence for the dual pathways model of gender differentiation. *Sex Roles, 75,* 301–313. http://dx.doi.org/10.1007/s11199-016-0624-z

Weisgram, E. S., Fulcher, M., & Dinella, L. M. (2014). Pink gives girls permission: Exploring the roles of explicit gender labels and gender-typed colors on preschool children's toy preferences. *Journal of Applied Developmental Psychology, 35,* 401–409. http://dx.doi.org/10.1016/j.appdev.2014.06.004

The White House of Barack Obama. (2016, April). *Breaking down gender stereotypes in media and toys so that our children can explore, learn, and dream without limits* [Fact sheet]. Washington, DC: Author. Retrieved from https://obamawhitehouse.archives.gov/the-press-office/2016/04/06/factsheet-breaking-down-gender-stereotypes-media-and-toys-so-our

Wong, W. I., Pasterski, V., Hindmarsh, P. C., Geffner, M. E., & Hines, M. (2013). Are there parental socialization effects on the sex-typed behavior of individuals with congenital adrenal hyperplasia? *Archives of Sexual Behavior, 42,* 381–391. http://dx.doi.org/10.1007/s10508-012-9997-4

Wood, E., Desmarais, S., & Gugula, S. (2002). The impact of parenting experience on gender stereotyped toy play of children. *Sex Roles, 47,* 39–49. http://dx.doi.org/10.1023/A:1020679619728

13

CONCLUSION: TOWARD A GREATER UNDERSTANDING OF CHILDREN'S GENDER-TYPED TOY PLAY

ERICA S. WEISGRAM AND LISA M. DINELLA

We designed this volume to make an evidence-based contribution to the recent societal conversation about gender and toys (see Chapter 1 for a review). Parents, corporate executives, feminist activists, and the popular press often debate the extent of gender differences in children's toy interests, the role of biological and social factors in children's interests and behaviors, and the degree to which gender-typed marketing should be used. Many topics in these discussions have been studied within the psychological literature, and thus we look to scientific evidence compiled by top experts in the field of developmental psychology to provide answers. A careful examination of the causes, consequences, and correlates of gender-typed toy play reveals the complexity of the issues at hand. In this volume, we have demonstrated that multiple factors lead a toy to be perceived as gender-typed, girls' and boys' interests may differ for multiple reasons, and children's gender-typed toy play has multiple consequences. In addition, this thorough review of the literature

http://dx.doi.org/10.1037/0000077-014
Gender Typing of Children's Toys: How Early Play Experiences Impact Development, E. S. Weisgram and L. M. Dinella (Editors)

and the recent conversations within the psychological field of gender development illustrate areas in which additional research is needed or viewpoints that previously have not been considered.

GENDER TYPING OF CHILDREN'S TOYS

Gender typing of children's toys generally refers to the process by which toys become deemed by society as appropriate for one gender or another. For example, our current American society deems fashion dolls as appropriate for play by girls but not boys, and action figures as appropriate for play by boys but not girls. As noted in Chapter 1, some toys historically have been gender typed as they matched onto gender-differentiated roles that were common among adults, but most toys used to be considered appropriate for both boys and girls. In the present day, gender typing of toys is prevalent with fewer toys considered appropriate for both boys and girls (Sweet, 2014). In their contributions to this volume, Cherney (see Chapter 4) and Liben, Schroeder, Borriello, and Weisgram (see Chapter 10) outlined the elements that contribute to the gender typing of toys and how research in psychology has investigated their use. Elements that contribute to children's gender schemata about toys include explicit gender labels, such as signs reading "Toys for Boys" or "Toys for Girls," and implicit gender markers, such as gender-stereotyped colors or depictions of only boys or only girls on packaging. Gender schemata then direct children's interests and behaviors via pathways described in cognitive models of gender stereotypes (see Chapter 7). It is not just the marketing of toys that contributes to gender typing but messages from others, such as peers, parents, teachers, and relatives (see Chapters 6 and 10). These social agents may reinforce and accept children with interests that conform to societal gender stereotypes and punish, reject, or victimize children with gender-nonconforming interests. Liben and colleagues in Chapter 10 also noted that the expressed interest and observed play of other children may contribute to gender stereotypes. Other children's interests may set social norms for what is acceptable play and reinforce existing gender stereotypes that are endorsed. The gender stereotypes that many individuals endorse may be both a cause or an effect of the elements discussed previously. That is, the endorsement of gender stereotypes about a toy may be the reason that explicit or implicit labels are used in marketing. However, it is possible that gender stereotypes develop because of gender-typed marketing. For example, both of first author Erica Weisgram's sons very much enjoyed the movie *Frozen* soon after its release, often quoting lines and singing songs long after watching the film. However, when they saw that the toys in the store were marketed toward girls, they developed a stereotype that the movie and associated toys were "for girls" and began to actively avoid anything related to the film.

The elements briefly described here all may contribute to boys' or girls' interests in toys; however, the degree to which each element contributes to gender typing is unknown. In our collaborative work with Megan Fulcher, we have begun to explore the combination of these elements with interesting results. Across two studies, one with familiar toys and one with novel toys, we found that preschool-aged boys were more swayed by explicit gender labels than gender-typed colors but that both the explicit and implicit labels affected girls' interest (Weisgram et al., 2014). In addition, some research has begun to examine the role of individual differences in the degree to which elements of gender typing of toys affects children's interests (Weisgram, 2016). Some children are particularly influenced by gender messages about toys (e.g., gender schematic children), whereas other children are less likely to be influenced (e.g., gender-aschematic children). Future research should continue to examine how these factors interact and how they may differentially contribute across various developmental stages. In addition, research should investigate which of these elements are necessary and/or sufficient for contributing to gender typing of children's toys. For example, does painting a toy pink make a toy "only for girls," or is other information about the toy needed to develop this stereotype? As the landscape on gender-typed marketing shifts (Fine & Rush, 2016), we need to continuously examine how these changes in everyday environments are affecting children's and adults' stereotypes and interests.

INFLUENCES ON GENDER DIFFERENCES IN CHILDREN'S INTERESTS

A primary goal of this volume was to gather experts who investigate gender differences in children's interests from a variety of psychological perspectives. Several studies conducted from a biological perspective have demonstrated that hormones, particularly prenatal testosterone, influence children's masculine toy preferences (see Chapter 5). In addition, social agents, such as peers, parents, and media, shape children's gender-typed toy interests through various mechanisms (see Chapter 6). A large body of research also has demonstrated that cognitive factors, such as children's gender schemas and gender identification, impact children's gender-typed toy play (see Chapter 7).

Although biological, social, and cognitive factors often are considered independently, these factors are not mutually exclusive and may simultaneously influence children's interests. In their biopsychosocial model of sex differences in cognitive skills, D. I. Miller and Halpern (2014) demonstrated that biological factors are one input into individuals' experiences but thoughts, behavior, and culture are additional inputs. Interestingly, D. F. Miller and Halpern also have suggested that the experiences children have further shape the brain, a hypothesis explored by Eliot in Chapter 8 that is in need of further investigation. Although some research has examined the intersection of parent socialization and prenatal testosterone in girls with congenital adrenal hyperplasia (Pasterski et al., 2005), little research has examined the intersection of the various biological, social, and cognitive factors that have been found individually to contribute to children's interest. Currently, in the field of developmental psychology, some theoretical approaches may broadly integrate these perspectives (e.g., Bronfenbrenner's bioecological model; see Chapter 12), but specific integrative, theoretical models related to gender-typed toys must be developed and tested to further explain gender differences in children's toy interests and play behaviors.

CONSEQUENCES OF CHILDREN'S GENDER-DIFFERENTIATED TOY PLAY

A second goal of this book was to outline the possible consequences of children's gender-differentiated toy play. Once again, we asked authors to review the literature in three broad domains: biological, cognitive, and social development. The findings in each of the different areas differed in their depth and breadth. Although research on brain development has supported the notion of experience-shaping synaptic development and higher levels of the central nervous system, the effects of specific toys or masculine and feminine toy types on brain development have not been studied thoroughly in the literature, thus leaving room for future research to explore these links (see Chapter 8). In social development, research has suggested links between some masculine toys (e.g., video games and toy weapons) and aggressive behaviors, and links between some feminine toys (e.g., baby dolls, fashion dolls) and nurturing and self-sexualization (for baby dolls and fashion dolls, respectively; see Chapter 9). Play with specific gender-typed and gender-neutral toys is linked to areas of cognitive development; play with blocks and construction toys is linked with the development of spatial and higher level math skills; and play with linear board games is linked to the development of early math skills (see Chapter 10). Play with gender-typed toys is linked also to children's perception of the gender-typed roles they may occupy as adults (see Chapter 11).

As noted throughout the chapters, some studies have demonstrated correlations between gender-typed play and developmental outcomes, but questions remain about the direction of the causal pathways between the constructs. Other studies have used experimental methods in controlled environments, such as laboratories, schools, or child care centers, to establish causal pathways but have been unable to establish external validity as to how the quality and quantity of children's play in natural environments (e.g., home, playgrounds) affects their development. Thus, we would like to reiterate Dinella's call in Chapter 2 for methodological pluralism and systematic approaches to further examine the links between children's play with gender-typed toys and how it may differentially impact boys' and girls' development. In addition, we found many areas in which little to no research has been conducted. For example, although research links play with video games and children's spatial skills in short-term intervention studies, no long-term intervention studies (to our knowledge) show positive effects later in development and across a variety of spatial tasks. One possible reason for the lack of published research showing links between gender-typed toys and domains of development is that such studies are difficult to conduct. In these cases, we suggest that future research be conducted to explore the correlational links and causal pathways between toy play and development. It is possible that such studies have been conducted, have not found significant effects, and thus were not published—a phenomenon known as the *file drawer effect*. If this is the case, we argue that these studies are worth publishing and still may make an important contribution to the psychological literature.

In Chapter 12, Leaper and Bigler emphasized how gender typing of children's toys impacts cognitive and social development but also contributes to perception of gender differences, endorsement of gender stereotypes, and beliefs about the social construct of gender more broadly. We echo their call for empirical research to investigate how to reduce gender stereotypes about toys and increase the diversity of children's play. This is not to say that children should not play with gender-typed toys or should abandon play with their favorite toys. Instead, we hope that parents, caregivers, and teachers will provide and engage children with a variety of toys (i.e., masculine, feminine, gender neutral) to enhance their development of a range of skills and experiences. We make the analogy to the importance of a healthy and diverse diet: Parents and caregivers typically would not allow their child to eat only apples, regardless of how healthy apples are. They would emphasize and encourage the child to eat a variety of healthy foods to maximize the benefits they receive from the food they eat. We argue that children's play should not be restricted by parents and caregivers—or by children themselves—but should be diverse to maximize the benefits that children will receive from playing with these toys.

WHERE DO WE GO FROM HERE?

In this volume, we have brought together top scientists in psychology who expertly reviewed the existing literature on gender typing of children's toys. In addition, the authors have identified many areas not addressed in the literature that need further research. As we conclude this volume, we identify and discuss issues that remain open to further study.

Exploring Reciprocal Effects

In many areas in this volume, authors have noted the difficulty of establishing the direction of effect between the constructs under investigation (see Chapters 2 and 10). As we consider the relations between gender-typed toy play and developmental outcomes, we also need to consider the possibility of reciprocal effects. As noted in Chapter 10, for example, children's play with spatially oriented toys (e.g., blocks, video games) may causally impact their spatial skills (as demonstrated by experimental work; see Chapter 10). Also, children who have better spatial skills may be more likely to choose spatially oriented toys during free play in their natural environment, thus creating a reciprocal relationship. In social development, a reciprocal relationship also may exist between girls' play with sexualized fashion dolls and their own self-sexualization (see Chapter 9). These examples demonstrate the need for longitudinal and experimental designs to unpack information about the pathways between these constructs. In addition, research investigating the mediators and moderators of the relationship between gender-typed toy play and developmental outcomes, such as self-efficacy, is needed to investigate the complexity of empirically established relationships.

Exploring Variation Within Key Constructs

As we and other authors within this volume describe gender-typed toys, children's toy choices, children's development, and many other constructs of interest, we often look at the constructs broadly and evaluate their relations to other constructs. We also often describe between-gender differences in interest and play behaviors. It is in this way that we can first describe how children's play is influenced and how it impacts their development. However, a closer investigation indicates that wide variation may exist within each of the constructs identified within the literature. For example, we often discuss "masculine toys" and "feminine toys" at the group level, yet there is wide variation in what is considered a masculine toy (e.g., professional wrestler action figure, toy weapon, small cars) and what is considered a feminine toy (e.g., play makeup, fashion doll, baby doll, toy vacuum). In their work, Blakemore and Centers (2005) had college students rate the degree to which a variety of toys were considered appropriate for boys or girls, rating them as "strongly masculine," "mostly masculine," "neutral," "mostly feminine," and "strongly feminine." As Hines and Davis noted in Chapter 5, one can study both between-gender variation and within-gender variation in children's interest to get a sense of how children's gender influences their toy interests and play.

Individual differences among children also merit further consideration. In their attitudinal pathway model of gender differentiation, Liben and Bigler (2002) noted that individual differences in the degree to which children use gender stereotypes to guide their decisions (i.e., *gender schematicity*) and the personal level of interest in a toy. Many children are influenced by the elements of gender typing described previously, but some children (e.g., gender-aschematic children) may not be influenced by gender-typed marketing, gender stereotypes, or social agents, and instead base their interest on features of the toy itself. In a recent study, Weisgram (2016) found that children who endorse more stereotypes about familiar toys were more likely to be influenced by gender labels applied to a novel toy than were children who endorse few gender stereotypes. Thus, the individual difference in gender schematicity could account for the level of impact gender typing has on children (see also C. L. Martin & Dinella, 2012). In addition, Liben and Bigler (2002) included a personal interest filter in their attitudinal pathway model. They noted that associations with one's own gender do not lead to guaranteed interest. For example, a boy may be interested in masculine toys, in general, but truly interested in only a subset of these toys (e.g., small cars, footballs) and uninterested in another subset of masculine toys (e.g., professional wrestler action figures). A thorough investigation of the variation within these constructs is beyond the scope of this volume but is a fruitful area for further research.

Investigating Contexts of Play

Throughout this volume, authors have discussed how the context in which children play may affect the degree of gender-typed play and the relationship between gender-typed play and development (see Chapters 2, 4, and 10). For example, the types of toys available to children in their environments may affect children's play. Within environments with many gender-neutral toys, such as day care and preschool environments, children's play may be less gender differentiated than environments in which many gender-typed toys are present. Interestingly, in an observational study, we found that when a variety of toys were available, children were more likely to play with gender-neutral toys than gender-typed toys (Dinella, Weisgram, & Fulcher, 2017).

In addition, the presence of other peers may impact children's play with gender-typed toys. Research has shown that both boys and girls were less likely to play with gender-stereotyped toys or engage in less stereotyped activities when playing in mixed-gender groups than when playing exclusively with children of their own gender (Fabes, Hanish, & Martin, 2003). Moreover, Wilansky-Traynor and Lobel (2008) found that gender-aschematic boys were more likely to play with masculine toys in the presence of an observer than when playing alone, even when the masculine toys were unattractive.

Interactions with parents and caregivers during play also may affect children's development. When playing with spatially oriented toys with their children, mothers who use more spatial language had children who also used more spatial language, a key factor in spatial skill development (Borriello & Liben, 2017). In addition, significant relationships between young children's quality of pretend play and language development could be mediated by attention from and verbal interactions with parents (Lillard et al., 2013). These verbal interactions may be more plentiful and supportive in parents' interactions with girls than with boys (Leaper, Anderson, & Sanders, 1998). Differences in children's interests also have been identified in interview versus observation settings, which raise methodological concerns (e.g., the need for diversity in methods to offset design advantages and disadvantages) but may indicate that children's thoughts about what toys they enjoy may differ than their free-play behaviors (Dinella et al., 2017). These findings demonstrate the importance of considering how children's gender-typed toy play is influenced by contextual factors and suggests that further research in this area is needed.

Developing Interventions

A common theme among many of the chapters within this volume is the need to develop interventions to reduce gender stereotypes about toys and increase children's play with cross-gender toys (e.g., see Chapter 12). One reason interventions are important is that play with gender-typed, gender-neutral, and cross-gender-typed toys may enhance a variety of different skills and prosocial behaviors that lead children to become more well-rounded and less gender differentiated. Another reason is that gender stereotypes about toys are limiting to children. A reduction of gender stereotypes would allow children to freely choose from a variety of toys and make choices based on features of the toy or the type of play it affords, rather than being limited to only a subset of toys.

Just as the elements described previously contribute to gender typing (see Chapters 4 and 10), these same elements can be leveraged to inform large- and small-scale interventions. For example, reducing the use of explicit gender labels in environments can reduce stereotypes. Bigler (1995) found that students assigned to a classroom in which teachers avoided the use of explicit gender labels had reduced gender stereotype endorsement after a few weeks compared with students in a classroom in which gender labels were used frequently (see also Hilliard & Liben, 2010). Thus, the elimination of explicit gender labels in Target's toy section and in other major retailers' toy sections may similarly reduce gender stereotypes about toys. Additionally, the reduction of implicit gender labels in toy marketing (e.g., colors, depictions of only boys or only girls on the box) also may attenuate children's gender stereotypes about toys and increase cross-gender play.

One trend aimed to increase girls' play with cross-gender-typed toys is to apply feminine-implicit gender labels, such as pink and purple colors, to masculine toys (see Chapter 1 for a review). In our research, we have found that adding pink to a masculine toy (e.g., monster truck, fighter jet) does increase girls' interest in the toy. The success of the LEGO Friends line also suggests that girls can be drawn to toys in this fashion. Although we support girls' crossing gender lines and expanding their cognitive skills through block play and play with other masculine toys, we also feel that this marketing strategy may enforce gender stereotypes and contribute to the exaggerated perception of gender differentiation rather than reduce gender stereotypes about toys. We argue that a better course of action would be to develop toys with diverse features in diverse colors and include both boys and girls in the marketing of the toy. In addition, interventions to reduce gender stereotypes and increase children's cross-gender toy play should be informed by the available psychological science and theoretical models of developmental psychology (Bigler, 1999; see also Chapter 2, this volume).

Broadening the Scope of Research in Gender Development

The call made by Dinella in Chapter 2 for a systematic investigation into single research questions using multiple methodologies applies to the need for similar investigations across contexts and individuals. Intersectional research serves to broaden the scope of research within developmental psychology as scientists consider intersections between gender, race, socioeconomic status, and other demographic factors. For example, the impact of implicit and explicit labels found in toy marketing strategies may not apply uniformly to all children. The Report of the APA Task Force on the Sexualization of Girls (American Psychological Association [APA], 2007) noted that girls of color are effective in resisting restrictive societal ideals of female sexuality and beauty. In addition, just as girls and boys may gain different skills by playing with different toys available to them based on cultural gender stereotypes, there may be differences in the different types of toys owned by children of lower and higher economic statuses. These differences also may differentially impact their development. For example, research by Ramani and Siegler

(2011) found positive effects of children's play with board games on their mathematic skills. This same study also demonstrated that children of lower economic status were less likely to own and play board games at home than children of middle economic status. Clearly, a need exists for intersectional research in understanding gender, toys, and children's development.

As with many areas within psychology, the literature on gender and toys is notably limited in regard to the inclusion of intersectional frameworks. Shields (2008) explained three common responses from psychologists when someone points out the absence of intersectionality in their work: Psychologists defer the responsibility of conducting intersectional research to other researchers, often in other fields, such as sociology; they respond in limited ways, such as studying the additive impacts of social identities (e.g., comparing and contrasting gender and racial or ethnic groups within their study); and they defer answering questions about intersectionality on the grounds that not enough information exists within the field on which to base a response. Shields (2008) pointed out that a "self-excusing paragraph that simultaneously acknowledges the central significance of intersectionality and absolves oneself of responsibility for attempting to incorporate intersectionality into the work" (p. 305) often is included in the discussion of empirical findings. Although we note the irony of making such a call for intersectionality in the conclusion of this volume, we would like to reiterate the call by Shields for researchers to have a purposeful focus on intersections of race, ethnicity, socioeconomic status, gender, and other identities within the literature on gender and toys. In addition, we echo the call made by Dinella (see Chapter 2) for the field to bridge the chasm between current gold-standard methodological approaches and progressive theoretical frameworks. As scientists in the gender development field, we can no longer espouse the importance of intersectionality and still respond with research that uses only quantitative, categorical approaches to studies conducted primarily with White, middle-class samples. Having an a priori focus on diverse methods, samples, and perspectives will allow scholars to expand the scientific knowledge of gender development in the area of toys and play, and beyond.

In addition to broadening the scope of this line of research through intersectional studies, there also is a need to consider whether the relations among key constructs differ with transgender and gender-nonconforming (TGNC) youths (APA, 2015). Research with cisgender, gender-nonconforming children has demonstrated that they may not endorse gender stereotypes or be as affected by cultural and marketing messages as their gender-conforming peers (Martin & Dinella, 2012). Research with transgender children has shown that their toy preferences, peer preferences, and gender attitudes are similar to those of cisgender children (Olson, 2016; Olson, Key, & Eaton, 2015). That is, transgender children who identify as girls (i.e., transgender girls) have feminine toy preferences that are similar to those of cisgender girls, and transgender children who identify as boys (i.e., transgender boys) have masculine toy preferences that are similar to cisgender boys. APA (2015) has emphasized the need for psychologists and other individuals to view gender as a nonbinary construct and has encouraged research "to promote social change that reduces the negative effects of stigma on the health and well-being of TGNC people" (p. 841). We feel that interventions aiming to reduce gender stereotypes about toys and play (as discussed previously) are one way that stigma can be reduced and that children of all genders will not feel limited by societal gender messages in their play. In addition, the field of gender development recognizes the need for increased dialogue about the way gender is conceptualized, discussed, and measured (see Chapter 2).

Recognizing the Need for Translation and Application

As mentioned in the Introduction to this volume, on April 6, 2016, the White House held a conference titled "Helping Our Children Explore, Learn, and Dream Without Limits: Breaking Down Gender Stereotypes in Media and Toys." The event brought together toy industry executives, media executives, youth-serving and parent organizations, and scientists. We attended this event, and Lisa Dinella was invited to speak on the scientific findings related to gender stereotypes, toys, and children's media. Many attendees remarked that the event felt momentous. The endorsement of the White House administration under President Barack Obama confirmed that gender stereotypes in children's toys and media deserve attention, and all of the attendees were in unique positions to make a positive difference in children's lives. The event illustrated the power of using scientific evidence to understand a situation, aid decision making, and guide actions.

The conference served as a reminder that it is important for the scientific community to communicate with stakeholders outside of academia, and it solidified our professional commitment as scholars to sharing scientific findings with a broad audience. Psychologists routinely have recognized the importance of informing the general public of scientific findings and helping apply psychology to address societal concerns (Klatzky, 2009; G. Miller, 1969), yet many may lack the time, training, or opportunities to disseminate their findings, especially given that these "outreach" efforts may not be valued for promotion and tenure decisions within their universities. We encourage colleges and universities to consider the importance of these outreach efforts and the time it takes faculty to engage in such activities. In addition, we encourage executives in the toy industry to reach out to members of the scientific community for guidance and support, and to continue the important conversations that began at the White House conference.

We can see that bridges between advocacy, media, industry, and science have begun to lead to positive changes and the reduction of gender stereotypes in children's toys. Examples of positive change include the removal of explicit gender labels in stores, such as Target; an increase in the presence of female superheroes, villains, and lead characters in active roles (e.g., DC Comics superhero girls, Harley Quinn, Moana); news articles and op-ed pieces in the mainstream media on gender and toys (e.g., Dinella, 2015; Weisgram, 2015); and support for social media campaigns, such as "Let Toys Be Toys." As noted in an op-ed by Dinella (2016), superhero Halloween costumes were more popular than princess costumes in October 2016 for the first time in 11 years, perhaps signifying a sign of a shift in at least one genre of gender-typed play that could provide an arena in which boys and girls may find common play interests. More studies are needed to understand the impact of advocacy and intervention so that the most effective strategies can be implemented and remove gendered barriers to full access to the benefits of toys (see Chapter 12).

CONCLUSION

As parents, we often say to our children, "There's no such thing as a 'boy toy' or 'girl toy.' Toys are toys, kids are kids." We contend that children should not be limited by societal gender messages when choosing toys, playing with friends, and engaging in play. In this volume and in our own research programs and outreach efforts, we seek to describe and understand children's gender-typed toy play, identify areas in need of further research, and advocate for the reduction of gender stereotypes about toys and the benefits of play with a variety of toys. We hope that this volume contributes to the current societal conversation about gender and toys; creates bridges between parents, caregivers, toy industry executives, and scholars; and inspires further investigation and conversations about gender and toys.

REFERENCES

American Psychological Association. (2007). *Report of the APA Task Force on the sexualization of girls* [Executive summary]. Retrieved from http://www.apa.org/pi/women/programs/girls/report-summary.pdf

American Psychological Association. (2015). Guidelines for psychological practice with transgender and gender nonconforming people. *American Psychologist, 70,* 832–864. http://dx.doi.org/10.1037/a0039906

Bigler, R. S. (1995). The role of classification skill in moderating environmental influences on children's gender stereotyping: A study of the functional use of gender in the classroom. *Child Development, 66*, 1072–1087. http://dx.doi.org/10.2307/1131799

Bigler, R. S. (1999). Psychological interventions designed to counter sexism in children: Empirical limitations and theoretical foundations. In W. B. Swann, Jr., J. H. Langlois, & L. A. Gilbert (Eds.), *Sexism and stereotypes in modern society: The gender science of Janet T. Spence* (pp. 129–151). Washington, DC: American Psychological Association. http://dx.doi.org/10.1037/10277-006

Blakemore, J. E. O., & Centers, R. E. (2005). Characteristics of boys' and girls' toys. *Sex Roles, 53*, 619–633. http://dx.doi.org/10.1007/s11199-005-7729-0

Borriello, G. A., & Liben, L. S. (2017). Effects of encouraging maternal guidance of preschoolers' spatial thinking during block play. *Child Development.* Advance online publication. http://dx.doi.org/10.1111/cdev.12779

Dinella, L. M. (2015, October 29). Wishing to be a mommy to a (girl) mummy this Halloween. *The Washington Post.* Retrieved from https://www.washingtonpost.com/news/parenting/wp/2015/10/29/wishing-to-be-a-mommy-to-a-girl-mummy-this-halloween/?utm_term=.461d8206e89b

Dinella, L. M. (2016, October 27). *This Halloween: Careful princess, your crown is slipping!* Retrieved from http://www.huffingtonpost.com/entry/this-halloween-careful-princess-your-crown-is-slipping_us_580f5c31e4b099c434319bd1

Dinella, L. M., Weisgram, E. S., & Fulcher, M. (2017). Children's gender-typed toy interests: Does propulsion matter? *Archives of Sexual Behavior, 46*, 1295–1305. http://dx.doi.org/10.1007/s10508-016-0901-5

Fabes, R. A., Hanish, L. D., & Martin, C. L. (2003). Children at play: The role of peers in understanding the effects of child care. *Child Development, 74*, 1039–1043. http://dx.doi.org/10.1111/1467-8624.00586

Fine, C., & Rush, E. (2016). "Why does all the girls have to buy pink stuff?" The ethics and science of the gendered toy marketing debate. *Journal of Business Ethics.* Advance online publication. http://dx.doi.org/10.1007/s10551-016-3080-3

Hilliard, L. J., & Liben, L. S. (2010). Differing levels of gender salience in preschool classrooms: Effects on children's gender attitudes and intergroup bias. *Child Development, 81*, 1787–1798. http://dx.doi.org/10.1111/j.1467-8624.2010.01510.x

Klatzky, R. L. (2009). Giving psychological science away: The role of applications courses. *Perspectives on Psychological Science, 4*, 522–530. http://dx.doi.org/10.1111/j.1745-6924.2009.01162.x

Leaper, C., Anderson, K. J., & Sanders, P. (1998). Moderators of gender effects on parents' talk to their children: A meta-analysis. *Developmental Psychology, 34*, 3–27. http://dx.doi.org/10.1037/0012-1649.34.1.3

Liben, L. S., & Bigler, R. S. (2002). The developmental course of gender differentiation: Conceptualizing, measuring, and evaluating constructs and pathways. *Monographs of the Society for Research in Child Development, 67*, i–viii.

Lillard, A. S., Lerner, M. D., Hopkins, E. J., Dore, R. A., Smith, E. D., & Palmquist, C. M. (2013). The impact of pretend play on children's development: A review of the evidence. *Psychological Bulletin, 139*, 1–34. http://dx.doi.org/10.1037/a0029321

Martin, C. L., & Dinella, L. M. (2012). Congruence between gender stereotypes and activity preference in self-identified tomboys and non-tomboys. *Archives of Sexual Behavior, 41*, 599–610. http://dx.doi.org/10.1007/s10508-011-9786-5

Miller, D. I., & Halpern, D. F. (2014). The new science of cognitive sex differences. *Trends in Cognitive Sciences, 18*, 37–45. http://dx.doi.org/10.1016/j.tics.2013.10.011

Miller, G. (1969). Psychology as a means of promoting human welfare. *American Psychologist, 24*, 1063–1075. http://dx.doi.org/10.1037/h0028988

Olson, K. R. (2016, October). *When sex and gender diverge: Gender development in transgender and gender nonconforming youth.* Paper presented at the Gender Development Research Conference, San Francisco, CA.

Olson, K. R., Key, A. C., & Eaton, N. R. (2015). Gender cognition in transgender children. *Psychological Science, 26*, 467–474. http://dx.doi.org/10.1177/0956797614568156

Pasterski, V. L., Geffner, M. E., Brain, C., Hindmarsh, P., Brook, C., & Hines, M. (2005). Prenatal hormones and postnatal socialization by parents as determinants of male-typical toy play in girls with congenital adrenal hyperplasia. *Child Development, 76*, 264–278. http://dx.doi.org/10.1111/j.1467-8624.2005.00843.x

Ramani, G. B., & Siegler, R. S. (2011). Reducing the gap in numerical knowledge between low-and middle-income preschoolers. *Journal of Applied Developmental Psychology, 32*, 146–159. http://dx.doi.org/10.1016/j.appdev.2011.02.005

Shields, S. (2008). Gender: An intersectionality perspective. *Sex Roles, 59*, 301–311. http://dx.doi.org/10.1007/s11199-008-9501-8

Sweet, E. (2014, December). Toys are more divided by gender now than they were 50 years ago. *The Atlantic.* Retrieved from https://www.theatlantic.com/business/archive/2014/12/toys-are-more-divided-by-gender-now-than-they-were-50-years-ago/383556

Weisgram, E. (2015, August 17). Now that Target won't label toys by gender, some alternatives [Web log post]. Retrieved from https://parenting.blogs.nytimes.com/2015/08/17/truth-in-signage-in-the-toy-aisle-after-target-removes-gender-labels-whats-next/

Weisgram, E. S. (2016). The cognitive construction of gender stereotypes: Evidence for the dual pathways model of gender differentiation. *Sex Roles, 75*, 301–313. http://dx.doi.org/10.1007/s11199-016-0624-z

Weisgram, E. S., Fulcher, M., & Dinella, L. M. (2014). Pink gives girls permission: Exploring the role of explicit gender labels and gender-typed colors on preschool children's toy preferences. *Journal of Applied Developmental Psychology, 35*, 401–409. http://dx.doi.org/10.1016/j.appdev.2014.06.004

Wilansky-Traynor, P., & Lobel, T. E. (2008). Differential effects of an adult observer's presence on sex-typed play behavior: A comparison between gender-schematic and gender-aschematic preschool children. *Archives of Sexual Behavior, 37*, 548–557. http://dx.doi.org/10.1007/s10508-008-9342-0

INDEX

Automated machinery, 13
Automatic-persuasion processing, 268

Baby dolls
    as gender-stereotyped toys, 190, 193
    girls' preferences for, 4, 37
    and heteronormativity, 273
    and nurturing behavior, 52, 195–196,
        295
Balance (video game), 232
Balls, 13
Bandura, A., 129, 261, 290
Barbie dolls
    accessories for, 77
    characteristics of, 190
    and child development, 37
    and children's future roles, 265
    creation of, 196
    in history of toys, 14
    social behavior promoted with, 193
Bartneck, C., 199
Basal ganglia, 171
Battlefield 4 (video game), 200
Bedroom decor, 267
Beltz, A. M., 155
Bem, S. L., 38, 39, 144, 150
Berenbaum, S. A., 155
Berkowitz, L., 199
Best, D. L., 216
Between-gender differences
    and classification of toys, 315
    in observational studies, 53–54,
        56, 57
Bias, confirmation, 25, 226
Bigler, R. S.
    and antecedents of gender typing of
        toys, 291
    dual pathways model developed by,
        268
    and explicit labels, 316
    and gender-free language, 40
    and individual differences, 315
    and social behavior, 193
    and stereotypic beliefs, 219
Biology. *See also* Sex hormones and
        gender-typed toy play
    and gender development, 12, 51,
        311–312
    of play, 173–175
    and study design, 37–38

Blakemore, J. E. O., 83, 218, 264,
        273–274, 314–315
Block, J. H., 83
Block design, 239
Blocks
    infant and toddler preferences for,
        56, 58
    and mathematics, 234–236, 312
    and spatial skills, 226–229, 239, 312
Board games, 131, 237–240, 312, 318
Body image
    and dolls, 28
    and social behavior, 194, 197, 198
    and sports-related toys, 295
Bomb toys, 83
Borriello, G. A., 243
Bradbard, M. R., 149
Brain adaptation (plasticity), 169–174
Brain structure, 39, 99
Bratz dolls, 196, 274
Breadwinner/caregiver ideal of paid and
        unpaid labor
    in children's creation of family roles,
        270
    family roles in, 269
    overview, 257, 258
    segregation of toys as parallel to,
        274–275
"Breaking Down Gender Stereotypes
    in Media and Toys So That Our
    Children Can Explore, Learn,
    and Dream Without Limits"
    (White House Fact Sheet), 167
Bronfenbrenner, U., 288
Brown, Christia Spears, 16
Brown, L. M., 204
Bryk, K., 155
Building sets
    boys' preference for, 74
    and neurological development, 179
    and socioemotional skills, 294–295
    and spatial skills, 294
    and STEM skills, 261
Bull, R., 238
Bussey, K., 290

CAH. *See* Congenital adrenal
        hyperplasia
CAIS (complete androgen insensitivity
        syndrome), 104–105

Online content, 31
Opioid transmitters, 174
Orbital prefrontal cortex, 174
Orenstein, Peggy, 15, 16
Ovary development, 98
Own-sex/own-gender schema
    overview, 147–148
    of transgender children, 158–159

Packaging of toys, 4
Paper folding tasks, 224
Parental involvement
    in children's culture, 204
    as factor in gender-typed toy play,
        122–126, 192
    and flexibility about play, 290–291
    in play with infants and toddlers,
        55–56
    research on effects of, 312
    and social partner messaging,
        217–218
Parent–child similarity, 30
*Parenting Beyond Pink and Blue: How
    to Raise Your Kids Free of Gender
    Stereotypes* (Brown), 16
Parents, 309
Parkinson's disease, 176
Pasterski, V., 109
Paternity leave, 271
Patriarchy, 194
Peers
    and children's future roles, 258–259
    and classifications, 218
    as factor in gender-typed toy play,
        126–128
    of infants and toddlers, 60
    as models, 263–264
    and transgender children, 318
Peirce, Charles S., 25
Pellegrini, A. D., 76
Peng, Y., 199–200
Penile growth, 108–109
Perception, 220
Personality differences, 194–195
Perspective taking, 133, 224
Phelps, P., 235
Phones, 57, 131, 232
Physical activity
    and neurological development,
        168–169

as positive behavior, 203
    practice of, 173
Physical appearance
    and characteristics of feminine toys,
        81
    and dolls, 196–197
    and gender-stereotyped toys, 189,
        190, 193
    and sex hormones, 107–109
Physical development, 300
Piaget, Jean, 10, 11, 144, 257
Pictorial (application), 232
Picture books, 31
Pike, J. J., 130
"Pinkification," 15
"Pink Stinks" campaign, 298
Pitcher, E. G., 76
Plasticity of brain, 169–174
Plato, 10
Play. *See also specific headings*
    biology of, 173–175
    contexts of, 315–316
    development of, 74–75
    importance of, 10–11
Play complexity, 82
Playful learning, 258
Play kitchens, 14
Playmobil, 265
Play Unlimited campaign, 204, 298
Pluralism, methodological, 32–34,
    313
Pokemon X (video game), 201
Power Rangers (TV show), 191
Predictive timing, 174
Prefrontal cortex
    and hippocampus, 176
    orbital, 174
Pre-School Activities Inventory
    (PSAI), 101, 106–109
Preschool children
    and marketing, 262
    and puzzles, 11
Preschool Embedded Figures Test,
    225
Preschool Occupation, Activity, and
    Traits scale, 291
Preschool programs, 258, 315
Prescribed hormones, 105–106
Pretend play, 73. *See also* Fantasy play
Primary activities, 259

Primate research
    on biological factors and gender, 51
    and environmental enrichment, 175
    and features of toy objects, 65
    on gender-stereotyped play, 53
    and sex hormones, 110–111
    on toy preference, 64
Princess toys, 130, 197–198, 320. *See
    also* Disney Princesses
Print advertisements, 31
Problem-solving, 175–176
PSAI (Pre-School Activities
    Inventory), 101, 106–109
Psychological androgyny, 38, 39, 150, 197
Puzzles
    jigsaw, 229–230
    and mathematics, 234–236
    outcomes of play with, 11
    and spatial skills, 229–230, 294

Qualitative research, 33–34
Quantitative research, 33–34
Quantity-estimation tasks, 239
Quasi-experimental designs, 29–30

Race, 317
Ramani, G. B., 28, 36, 238, 317–318
RapeLay (video game), 202
Rape myths, 202
Rats, 174, 175, 177
Rattles, 13
Reading skills
    gender differences in performance
        on, 297–298
    and neurological development,
        179–180
Reasoning skills, 220
Reciprocal effects, 314
*Redefining Girly: How Parents Can Fight
    the Stereotyping and Sexualizing
    of Girlhood, From Birth to Tween*
    (Wardy), 16
Reflex circuits, 171
Reilly, D., 222
Replication, 34, 35
Representation skills, 294
Reproductive behaviors, 100
Research methods for study of gender
        and toy preferences, 23–40
    challenges with, 35–40
    content analysis, 31–32

correlational designs, 26–28
experimental designs, 28–29, 35
importance of, 24–26
meta-analysis, 30–31
mixed-methods and pluralistic
    approaches to, 32–34
quasi-experimental designs, 29–30
systemic approaches to, 32–35
Rheingold, H. L., 77
Rhesus monkeys, 51
Riskiness, 189, 198–199
Risley, T. R., 219
Rod and frame task, 224
Rogoff, B., 296
Role-playing activities
    of infants and toddlers, 65
    and social factors in gender-typed toy
        play, 122
Romney, D. M., 218
Rose, H., 216
Rosenzweig, Mark, 175
Rough-and-tumble play
    as gender-differentiated play style,
        75, 76
    in rats, 174
    research on, 65
    and sex hormones, 101, 102
    and social factors in gender-typed toy
        play, 124
Ruane, A., 198
Rush, E., 191, 297, 298
Ryalls, B. O., 198

Saenz, J., 58
Sala, G., 236, 237
Schau, C. G., 219
Scholastic Aptitude Test (SAT), 223
School environment
    gender in, 216
    opportunities for play in, 243
    peer influence in. *See* Peers
    use of explicit gender labels in,
        316–317
Schultz, L. H., 76
Science, 39, 222
Science, technology, engineering, and
        mathematics (STEM) workforce
    building of skills for, 261–263
    and dolls, 265–266, 274
    and family roles, 270–271

ABOUT THE EDITORS

Erica S. Weisgram, PhD, is a professor of psychology at University of Wisconsin–Stevens Point (UWSP). Her research focuses broadly on gender development in children, adolescents, and young adults. Her recent work explores the cognitive construction of stereotypes in preschool children and how cultural stereotypes affect children's interest in toys. She also examines how gender and gender-related factors (e.g., stereotypes, values, familial roles) affect individuals' occupational and academic interests with a specific focus on girls' and women's interest in math and science occupations. Dr. Weisgram earned her bachelor's degree at Luther College and her PhD at The University of Texas at Austin. She is the 2016 winner of the UWSP Justus Paul Sabbatical Award, the UWSP Excellence in Teaching Award, and the 2017 UWSP University Scholar Award.

Lisa M. Dinella, PhD, is a research scientist who investigates the relations between gender, academic achievement, and career development. Dr. Dinella studies children's toy play and media exposure, and how gendered experiences shape academic and career pursuits across the lifespan. She is principal investigator of the Gender Development Laboratory at Monmouth University, where she is an associate professor of psychology and an affiliated faculty member of Gender Studies. Her school-based research endeavors led to her edited book *Conducting Science-Based Psychology Research in Schools*. Dr. Dinella recently presented on gender disparities in children's media and toys at the White House in Washington, DC. She drew from her research to provide key recommendations to toy, media, and youth-serving organizations on how to break down gender stereotypes.

3